THE SHORT
PROSE READER

THE SHORT PROSE READER

SIXTH EDITION

Gilbert H. Muller
The City University of New York
LaGuardia

Harvey S. Wiener
The City University of New York

McGRAW-HILL, INC.

New York St. Louis San Francisco Auckland Bogotá Caracas
Hamburg Lisbon London Madrid Mexico Milan Montreal New Delhi
Paris San Juan São Paulo Singapore Sydney Tokyo Toronto

This book was set in Goudy Old Style by the
College Composition Unit in cooperation with
General Graphics Services, Inc.
The editors were Lesley Denton and David Dunham;
the production supervisor was Friederich W. Schulte.
The cover was designed by Amy Becker.
R. R. Donnelley & Sons Company was printer and binder.
Cover painting: Young Girl Reading by Fragonard, courtesy of
Art Resource.

Acknowledgments appear on pages 494–498,
and on this page by reference.

THE SHORT PROSE READER

1 2 3 4 5 6 7 8 9 0 DOC DOC 9 5 4 3 2 1 0

ISBN 0-07-044135-9

Library of Congress Cataloging-in-Publication Data

The Short prose reader / [compiled by] Gilbert H. Muller, Harvey S. Wiener.—
  6th ed.
    P.   cm.
  ISBN 0-07-044135-9
  1. College readers.   2. English language—Rhetoric.   I. Muller, Gilbert
H., (date).   II. Wiener, Harvey S.
PE1417.S446   1991
808'.0427—dc20   90–6354

ABOUT THE AUTHORS

Gilbert H. Muller, who received a Ph.D. in English and American Literature from Stanford University, is currently professor of English at LaGuardia Community College of the City University of New York and adjunct professor at the Graduate Center. He has also taught at Stanford, Vassar, and several universities overseas. Dr. Muller is the author of the award-winning study *Nightmares and Visions: Flannery O'Connor and the Catholic Grotesque, Chester Himes,* and other critical texts. His essays and reviews have appeared in *The New York Times, The New Republic, The Nation, The Sewanee Review, The Georgia Review,* and elsewhere. He is also a noted author and editor of textbooks in English and composition, including *The McGraw-Hill Reader* and, with John Williams, *The McGraw-Hill Introduction to Literature.* Among Dr. Muller's awards are a National Endowment for the Humanities Fellowship, a Fulbright Fellowship, and a Mellon Fellowship.

Harvey S. Wiener, University Associate Dean for Academic Affairs of the City University of New York, codirects the National Testing Network in Writing (NTNW). He was founding president of the Council of Writing Program Administrators. Dr. Wiener is the author of many books on reading and writing for college students and their teachers, including *The Writing Room* (Oxford, 1981). He is coauthor of *The McGraw-Hill College Handbook,* a reference grammar and rhetoric text.

Dr. Wiener is a member of the Standing Committee on Assessment for the National Council of Teachers of English, and has chaired the Teaching of Writing Division of the Modern Language Association (1987). He has taught writing at every level of education from elementary school to graduate school. A Phi Beta Kappa graduate of Brooklyn College, he holds a Ph.D. in Renaissance literature. He currently teaches as an adjunct in the doctoral program at Columbia Teachers College. Dr. Wiener has won grants from the National Endowment for the Humanities, the Fund for the Improvement of Postsecondary Education, and the Exxon Education Foundation.

CONTENTS

ALTERNATE THEMATIC CONTENTS   **xv**
PREFACE   **xxi**

CHAPTER 1

On Writing   1

William Saroyan   *Why I Write*   5
A Pulitzer Prize–winning author explains how his determination "to un-derstand the meaning of his own life" led him to live "in a special way" since the age of nine.

William Stafford   *Writing*   13
William Stafford offers his "process-rather-than-substance view of writ-ing," in which we must be willing to fail, cannot bother to insist on high standards, and will often be baffled about what "skill" has to do with it.

William Zinsser   *Simplicity*   22
According to this writer-teacher, "clutter is the disease of American writ-ing." We must simplify. In this essay, Zinsser connects clear writing to clear thinking, which, he declares, doesn't appear nearly enough these days.

Joan Didion   *On Keeping a Notebook*   32
"Our notebooks give us away," claims Joan Didion, who shares with us the intimacies of her own notebooks over the years.

Summing Up: Chapter 1   47

CHAPTER 2

On Reading   49

Eudora Welty   *Moon on a Silver Spoon*   51
One of America's best fiction writers reveals a long-standing love affair—
with books! "Long before I wrote stories, I listened to stories," she tells us.

Malcolm X   *Prison Studies*   61
"Reading had changed the course of my life forever," writes Malcolm X,
who explains movingly how reading is both an activity of love and a tool
of power.

Margaret Atwood   *Survival*   71
Canadian author Margaret Atwood relates how, almost against the odds,
she came to delight in reading the stories of her own country.

Donald Hall   *Four Ways of Reading*   81
An eclectic writer claims that although there are different ways to read,
"most reading is no more cultural nor intellectual than shooting pool or
watching What's My Line."

Summing Up: Chapter 2   90

CHAPTER 3

Description   92

Margaret Laurence   *The Shack*   94
A small cabin on the Otonabee River in southern Ontario, Canada, is
the focal point for one writer's environmentally lush workplace where
she's entirely "content to be alone."

William Least Heat Moon   *Arizona 87*   103
Drive with this writer through the Arizona desert and into its mountains.
The landscape is sometimes "reminiscent of old Chinese woodblock
prints," but the towns have "no center, no focus for the eye and soul."

Richard Selzer   *The Discus Thrower*   111
A surgeon and an author offers a chilling, yet moving and dignified, description of a patient's last day.

Gretel Ehrlich   *A River's Route*   119
"To find wildness, I must first offer myself up, accepting all that comes

before me" writes an environmentalist of her often spiritual journey to find the source of a river.

Summing Up: Chapter 3   127

CHAPTER 4

Narration   129

Elizabeth Wong   *The Struggle to Be an All-American Girl*   131
In a narrative of her youth, a writer remembers her efforts to obtain "a cultural divorce" from the heritage into which she was born.

Langston Hughes   *Salvation*   139
One of America's foremost poets tells of his childhood disillusionment as he struggled desperately to see Jesus.

Roger Wilkins   *I Became Her Target*   146
"Dead-Eye" Bean was the first teacher to make this present-day scholar aware that thinking was educational and that his opinions were valuable.

George Orwell   *A Hanging*   154
The renowned author of 1984 discovers how precious human life is as he tells of witnessing an execution in Burma. "It is curious," he recalls, "but 'til that moment, I had never realized what it meant to destroy a healthy, conscious man."

Summing Up: Chapter 4   165

CHAPTER 5

Illustration   167

Randall Williams   *Daddy Tucked the Blanket*   169
A contemporary journalist shows what it means to be poor and how the environment of poverty can destroy families.

Ray Bradbury   *Tricks! Treats! Gangway!*   178
Here from the noted science fiction writer is the wonder of Halloween, 1928, with all its gorilla fangs, pumpkin pies, creaking stairs, black confetti, banshee trains, and much more.

Brent Staples   *Night Walker*   189
An "avid night walker" explains how his seemingly innocent habit has turned him into "an accomplice in tyranny."

Lewis Thomas   *Death in the Open*   198
*This biologist and popular writer says that death "is a natural marvel"
throughout the universe of animals and plants; and that humans, sharing a
kinship with other life forms, will have to stop seeing death as a catastrophe.*

Summing Up: Chapter 5   207

CHAPTER 6

Comparison and Contrast   209

Rachel Carson   *A Fable for Tomorrow*   211
*One of America's most celebrated naturalists warns us of the future in a
grim contrast between a flourishing environment and a destroyed landscape plagued by a mysterious curse.*

Russell Baker   *The Two Ismo's*   217
*The ammunition in this columnist's "urban war zone" includes quiche,
kiwi fruit, zippered plastic briefcases, and gourmet Swedish toothpaste, as
he explores two social doctrines: machismo and quichismo.*

Ellen Goodman   *The Tapestry of Friendships*   225
*This piece, in which columnist Ellen Goodman talks about the difference
between "buddies" and "friends," may heat up the battle between the
sexes, but it certainly raises some important questions about the ways in
which people relate to one another.*

Bruno Bettelheim   *Fairy Tales and Modern Stories*   234
*One of the world's foremost child psychologists explains that traditional
fairy tales give solace to children, but that modern tales "fail to provide
the escape and consolation that children need."*

Summing Up: Chapter 6   241

CHAPTER 7

Definition   242

Jack Denton Scott   *What's a Bagel?*   244
*What's next? McBagel?! A fan of "Brooklyn jawbreakers" explains why
we may one day say, "As American as a sesame seed bagel."*

Suzanne Britt Jordan   *Fun, Oh Boy. Fun. You Could Die from It.*   253
If you've ever felt that you should have been having fun but that somehow you weren't, this essay proves that you're not alone.

Gregg Easterbrook   *Escape Valve*   261
One of the results of modern living, according to this writer, is the "automatic-out," a means for avoiding long-term commitments. Here, he explains this trend toward escaping responsibilities, a trend that produces serious results in the way we develop relationships.

Rita Mae Brown   *To the Victor Belongs the Language*   269
Revolution! Rebellion! Strong words, which form the basis for an essay that proves that "whoever wins the war redefines the language."

Summing Up: Chapter 7   277

CHAPTER 8

Classification   279

Judith Viorst   *Friends, Good Friends—and Such Good Friends*   281
This popular writer believes that friendships "are conducted at many levels of intensity" and "meet different needs." Here she categorizes eight types of friends, including Convenience friends, Historical friends, and Crossroads friends.

E. B. White   *The Three New Yorks*   290
Natives, commuters, and those who come searching: These are the inhabitants of E. B. White's three cities in one in this fascinating look at the world's most talked about city.

James T. Baker   *How Do We Find the Student in a World of Academic Gymnasts and Worker Ants?*   297
This gently cynical essay introduces twelve types of students everyone knows and loves—including among others, the Performer, the Jock, the Lost Soul, the Worker Ant, and finally, the Student.

Aaron Copland   *What to Listen for in Music*   306
One of America's foremost composers appeals to the average music listener to become more active—not just to listen, but to listen "for something."

Summing Up: Chapter 8   318

CHAPTER 9

Process Analysis   320

Garrison Keillor   *How to Write a Personal Letter*   322
Do you feel a "burning shame" whenever you see unanswered mail piled up on your desk? Fear not—Garrison Keillor tells you how to "take a deep breath and plunge in."

Bruce Jay Friedman   *Eating Alone in Restaurants*   331
The author explains to us how to perform one of the most dreaded activities on earth—and live through it.

Grace Lichtenstein   *Coors Beer*   340
Investigating the most famous beer in the West, this reporter unlocks the secret to "the Coors mystique."

Ernest Hemingway   *Camping Out*   347
Avoiding insects. Getting a good rest. Cooking trout just right. This essay can make anyone's next camping trip a success.

Summing Up: Chapter 9   354

CHAPTER 10

Cause-and-Effect Analysis   356

Anne Roiphe   *Why Marriages Fail*   359
In the United States, new marriages have a 50 percent chance of succeeding—or failing, depending on your outlook. A contemporary novelist explains in this essay why "happily ever after" may become an extinct phrase.

Arthur Miller   *Rite of Spring*   370
This famous playwright claims that a small garden plot with rows of hot dogs and pastrami vines sounds good to him. Yet, yearly he goes through the "back-breaking make-believe" of planting a vegetable garden. Why? "I garden," he writes, "because I must."

Linda Bird Francke   *The Ambivalence of Abortion*   380
Political convictions and personal experience make an unforgettable mix in this haunting essay about abortion.

Susan Jacoby   *When Bright Girls Decide That Math Is "A Waste of Time"*   391

A one-time straight-A algebra student explains why math and science are a no-woman's-land for promising young scholars.

Summing Up: Chapter 10   400

CHAPTER 11

Argumentation and Persuasion   402

Judy Syfers   *I Want a Wife*   405
Author, wife, and mother, Judy Syfers ironically argues that men often take wives for granted. "My God," she concludes, "who wouldn't want a wife?"

Jonathan Kozol   *Are the Homeless Crazy?*   412
With biting precision, a noted educator and social critic disputes a commonly accepted "denial of reality" about the cause of the ever-increasing problem of homelessness.

Joseph Wood Krutch   *The Vandal and the Sportsman*   425
Sports hunters are evil and their joy lies in the destruction of God's creatures. So argues a lifelong naturalist in this emotionally charged essay.

Leonid Fridman   *America Needs Its Nerds*   433
What value should we place on intellectuals in our society? A graduate student argues that nerds and geeks are vital to our future.

Summing Up: Chapter 11   440

CHAPTER 12

Prose for Further Reading   442

Maxine Kumin   *In Deep*   443
Kumin shares with us an idyll of early winter, in the forest, moving in deep in a quest of the perfect trail—the other side.

Annie Dillard   *An American Childhood*   445
In this haunting "dreaming memory of land," the author takes us back past her own American childhood to the childhood of America.

James Baldwin   *If Black English Isn't a Language, Then Tell Me, What Is?*   447
"A language comes into existence by means of brutal necessity, and the

rules of the language are dictated by what the language must convey." *So saying, James Baldwin argues that black English isn't a dialect, but a language.*

Maya Angelou *The Fight* 451
When Joe Louis defeated Max Schmeling for the heavyweight championship in 1936, more than just a boxing title was at stake.

Jamaica Kincaid *The Ugly Tourist* 454
"From day to day, you are a nice person," the author assures us. But, she warns, "the minute you become a tourist" you become "an ugly human being."

Tama Janowitz *He Rocked, I Reeled* 457
Which of your teachers have spoken to their classes "with the honesty of one adult talking to others"? Which were really "in love" with their subjects? Fiction writer Janowitz tells us how a few of her teachers have sparked an excitement about subjects that she thought would put her to sleep.

Stephen King *"Ever Et Raw Meat?" and Other Weird Questions* 460
"Do you ever write in the nude?" Strange question? Stephen King, master of horror and suspense, has heard stranger, yet at least he feels comfortable giving that one an honest answer.

Nora Ephron *Living with My VCR* 465
Confessions of "a compulsive videotaper"! Simultaneously addicted to and hateful of her VCR, Ephron nevertheless goes on taping, hoping she'll live long enough to be able to watch everything she's recorded.

Mordecai Richler *My Grandmother's Illness* 469
For a young Jewish boy in Montreal fifty years ago, life turns sad and mysterious when his grandmother dies. But, he finds, it doesn't end!

Richard Rodriguez *Complexion* 474
A man labeled feo as a child (feo means "ugly" in Spanish) remembers how his dark skin set him apart from those around him.

GLOSSARY **479**

ACKNOWLEDGMENTS **494**

ALTERNATE THEMATIC CONTENTS

Childhood and Family

William Saroyan   *Why I Write*   5

Eudora Welty   *Moon on a Silver Spoon*   51

Margaret Atwood   *Survival*   71

Elizabeth Wong   *The Struggle to Be an All-American Girl*   131

Langston Hughes   *Salvation*   139

Roger Wilkins   *I Became Her Target*   146

Randall Williams   *Daddy Tucked the Blanket*   169

Ray Bradbury   *Tricks! Treats! Gangway!*   178

Bruno Bettelheim   *Fairy Tales and Modern Stories*   234

Annie Dillard   *An American Childhood*   445

Maya Angelou   *The Fight*   451

Mordecai Richler   *My Grandmother's Illness*   469

Richard Rodriguez   *Complexion*   474

Social Problems and Issues

Malcolm X   *Prison Studies*   61

Richard Selzer   *The Discus Thrower*   111

Elizabeth Wong   *The Struggle to Be an All-American Girl*   131

Roger Wilkins   *I Became Her Target*   146

George Orwell   *A Hanging*   154

Randall Williams   *Daddy Tucked the Blanket*   169

Brent Staples   *Night Walker*   189

Rachel Carson   *A Fable for Tomorrow*   211

Gregg Easterbrook   *Escape Valve*   261

Anne Roiphe   *Why Marriages Fail*   359

Linda Bird Francke   *The Ambivalence of Abortion*   380

Judy Syfers   *I Want a Wife*   405

Jonathan Kozol   *Are the Homeless Crazy?*   412

James Baldwin   *If Black English Isn't a Language, Then Tell Me, What Is?*   447

Leonid Fridman   *America Needs Its Nerds*   433

Jamaica Kincaid   *The Ugly Tourist*   454

Richard Rodriguez   *Complexion*   474

Men and Women Today

Ellen Goodman   *The Tapestry of Friendships*   225

Judith Viorst   *Friends, Good Friends—and Such Good Friends*   281

Anne Roiphe   *Why Marriages Fail*   359

Linda Bird Francke   *The Ambivalence of Abortion*   380

Susan Jacoby   *When Bright Girls Decide That Math Is "A Waste of Time"*   391

Judy Syfers   *I Want a Wife*   405

The Minority Experience

Malcolm X   *Prison Studies*   61

Elizabeth Wong   *The Struggle to Be an All-American Girl*   131

Roger Wilkins   *I Became Her Target*   146

George Orwell   *A Hanging*   154

Brent Staples   *Night Walker*   189

James Baldwin   *If Black English Isn't a Language, Then Tell Me, What Is?*   447

Maya Angelou   *The Fight*   451

Richard Rodriguez   *Complexion*   474

City and Country

Margaret Laurence   *The Shack*   94

William Least Heat Moon   *Arizona 87*   103

Gretel Ehrlich   *A River's Route*   119

Brent Staples   *Night Walker*   189

Lewis Thomas   *Death in the Open*   198

Rachel Carson   *A Fable for Tomorrow*   211

Russell Baker   *The Two Ismo's*   217

E. B. White   *The Three New Yorks*   290

Ernest Hemingway   *Camping Out*   347

Arthur Miller   *Rite of Spring*   370

Jonathan Kozol   *Are the Homeless Crazy?*   412

Maxine Kumin   *In Deep*   443

Annie Dillard   *An American Childhood*   445

Sports, Travel, and Leisure

William Least Heat Moon   *Arizona 87*   103

Gretel Ehrlich   *A River's Route*   119

Aaron Copland   *What to Listen for in Music*   306

Garrison Keillor   *How to Write a Personal Letter*   322

Bruce Jay Friedman   *Eating Alone in Restaurants*   331

Grace Lichtenstein   *Coors Beer*   340

Ernest Hemingway   *Camping Out*   347

Arthur Miller   *Rite of Spring*   370

Joseph Wood Krutch   *The Vandal and the Sportsman*   425

Jamaica Kincaid   *The Ugly Tourist*   454
Nora Ephron   *Living with My VCR*   465

Psychology and Behavior

Joan Didion   *On Keeping a Notebook*   32
Donald Hall   *Four Ways of Reading*   81
Lewis Thomas   *Death in the Open*   198
Ellen Goodman   *The Tapestry of Friendships*   225
Russell Baker   *The Two Ismo's*   217
Bruno Bettelheim   *Fairy Tales and Modern Stories*   234
Suzanne Britt Jordan   *Fun, Oh Boy. Fun. You Could Die from It.*   253
Gregg Easterbrook   *Escape Valve*   261
Judith Viorst   *Friends, Good Friends—and Such Good Friends*   281
Bruce Jay Friedman   *Eating Alone in Restaurants*   331
Stephen King   *"Ever Et Raw Meat?" and Other Weird Questions*   460
Jamaica Kincaid   *The Ugly Tourist*   454
Nora Ephron   *Living with My VCR*   465

Science, Technology, and Medicine

Richard Selzer   *The Discus Thrower*   111
Lewis Thomas   *Death in the Open*   198
Rachel Carson   *A Fable for Tomorrow*   211
Grace Lichtenstein   *Coors Beer*   340

Language and Thought

William Saroyan   *Why I Write*   5
William Stafford   *Writing*   13

William Zinsser   *Simplicity*   22

Joan Didion   *On Keeping a Notebook*   32

Eudora Welty   *Moon on a Silver Spoon*   51

Malcolm X   *Prison Studies*   61

Margaret Atwood   *Survival*   71

Donald Hall   *Four Ways of Reading*   81

Bruno Bettelheim   *Fairy Tales and Modern Stories*   234

Rita Mae Brown   *To the Victor Belongs the Language*   269

Garrison Keillor   *How to Write a Personal Letter*   322

James Baldwin   *If Black English Isn't a Language, Then Tell Me, What Is?*   447

Humor and Satire

Langston Hughes   *Salvation*   139

Ellen Goodman   *The Tapestry of Friendships*   225

Russell Baker   *The Two Ismo's*   217

Jack Denton Scott   *What's a Bagel?*   244

Suzanne Britt Jordan   *Fun, Oh Boy. Fun. You Could Die from It.*   253

James T. Baker   *How Do We Find the Student in a World of Academic Gymnasts and Worker Ants?*   297

Garrison Keillor   *How to Write a Personal Letter*   322

Bruce Jay Friedman   *Eating Alone in Restaurants*   331

Arthur Miller   *Rite of Spring*   370

Judy Syfers   *I Want a Wife*   405

Tama Janowitz   *He Rocked, I Reeled*   457

PREFACE

Now in its sixth edition, *The Short Prose Reader* continues to offer lively reading selections for college composition courses. Its twelve chapters cover all-important patterns of writing, offering students concise and lively prose models for analysis, discussion, and imitation. Designed as a practical text, it addresses the challenge that faces today's college students in reading and writing short essays.

The organization of *The Short Prose Reader* is one of its major strengths. In this edition we offer a new feature at the end of each chapter. "Summing Up" provides a means for students to focus their attention on comparative issues and writing topics. Chapter 1, "On Writing," is followed by a chapter offering four unique views of the craft of reading by well-known authors. Each of the following nine chapters contains four short essays that illustrate clearly a specific pattern or technique—description, narration, illustration, comparison and contrast, definition, classification, process analysis, causal analysis, or argumentation. For this edition we offer many new selections. We organize the text by starting with the forms of prose mastered most readily by college students, and by then moving carefully to more difficult types of analytical and argumentative writing. Students learn to build upon earlier techniques and patterns as they progress through the book. The last chapter, consisting of ten essays, offers students the opportunity to read and to discuss short prose pieces that reflect the various rhetorical strategies.

Teachers and students will discover that the essays appeal to a broad audience. Readers will be excited by William

Least Heat Moon's "Arizona 87," Malcolm X's "Prison Studies," Leonid Fridman's "America Needs Its Nerds," Ernest Hemingway's "Camping Out," Judy Syfer's "I Want a Wife," Jonathan Kozol's "Are the Homeless Crazy?" and the many other timely or controversial pieces included in the text. This is a readable text, and one that has ample representation by many different types of writers. Moreover, the essays, which range typically between 300 to 1,200 words, achieve their goals succinctly and clearly and are easy to read and to understand. The essays will alert students both to the *types* of college writing expected of them and to the *length* of an essay required frequently by teachers.

Finally, the exercises we have included for each essay are comprehensive and integrated—designed to develop and reinforce the key skills required in college writing. We have included two vocabulary exercises for each selection; the Words to Watch exercise alerts students to words they will read in context, and the Building Vocabulary exercise uses other effective methods (prefix/suffix, context clues, synonym/antonym, abstract/concrete) of teaching vocabulary. A section called Understanding the Writer's Ideas reinforces reading comprehension. Sections entitled Understanding the Writer's Techniques and Exploring the Writer's Ideas provide an excellent basis for class discussion and independent reading and analysis. The last exercise for each essay involves a dynamic approach to writing projects. Guided writing activities—a novel feature of *The Short Prose Reader*—tie the writing projects to the reading selections. Instead of simply being told to write an essay on a certain topic, students through Guided Writing will be able to move from step to step in the process of composition.

The Short Prose Reader can be used flexibly and effectively by students and teachers alike. The text is simple yet sophisticated, presenting essays and exercises that are easy to follow but never condescending. Weighing the needs and expectations of today's college freshmen, we have designed a rhetoric reader that can serve as the major text for the composition course.

We wish to thank our friend and aide, Don Linder, for

the invaluable assistance he gave us in developing the text. Next, we wish to thank our colleagues over the country for their support and are especially grateful to those who read the manuscript for this and previous editions and offered helpful suggestions: Mary Bisney, California State Polytechnic University, Pomona; Marilyn Collins, Glassboro State College; Kathy Cowan, Cabrillo College; Harry Crosby, Boston University; Mary Daly, College of DuPage; Morgan Desmond, State University of New York–ATC; Robert Esch, University of Texas, El Paso; Mary Frances Everhart, City College of San Francisco; Rowena Flanagan, Kansas City, Kansas Community College; Doug Fossek, Santa Barbara City College; Albert Geritz, Ft. Hays State College; Sister Madonna Giesilman, Donnelley College; Owen W. Gilman, Jr., St. Joseph's University; Bernard M. Goldman, Los Angeles Trade Tech College; Marc H. Goldsmith, Mitchell College; Wallace Goldstein, Westfield State College; Lillian Gottesman, Bronx Community College; Peggy-Joyce Grable, Walla Walla Community College; Wilma H. Hasse, Mitchell College; Roland Holmes, University of Illinois, Champaign-Urbana; Sharon Katz, Iona College; Isabel Kidder, Holyoke Community College; Elizabeth Latosi-Sawin, Missouri Western State College; Joseph V. Meduros, Mitchell Junior College; Robert Reising, Pembroke State University; Michael H. Riley, West Virginia Northern Community College; J. C. Searles, Pennsylvania State University; Mike Walker, Cabrillo College; and Ann N. Weisner, New York Institute of Technology.

Gilbert H. Muller

Harvey S. Wiener

THE SHORT
PROSE READER

CHAPTER 1

On Writing

Writing is not an isolated act. It is a definitive and integral part of daily human communication.

Writing is historic. Whether we try to imagine the "meanings" of prehistoric cave drawings or we plow through a satellite-transmitted newspaper each Sunday morning, we are participating in the same human impulse to communicate ideas to other people.

Writing is a product—whether that product is Thoreau's *Walden* or a student's essay calling for a ban on smoking in the college cafeteria.

And, perhaps most crucially, writing is a process—a process of transferring ideas from head to hand. Certainly that process is not absolute; the steps in producing a written piece vary from writer to writer and follow no exact order. Still, considering some of the common elements in this process is instructive for anyone embarking on a study of writing.

Few writers begin without some warmup activity. Generally called prewriting, the steps they take before producing a draft almost always start with thinking about their topic. They talk to friends and colleagues; they browse in libraries and rifle through reference books; they read newspaper and magazine articles. Sometimes they jot down notes and lists in order to put on paper some of their thoughts in very rough form. Some writers use free-association: they record as thoroughly as possible their random, unedited ideas about the topic. Using the raw, often disorganized materials produced in this preliminary stage, many writers try to group related thoughts with a scratch outline or some other effort to bring order to their written notes.

In these early stages, serious writers consider their *purpose* and their *audience*. Purpose means "intent," and all writers must know clearly what they intend to accomplish in a particular piece. Often the purpose evolves as the writer continues to think and write about the topic. The issue of audience is important too. Whom does the writer want to read the work? A clear sense of what readers may know and what they may expect helps a writer identify essential issues and choose appropriate language that can win the audience's support.

Prewriting efforts lead to a first draft. Like all works in progress, drafts are generally messy affairs—words crossed out or erased, loops and arrows drawn from one phrase to another, sentences scrawled in the margin.

As they read over their drafts, writers check for clarity of ideas and expression. Are thoughts *unified:* do they relate to an obvious main point? Are thoughts *coherent:* do they follow a logical plan, one idea flowing smoothly into the next? Which ideas require expansion with details? Which ideas should be eliminated? Which thoughts and words are vague or imprecise? In attempting to answer these questions, writers often try to find a friendly reader to look over the draft and to give advice. Whatever else they may look for at this stage, they do not pay much attention to spelling or other matters of correctness. Scissors and paste help in the transfer of one part of the text to another. A good word-processing program that can move blocks of sentences around saves time and simplifies revision.

One draft invariably leads to another. Of course, no one can predict how many drafts a piece of writing will require, but not many writers get by with fewer than two or three attempts. It's always necessary to produce a final copy—the manuscript that a writer will allow others to read and perhaps evaluate. At this point, careful attention to sentence structure, grammar, and spelling is very important. The final copy is the writer's best, cleanest effort.

This brief overview sketches in some of the important elements in the writing process. But you don't want to lose the idea that writing is both a process of inspiration and of craft. Many writers have tried to explain how the two connect in their own particular efforts to create. The novelist and short story writer Katherine Anne Porter, for example, tells how inspiration becomes communication in her writing: "Now and again thousands of memories converge, harmonize, and arrange themselves around a central idea in a coherent form, and I write...." Jean Cocteau, the playwright, asserts the need to shape inspiration into language for a page of writing: "To write, to conquer ink and paper, accumulate letters and paragraphs, divide them with periods and commas, is a different matter from carrying around the dream of a play or a book." The point made by Porter and Cocteau is that writing emerges from both creativity and skill, instruction and technique, talent and effort. As we said, writing is a process of inspiration *and* craft.

Why do people write?

We all (and we *all* can consider ourselves writers) attempt to explain things—what we see, what we feel, what we understand, what we experience, what we dream—so that we and others may better know the world and each other. We all—whether we are writing essays, poems, or stories, whether we are second graders attempting to describe a snowfall or philosophers attempting to explain the meaning of life—have an impulse, as James Baldwin states, "to examine attitudes, to go beneath the surface, to tap the source."

Because communication involves an audience, we need to be aware of a certain communal responsibility as writers. This is a responsibility to both form and content. As for content, we must be accurate—truthful, faithful to facts and details. As for form, we must carefully shape our words and sentences so that they represent what we perceive in our unique, exact, and precise way of viewing things.

It is no wonder that the four writers included in this chapter—four writers who represent a broad spectrum of personal histories, stylistic methods, and intellectual concerns—are all dedicated to exactitude and precision. Whether it's Joan Didion's desire to have "an accurate factual record of what I have been doing or thinking" or William Zinsser's pleas for the preciseness that comes only with simplicity, all are minutely concerned with the nuts and bolts of the process of shaping what Baldwin terms the "explicit medium of language."

The four writers represented here also run the gamut of expository techniques discussed in subsequent chapters. None of their essays is simply a "set piece." For example, William Saroyan combines personal reminiscence with theories of art, while William Stafford urges paying much more attention to the process than to the product. It can even be suggested that for some of the most successful writers, the process of writing may be even more important than the product.

Finally, although in the future a floppy disk may become more easily recognizable than a printed page, the basic medium of communication is still words. And, in order for these words to survive from generation to generation, there must be writing. It will always be true, in the words of Henry Miller, that "[w]riting, like life itself, is a voyage of discovery."

Why I Write

William Saroyan

William Saroyan (1908–1981) won the 1939 Pulitzer Prize for his play *The Time of Your Life*. His novel *The Human Comedy* (1942) is both an ironic and optimistic look at the human condition. In this essay, Saroyan writes of how tragedy, memory, and art have combined to bring meaning to his life.

Words to Watch

isolated (par. 2) set apart
vineyards (par. 4) fields for growing wine grapes
sorrow (par. 5) sadness
impelled (par. 6) driven to do something
impulse (par. 7) sudden inclination prompting action
gradual (par. 10) by degrees; little by little

1   It is a quarter of a century, almost, since my first book was published, but as I began to write when I was nine, I have been writing for forty years: that is to say, I have lived in a special way for forty years—the way that takes hold of a man who is determined to understand the meaning of his own life, and to be prepared to write about it.

2   But I think it goes even farther back than forty years. I think I began to live in my own special way when I became aware that I had memory. That happened before I was three. I also had a memory that went back to a time before I was *two,* but it was an isolated one. At that age I wasn't given to remembering *everything,* or rather I hadn't yet noticed that it had come to pass that I remembered.

3   In the past were some of the best things I had, several of them gone: my father, for instance, who had died before I was three.

4   My first memory, the one that went back to a time when I was not yet two, was of my father getting up onto a wagon, sitting beside my mother, and making a sound that told the horse to go. My two sisters and my brother and I sat in the

5

back of the wagon as it moved slowly down a dusty road between vineyards on a hot afternoon in the summertime. I remembered sensing sorrow and feeling *with*—with mine, my people—a father, a mother, two sisters, a brother, our horse, our wagon, our pots and pans and books. The rest is lost in the sleep that soon carried me away. The next thing I knew my father was gone, which I didn't understand.

I was fascinated by having memory, and troubled by the 5 sorrow of it. I refused to accept the theory that things end, including people, including my father. I refused to believe that my father was dead. (In the sense that every man *is* his father, I wasn't much mistaken.)

All the same, I felt impelled from the time I knew I had 6 memory to do something about the past, about endings, about human death.

My first impulse was simple. I wanted to cause the im- 7 possible to happen, because if I was able to do that, I knew I would be able to cause *anything* to happen. Thus, death would not be death, if anybody wanted it not to be.

I found two large empty cans. One I filled with water. 8 The empty can I placed two feet from the full can. I asked myself to cause the water in the full can to pass into the empty can, by itself, because I wanted it to.

The experiment failed. I had begun with the maximum, I 9 had failed, and so I began to consider what might be the next best.

For a long time there didn't appear to be *any* next best at 10 all. It was a matter of all or nothing, or at any rate the equivalent of nothing: continuous *gradual* loss, and finally total loss, or death.

What could a man do about this? Wait? That didn't seem 11 to be enough.

Why should I be troubled by memory at all if all memory 12 told me was that things change, fail, decline, end, and die? I didn't want good things to do that, and I didn't think they should. How could I seize a good thing when I saw it and halt its decline and death? As far as people were concerned, there just didn't seem to be *any* way.

And so I came to accept the theory that as far as I knew, 13 as far as *anybody* knew, as far as there appeared to be any order to the action of things at all, the end of the order was invariably and inevitably decline, disappearance, and death.

And yet the world was full of people all the time. And 14 the earth, the sea, and the sky were full of all manner of other living things: plants, animals, fish, birds.

Thus, something *did* stay, something *was* constant, or 15 appeared to be. It was the *kind* that stayed. *One* of a kind couldn't stay, and couldn't apparently be made to. I myself was one of a kind, and everybody I knew and loved was one of a kind, and so what about us? What could I do about our impermanence?

How could I halt this action? How had other men halted it? 16

I learned that they never had halted it. They had only 17 pretended to.

They had done this by means of art, or the putting of lim- 18 its upon the limitless, and thereby holding something fast and making it seem constant, indestructible, unstoppable, unkillable, deathless.

A great painter painted his wife, his son, his daughter, 19 and himself, and then one by one they all moved along and died. But the painting remained. A sculptor did the same thing with stone, a composer with musical sounds, and a writer with words.

Therefore, as the next best thing, art in one form or an- 20 other would have to be the way of my life, but which form of art?

Before I was eight I didn't think it could possibly be writ- 21 ing, for the simple reason that I couldn't read, let alone write, and everybody else I knew could do both. At last, though, I got the hang of reading and writing, and I felt (if I didn't think), "This is for me."

It had taken me so long to learn to write that I consid- 22 ered being able to write the greatest thing that could happen to anybody.

If I wrote something, it *was* written, it was itself, and it 23 might continue to be itself forever, or for what passes as forever.

Thus, I could halt the action of things, after all, and at 24 the same time be prepared to learn new things, to achieve new forms of halting, or art.

That is roughly how and why I became a writer.   25

In short, I began to write in order to get even on death.   26

I have continued to write for many reasons.   27

A long time ago I said I write because it is the only way   28
I am willing to survive.

Mainly, though, I write because I want to.   29

BUILDING VOCABULARY

1. The words below from the essay contain prefixes and suffixes that can help you determine the meanings of the words themselves. (See Glossary.) For each word define the prefix or suffix in italics and then define the word.

   a. *de*cline (par. 12)
   b. *in*vari*ably* (par. 13)
   c. *in*evit*ably* (par. 13)
   d. *dis*appear*ance* (par. 13)
   e. *im*perman*ence* (par. 15)
   f. limit*less* (par. 18)
   g. *in*destruct*ible* (par. 18)
   h. *un*stopp*able* (par. 18)
   i. *un*kill*able* (par. 18)
   j. death*less* (par. 18)

2. Write the *antonyms* (opposite meanings) for any five of the words in the exercise above. Then, use each antonym in an original sentence.

UNDERSTANDING THE WRITER'S IDEAS

1. How old is Saroyan at the time of writing this essay? How do you know?

2. In your own words, describe the "special way" in which Saroyan has lived? When did this "special way" of living begin for the author?

3. From what age does Saroyan remember his first memory? Summarize the memory in your own words. What is the importance of memory for this writer?

4. In what sort of environment did Saroyan live as a child?

5. How was Saroyan affected by his father's death? Explain the meaning of the parenthetical sentence: "(In the sense that every man *is* his father, I wasn't much mistaken.)" (par. 5).

6. In paragraph 7, Saroyan writes, "I wanted to cause the impossible to happen." Why? How did this desire relate to his father's death? How did he go about trying to cause the impossible? Did he succeed?

7. What *definition* does Saroyan offer of "art"? Why did he choose art as a way of life? What relationship did this choice have to memory? To his father's death? How did he come to choose writing among all the arts?

8. The title may be read in two ways: (a) Why Saroyan *started* to write, and (b) why he *continues* to write. Which seems predominant? Why? Cite the author's own reasons for both (a) and (b).

UNDERSTANDING THE WRITER'S TECHNIQUES

1. Is there a *thesis statement* (see Glossary) in this essay? Explain. Describe Saroyan's *purpose* for writing this essay. Who is his intended *audience?* Explain.

2. *Tone* refers to the writer's attitude or stance toward his or her subject (see Glossary) and is expressed in the word choices, rhythms, and overall "voice" of a piece of writing. How would you describe the *tone* of this essay? Point to three places in the essay that are particularly expressive of the tone.

3. What was your emotional response to reading the first

paragraph of this essay? Explain what it was about Saroyan's writing that made you feel that way.

4. What idea is repeated in paragraphs 1 and 2? Why? For
   what effect?

5. A *process analysis* (see Chapter 9) tells the reader step-
   by-step how to do something. Trace the steps whereby
   Saroyan dealt with his father's death.

6. Paragraph 18 (just one sentence long) contains at least five
   words built from prefix, root, suffix combinations. What is
   the cumulative effect of all these words? Why do you
   think Saroyan has used them here?

7. Throughout this essay, Saroyan makes liberal use of *italics*. For what reason does he use them? Which uses are
   most effective? Are there any which you feel are unnecessary? Why?

8. This essay is composed of a series of relatively short paragraphs, some only one or two sentences long. What is the
   effect of this type of writing? Do you feel any choppiness
   or incompleteness? Why or why not?

9. Throughout the essay, the author asks a number of questions, especially in paragraphs 15 and 16. What is his purpose in asking these questions? To whom are they addressed? What effect do they create?

10. Do you think the title is meant as a question or as a state-
    ment? Explain your answer in the context of the essay.

EXPLORING THE WRITER'S IDEAS

1. What is your earliest memory? How old were you? What
   lasting effect has the memory had on you?

2. Compare the environment in which Saroyan lived with
   your own childhood surroundings.

3. Was Saroyan's reaction to his father's death typical? How

does it compare with the way in which you have had to handle the loss of a loved one?

4. Have any of the arts given you the sort of consolation or life direction that they have provided for Saroyan? For example, at a time of stress or sadness, has anything in music, literature, or the visual arts ever changed your mood? Do you practice any art form, either professionally or as a hobby? If so, explain why you do it and how it makes you feel.

IDEAS FOR WRITING

Guided Writing

Write an essay entitled "Why I _____." Fill in the blank with an activity that is very important to you, that you believe will remain so throughout your life, and that reflects your creative talents. For example, you might want to write about "Why I Paint," "Why I Play the Piano," or "Why I Cook"—or, if you prefer, "Why I Write."

1. Begin with a statement of why and for how long this activity has been important to you.

2. Dig deeply into your memory to relate an early memory that is tied to your choice to pursue this activity.

3. Tell about a particular incident or person that especially affected your choice of this activity.

4. Relate the process whereby you chose this "special way of living."

5. Throughout your essay use questions to help your reader understand your thought processes as you developed this way of life.

6. Write in a simple, direct way using mainly very short paragraphs.

7. Try to maintain an emotionally charged, serious tone.

8. End your essay with a series of quick, direct statements, the last of which should relate positively to your future in this activity.

More Writing Projects

1. Start a journal for the term. In your first entry, record some of your earliest memories of various creative acts—for instance, writing out letters of the alphabet, toying with a musical instrument, playing with crayons and paint, and so forth. Try to capture the original sensations.

2. Summarize the main ideas presented by Saroyan in a paragraph of no more than 100 words. Then write another paragraph condensing the summary to 50 words.

3. Write a brief essay on what Saroyan calls the "fascination" and "sorrow" of memory.

Writing
William Stafford

In this 1970 essay on writing, author William Stafford presents an important message to writers at all levels. Writing, he insists, is foremost a *process*. It is not, according to Stafford, "negotiable," not to be considered for its value as a product. And, he suggests, the ultimate guide for a writer must be "the self." Stafford's "process-rather-than-substance" message also relates well to creative endeavors other than writing, as well as to less-exalted processes like *fishing,* for example, which Stafford offers as an analogy.

Words to Watch

unforeseen (par. 1)   unexpected; not anticipated
succession (par. 1)   series; sequence
interval (par. 3)   fixed period of time
trivial (par. 3)   unimportant; superficial
resolutely (par. 4)   purposefully; in a determined manner
headlong (par. 4)   without pause or delay
justification (par. 5)   defense; vindication
successive (par. 6)   one after another
baffled (par. 7)   confused; dazed
stalled (par. 7)   temporarily stopped
negotiable (par. 9)   marketable; usable
eventuates (par. 9)   makes happen in the end
scope (par. 12)   range; area
elation (par. 12)   joy; great happiness
realm (par. 12)   domain; zone

A writer is not so much someone who has something to 1
say as he is someone who has found a process that will bring
about new things he would not have thought of if he had not
started to say them. That is, he does not draw on a reservoir;
instead, he engages in an activity that brings to him a whole

succession of unforeseen stories, poems, essays, plays, laws, philosophies, religions, or—but wait!

Back in school, from the first when I began to try to 2 write things, I felt this richness. One thing would lead to another; the world would give and give. Now, after twenty years or so of trying, I live by that certain richness, an idea hard to pin, difficult to say, and perhaps offensive to some. For there are strange implications in it.

One implication is the importance of just plain receptiv- 3 ity. When I write, I like to have an interval before me when I am not likely to be interrupted. For me, this means usually the early morning, before others are awake. I get pen and paper, take a glance out the window (often it is dark out there), and wait. It is like fishing. But I do not wait very long, for there is always a nibble—and this is where receptivity comes in. To get started I will accept anything that occurs to me. Something always occurs, of course, to any of us. We can't keep from thinking. Maybe I have to settle for an immediate impression: it's cold, or hot, or dark, or bright, or in between! Or—well, the possibilities are endless. If I put down something, that thing will help the next thing come, and I'm off. If I let the process go on, things will occur to me that were not at all in my mind when I started. These things, odd and trivial as they may be, are somehow connected. And if I let them string out, surprising things will happen.

If I let them string out.... Along with initial receptivity, 4 then, there is another readiness: I must be willing to fail. If I am to keep on writing, I cannot bother to insist on high standards. I must get into action and not let anything stop me, or even slow me much. By "standards" I do not mean "correctness"—spelling, punctuation, and so on. These details become mechanical for anyone who writes for a while. I am thinking about what many people would consider "important" standards, such matters as social significance, positive values, consistency, etc. I resolutely disregard these. Something better, greater, is happening! I am following a process that leads so wildly and originally into new territory that no judgment can at the moment be made about values, significance, and so on. I am making something new, something that has not been judged before. Later others—and maybe I myself—will make judgments. Now, I am headlong to discover. Any distraction may harm the creating.

So, receptive, careless of failure, I spin out things on the 5 page. And a wonderful freedom comes. If something occurs to me, it is all right to accept it. It has one justification: it occurs to me. No one else can guide me. I must follow my own weak, wandering, diffident impulses.

A strange bonus happens. At times, without my insisting 6 on it, my writings become coherent; the successive elements that occur to me are clearly related. They lead by themselves to new connections. Sometimes the language, even the syllables that happen along, may start a trend. Sometimes the materials alert me to something waiting in my mind, ready for sustained attention. At such times, I allow myself to be eloquent, or intentional, or for great swoops (treacherous! not to be trusted!) reasonable. But I do not insist on any of that; for I know that back of my activity there will be the coherence of my self, and that indulgence of my impulses will bring recurrent patterns and meanings again.

This attitude toward the process of writing creatively 7 suggests a problem for me, in terms of what others say. They talk about "skills" in writing. Without denying that I do have experience, wide reading, automatic orthodoxies and maneuvers of various kinds, I still must insist that I am often baffled about what "skill" has to do with the precious little area of confusion when I do not know what I am going to say and then I found out what I am going to say. That precious interval I am unable to bridge by skill. What can I witness about it? It remains mysterious, just as all of us must feel puzzled about how we are so inventive as to be able to talk along through complexities with our friends, not needing to plan what we are going to say, but never stalled for long in our confident forward progress. Skill? If so, it is the skill we all have, something we must have learned before the age of three or four.

A writer is one who has become accustomed to trusting 8 that grace, or luck, or—skill.

Yet another attitude I find necessary: most of what I 9 write, like most of what I say in casual conversation, will not amount to much. Even I will realize, and even at the time, that it is not negotiable. It will be like practice. In conversation, I allow myself random remarks—in fact, as I recall, that is the way I learned to talk—so in writing I launch many expendable efforts. A result of this free way of writing is that I am not writing for others, mostly; they will not see the product at all unless the activity eventuates in something that later appears to be worthy. My guide is the self, and its adventuring in the language brings about communication.

This process-rather-than-substance view of writing in- 10 vites a final, dual reflection:

1. Writers may not be special—sensitive or talented in 11 any usual sense. They are simply engaged in sustained use of a language skill we all have. Their "creations" come about through confident reliance on stray impulses that will, with trust, find occasional patterns that are satisfying.

2. But writing itself is one of the great, free human ac- 12 tivities. There is scope for individuality, and elation, and discovery, in writing. For the person who follows with trust and forgiveness what occurs to him, the world remains always ready and deep, an inexhaustible environment, with the combined vividness of an actuality and flexibility of a dream. Working back and forth between experience and thought, writers have more than space and time can offer. They have the whole unexplored realm of human vision.

BUILDING VOCABULARY

1. Use *context clues* (see Glossary) to determine the meanings of the words in italics below. Use a dictionary to check your definitions.

   a. strange *implications* (par. 2)
   b. initial *receptivity* (par. 4)
   c. *diffident* impulses (par. 5)
   d. strange *bonus* (par. 6)
   e. *sustained* attention (par. 6)
   f. *recurrent* patterns (par. 6)

    g. automatic *orthodoxies* (par. 7)
    h. *expendable* efforts (par. 9)
    i. stray *impulses* (par. 11)
    j. *inexhaustible* environment (par. 12)

2. Select five words from the Words to Watch section and
write original sentences that use each word correctly.

UNDERSTANDING THE WRITER'S IDEAS

1. In your own words, explain the meaning of the first two
sentences.

2. What is the "richness" Stafford refers to in paragraph 2?
Why is it "hard to pin"? Why "perhaps offensive to
some"?

3. What does Stafford mean by "just plain receptivity" (par.
3)?

4. Outline the main steps in Stafford's process of writing.
What does he mean when he writes of the first step that
"It is like fishing" (par. 3)? What is his general attitude
toward the overall process? When and how does he usually begin the process? Why?

5. According to Stafford, what are the important "standards" in writing? Which are *not* important? What is his
attitude toward these standards? Why?

6. Why does Stafford say: "I must be willing to fail" (par.
4)?

7. Explain Stafford's use of the phrase "great swoops" (par.
6). Why does he follow the phrase with parenthetical
"(treacherous! not to be trusted!)"?

8. What is "that indulgence" of paragraph 6?

9. What is the author's opinion of the "skills" to which people refer when they talk about writing? What skill does he
feel is the most valuable? Why?

10. What is Stafford's attitude toward his writing while he is in the midst of the process? Explain. What is his attitude toward his readers while he is writing? Explain.

11. Stafford offers two definitions of a writer. What are they? How do they relate to each other? In what ways are they similar? In what ways different? What relation does their placement in the essay have to Stafford's purpose in writing the essay? What relation to his main idea?

12. What does Stafford mean by "an inexhaustible environment, with the combined vividness of an actuality and flexibility of a dream" (par. 12)?

UNDERSTANDING THE WRITER'S TECHNIQUES

1. What is the effect of "—but wait!" which ends paragraph 1? What relation does it have to the reader? Who is the intended audience (readership) for this essay?

2. In what ways does the first sentence of paragraph 3 serve as an effective *transition* (see Glossary) from the introduction to the body of this essay?

3. Throughout the essay, Stafford uses dashes. What is the usual purpose of this form of punctuation? How does Stafford's use of dashes affect meaning in this essay? How does it affect *tone* (see Glossary)?

4. Why does Stafford repeat the statement "if I let them string out" at the end of paragraph 3 and the beginning of paragraph 4? What does he mean by that clause?

5. What comparison does Stafford make between the process of writing and conversation? Explain the comparison in your own words.

6. Although most of the paragraphs in this essay are quite fully developed, Stafford makes use of two, one-sentence

paragraphs. Locate them and discuss their usefulness and effectiveness.

7. To whom is the one-word question "Skill?" addressed in paragraph 7?

8. The title of this essay is simple and direct. Do you find it appropriate? If you were to give this essay a new title, what would it be?

9. What is the relation between the two aspects of the "dual reflection" (pars. 10–12) that concludes this essay?

10. Is there one sentence in this essay that states the *main idea?* If so, what is it? Where does it appear in the development of the essay? Why?

11. Compare the tone of the opening (pars. 1–2), middle (pars. 3–9), and closing (pars. 10–12) sections of the essay. Are there any changes in tone? Support your answer with specific references to the text.

12. What is Stafford's purpose in writing this essay? How do you know?

13. In paragraph 1, Stafford refers to "A writer" and "he." But, in paragraph 12, the references are to "Writers" and "They." What is the effect of this change in reference?

EXPLORING THE WRITER'S IDEAS

1. In the first sentence, Stafford indicates that the *process* of writing itself calls forth ideas that even the writer may not have been aware of. Do you believe this is true? How have your experiences of writing—essays, letters, stories, poems—confirmed or challenged this assertion?

2. Many writers, and creative artists in general, have a less-than-favorable view of critics. Based on your reading of Stafford's essay about the process of writing, what would

you guess is his attitude toward literary critics? Explain your response.

3. In paragraph 10, Stafford relates to his "process-rather-than-substance view of writing." Throughout the essay, he is clearly more concerned with the creative process than with the creative product. Find examples throughout the essay that support this attitude.

4. Stafford states: "Writers may not be special." Do you feel this honestly sums up his attitude toward writers? Why? Compare Stafford's attitude to William Saroyan's attitude that as a writer, he felt that he has "lived in a special way" (page 5 in the essay "Why I Write"). Would Stafford agree with the last sentence in Saroyan's essay, in which he states: "Mainly, though, I write because I want to" (page 8)?

5. In general, do you think that creative processes such as writing, painting, making music, and so on can be learned—or do you think that people must be born with certain talents and abilities? Discuss examples of talented people you know personally.

IDEAS FOR WRITING

Guided Writing

Write an essay about something that you do well in which the process is more important to you than the product. For example, you might choose singing, painting, weight lifting, public speaking, cooking, gardening, and so on.

1. Begin your essay with a definition of a person (for example, a singer, a painter, a weight lifter) who engages in this activity. Relate your definition to the process.

2. Briefly state the most important feature of this process and comment on how others may view it.

3. In well-developed paragraphs, outline the steps and most

important concerns that guide you in the process. Explain how your concerns might contradict the more usually accepted attitudes toward the process of this activity.

4. Pay close attention to the ways in which you feel that you are developing your skills or achieving personal satisfaction while you are engaged in the process.

5. Use dashes here and there to set off parenthetical reflections.

6. Before beginning your conclusion, write another, more concise, one-sentence definition of a person who engages in this activity.

7. Organize your conclusion into two generalized, yet important, summary observations about the process of this activity.

8. Give your essay a simple, one- or two-word title.

More Writing Projects

1. In your journal, list the skills that you possess as a writer—as well as those skills that you would like to acquire.

2. Outline in a paragraph the processes you use in approaching a writing assignment. Explain which is the most satisfying and enjoyable. Which is the least so? Why?

3. Write a short essay to describe an activity in which the product, or end result, is *definitely more important* than the process by which you achieve it.

Simplicity

William Zinsser

In this chapter from *On Writing Well,* William Zinsser begins with a fairly pessimistic analysis of the clutter that pervades and degrades American writing, and he offers many examples to prove his point. Zinsser deals with almost all major aspects of the writing process—thinking, composing, awareness of the reader, self-discipline, rewriting, and editing—and concludes that simplicity is the key to them all.

Words to Watch

decipher (par. 2)   to make out the meaning of something obscure

adulterants (par. 3)   added substances which make something impure or inferior

mollify (par. 4)   to appease; to soothe

spell (par. 4)   a short period of time

assailed (par. 8)   attacked with words or physical violence

spruce (par. 8)   neat or smart in appearance

rune (par. 11)   character in an ancient alphabet

surfeit (par. 14)   an overabundant supply

superfluous (par. 15)   extra; more than is needed; wasteful

enumerate (par. 16)   to count or list in order

Clutter is the disease of American writing. We are a society strangling in unnecessary words, circular constructions, pompous frills and meaningless jargon. 1

Who really knows what the average businessman is trying to say in the average business letter? What member of an insurance or medical plan can decipher the brochure that tells him what his costs and benefits are? What father or mother can put together a child's toy—on Christmas Eve or any other eve—from the instructions on the box? Our national tendency is to inflate and thereby sound important. The airline pilot who wakes us to announce that he is presently anticipating experiencing considerable weather wouldn't dream of saying that 2

初搭

there's a storm ahead and it may get bumpy. The sentence is too simple—there must be something wrong with it.

But the secret of good writing is to strip every sentence 3 to its cleanest components. Every word that serves no function, every long word that could be a short word, every adverb which carries the same meaning that is already in the verb, every passive construction that leaves the reader unsure of who is doing what—these are the thousand and one adulterants that weaken the strength of a sentence. And they usually occur, ironically, in proportion to education and rank.

During the late 1960's the president of Princeton Univer- 4 sity wrote a letter to mollify the alumni after a spell of campus unrest. "You are probably aware," he began, "that we have been experiencing very considerable potentially explosive expressions of dissatisfaction on issues only partially related." He meant that the students had been hassling them about different things. As an alumnus I was far more upset by the president's syntax than by the students' potentially explosive expressions of dissatisfaction. I would have preferred the presidential approach taken by Franklin D. Roosevelt when he tried to convert into English his own government's memos, such as this blackout order of 1942:

> Such preparations shall be made as will completely obscure all Federal buildings and non-Federal buildings occupied by the Federal government during an air raid for any period of time from visibility by reason of internal or external illumination.

"Tell them," Roosevelt said, "that in buildings where 5 they have to keep the work going to put something across the windows."

Simplify, simplify. Thoreau said it, as we are so often re- 6 minded, and no American writer more consistently practiced what he preached. Open *Walden* to any page and you will find a man saying in a plain and orderly way what is on his mind:

> I love to be alone. I never found the companion that was so companionable as solitude. We are for the most part more lonely when we go abroad among men than when we stay in

our chambers. A man thinking or working is always alone, let him be where he will. Solitude is not measured by the miles of space that intervene between a man and his fellows. The really diligent student in one of the crowded hives of Cambridge College is as solitary as a dervish in the desert.

How can the rest of us achieve such enviable freedom 7 from clutter? The answer is to clear our heads of clutter. Clear thinking becomes clear writing: one can't exist without the other. It is impossible for a muddy thinker to write good English. He may get away with it for a paragraph or two, but soon the reader will be lost, and there is no sin so grave, for he will not easily be lured back.

Who is this elusive creature, the reader? He is a person 8 with an attention span of about twenty seconds. He is assailed on every side by forces competing for his time: by newspapers and magazines, by television and radio and stereo, by his wife and children and pets, by his house and his yard and all the gadgets that he has bought to keep them spruce, and by that most potent of competitors, sleep. The man snoozing in his chair with an unfinished magazine open on his lap is a man who is being given too much unnecessary trouble by the writer.

It won't do to say that the snoozing reader is too dumb 9 or too lazy to keep pace with the train of thought. My sympathies are with him. If a reader is lost, it is generally because the writer has not been careful enough to keep him on the path.

This carelessness can take any number of forms. Per- 10 haps a sentence is so excessively cluttered that the reader, hacking his way through the verbiage, simply doesn't know what it means. Perhaps a sentence has been so shoddily constructed that the reader could read it in any of several ways. Perhaps the writer has switched pronouns in mid-sentence, or has switched tenses, so the reader loses track of who is talking or when the action took place. Perhaps Sentence B is not a logical sequel to Sentence A—the writer, in whose head the connection is clear, has not bothered to provide the missing link. Perhaps the writer has used an important word incorrectly by not taking the trouble to look it up. He may think that "sanguine" and "sanguinary" mean the same thing, but the difference is a bloody big one. The reader can only infer (speaking of big differences) what the writer is trying to imply.

Faced with these obstacles, the reader is at first a re- 11 markably tenacious bird. He blames himself—he obviously missed something, and he goes back over the mystifying sentence, or over the whole paragraph, piecing it out like an ancient rune, making guesses and moving on. But he won't do this for long. The writer is making him work too hard, and the reader will look for one who is better at his craft.

The writer must therefore constantly ask himself: What 12 am I trying to say? Surprisingly often, he doesn't know. Then he must look at what he has written and ask: Have I said it? Is it clear to someone encountering the subject for the first time? If it's not, it is because some fuzz has worked its way into the machinery. The clear writer is a person clear-headed enough to see this stuff for what it is: fuzz.

I don't mean that some people are born clear-headed and 13 are therefore natural writers, whereas others are naturally fuzzy and will never write well. Thinking clearly is a conscious act that the writer must force upon himself, just as if he were embarking on any other project that requires logic: adding up a laundry list or doing an algebra problem. Good writing doesn't come naturally, though most people obviously think it does. The professional writer is forever being bearded by strangers who say that they'd like to "try a little writing some time" when they retire from their real profession. Good writing takes self-discipline and, very often, self-knowledge.

Many writers, for instance, can't stand to throw any- 14 thing away. Their sentences are littered with words that mean essentially the same thing and with phrases which make a point that is implicit in what they have already said. When students give me these littered sentences I beg them to select from the surfeit of words the few that most precisely fit what they want to say. Choose one, I plead, from among the three almost identical adjectives. Get rid of the unnecessary adverbs. Eliminate "in a funny sort of way" and other such qualifiers—they do no useful work.

The students look stricken—I am taking all their wonder- 15

ful words away. I am only taking their superfluous words
away, leaving what is organic and strong.

"But," one of my worst offenders confessed, "I never 16
can get rid of anything—you should see my room." (I didn't
take him up on the offer.) "I have two lamps where I only need
one, but I can't decide which one I like better, so I keep them
both." He went on to enumerate his duplicated or unnecessary
objects, and over the weeks ahead I went on throwing away his
duplicated and unnecessary words. By the end of the term—a
term that he found acutely painful—his sentences were clean.

"I've had to change my whole approach to writing," he 17
told me. "Now I have to *think* before I start every sentence
and I have to *think* about every word." The very idea amazed
him. Whether his room also looked better I never found out. I
suspect that it did.

Two pages of the final manuscript of this chapter. Although they look
like a first draft, they have already been rewritten and retyped—like
almost every other page—four or five times. With each rewrite I try
to make what I have written tighter, stronger and more precise, elim-
inating every element that is not doing useful work, until at last I
have a clean copy for the printer. Then I go over it once more, reading it aloud, and am always amazed at how much clutter can still be
profitably cut.

---

is too dumb or too lazy to keep pace with the ~~writer's~~ train
of thought. My sympathies are ~~entirely~~ with him.) ~~He's not
so dumb~~. (If the reader is lost, it is generally because the
writer ~~of the article~~ has not been careful enough to keep
him on the ~~proper~~ path.

(This carelessness can take any number of ~~different~~ forms.
Perhaps a sentence is so excessively ~~long and~~ cluttered that
the reader, hacking his way through ~~all~~ the verbiage, simply
doesn't know what _it_ ~~the writer~~ means. Perhaps a sentence has
been so shoddily constructed that the reader could read it in
any of _several_ ~~two or three different~~ ways. ~~He thinks he knows what
the writer is trying to say, but he's not sure.~~ Perhaps the
writer has switched pronouns in mid-sentence, or ~~perhaps he~~
has switched tenses, so the reader loses track of who is
talking ~~to whom,~~ or ~~exactly~~ when the action took place. Perhaps Sentence B is not a logical sequel to Sentence A -- the
writer, in whose head the connection is ~~perfectly~~ clear, has
not _bothered to provide_ ~~given enough thought to providing~~ the missing link. Perhaps the writer has used an important word incorrectly by not
taking the trouble to look it up ~~and make sure.~~ He may think
that "sanguine" and "sanguinary" mean the same thing, but)
~~I can assure you that~~(the difference is a bloody big one~~to the~~

The reader can only infer (speaking of big differences) what the writer is trying to imply.

Faced with these obstacles, the reader is at first a remarkably tenacious bird. He blames himself. He obviously missed something, and he goes back over the mystifying sentence, or over the whole paragraph, piecing it out like an ancient rune, making guesses and moving on. But he won't do this for long. The writer is making him work too hard, and the reader will look for one who is better at his craft.

The writer must therefore constantly ask himself: What am I trying to say? Surprisingly often, he doesn't know. Then he must look at what he has written and ask: Have I said it? Is it clear to someone encountering the subject for the first time? If it's not, it is because some fuzz has worked its way into the machinery. The clear writer is a person clear-headed enough to see this stuff for what it is: fuzz.

I don't mean that some people are born clear-headed and are therefore natural writers, whereas others are naturally fuzzy and will never write well. Thinking clearly is a conscious act that the writer must force upon himself, just as if he were embarking on any other project that requires logic: adding up a laundry list or doing an algebra problem. Good writing doeesn't come naturally, though most people obviously think it does. The professional

BUILDING VOCABULARY

1. Zinsser uses a number of words and expressions drawn from areas other than writing; he uses them to make interesting combinations or comparisons in such expressions as *elusive creature* (par. 8), *hacking his way through the verbiage* (par. 10), and *a remarkably tenacious bird* (par. 11). Find other such expressions in this essay. Write simple explanations for the three above and the others that you find.

2. List words or phrases in this essay that pertain to writing—the process, the results, the faults, the successes. Explain any with which you were unfamiliar.

UNDERSTANDING THE WRITER'S IDEAS

1. State simply Zinsser's meaning in the opening paragraph. What faults of "bad writing" does he mention in this paragraph?

2. To what is Zinsser objecting in paragraph 2?

3. What, according to the author, is the "secret of good writing"? Explain this "secret" in a few simple words of your own. What does Zinsser say detracts from good writing? What is the meaning of the word *ironically?* Why does Zinsser write that the incidence of these writing faults "occur, *ironically,* in proportion to education and rank"?

4. What was the "message" in the letter from the president of Princeton to the alumni? Why does Zinsser object to it? Was it more objectionable in form or content?

5. Who was Thoreau? What is *Walden?* Why are references to the two especially appropriate to Zinsser's essay?

6. What, according to Zinsser, is the relation between clear thinking and good writing? Can you have one without the other? What is meant by a "muddy thinker" (par. 7)? Why is it "impossible for a muddy thinker to write good English"?

7. Why does the author think most people fall asleep while reading? What is his attitude toward such people?

8. Look up and explain the "big differences" between the words *sanguine* and *sanguinary*; *infer* and *imply*. What is Zinsser's point in calling attention to these differences?

9. In paragraph 12, Zinsser writes about a writer's necessary awareness of the composing process. What elements of the *process* of writing are included in that paragraph? In that discussion, Zinsser speaks of *fuzz* in writing. What does he mean by that word as it relates to the writing process? To what does Zinsser compare the writer's thinking process? Why does he use such simple comparisons?

10. Explain the meaning of the last sentence. What does it indicate about Zinsser's attitude toward his work?

UNDERSTANDING THE WRITER'S TECHNIQUES

1. Explain the use of the words *disease* and *strangling* in paragraph 1. Why does Zinsser use these words in an essay about writing?

2. For what purpose does Zinsser use a series of questions in paragraph 2?

3. Throughout this essay, Zinsser makes extensive use of examples to support general opinions and attitudes. What attitude or opinion is he supporting in paragraphs 2, 3, 4, 5, and 10? How does he use examples in each of those paragraphs?

4. Analyze the specific structure and organization of paragraph 3:
    a. What general idea about writing does he propose?
    b. Where does he place that idea in the paragraph?
    c. What examples does he offer to support his general idea?

   d. With what new idea does he conclude the paragraph?
   How is it related to the beginning idea?

5. Why does Zinsser reproduce exactly portions of the writings of a past president of Princeton University, President Franklin D. Roosevelt, and Henry David Thoreau? How do these sections makes Zinsser's writing clearer, more understandable, or more important?

6. What is the effect on the reader of the words, "Simplify, simplify," which begin paragraph 6? Why does Zinsser use them at that particular point in the essay? What do they indicate about his attitude toward his subject? Explain.

7. Why does the author begin so many sentences in paragraph 10 with the word *Perhaps?* How does that technique help to *unify* (see page 2) the paragraph?

8. For what reasons does Zinsser include the two pages of "rough" manuscript as a part of the finished essay? What is he trying to show the reader in this way? How does seeing these pages help you to understand better what he is writing about in the completed essay?

9. Overall, how would you describe Zinsser's attitude toward the process and craft of writing? What would you say is his overall attitude toward the future of American writing? Is he generally optimistic or pessimistic? On what does his attitude depend? Refer to specifics in the essay to support your answer.

10. Do you think Zinsser expected other writers, or budding writers, to be the main readers of this essay? Why or why not? If so, with what main idea do you think he would like them to come away from the essay? Do you think readers who were not somehow involved in the writing process would benefit equally from this essay? Why?

EXPLORING THE WRITER'S IDEAS

1. Do you think that Zinsser is ever guilty in this essay of the very "sins" against writing about which he is upset? Could

he have simplified any of his points? Select one of Zinsser's paragraphs in the finished essay and explain how you might rewrite it more simply.

2. In the reading that you do most often, have you noticed overly cluttered writing? Or, do you feel that the writing is at its clearest level of presentation and understanding for its audience? Bring to class some examples of this writing and be prepared to discuss it. In general, what do you consider the relation between the simplicity or complexity of a piece of writing and its intended readership?

3. In the note to the two rough manuscript pages included with this essay, Zinsser implies that the process of rewriting and simplifying may be endless. How do you know when to stop trying to rewrite an essay, story, or poem? Do you ever really feel satisfied that you've reached the end of the rewriting process?

4. Choose one of the rough manuscript paragraphs and compare it to the finished essay. Which do you feel is better? Why? Is there anything Zinsser deleted from the rough copy that you feel he should have retained? Why?

5. Comment on Zinsser's assertion that "Thinking clearly is a conscious act that the writer must force upon himself" (par. 13). How does this opinion compare with the opinions of the three other writers in this chapter?

6. Reread William Stafford's essay "Writing" (pages 13–16). What similarities and differences do you note in Zinsser's and Stafford's writing processes?

IDEAS FOR WRITING

Guided Writing

In a 500- to 750-word essay, write about what you feel are some of the problems that you face as a writer.

1. In the first paragraph, identify the problems that you plan to discuss.

2. In the course of your essay, relate your problems more generally to the society-at-large.

3. Identify what, in your opinion, is the "secret" of good writing. Give specific examples of what measures to take to achieve that secret process and thereby to eliminate some of your problem.

4. Try to include one or two accurate reproductions of your writing to illustrate your composing techniques.

5. Point out what you believe were the major causes of your difficulties as a writer.

6. Toward the end of your essay, explain the type of writer that you would like to be in order to succeed in college.

More Writing Projects

1. Over the next few days, listen to the same news reporter or talk-show host on television or radio. Record in your journal at least ten examples that indicate the use of "unnecessary words, circular constructions, pompous frills, and meaningless jargon." Or, compile such a list from an article in a newspaper or magazine you read regularly. Then write an essay presenting and commenting on these examples.

2. Respond in a paragraph to Zinsser's observation, "Good writing takes self-discipline and, very often, self-knowledge."

3. In preparation for a writing assignment, collect with other class members various samples of junk mail and business correspondence that confirm Zinsser's statement that these tend to be poorly written. Write an essay describing your findings. Be certain to provide specific examples from the documents you have assembled.

On Keeping a Notebook

Joan Didion

Joan Didion is an American novelist and essayist whose works include the novel *Play It As It Lays* (1970) and the essay collection *The White Album* (1979). Much of her writing deals with what she considers an inherent lack of fulfillment in contemporary American life. In the essay that follows, Didion discusses the meanings and processes of keeping a notebook—what she describes as a "compulsive" and "inexplicable" impulse—which, nevertheless, is a valuable and often crucial prewriting activity. As you read this essay, consider what might prompt you to make notes on your experiences, thoughts, and feelings.

Words to Watch

crepe-de-Chine (par. 1)   a fine, soft, crinkly cloth

presentiment (par. 4)   a feeling that something is about to happen

verisimilitude (par. 7)   the appearance of truth; realism

delude (par. 8)   mislead

aperçus (par. 8)   insights

diffident (par. 10)   timid; unassertive

self-effacing (par. 10)   shy; expressing a negative self-image

affect (par. 10)   to put on a pretense

absorption (par. 10)   intense interest

patently (par. 11)   openly

indiscriminate (par. 11)   without plan or pattern

marginal (par. 12)   at the outer fringes of importance

ambergris (par. 13)   a waxy substance used in perfumery

magpie (par. 14)   a person who chatters noisily

" 'That woman Estelle,' " the note reads, " 'is partly the 1 reason why George Sharp and I are separated today.' *Dirty crepe-de-Chine wrapper, hotel bar, Wilmington RR, 9:45 A.M. August Monday morning.*"

Since the note is in my notebook, it presumably has 2 some meaning to me. I study it for a long while. At first I have only the most general notion of what I was doing on an August Monday morning in the bar of the hotel across from the Pennsylvania Railroad station in Wilmington, Delaware (waiting for a train? missing one? 1960? 1961? why Wilmington?), but I do remember being there. The woman in the dirty crepe-de-Chine wrapper had come down from her room for a beer, and the bartender had heard before the reason why George Sharp and she were separated today. "Sure," he said, and went on mopping the floor. "You told me." At the other end of the bar is a girl. She is talking, pointedly, not to the man beside her but to a cat lying in the triangle of sunlight cast through the open door. She is wearing a plaid silk dress from Peck & Peck, and the hem is coming down.

Here is what it is: the girl has been on the Eastern Shore, 3 and now she is going back to the city, leaving the man beside her, and all she can see ahead are the viscous summer sidewalks and the 3 A.M. long-distance calls that will make her lie awake and then sleep drugged through all the steaming mornings left in August (1960? 1961?). Because she must go directly from the train to lunch in New York, she wishes that she had a safety pin for the hem of the plaid silk dress, and she also wishes that she could forget about the hem and the lunch and stay in the cool bar that smells of disinfectant and malt and make friends with the woman in the crepe-de-Chine wrapper. She is afflicted by a little self-pity, and she wants to compare Estelles. That is what that was all about.

Why did I write it down? In order to remember, of 4 course, but exactly what was it I wanted to remember? How much of it actually happened? Did any of it? Why do I keep a notebook at all? It is easy to deceive oneself on all those scores. The impulse to write things down is a peculiarly compulsive one, inexplicable to those who do not share it, useful only accidentally, only secondarily, in the way that any compulsion tries to justify itself. I suppose that it begins or does not begin in the cradle. Although I have felt compelled to write things down since I was five years old, I doubt that my daughter ever will, for she is a singularly blessed and accepting child, delighted with life exactly as life presents itself to her, unafraid to go to sleep and unafraid to wake up. Keepers of private notebooks are a different breed altogether, lonely and resistant rearrangers of things, anxious malcontents, children afflicted apparently at birth with some presentiment of loss.

My first notebook was a Big Five tablet, given to me by 5 my mother with the sensible suggestion that I stop whining and learn to amuse myself by writing down my thoughts. She returned the tablet to me a few years ago; the first entry is an account of a woman who believed herself to be freezing to death in the Arctic night, only to find, when day broke, that she had stumbled onto the Sahara Desert, where she would die of the heat before lunch. I have no idea what turn of a five-year-old's mind could have prompted so insistently "ironic" and exotic a story, but it does reveal a certain predilection for the extreme which has dogged me into adult life; perhaps if I were analytically inclined I would find it a truer story than any I might have told about Donald Johnson's birthday party or the day my cousin Brenda put Kitty Litter in the aquarium.

So the point of my keeping a notebook has never been, 6 nor is it now, to have an accurate factual record of what I have been doing or thinking. That would be a different impulse entirely, an instinct for reality which I sometimes envy but do not possess. At no point have I ever been able successfully to keep a diary; my approach to daily life ranges from the grossly negligent to the merely absent, and on those few occasions when I have tried dutifully to record a day's events, boredom has so overcome me that the results are mysterious at best. What is this business about "shopping, typing piece, dinner with E, depressed"? Shopping for what? Typing what piece? Who is E? Was this "E" depressed, or was I depressed? Who cares?

In fact I have abandoned altogether that kind of pointless 7 entry; instead I tell what some would call lies. "That's simply not true," the members of my family frequently tell me when they come up against my memory of a shared event. "The party was *not* for you, the spider was *not* a black widow, *it wasn't that way at all*." Very likely they are right, for not only have I always had trouble distinguishing between what happened and what merely might have happened, but I remain unconvinced that the distinction, for my purposes, matters. The cracked crab that I recall having for lunch the day my father came home from Detroit in 1945 must certainly be embroidery, worked into the day's pattern to lend verisimilitude; I was ten years old and would not now remember the cracked crab. The day's events did not turn on cracked crab. And yet it is precisely that fictitious crab that makes me see the afternoon all over again, a home movie run all too often, the father bearing gifts, the child weeping, an exercise in family love and guilt. Or that is what it was to me. Similarly, perhaps it never did snow that August in Vermont; perhaps there never were flurries in the night wind, and maybe no one else felt the ground hardening and summer already dead even as we pretended to bask in it, but that was how it felt to me, and it might as well have snowed, could have snowed, did snow.

How it felt to me: that is getting closer to the truth about **8** a notebook. I sometimes delude myself about why I keep a notebook, imagine that some thrifty virtue derives from preserving everything observed. See enough and write it down, I tell myself, and then some morning when the world seems drained of wonder, some day when I am only going through the motions of doing what I am supposed to do, which is write—on that bankrupt morning I will simply open my notebook and there it will all be, a forgotten account with accumulated interest, paid passage back to the world out there: dialogue overheard in hotels and elevators and at the hatcheck counter in Pavillon (one middle-aged man shows his hat check to another and says, "That's my old football number"); impressions of Bettina Aptheker and Benjamin Sonnenberg and Teddy ("Mr. Acapulco") Stauffer; careful *aperçus* about tennis bums and failed fashion models and Greek shipping heiresses, one of whom taught me a significant lesson (a lesson I could have learned from F. Scott Fitzgerald, but perhaps we all must meet the very rich for ourselves) by asking, when I arrived to interview her in her orchid-filled sitting room on the second day of a paralyzing New York blizzard, whether it was snowing outside.

I imagine, in other words, that the notebook is about **9** other people. But of course it is not. I have no real business with what one stranger said to another at the hatcheck counter in Pavillon; in fact I suspect that the line "That's my old football number" touched not my own imagination at all, but merely some memory of something once read, probably "The Eighty-Yard Run." Nor is my concern with a woman in a dirty crepe-de-Chine wrapper in a Wilmington bar. My stake is always, of course, in the unmentioned girl in the plaid silk dress. *Remember what it was to be me:* that is always the point.

It is a difficult point to admit. We are brought up in the 10 ethic that others, any others, all others, are by definition more interesting than ourselves; taught to be diffident, just this side of self-effacing. ("You're the least important person in the room and don't forget it," Jessica Mitford's governess would hiss in her ear on the advent of any social occasion; I copied that into my notebook because it is only recently that I have been able to enter a room without hearing some such phrase in my inner ear.) Only the very young and the very old may recount their dreams at breakfast, dwell upon self, interrupt with memories of beach picnics and favorite Liberty lawn dresses and the rainbow trout in a creek near Colorado Springs. The rest of us are expected, rightly, to affect absorption in other people's favorite dresses, other people's trout.

. And so we do. But our notebooks give us away, for how- 11 ever dutifully we record what we see around us, the common denominator of all we see is always, transparently, shamelessly, the implacable "I." We are not talking here about the kind of notebook that is patently for public consumption, a structural conceit for binding together a series of graceful *pensées*; we are talking about something private, about bits of the mind's string too short to use, an indiscriminate and erratic assemblage with meaning only for its maker.

And sometimes even the maker has difficulty with the 12 meaning. There does not seem to be, for example, any point in my knowing for the rest of my life that, during 1964, 720 tons of soot fell on every square mile of New York City, yet there it is in my notebook, labeled "FACT." Nor do I really need to remember that Ambrose Bierce liked to spell Leland Stan-

ford's name "£eland $tanford" or that "smart women almost
always wear black in Cuba," a fashion hint without much potential for practical application. And does not the relevance of
these notes seem marginal at best?:

> In the basement museum of the Inyo County Courthouse in In-
> dependence, California, sign pinned to a mandarin coat: "This
> MANDARIN COAT was often worn by Mrs. Minnie S. Brooks
> when giving lectures on her TEAPOT COLLECTION."

> Redhead getting out of car in front of Beverly Wilshire Hotel,
> chinchilla stole, Vuitton bags with tags reading:

> MRS LOU FOX
HOTEL SAHARA
VEGAS

Well, perhaps not entirely marginal. As a matter of fact,   13
Mrs. Minnie S. Brooks and her MANDARIN COAT pull me
back into my own childhood, for although I never knew Mrs.
Brooks and did not visit Inyo County until I was thirty, I grew
up in just such a world, in houses cluttered with Indian relics
and bits of gold ore and ambergris and the souvenirs my Aunt
Mercy Farnsworth brought back from the Orient. It is a long
way from that world to Mrs. Lou Fox's world, where we all
live now, and is it not just as well to remember that? Might not
Mrs. Minnie S. Brooks help me to remember what I am?
Might not Mrs. Lou Fox help me to remember what I am not?

But sometimes the point is harder to discern. What ex-   14
actly did I have in mind when I noted down that it cost the
father of someone I know $650 a month to light the place on
the Hudson in which he lived before the Crash? What use was
I planning to make of this line by Jimmy Hoffa: "I may have
my faults, but being wrong ain't one of them"? And although
I think it interesting to know where the girls who travel with
the Syndicate have their hair done when they find themselves
on the West Coast, will I ever make suitable use of it? Might I
not be better off just passing it on to John O'Hara? What is a
recipe for sauerkraut doing in my notebook? What kind of
magpie keeps this notebook? *"He was born the night the Ti-*

tanic went down.'' That seems a nice enough line, and I even
recall who said it, but is it not really a better line in life than it
could ever be in fiction?

But of course that is exactly it: not that I should ever use 15
the line, but that I should remember the woman who said it
and the afternoon I heard it. We were on her terrace by the
sea, and we were finishing the wine left from lunch, trying to
get what sun there was, a California winter sun. The woman
whose husband was born the night the *Titanic* went down
wanted to rent her house, wanted to go back to her children in
Paris. I remember wishing that I could afford the house, which
cost $1,000 a month. "Someday you will," she said lazily.
"Someday it all comes." There in the sun on her terrace it
seemed easy to believe in someday, but later I had a low-grade
afternoon hangover and ran over a black snake on the way to
the supermarket and was flooded with inexplicable fear when
I heard the checkout clerk explaining to the man ahead of me
why she was finally divorcing her husband. "He left me no
choice," she said over and over as she punched the register.
"He has a little seven-month-old baby by her, he left me no
choice." I would like to believe that my dread then was for
the human condition, but of course it was for me, because I
wanted a baby and did not then have one and because I
wanted to own the house that cost $1,000 a month to rent and
because I had a hangover.

It all comes back. Perhaps it is difficult to see the value 16
in having one's self back in that kind of mood, but I do see it;
I think we are well advised to keep on nodding terms with the
people we used to be, whether we find them attractive company or not. Otherwise they turn up unannounced and surprise us, come hammering on the mind's door at 4 A.M. of a
bad night and demand to know who deserted them, who be-
trayed them, who is going to make amends. We forget all too
soon the things we thought we could never forget. We forget
the loves and the betrayals alike, forget what we whispered
and what we screamed, forget who we were. I have already
lost touch with a couple of people I used to be; one of them, a
seventeen-year-old, presents little threat, although it would be

of some interest to me to know again what it feels like to sit on a river levee drinking vodka-and-orange-juice and listening to Les Paul and Mary Ford and their echoes sing "How High the Moon" on the car radio. (You see I still have the scenes, but I no longer perceive myself among those present, no longer could even improvise the dialogue.) The other one, a twenty-three-year-old, bothers me more. She was always a good deal of trouble, and I suspect she will reappear when I least want to see her, skirts too long, shy to the point of aggravation, always the injured party, full of recriminations and little hurts and stories I do not want to hear again, at once saddening me and angering me with her vulnerability and ignorance, an apparition all the more insistent for being so long banished.

It is a good idea, then, to keep in touch, and I suppose 17 that keeping in touch is what notebooks are all about. And we are all on our own when it comes to keeping those lines open to ourselves: your notebook will never help me, nor mine you. *"So what's new in the whiskey business?"* What could that possibly mean to you? To me it means a blonde in a Pucci bathing suit sitting with a couple of fat men by the pool at the Beverly Hills Hotel. Another man approaches, and they all regard one another in silence for a while. "So what's new in the whiskey business?" one of the fat men finally says by way of welcome, and the blonde stands up, arches one foot and dips it in the pool, looking all the while at the cabana where Baby Pignatari is talking on the telephone. That is all there is to that, except that several years later I saw the blonde coming out of Saks Fifth Avenue in New York with her California complexion and a voluminous mink coat. In the harsh wind that day she looked old and irrevocably tired to me, and even the skins in the mink coat were not worked the way they were doing them that year, not the way she would have wanted them done, and there is the point of the story. For a while after that I did not like to look in the mirror, and my eyes would skim the newspapers and pick out only the deaths, the cancer victims, the premature coronaries, the suicides, and I stopped riding the Lexington Avenue IRT because I noticed for the first time that all the strangers I had seen for years—the man with the seeing-eye dog, the spinster who read the classified pages every day, the fat girl who always got off with me at Grand Central—looked older than they once had.

It all comes back. Even that recipe for sauerkraut: even **18** that brings it back. I was on Fire Island when I first made that sauerkraut, and it was raining, and we drank a lot of bourbon and ate the sauerkraut and went to bed at ten, and I listened to the rain and the Atlantic and felt safe. I made the sauerkraut again last night and it did not make me feel any safer, but that is, as they say, another story.

BUILDING VOCABULARY

1. Didion makes references to numerous people, places, events, books, and groups. The following is a list of twenty such references. From this list, select ten to research and write explanations for. Then, discuss your definitions with the class.

   a. Peck & Peck (par. 2)
   b. the Arctic (par. 5)
   c. Sahara Desert (par. 5)
   d. F. Scott Fitzgerald (par. 8)
   e. the Pavillon (par. 8)
   f. "The Eighty-Yard Run" (par. 9)
   g. Colorado Springs (par. 10)
   h. Ambrose Bierce (par. 12)
   i. Leland Stanford (par. 12)
   j. the Crash (par. 14)
   k. Jimmy Hoffa (par. 14)
   l. John O'Hara (par. 14)
   m. the Syndicate (par. 14)
   n. Les Paul (par. 16)
   o. Mary Ford (par. 16)
   p. Pucci (par. 17)
   q. Beverly Hills Hotel (par. 17)
   r. Lexington Avenue IRT (par. 17)

    s. Grand Central (par. 17)
    t. Fire Island (par. 18)

2. *Figurative language* creates images through imaginative comparisons and descriptions. The following are but a few examples of the startlingly original figurative language that Didion uses throughout this essay. For each, look back to the point in the essay where it occurs and explain it in more *literal* (or realistic) terms. Then, find and list five more examples of figurative language in the essay.

    a. triangle of sunlight (par. 2)
    b. steamy mornings (par. 3)
    c. the viscous summer sidewalks (par. 3)
    d. afflicted by a little self-pity (par. 3)
    e. afflicted apparently at birth with some presentiment of loss (par. 4)
    f. some morning when the world seems drained of wonder (par. 8)
    g. that bankrupt morning (par. 8)
    h. a structural conceit for binding together a series of graceful *pensées* (par. 11)
    i. bits of the mind's string too short to use (par. 11)
    j. come hammering on the mind's door at 4 A.M. of a bad night (par. 16)

UNDERSTANDING THE WRITER'S IDEAS

1. What is the meaning of the first paragraph? If you hadn't read the second paragraph, would the first have had the same meaning? Any meaning? Explain.

2. Who is the woman "wearing a plaid silk dress from Peck & Peck" mentioned in paragraph 2? How do you know? Summarize the woman's situation. What does the author mean when she writes, "She wants to compare Estelles"?

3. What is Didion's opinion about "the impulse to write things down"? When did it begin for her? Does she feel that her daughter will do the same? Why? Does this please or displease Didion? Why? For what reason did Didion's mother first encourage her to write things down? What was her first story?

4. Summarize as clearly as possible Joan Didion's *reasons* for keeping a notebook. Then, summarize her *attitude* about keeping a notebook. Draw your answers from the essay and quote at least three specific statements in support of each summary.

5. What does the author specifically mention as *not* a good reason to keep a notebook? Why? What is Didion's distinction between keeping a notebook and keeping a diary? What is her attitude toward diaries? What have been the results of her attempts to keep diaries?

6. According to the author, how important is the distinction between what happened in the past and what might have happened? Why?

7. In paragraph 8, what lesson does the author learn from a "Greek shipping heiress" and how does she learn it? Do you know to whom she is referring? What does she mean when she writes parenthetically: "(a lesson I could have learned from F. Scott Fitzgerald, but perhaps we all must meet the very rich for ourselves)"?

8. According to Didion, what is the relation between the way we see others and the way we see ourselves? What does she mean by "*Remember what it was to be me:* that is always the point" (par. 9)? What does that process say about the process of writing? Why is it "a difficult point to admit" (par. 10)?

9. Throughout the essay, Didion stresses the critical necessity for a writer to know herself, "the implacable 'I'" (par. 11), very well. Why is this so important? Does Didion always seem comfortable with this emphasis on the self? Explain your answers with specific references to the essay.

10. In her memory, does she prefer herself at age seventeen

or at age twenty-three? Explain. Why is it so important to "keep in touch" with past eras in one's life?

11. What is the "It" of the sentence that begins paragraph 16: "It all comes back"? Why does Didion repeat this statement at the beginning of the final paragraph? Does "It" have a different meaning there?

UNDERSTANDING THE WRITER'S TECHNIQUES

1. What is Didion's main point here? Why is she writing this essay?

2. Throughout the essay, Didion is extremely thorough in her use of *details*. What is the effect of such thoroughness? Which descriptions do you find especially well detailed?

3. For what reasons does Didion begin the essay with a short entry from one of her notebooks? On first reading, did the opening paragraph make sense to you? Why? In your own words, explain the relationship between paragraphs 1 and 2.

4. What is the significance of the five questions and one answer which begin paragraph 4?

5. *Hyperbole* (see Glossary) in writing is exaggeration used figuratively to make a point. Does Didion use hyperbole in this essay? Why? List five examples of hyperbolic writing from this essay and explain the point they are used to make.

6. Why does the author put quotation marks around the word "ironic" in paragraph 5?

7. In paragraph 7, Didion discusses *lies*. What is her meaning for that word as it is used in this paragraph? How is the technique useful to her as a fiction writer? Support your answer with an example.

8. A *metaphor* is a figure of speech that imaginatively compares items from different categories (see Glossary). An *extended metaphor* carries the figure of speech past the initial comparison. How is the following citation from the essay an example of an extended metaphor: "...—on that bankrupt morning I will simply open my notebook and there it will all be, a forgotten account with accumulated interest"? Explain the meaning of the full extended metaphor.

9. How does Didion use short, introductory phrases as transitional devices between paragraphs and sections of this essay? Give examples. How does she use *repetition* as a transitional device between paragraphs 9 and 10? Where else in the essay does repetition play a significant role?

10. *Dialogue* is the written reproduction of speech or conversation (see Glossary). Where does Didion use dialogue in this essay? For what reason and to gain what effect?

11. *Narration* (see Chapter 4) is the telling of a story or series of events. *Anecdotes* are very short narrations, usually of an amusing or autobiographical nature. How does the author use an anecdote in paragraph 15? List at least three other uses of anecdotes and narration in the essay.

12. Based on Didion's essay, in what ways would keeping a notebook be a very valuable prewriting tool (see pages 1–2)?

13. What purpose of keeping a notebook answers the two questions at the end of paragraph 13: "Might not Mrs. Minnie S. Brooks help me to remember what I am? Might not Mrs. Lou Fox help me to remember what I am not?"

14. Describe what you think is the intended *audience* for this essay.

15. *Conclusions* (see Glossary) for essays should ideally make the reader feel that he or she has reached some logical endpoint of the discussion and that nothing important has been omitted. Do you feel that Didion's conclusion is a

good one? Does she have in mind any other purpose than simply "closing" the essay? Explain.

EXPLORING THE WRITER'S IDEAS

1. In this selection, Didion explores the relation between fact and fiction. She first relates one perception of people and events as recorded in her notebook, and another perception as the initial entry is "fleshed out" as a piece of writing. She states: "I tell what some would call lies.... I always had trouble distinguishing between what happened and what merely might have happened, but I remain unconvinced that the distinction, for my purposes, matters."

   Raymond Carver, another leading American fiction writer, says: "None of my stories really *happened,* of course—I'm not writing autobiography—but most of them bear a resemblance, however faint, to certain life occurrences or situations." A collection of short stories by the renowned Argentine writer Jorge Luis Borges is entitled *Ficciones,* which literally translates as "Fictions," but has the nuance of "Lies."

   Why do you think these writers see a connection between lies and fiction? Is it possible to view fiction as lies used in the service of telling the truth? Explain. How does the issue of "lies" enter nonfiction writing?

2. Reread this essay and pay special attention to the notebook entries that Didion quotes. Do you find any particular pattern in what she chooses to note? Do the entries represent a particular *point of view* (see Glossary) or outlook on life? Explain.

3. Do you keep a diary, journal, or notebook? If so, how do you choose what to include as entries? What is most valuable to you about keeping a notebook? When did you begin? Why? Would you ever share your notebooks with others? Why or why not? Do you agree with Didion's statement that "our notebooks give us away"? What would someone learn about you from your notebooks?

IDEAS FOR WRITING

Guided Writing

Write an essay entitled "On Writing an Essay." Base your essay on the writing of the essay that you plan to write for this Guided Writing assignment.

1. Begin with some notes or a section of a rough draft for a paragraph of this essay.

2. Follow with an example from the finished paragraph. Briefly elaborate on how you transformed your prewriting notes into a final draft.

3. Discuss the first essay you remember writing. Tell about the process you used then.

4. Use narration to explain by what means you got from the rough to the finished draft of this essay. Include plenty of details, even if they don't seem directly related to writing: fixing a snack; watching the clock; watering the plants; blasting out some Springsteen; desperately searching for your lucky hat.

5. Try to use imaginative, original figurative language and metaphors. Use at least one extended metaphor (see Glossary).

6. Tell about the personal effects of writing this essay (*besides* fulfilling the assignment!). How did you feel while writing it? When finishing it?

7. Write a conclusion that is purposefully somewhat open-ended.

More Writing Projects

1. In your journal, record your dreams for one week. Attempt at least once or twice to wake yourself at the end of a dream and write it down before you experience any inter-

ruptions. At the end of the week, reread your entries and try to discover a pattern in your dreams. Use one as the basis for a short story or essay.

2. Write nonstop for five minutes (this is called "freewriting"), explaining all the reasons you can think of for keeping a journal. Be certain to write continuously. Don't correct, look back, revise, or check what you have written. Develop an extended paragraph using this technique.

3. In the library, find a published journal by a writer who interests you. Write a brief essay in which you explain what the journal reveals about the writer's interests, beliefs, character, and philosophy.

SUMMING UP: CHAPTER 1

1. It sounds simple enough. Many writers, famous and unknown, have tried it at one time or another. Now, it's your turn.

   Write an essay simply titled, "On Writing." Develop the essay in any way you please: you may deal with abstract or concrete ideas, philosophical or practical issues, emotional or intellectual processes, and so forth. Just use this essay to focus your own thoughts and to give your readers a clear idea of what writing means to you.

2. William Zinsser ("Simplicity") tells writers to simplify their writing. Select any writer from this section and write an essay about whether you think the writer achieved (or did not achieve) simplicity. How did the writer achieve it? Where in the selection would you have preferred even more simplicity? Make specific references to the text.

3. Follow the advice implicit in Joan Didion's essay "On Keeping a Notebook." In your own notebook or journal, *write at least one entry every day* for one week. Record interesting observations, daydreams, sudden thoughts, unusual events, or people that strike you as noteworthy. After a week, reread your notebook entries and write an

essay in which you explain what they reveal about your character. John Berger in his book *Ways of Seeing* says, "We only see what we look at. To look is an act of choice." What does what *you* see reveal about your choices?

4. Write a letter from William Stafford to Joan Didion in which Stafford reacts to Didion's belief in keeping a notebook. Draw upon what you understand as Stafford's philosophy of writing from his essay "Writing."

5. The writers in this chapter all give some sense of *why* they write. For the most part, their reasons are very personal. For example, William Stafford writes of the "scope for individuality, and elation, and discovery," while William Saroyan simply states, "I write because I want to." However, many writers (including many represented in this book) feel that writing entails a certain social responsibility. For example, when Albert Camus received the 1957 Nobel Prize for Literature, he was cited for "illuminating the problems of the human conscience of our time." And, in his acceptance speech, he stated, "[T]he writer's function is not without arduous duties. By definition, he cannot serve today those who make history; he must serve those who are subject to it."

What do you feel are writers' responsibilities to themselves and to others? Do you agree with Camus? Do you prefer writing that deals primarily with an individual's experience or with more general social issues?

Write an essay concerning the social responsibilities of writers. As you consider the issue, refer to points made by writers in this section.

CHAPTER 2

On Reading

The educator Mortimer J. Adler once observed in a celebrated essay, "How to Make a Book Your Own," that reading is like a conversation between you and the author. This "conversation" opens new universes, challenges your opinions, enhances your understanding of yourself and of others, of your past, present, and future. Knowledge of books—your ability to engage actively the minds of many writers who have much to tell you—is the mark of a literate person.

Just as you cannot be literate in today's complex world with weak writing skills, you cannot be literate with mediocre reading abilities. Admittedly, today we are surrounded by 150-channel cablevision, remote-control VCRs, and other high-tech video forms that tempt our eyes and compete for our attention. Some even argue that reading is rapidly becoming a lost art. Yet precisely because we are in a challenging and potentially dangerous high-tech era, the ability to understand and learn from what others have written over time is an indispensable resource. After all, not everyone communicates by electronic media alone.

Of course, when we first learn to read as children we are not exclusively interested in practical knowledge that will help us prosper in today's society, but more perhaps in the mystery, magic, and enchantment of words that Eudora Welty describes in her essay in this section. As youngsters, many of us learned to read in much the same way as Scout Finch, the main character in Harper Lee's *To Kill a Mockingbird*. Sitting on her father's lap, she would follow the words on the page as he read aloud to her. Gradually, she came to know many words, and from the sounds or "phonics" that she internalized, she reached a point at which she had enough knowledge and information to figure out new words for herself.

As adults, we must strive for the same active, inquiring, critical intelligence that young people seem naturally blessed with during the act of reading. We must constantly engage ourselves with the text at hand. Of course, not everything we read demands equally careful thought, but with important reading material we should ask ourselves certain key questions:

- What is the writer's primary purpose?
- What is the precise issue or problem that the writer treats?
- Who is the writer? For whom is he or she writing?
- What information, conclusions, and recommendations does the writer present?
- What substantiating evidence does the writer provide to "prove" his or her case?
- Is the total message successful, objective, valid, or persuasive?

These are the minimal expectations that we should have of ourselves as we engage any writer in an active dialogue or debate over ideas.

In this chapter, each of the authors tells us something about his or her own relation to reading. For Eudora Welty, words came to her "as though fed...out of a silver spoon." Malcolm X tells us how reading was so powerful for him that it allowed him to tear down prison walls. Margaret Atwood writes of her bittersweet discovery of literature in her native Canada. And Donald Hall warns us not to become too snobbish about the intellectual or social value of reading.

Moon on a Silver Spoon

Eudora Welty

Eudora Welty, born in 1909, is among America's foremost writers, often focusing on the ways of life in rural Mississippi. Her novel *The Optimist's Daughter* won the 1972 Pulitzer Prize, and her *Collected Stories* (1980) has been widely acclaimed. In this selection from her autobiography, *One Writer's Beginnings* (1984), Welty uses delightful descriptions and narrations of her childhood to tell how she developed her love for reading.

Words to Watch

sap (par. 4)   to drain away

gratitude (par. 10)   thankfulness

essential (par. 10)   absolutely necessary

keystone (par. 10)   something on which associated things depend for support

wizardry (par. 11)   magic

acute (par. 13)   very specific or serious

elders (par. 13)   older people

ailment (par. 14)   illness

insatiability (par. 16)   inability to be satisfied

lingers (par. 18)   stays with

1   On a visit to my grandmother's in West Virginia, I stood inside the house where my mother had been born and where she grew up.

2   "Here's where I first began to read my Dickens," Mother said, pointing. "Under that very bed. Hiding my candle. To keep them from knowing I was up all night."

3   "But where did it all *come* from?" I asked her at last. "All that Dickens?"

4   "Why, Papa gave me that set of Dickens for agreeing to let them cut off my hair," she said. "In those days, they thought very long, thick hair like mine would sap a child's strength. I said *No!* I wanted my hair left the very way it was.

They offered me gold earrings first. I said *No!* I'd rather keep
my hair. Then Papa said, 'What about books? I'll have them
send a whole set of Charles Dickens to you, right up the river
from Baltimore, in a barrel.' I agreed.''

My mother had brought that set of Dickens to our house 5
in Jackson, Miss.; those books had been through fire and water before I was born, she told me, and there they were, lined
up—as I later realized, waiting for *me*.

I learned from the age of two or three that any room in 6
our house, at any time of day, was there to read in, or to be
read to. My mother read to me. She'd read to me in the big
bedroom in the mornings, when we were in her rocker together, which ticked in rhythm as we rocked, as though we
had a cricket accompanying the story. She'd read to me in the
dining room on winter afternoons in front of the coal fire, with
our cuckoo clock ending the story with "Cuckoo," and at
night when I'd got in my own bed. I must have given her no
peace.

It had been startling and disappointing to me to find out 7
that storybooks had been written by *people,* that books were
not natural wonders, coming up of themselves like grass. Yet
regardless of where they came from, I cannot remember a
time when I was not in love with them—with the books themselves, cover and binding and the paper they were printed on,
with their smell and their weight and with their possession in
my arms, captured and carried off to myself.

Neither of my parents had come from homes that could 8
afford to buy many books, but though it must have been something of a strain on his salary, my father was all the while carefully selecting and ordering away for what he and Mother
thought we children should grow up with.

Besides the bookcase in the living room, which was al- 9
ways called the library, there were the encyclopedia tables
and dictionary stand under windows in our dining room. There
was a full set of Mark Twain and a short set of Ring Lardner in
our bookcase, and those were the volumes that in time united
us as parents and children.

I live in gratitude to my parents for initiating me—and as 10

early as I begged for it, without keeping me waiting—into
knowledge of the word, into reading and spelling, by way of
the alphabet. They taught it to me at home in time for me to
begin to read before starting school. I believe the alphabet is
no longer considered an essential piece of equipment for traveling through life. In my day it was the keystone to knowledge. You learned the alphabet as you learned "Now I lay
me" and the Lord's Prayer, and your father's and mother's
name and address and telephone number, all in case you were
lost.

My love for the alphabet, which endures, grew out of re-   11
citing it, but before that, out of seeing the letters on the page.
In my own storybooks, before I could read them for myself, I
fell in love with various winding, enchanted-looking initials at
the heads of fairy tales. In "Once upon a time," an "O" had
a rabbit running it as a treadmill, his feet upon flowers. When
the day came, years later, for me to see the Book of Kells,
Gospels from the ninth century, all the wizardry of letter, initial and word swept over me, a thousand times over, and the
illustration, the gold, seemed a part of the word's beauty and
holiness that had been there from the start.

In my sensory education I include my physical aware-   12
ness of the word. Of a certain word, that is; the connection it
has with what it stands for. Around age six, perhaps, I was
standing by myself in our front yard waiting for supper, just at
that hour in a late summer day when the sun is already below
the horizon and the risen full moon in the visible sky stops being chalky and begins to take on light. There comes the moment, and I saw it then, when the moon goes from flat to
round. For the first time it met my eyes as a globe. The word
"moon" came into my mouth as though fed to me out of a silver spoon. Held in my mouth the moon became a word. It had
the roundness of a Concord grape that Grandpa took off his
vine and gave me to suck out of its skin and swallow whole, in
Ohio.

Long before I wrote stories, I listened for stories. Lis-   13
tening *for* them is something more acute than listening *to*
them. I supposed it's an early form of participation in what
goes on. Listening children know stories are *there*. When their

elders sit and begin, children are just waiting and hoping for one to come out, like a mouse from its hole.

When I was six or seven, I was taken out of school and 14
put to bed for several months for an ailment the doctor described as "fast-beating heart." I never dreamed I could learn away from the schoolroom, and that bits of enlightenment far-reaching in my life went on as ever in their own good time.

An opulence of storybooks covered my bed. As I read 15
away, I was Rapunzel, or the Goose Girl, or the princess in one of the *Thousand and One Nights* who mounted the roof of her palace every night and of her own radiance faithfully lighted the whole city just by reposing there.

My mother was very sharing of this feeling of insatiabil- 16
ity. Now, I think of her as reading so much of the time while doing something else. In my mind's eye *The Origin of Species* is lying on the shelf in the pantry under a light dusting of flour—my mother was a bread maker; she'd pick it up, sit by the kitchen window and find her place, with one eye on the oven.

I'm grateful, too, that from my mother's example, I 17
found the base for worship—that I found a love of sitting and reading the Bible for myself and looking up things in it.

How many of us, the Southern writers-to-be of my gen- 18
eration, were blessed in one way or another if not blessed alike, in not having gone deprived of the King James Version of the Bible. Its cadence entered into our ears and our memories for good. The evidence, or the ghost of it, lingers in all our books.

"In the beginning was the Word."   19

BUILDING VOCABULARY

1. Identify the following references to authors, books, and stories from Welty's essay:

   a. Charles Dickens
   b. Mark Twain

   c. Ring Lardner
   d. the Book of Kells
   e. Gospels
   f. Rapunzel
   g. the Goose Girl
   h. the *Thousand and One Nights*
   i. *The Origin of Species*
   j. the King James version of the Bible

2. Write definitions and your own sentences for the following
    words:

   a. initiating (par. 10)
   b. enchanted-looking (par. 11)
   c. treadmill (par. 11)
   d. holiness (par. 11)
   e. enlightenment (par. 14)
   f. opulence (par. 15)
   g. radiance (par. 15)
   h. reposing (par. 15)
   i. deprived (par. 18)
   j. cadence (par. 18)

UNDERSTANDING THE WRITER'S IDEAS

1. Where did Welty's grandmother come from? Where was
    Welty herself brought up? Why did Welty's grandparents
    want to cut off their daughter's hair?

2. For what reason did Welty's mother receive a set of
    Charles Dickens's works? What does this tell you about
    the attitude toward reading in Welty's family? What hap-
    pened to the set of Dickens? Although Welty doesn't say
    so, what do you think she did with the books? Why?

3. How did the way Welty's mother felt toward books affect
    her child's attitude toward reading? In what ways did the
    conditions in Welty's home contribute to her attitude to-
    ward books?

4. Why does the author write of her mother, "I must have given her no peace" (par. 6)?

5. Why was it "startling and disappointing" for Welty to find out that story books were written *by people?* Where did she think they came from? Aside from the stories themselves, what is it that the author loves so much about books?

6. For what reasons does Welty feel that learning the alphabet is so important? To what other learning processes does she compare it? Before she learned to recite her alphabet, why was it so important to her?

7. Explain in your own words what Welty considers to be the relation between physical sensations and learning words. According to the author, why is it important for parents to read to their children?

8. For what reason was the young Welty taken out of school? How did this affect her attitude toward reading? How did her mother influence her at this time?

9. At the time of writing this piece, Welty was in her mid-seventies. Explain what she sees as the relation between the Bible and southern writers of her generation. By what descriptions and references in the essay does she indicate her feelings for the Bible?

10. Identify the source of the final sentence. Why is it especially significant to this essay?

UNDERSTANDING THE WRITER'S TECHNIQUES

1. Why does Welty use an image (see Glossary) for her title instead of choosing a more straightforward one, such as Joan Didion's "On Keeping a Notebook" (pages 34–42), William Stafford's "Writing" (pages 13–16), or William Saroyan's "Why I Write" (pages 5–8)? What effect does Welty achieve with the title? What does the title mean?

2. A *reminiscence* is a narrative account of a special memory. How does Welty use reminiscence in this essay?

3. What is the main idea of Welty's essay? Is there any point at which she directly states that main idea? Explain.

4. The *tone* of an essay is the expression of the writer's attitude toward the topic (see Glossary). Describe the tone of this essay. What specifically about the writing contributes to that tone?

5. *Description* helps the reader to "see" objects and scenes, and to feel their importance through the author's eyes. *Narration*—the telling of a story—helps the reader follow a sequence of events. (See Chapters 3 and 4.) Both techniques rely on the writer's skill in choosing and presenting *details*. In what way does Welty make use of description and narration in this essay? How would you evaluate her use of details?

6. Placing words in *italics* emphasizes them. Where does the author use italics in this essay? Why does she use them?

7. What does Welty mean by the italicized phrase in the statement "Those books had been *through fire and water* before I was born" (par. 5)? How does the image contribute to the point she's making?

8. The writing of *dialogue,* often used as part of a narration, is the technique whereby a writer either reproduces words actually spoken or invents speech that logically fits into the essay or story. How does Welty use dialogue here? In what ways does it affect your understanding or enjoyment of the writing?

9. *Similes* are imaginative comparisons using the words "like" or "as" (see Glossary). Use of similes often enlivens the writing and makes it memorable.

In your own words explain what is being compared in the following similes drawn from Welty's essay, and tell how they contribute to the essay:

   a. . . . we were in her rocker together, which ticked in

> rhythm as we rocked, *as though we had a cricket ac-
> companying the story.* (par. 6)
>
> **b.** The word "moon" came into my mouth *as though fed
> to me out of a silver spoon.* (par. 12)
>
> **c.** Listening children know stories are *there.* When their
> elders sit and begin, children are just waiting for one
> to come out, *like a mouse from its hole.* (par. 13)

10. Throughout this essay, Welty refers to "the word." Is she
referring to a specific word or to a more abstract concept?
Explain. Reread the essay and find and list all references
to "the word." What is the relation between them all?
How do they work to keep the essay *coherent* and *unified*
(see Glossary)? How do they build to the reference in the
final sentence? Why is "the Word" capitalized there?

EXPLORING THE WRITER'S IDEAS

1. Welty believes that it is very important for parents to read
to their children. Some specialists in child development
even advocate reading to infants still in the womb and to
babies before they've spoken their first words. For what
reasons might such activities be important? Do you personally feel they are important or useful? Would you read to an
unborn infant? Why or why not? If you would, *what* would
you read?

2. Welty was born in 1909 and obviously belongs to a different generation from the vast majority of college students
today. Do you feel that her type of love and advocacy of
reading are as valid for the current generation, raised on
television, video, cassettes, VCRs, CDs, satellite dishes,
and MTV? Explain.

3. Welty describes her love of books as going beyond the
words and stories they contain to their physical and visual
attributes. What objects—not other people—do you love or
respect with that intensity? Tell a little about why and how
you have developed this feeling.

IDEAS FOR WRITING

Guided Writing

Write an essay that describes your own attitude toward reading.

1. In order to set the stage for the discussion of your attitude, begin by recalling details about a moment with a parent or other adult.

2. Use dialogue as part of this scene.

3. Go as far back in your childhood as you can possibly remember and narrate two or three incidents that help explain the formation of your current attitude toward reading.

4. Use sensory language (color, sound, smell, touch, and taste) to show how the environment of the home where you grew up helped shape your attitude.

5. Tell about a particular, special childhood fascination with something you *saw*—not read—in a book.

6. Try to describe the first time you were conscious of the *meaning* of a particular word.

7. Use at least one *simile* in your essay.

8. Create and keep a consistent *tone* throughout the essay.

9. End your essay with an explanation of how a particular book has been continually influential to you, as well as to others of your generation.

10. Give your essay an unusual title that derives from some description in your essay.

More Writing Projects

1. Enter in your journal early memories of people who read to you or of books that you read on your own. Try to capture

the sensation and importance of these early reading experiences.

2. Return to question 2 in Exploring the Writer's Ideas and write a one-paragraph response to it.

3. Write an essay on the person who most influenced your childhood education. Did this person read to you, give you books, make you do your homework? Assess the impact of this person on your life.

Prison Studies

Malcolm X

Born Malcolm Little in Omaha, Nebraska, Malcolm X (1925–1965) was a charismatic leader of the black power movement and founded the Organization of Afro-American Unity. In prison, he became a Black Muslim. (He split with this faith in 1963 to convert to orthodox Islam.) "Prison Studies" is excerpted from the popular and fascinating *Autobiography of Malcolm X,* which he cowrote with *Roots* author Alex Haley. The essay describes the writer's struggle to learn to read, as well as the joy and power he felt when he won that struggle.

Words to Watch

emulate (par. 2)   imitate, especially from respect

motivation (par. 2)   reason to do something

tablets (par. 3)   writing notebooks

bunk (par. 9)   small bed

rehabilitation (par. 10)   the process of restoring to a state of usefulness or constructiveness

inmate (par. 10)   prisoner

corridor (par. 13)   hallway; walkway

vistas (par. 15)   mental overviews

confers (par. 15)   bestows; gives ceremoniously

alma mater (par. 15)   the college that one has attended

Many who today hear me somewhere in person, or on 1 television, or those who read something I've said, will think I went to school far beyond the eighth grade. This impression is due entirely to my prison studies.

It had really begun back in the Charlestown Prison, 2 when Bimbi first made me feel envy of his stock of knowledge. Bimbi had always taken charge of any conversation he was in, and I had tried to emulate him. But every book I picked up had few sentences which didn't contain anywhere from one to nearly all of the words that might as well have been in Chinese. When I just skipped those words, of course, I really ended up with little idea of what the book said. So I had come to the Norfolk Prison Colony still going through only book-reading motions. Pretty soon, I would have quit even these motions, unless I had received the motivation that I did.

I saw that the best thing I could do was get hold of a dic- 3 tionary—to study, to learn some words. I was lucky enough to reason also that I should try to improve my penmanship. It was sad. I couldn't even write in a straight line. It was both ideas together that moved me to request a dictionary along with some tablets and pencils from the Norfolk Prison Colony school.

I spent two days just riffling uncertainly through the dic- 4 tionary's pages. I'd never realized so many words existed! I didn't know which words I needed to learn. Finally, to start some kind of action, I began copying.

In my slow, painstaking, ragged handwriting, I copied 5 into my tablet everything printed on that first page, down to the punctuation marks.

I believe it took me a day. Then, aloud, I read back, to 6 myself, everything I'd written on the tablet. Over and over, aloud, to myself, I read my own handwriting.

I woke up the next morning, thinking about those 7 words—immensely proud to realize that not only had I written so much at one time, but I'd written words that I never knew were in the world. Moreover, with a little effort, I also could remember what many of these words meant. I reviewed the words whose meanings I didn't remember. Funny thing, from the dictionary first page right now, that "aardvark" springs to my mind. The dictionary had a picture of it, a long-tailed, long-eared, burrowing African mammal, which lives off ter-mites caught by sticking out its tongue as an anteater does for ants.

I was so fascinated that I went on—I copied the dictio- 8 nary's next page. And the same experience came when I stud-ied that. With every succeeding page, I also learned of people and places and events from history. Actually the dictionary is like a miniature encyclopedia. Finally the dictionary's A sec-tion had filled a whole tablet—and I went on into the B's. That was the way I started copying what eventually became the entire dictionary. It went a lot faster after so much practice helped me to pick up handwriting speed. Between what I wrote in my tablet, and writing letters, during the rest of my time in prison I would guess I wrote a million words.

I suppose it was inevitable that as my word-base broad- 9 ened, I could for the first time pick up a book and read and now begin to understand what the book was saying. Anyone who has read a great deal can imagine the new world that opened. Let me tell you something; from then until I left that prison, in every free moment I had, if I was not reading in the library, I was reading on my bunk. You couldn't have gotten me out of books with a wedge. Between Mr. Muhammad's teachings, my correspondence, my visitors—usually Ella and Reginald—and my reading of books, months passed without my even thinking about being imprisoned. In fact, up to then, I never had been so truly free in my life....

As you can imagine, especially in a prison where there 10 was heavy emphasis on rehabilitation, an inmate was smiled upon if he demonstrated an unusually intense interest in books. There was a sizable number of well-read inmates, especially the popular debaters. Some were said by many to be practically walking encyclopedias. They were almost celebrities. No university would ask any student to devour literature as I did when this new world opened to me, of being able to read and *understand*.

I read more in my room than in the library itself. An in- 11 mate who was known to read a lot could check out more than the permitted maximum number of books. I preferred reading in the total isolation of my own room.

When I had progressed to really serious reading, every 12 night at about ten P.M. I would be outraged with the "lights out." It always seemed to catch me right in the middle of something engrossing.

Fortunately, right outside my door was a corridor light 13 that cast a glow into my room. The glow was enough to read by, once my eyes adjusted to it. So when "lights out" came, I would sit on the floor where I could continue reading in that glow.

At one-hour intervals the night guards paced past every- 14
room. Each time I heard the approaching footsteps, I jumped
into bed and feigned sleep. And as soon as the guard passed, I
got back out of bed onto the floor area of that light-glow,
where I would read for another fifty-eight minutes—until the
guard approached again. That went on until three or four every morning. Three or four hours of sleep a night was enough
for me. Often in the years in the streets I had slept less than
that.

I have often reflected upon the new vistas that reading 15
opened to me. I knew right there in prison that reading had
changed forever the course of my life. As I see it today, the
ability to read awoke inside me some long dormant craving to
be mentally alive. I certainly wasn't seeking any degree, the
way a college confers a status symbol upon its students. My
homemade education gave me, with every additional book
that I read, a little bit more sensitivity to the deafness, dumbness, and blindness that was afflicting the black race in America. Not long ago, an English writer telephoned me from London, asking questions. One was, "What's your alma mater?"
I told him, "Books." You will never catch me with a free fifteen minutes in which I'm not studying something I feel might
be able to help the black man....

Every time I catch a plane, I have with me a book that I 16
want to read—and that's a lot of books these days. If I weren't
out here every day battling the white man, I could spend the
rest of my life reading, just satisfying my curiosity—because
you can hardly mention anything I'm not curious about. I
don't think anybody ever got more out of going to prison than
I did. In fact, prison enabled me to study far more intensively
than I would have if my life had gone differently and I had attended some college. I imagine that one of the biggest troubles
with colleges is there are too many distractions, too much
panty-raiding, fraternities, and boola-boola and all of that.
Where else but in prison could I have attacked my ignorance
by being able to study intensely sometimes as much as fifteen
hours a day?

BUILDING VOCABULARY

1. Throughout the selection, Malcolm X uses *figurative* and *colloquial language* (see Glossary). As you know, *figurative language* involves imaginative comparisons, which go beyond plain or ordinary statements. *Colloquial language* involves informal or conversational phrases and expressions.

   The following are examples of some of the figurative and colloquial usages in this essay. Explain each italicized word group in your own words.

   a. *going through* only *book-reading motions* (par. 2)
   b. I was *lucky enough* (par. 3)
   c. *Funny thing* (par. 7)
   d. can imagine *the new world that opened* (par. 9)
   e. *You couldn't have gotten me out of books with a wedge* (par. 9)
   f. an inmate was *smiled upon* (par. 10)
   g. to be practically *walking encyclopedias* (par. 10)
   h. ask any student *to devour literature* (par. 10)
   i. changed forever *the course of my life* (par. 15)
   j. *some long dormant craving* to be *mentally alive* (par. 15)
   k. *the deafness, dumbness, and blindness that was afflicting* the black race in America (par. 15)
   l. Every time I *catch a plane* (par. 16)
   m. every day *battling the white man* (par. 16)
   n. just *satisfying my curiosity* (par. 16)
   o. *boola-boola and all of that* (par. 16)
   p. I have *attacked my ignorance* (par. 16)

2. Find the following words in the essay. Write brief definitions for them without using a dictionary. If they are unfamiliar to you, try to determine their meaning based on the context in which they appear.

   a. riffling (par. 4)
   b. painstaking (par. 5)

    c. ragged (par. 5)
    d. burrowing (par. 7)
    e. inevitable (par. 9)
    f. emphasis (par. 10)
    g. distractions (par. 16)

UNDERSTANDING THE WRITER'S IDEAS

1. What was the highest level of formal education that the writer achieved? How is this different from the impression most people got from him? Why?

2. Who was Bimbi? Where did Malcolm X meet him? How was Bimbi important to the writer?

3. What does the author mean by writing that when he tried to read, most of the words "might as well have been in Chinese"? What happened when he skipped over such words? What motivated him to change his way of reading?

4. Why did Malcolm X start trying to improve his handwriting? How was it connected to his desire to improve his reading ability? Briefly describe how he went about this dual process. How did he feel after the first day of this process? Why?

5. How is the dictionary "like a miniature encyclopedia"?

6. Judging from this essay and his description of his "home-made education," how much time did Malcolm X spend in prison? Does the fact that he was in prison affect your appreciation of his learning process? How?

7. What is a "word-base" (par. 9)? What happened once the author's word-base expanded? How did this give him a sense of freedom?

8. Who is "Mr. Muhammad"?

9. Why did the prison officials like Malcolm X? What special privileges came to him as a result of this favorable opinion?

10. Why was Malcolm X angered with the "lights out" procedure? How did he overcome it?

11. What does the following sentence tell you about Malcolm X's life: "Often in the years in the streets I had slept less than that" (par. 14)?

12. Characterize the writer's opinion of a college education. How does he compare his education to a college degree? How did his education influence his understanding of his place and role in American society?

13. In your own words, describe the writer's attitude toward American blacks. Toward the relation between blacks and whites?

14. To what main purpose in life does the writer refer? What was the relation between this purpose and his feelings about reading? Use one word to describe Malcolm X's attitude toward reading.

15. What is the meaning of the conclusion?

UNDERSTANDING THE WRITER'S TECHNIQUES

1. Later in the book, you will learn about the techniques of *Process Analysis* (Chapter 9) and *Cause-and-Effect Analysis* (Chapter 10). Briefly, process analysis tells the reader *how* something is done, while cause-and-effect analysis explains *why* one thing leads to or affects another.

   For this essay, outline step-by-step the process whereby Malcolm X developed his ability to read and enthusiasm for reading. Next, for each step in your outline, explain why one step led to the next.

2. *Narration* (Chapter 4) is the telling of a story or the orderly relating of a series of events. How does Malcolm X use narration in this essay? How does he order the events of his narration?

3. What is the effect of the author writing "Let me tell you something" in paragraph 9?

4. How is the author's memory of the first page of the dictionary like a dictionary entry itself? What does this say about the importance of this memory to the author?

5. *Tone* is a writer's attitude toward his or her subject (see Glossary). Characterize the *tone* of this essay. What elements of the writing contribute to that tone? Be specific.

6. Which paragraphs make up the conclusion of this essay? How does the author develop his conclusion? How does he relate it to the main body of the essay? Do you feel that there is a change in *tone* (see Question 5) in the conclusion? Explain, using specific examples.

7. What is Malcolm X's main purpose in writing this essay? For whom is it intended? How do you know?

EXPLORING THE WRITER'S IDEAS

1. Malcolm X writes about his newly found love of reading and ability to read: "In fact, up to then, I never had been so truly free in my life." Has learning any particular skill or activity ever given you such a feeling of freedom or joy? Explain.

2. What do you feel was the source of Malcolm X's attitude toward a college education? Do you think any of his points here are valid? Why? What are your opinions about the quality of the college education you are receiving?

3. The writer also implies that, in some ways, the educational opportunities of prison were superior to those he would have had at college. What is his basis for this attitude? Have you ever experienced a circumstance in which being restricted actually benefited you? Explain.

4. Malcolm X held very strong opinions about the relations between blacks and whites in America. Do some library re-

search on him to try to understand his opinions. You might begin by reading *The Autobiography of Malcolm X,* from which this essay was excerpted. Do you agree or disagree with his feelings? Why?

5. Following Malcolm X's example, handwrite a page from a dictionary (a pocket dictionary will be fine), copying everything—including punctuation—*exactly!*

How long did it take you? How did it make you feel? Did you learn anything from the experience?

IDEAS FOR WRITING

Guided Writing

Write an essay in which you tell about an activity that you can now perform but that once seemed impossible to you.

1. Open your essay with an example in which you compare what most people assume about your skill or background in the activity to what the reality is.

2. Mention someone who especially influenced you in your desire to master this activity.

3. Tell what kept you from giving up on learning this activity.

4. Explain step-by-step the *process* by which you learned more and more about the activity. Explain how and why one step led to the next.

5. Use *figurative* and *colloquial* language where you think it appropriate in your essay.

6. Describe in some detail how you overcame an obstacle, imposed by others, which could have impeded your learning process.

7. Use your conclusion to express a deeply felt personal opinion and to generalize your learning of this skill to the population at large.

More Writing Projects

1. Select any page of a standard dictionary and copy in your journal at least ten words with definitions that are new or somewhat unfamiliar to you. Then jot down some thoughts on the process.

2. Ask yourself formal, journalistic questions about Malcolm X's essay: *What* happened? *Who* was involved? *How* was it done? *Where* did it occur? *When* did it occur? *Why* did it happen? Write out answers to these questions, and then assemble them in a unified, coherent paragraph.

3. Form a group with three other classmates. Focus on the context of Malcolm X's essay and on his comment on "the deafness, dumbness, and blindness that was afflicting the black race in America" (par. 15). Discuss this issue and its connection to education. Then prepare a collaborative essay on the topic.

Survival

Margaret Atwood

Margaret Atwood is a Canadian poet and novelist whose works, such as *The Edible Woman* (1969) and *Bodily Harm* (1981), often deal with alienation and people's insensitivities toward one another and the environment. In this selection from her 1972 book, *Survival: A Thematic Guide to Canadian Literature,* Atwood explains how, even as a budding Canadian writer, she was almost ignorant of Canadian literature. However, through her richly detailed descriptions, she also communicates the delight she came to experience—and still experiences—in reading Canadian authors.

Words to Watch

enhanced (par. 1)   made more valuable

sniveled (par. 2)   acted in a whining or emotionally weak manner

artifacts (par. 3)   simple, usually hand-made objects such as tools or ornaments (often refers to ancient objects)

stress (par. 4)   emphasis

snares (par. 4)   animal traps

posthaste (par. 4)   immediately

domestic (par. 5)   family- or home-related

menace (par. 5)   threat; danger

curricula (par. 6)   sets of academic courses

I started reading Canadian literature when I was young, 1 though I didn't know it was that; in fact I wasn't aware that I lived in a country with any distinct existence of its own. At school we were being taught to sing "Rule, Britannia" and to draw the Union Jack; after hours we read stacks of Captain Marvel, Plastic Man and Batman comic books, an activity delightfully enhanced by the disapproval of our elders. However, someone had given us Charles G. D. Roberts' *Kings in Exile* for Christmas, and I sniveled my way quickly through these heart-wrenching stories of animals caged, trapped and tormented. That was followed by Ernest Thompson Seton's *Wild Animals I Have Known,* if anything more upsetting because the animals were more actual—they lived in forests, not circuses—and their deaths more mundane: the deaths, not of tigers, but of rabbits.

No one called these stories Canadian literature, and I wouldn't have paid any attention if they had; as far as I was concerned they were just something else to read, along with Walter Scott, Edgar Allan Poe and Donald Duck. I wasn't discriminating in my reading, and I'm still not. I read then primarily to be entertained, as I do now. And I'm not saying that apologetically: I feel that if you remove the initial gut response from reading—the delight or excitement or simply the enjoyment of being told a story—and try to concentrate on the meaning or the shape or the "message" first, you might as well give up, it's too much like all work and no play.

But then as now there were different levels of entertainment. I read the backs of Shredded Wheat boxes as an idle pastime, Captain Marvel and Walter Scott as fantasy escape—I knew, even then, that wherever I lived it wasn't *there,* since I'd never seen a castle and the Popsicle Pete prizes advertised on the comic book covers either weren't available in Canada, or cost more—and Seton and Roberts as, believe it or not, something closer to real life. I *had* seen animals, quite a few of them; a dying porcupine was more real to me than a knight in armor or Clark Kent's Metropolis. Old mossy dungeons and Kryptonite were hard to come by where I lived, though I was quite willing to believe they existed somewhere else; but the materials for Seton's stick-and-stone artifacts and live-off-the-land recipes in *Wildwood Wisdom* were readily available, and we could make them quite easily, which we did. Most of the recipes were somewhat inedible, as you'll see if you try Cattail Root Stew or Pollen Pancakes, but the raw ingredients can be collected around any Canadian summer cottage.

However, it wasn't just the content of these books that felt more real to me; it was their shapes, their patterns. The animal stories were about the struggle to survive, and Seton's practical handbook was in fact a survival manual: it laid much stress on the dangers of getting lost, eating the wrong root or berry, or angering a moose in season. Though it was full of helpful hints, the world it depicted was one riddled with pitfalls, just as the animal stories were thickly strewn with traps and snares. In this world, no Superman would come swooping out of the sky at the last minute to rescue you from the catastrophe; no rider would arrive posthaste with a pardon from the King. The main thing was to avoid dying, and only by a mixture of cunning, experience and narrow escapes could the animal—or the human relying on his own resources—manage that. And, in the animal stories at any rate, there were no final happy endings or ultimate solutions; if the animal happened to escape from the particular crisis in the story, you knew there would be another one later on from which it wouldn't escape.

I wasn't making these analytical judgments at the time, of course. I was just learning what to expect: in comic books and things like *Alice in Wonderland* or Conan Doyle's *The Lost World,* you got rescued or you returned from the world of dangers to a cozy safe domestic one; in Seton and Roberts, because the world of dangers was *the same* as the real world, you didn't. But when in high school I encountered—again as a Christmas present—something labeled more explicitly as Canadian Literature, the Robert Weaver and Helen James anthology, *Canadian Short Stories,* I wasn't surprised. There they were again, those animals on the run, most of them in human clothing this time, and those humans up against it; here was the slight mistake that led to disaster, here was the fatal accident; this was a world of frozen corpses, dead gophers, snow, dead children, and the ever-present feeling of menace, not from an enemy set over against you but from everything surrounding you. The familiar peril lurked behind every bush, and *I knew the names of the bushes*. Again, I wasn't reading this as Canlit, I was just reading it; I remember being elated by some stories (notably James Reaney's "The Bully") and not very interested in others. But these stories felt real to me in a way that Charles Dickens, much as I enjoyed him, did not.

I've talked about these early experiences not because I think that they were typical but because I think that—significantly—they weren't: I doubt that many people my age had even this much contact, minimal and accidental though it was, with their own literature. (Talking about this now makes me feel about 102, because quite a lot has changed since then. But though new curricula are being invented here and there across the country, I'm not convinced that the *average* Canadian child or high school student is likely to run across much more Canadian literature than I did. *Why* this is true is of course one of our problems.)

Still, although I didn't read much Canadian writing, what   7
I did read had a shape of its own that felt different from the shapes of the other things I was reading. What that shape turned out to be, and what I felt it meant in terms of this country, became clearer to me the more I read.

BUILDING VOCABULARY

1. A writer will often use *allusions* (see Glossary) and references to people, events, places, literature, and aspects of a particular culture or era. In order to better understand Atwood's essay, try to identify as many of the following allusions as you can:

   a. "Rule, Britannia," the Union Jack, Captain Marvel, Plastic Man, Batman, G. D. Roberts, Ernest Thompson Seton (par. 1)
   b. Walter Scott, Edgar Allan Poe, Donald Duck (par. 2)
   c. Shredded Wheat, Popsicle Pete, Clark Kent's Metropolis, Kryptonite (par. 3)
   d. *Alice in Wonderland,* Conan Doyle, Charles Dickens (par. 5)

2. Select the letter of the word following it that best defines the word in italics.

   1. *distinct*
      a. wonderful   b. cloudy   c. well-defined   d. careful

   2. *mundane*
      a. common   b. tragic   c. horrible   d. timely
   3. *initial*
      a. nervous   b. warm   c. first   d. alphabetic
   4. *readily*
      a. inexpensively   b. speedily   c. willingly   d. really

5. *inedible*
    a. unfit for consumption **b.** delicious **c.** difficult
    d. different

6. *depicted*
    a. ridiculed **b.** represented **c.** longed for **d.** hated

7. *cunning*
    a. speed **b.** trickery **c.** cleverness **d.** cuteness

8. *cozy*
    a. comfortable **b.** limited **c.** familiar **d.** boring

9. *explicitly*
    a. precisely **b.** sexually **c.** unhappily **d.**
    hopelessly

10. *fatal*
    a. deadly **b.** fated **c.** tragic **d.** weary

11. *elated*
    a. sad **b.** gleeful **c.** confused **d.** welcome

12. *minimal*
    a. short-lived **b.** fortunate **c.** minor **d.** major

UNDERSTANDING THE WRITER'S IDEAS

1. What point about the sense of national identity for Canadians of her generation (she was born in 1939) does Atwood make in the opening sentence? How does the next sentence illustrate that point? With what nation are "Rule, Britannia" and the Union Jack associated?

2. How did Atwood's parents' attitude toward comic books affect her enjoyment of them?

3. What nationality were the writers Charles G. D. Roberts and Ernest Thompson Seton? What did Atwood feel when she read them for the first time? Why did she read them? What were their respective subject matters?

4. Did the young Atwood enjoy reading? Was she choosy about what she read? What was her main reason for reading? What is it as an adult?

5. According to the writer, what happens if you concentrate too much on the "meaning" of what you are reading?

6. For what purpose would Atwood read things like Walter Scott or Captain Marvel? To where does the italicized *there* in paragraph 3 refer? How did writers such as Seton and Roberts, and the environments they described, feel to Atwood when she first read them? Why? Explain how her references to "Cat-tail Root Stew" and "Pollen Pancakes" connect with this feeling.

7. Summarize in your own words why it was not just Seton's and Roberts's subject matter, but also the "shapes" and "patterns" of their writing that held special significance for Atwood. What was their overview of life? What does their appeal tell you about Atwood's outlook as a child?

8. Contrast the two different types of "worlds of danger" discussed in paragraph 5.

9. How did Atwood react upon reading the anthology *Canadian Short Stories* when in high school? Why? Who are "those animals" (par. 5)? What is "Canlit"?

10. Does Atwood think that the majority of Canadians have a good sense of their national literature? Explain. How has the situation changed since she was a child? How has it remained the same? What is her idea about the connection between reading and self-image? Based on your understanding of the entire essay, what would you assume Atwood sees as "the shape" of Canadian literature as she refers to it in her conclusion?

UNDERSTANDING THE WRITER'S TECHNIQUES

1. Is there a single statement of the main idea of this essay? Explain. Which paragraphs comprise the introduction, body, and conclusion of this essay?

2. For whom did Atwood write this essay? Is it equally sig-

nificant to both Canadian and non-Canadian readers? Why?

3. *Transitions* (see Glossary) enable writers to move from one idea to the next, or one paragraph to the next, while maintaining the *coherence* (logical connections) of their ideas. It is interesting to note that Atwood consistently uses grammatical negatives in the first sentences of the paragraphs of this selection.

Go through the essay and list some of the grammatical negatives that appear in the opening sentence of selected paragraphs. How does this pattern serve as a transition device? For what other reasons might she be using these constructions?

4. At the end of paragraph 2, why does the writer place the word "message" in quotation marks?

5. In paragraph 5, Atwood italicizes a statement of seemingly not much importance on its own: "*I knew the names of the bushes.*" Why does she place it in italics? How is it so significant to the paragraph or the essay?

6. The techniques of *description* and *illustration* (see Glossary) go hand in hand to make a writer's abstract ideas clear and vivid for readers. Generally, how does Atwood use description and illustration in this essay? Choose a particular paragraph and explain in detail what ideas the author's descriptions and illustrations make clear for you.

7. In the Building Vocabulary section, you identified various *allusions* (see page 76) in this essay. For what purpose did the author include so many allusions? Which were the most important to your understanding of the essay? Why?

8. Atwood uses four adjectives composed of between two and four words linked by hyphens. (*Stick-and-stone* in paragraph 3 is one example.) Find and list the other three. What single word adjectives could she have used instead? How would that have altered the tone of the sentences in which these adjectives appear?

9. Paragraph 6 is at least half composed of an explanation in *parentheses*. What is the main point of paragraph 6? What is Atwood's reason for the parenthetical explanation? How would it have affected the paragraph's meaning if she had written all the same sentences but had omitted the parentheses?

10. What is the significance of the title of this essay? Are there possible multiple meanings? Explain your answer with specific references to the essay.

EXPLORING THE WRITER'S IDEAS

1. Clearly, Atwood is proud of her heritage as a Canadian, as well as of her status as a Canadian writer. Look up and define the following words: *nationalist, patriot, chauvinist.* Which word most closely describes Atwood's attitude in this essay? Why?

2. Atwood makes the point that if you try too hard to understand the "message" of a story, you are likely to miss its "delight or excitement." What different responses do you experience when reading for an assignment versus reading for your own reasons? Describe the differences. Which do you enjoy more? From which do you learn more? Explain. How do you feel that school reading assignments can be made more pleasurable?

3. Do you believe that different countries produce significantly different types of literature? Explain. Discuss some of the best-known authors from countries other than your own. How many have you read? In general, do you more enjoy reading works by authors from your own country (or region) or from elsewhere? Why? How are the two reading experiences different for you?

IDEAS FOR WRITING

Guided Writing

Write an essay that explains how you came to appreciate a particular aspect of your own national culture or ethnic background.

1. Begin by telling when you first became aware of this aspect of your culture. Tell how circumstances or the environment around you did not necessarily encourage your appreciation.

2. Introduce specific examples of this cultural aspect that were important in shaping your appreciation.

3. Where appropriate, use allusions as examples of other things that were more available to you than your own culture.

4. Use specific examples to support your point.

5. Throughout the essay, keep as an unstated purpose to educate your readers to the value and joy of this aspect of your culture.

6. Use clear transitions between paragraphs.

7. Describe how your initial attraction blossomed into a deep appreciation.

8. Explain to your readers your main reason for relating these early experiences. In this overall explanation, include a long parenthetical explanation.

9. Give your essay a one-word title.

More Writing Projects

1. Atwood writes about reading to be entertained rather than instructed. Write in your journal about books, television

shows, and films that you have found entertaining —even if they haven't had a serious "message."

2. Describe in a paragraph your favorite story, book, or television program from childhood.

3. Do you think that publishers, film studios, and television producers have a responsibility to present entertainment reflecting the cultural diversity of the United States? Take a position on this issue and write an essay on it.

Four Ways of Reading

Donald Hall

Donald Hall is a prolific writer who wears many hats. He has published numerous books of poetry and literary criticism, as well as books on writing (among which is the well-known *Writing Well*). Hall has also edited several anthologies. In this essay, which first appeared in *The New York Times,* he suggests that the activity of reading is not as sacred as some would like us to believe. He insists that the four types of reading that he outlines serve different purposes and yield very different results.

Words to Watch

advent (par. 1)   arrival; appearance

piety (par. 1)   reverent belief; religiosity

literacy (par. 2)   condition of being able to read and write

irrelevant (par. 3)   pointless; extraneous

decodes (par. 4)   explains meaning in ordinary language

discipline (par. 5)   field of study

embodiments (par. 5)   forms; shapes; manifestations

narcotic (par. 6)   something that soothes or dulls the senses

injurious (par. 6)   harmful; hurtful

lethargy (par. 6)   extreme tiredness; chronic fatigue

narcolepsy (par. 7)   a condition characterized by brief attacks of deep sleep

lavish (par. 8)   extravagant; full of richness

narcissism (par. 8)   egoistical self-love

Everywhere one meets the idea that reading is an activity desirable in itself. It is understandable that publishers and librarians—and even writers—should promote this assumption, but it is strange that the idea should have general currency. People surround the idea of reading with piety, and do not take into account the purpose of reading or the value of what is being read. Teachers and parents praise the child who reads, and praise themselves, whether the text be *The Read-*

83

er's Digest or *Moby Dick*. The advent of TV has increased the
false values ascribed to reading, since TV provides a vulgar
alternative. But this piety is silly; and most reading is no more
cultural nor intellectual nor imaginative than shooting pool or
watching *What's My Line*.

It is worth asking how the act of reading became some-   2
thing to value in itself, as opposed for instance to the act of
conversation or the act of taking a walk. Mass literacy is a recent phenomenon, and I suggest that the aura which decorates
reading is a relic of the importance of reading to our great-
great-grandparents. Literacy used to be a mark of social distinction, separating a small portion of humanity from the rest.
The farm laborer who was ambitious for his children did not
daydream that they would become schoolteachers or doctors;
he daydreamed that they would learn to read, and that a world
would therefore open up to them in which they did not have to
labor in the fields fourteen hours a day for six days a week in
order to buy salt and cotton. On the next rank of society, ample time for reading meant that the reader was free from the
necessity to spend most of his waking hours making a living of
any kind. Reading is an inactivity, and therefore a badge of
social class. Of course, these reasons for the piety attached to
reading are never acknowledged. They show themselves in
the shape of our attitudes toward books; reading gives off an
air of gentility.

It seems to me possible to name four kinds of reading,   3
each with a characteristic manner and purpose. The first is
reading for information—reading to learn about a trade, or
politics, or how to accomplish something. We read a newspaper this way, or most textbooks, or directions on how to assemble a bicycle. With most of this sort of material, the reader
can learn to scan the page quickly, coming up with what he
needs and ignoring what is irrelevant to him, like the rhythm
of the sentence, or the play of metaphor. Courses in speed
reading can help us read for this purpose, training the eye to
jump quickly across the page. If we read *The New York Times*
with the attention we should give a novel or a poem, we will
have time for nothing else, and our mind will be cluttered with
clichés and dead metaphor. Quick eye-reading is a necessity

to anyone who wants to keep up with what's happening, or learn much of what has happened in the past. The amount of reflection, which interrupts and slows down the reading, depends on the material.

But it is not the same activity as reading literature. There 4 ought to be another word. If we read a work of literature properly, we read slowly, and we hear all the words. If our lips do not actually move, it's only laziness. The muscles in our throats move, and come together when we see the word "squeeze." We hear the sounds so accurately that if a syllable is missing in a line of poetry we hear the lack, though we may not know what we are lacking. In prose we accept the rhythms, and hear the adjacent sounds. We also register a track of feeling through the metaphors and associations of words. Careless writing prevents this sort of attention, and becomes offensive. But the great writers reward this attention. Only by the full exercise of our powers to receive language can we absorb their intelligence and their imagination. This kind of reading goes through the ear—though the eye takes in the print, and decodes it into sound—to the throat and the understanding, and it can never be quick. It is slow and sensual, a deep pleasure that begins with touch and ends with the sort of comprehension that we associate with dream.

Too many intellectuals read in order to reduce images to 5 abstractions. With a philosopher one reads slowly, as if it were literature, but much time must be spent with the eyes turned away from the pages, reflecting on the text. To read literature this way is to turn it into something it is not—to concepts clothed in character, or philosophy sugar-coated. I think that most literary intellectuals read this way, including the brighter Professors of English, with the result that they miss literature completely, and concern themselves with a minor discipline called the history of ideas. I remember a course in Chaucer at my University in which the final exam largely required the identification of a hundred or more fragments of Chaucer, none as long as a line. If you liked poetry, and read Chaucer through a couple of times slowly, you found yourself knowing them all. If you were a literary intellectual, well-informed about the great chain of being, chances are you had

a difficult time. To read literature is to be intimately involved
with the words on the page, and never to think of them as the
embodiments of ideas which can be expressed in other terms.
On the other hand, intellectual writing—closer to mathematics
on a continuum that has at its opposite pole lyric poetry—requires intellectual reading, which is slow because it is reflec-
tive and because the reader must pause to evaluate concepts.

But most of the reading which is praised for itself is nei-   6
ther literary nor intellectual. It is narcotic. Novels, stories and
biographies—historical sagas, monthly regurgitations of book
clubs, four- and five-thousand word daydreams of the magazines—these are the opium of the suburbs. The drug is not
harmful except to the addict himself, and is no more injurious
to him than Johnny Carson or a bridge club, but it is nothing to
be proud of. This reading is the automated daydream, the mild
trip of the housewife and the tired businessman, interested not
in experience and feeling but in turning off the possibilities of
experience and feeling. Great literature, if we read it well,
opens us up to the world, and makes us more sensitive to it, as
if we acquired eyes that could see through things and ears that
could hear smaller sounds. But by narcotic reading, one can
reduce great literature to the level of *The Valley of the Dolls*.
One can read *Anna Karenina* passively and inattentively, and
float down the river of lethargy as if one were reading a confession magazine: "I Spurned My Husband for a Count."

I think that everyone reads for narcosis occasionally,   7
and perhaps most consistently in late adolescence, when great
readers are born. I remember reading to shut the world out,
away at a school where I did not want to be; I invented a word
to name my disease: "bibliolepsy," on the analogy of narcolepsy. But after a while the books became a window on the
world, and not a screen against it. This change doesn't always
happen. I think that late adolescent narcotic reading accounts
for some of the badness of English departments. As a college
student, the boy loves reading and majors in English because
he would be reading anyway. Deciding on a career, he takes
up English teaching for the same reason. Then in graduate
school he is trained to be a scholar, which is painful and irrelevant, and finds he must write papers and publish them to be

a Professor—and at about this time he no longer requires reading for narcosis, and he is left with nothing but a Ph.D. and the prospect of fifty years of teaching literature; and he does not even like literature.

Narcotic reading survives the impact of television, because this type of reading has even less reality than melodrama; that is, the reader is in control: once the characters reach into the reader's feelings, he is able to stop reading, or glance away, or superimpose his own daydream. The trouble with television is that it writes its own script. Literature is often valued precisely because of its distance from the tangible. Some readers prefer looking into the text of a play to seeing it performed. Reading a play, it is possible to stage it oneself by an imaginative act; but it is also possible to remove it from real people. Here is Virginia Woolf, who was lavish in her praise of the act of reading, talking about reading a play rather than seeing it: "Certainly there is a good deal to be said for reading *Twelfth Night* in the book if the book can be read in a garden, with no sound but the thud of an apple falling to the earth, or of the wind ruffling the branches of the trees." She sets her own stage; the play is called *Virginia Woolf Reads Twelfth Night in a Garden*. Piety moves into narcissism, and the high metaphors of Shakespeare's lines dwindle into the flowers of an English garden; actors in ruffles wither, while the wind ruffles branches.

BUILDING VOCABULARY

1. Determine the meanings of the following phrases and in your own words explain them as they relate to the essay.

   a. the idea should have general currency (par. 1)
   b. a vulgar alternative (par. 1)
   c. the aura which decorates reading (par. 2)
   d. a mark of social distinction (par 2.)
   e. gives off an air of gentility (par. 2)
   f. speed reading (par. 3)
   g. our minds will be cluttered with clichés and dead metaphor (par. 3)

   h. the full exercise of our powers to receive language (par. 4)

   i. concepts clothed in character (par. 5)

   j. philosophy sugar-coated (par. 5)

   k. the great chain of being (par. 5)

   l. to be intimately involved with the words on the page (par. 5)

   m. the opium of the suburbs (par. 6)

   n. the books became a window on the world (par. 7)

   o. superimpose his own daydream (par. 8)

2. Identify these references from literature and popular culture that appear in the essay:

   a. *The Reader's Digest*; *Moby Dick*

   b. *What's My Line*; *The New York Times*

   c. Chaucer; Johnny Carson

   d. *The Valley of the Dolls*; *Anna Karenina*

   e. Virginia Woolf; Shakespeare

UNDERSTANDING THE WRITER'S IDEAS

1. What is Hall's opinion about how most people regard the activity of reading? Explain in your own words what Hall is saying in the first two sentences of his essay. Why is it "understandable that publishers and librarians—and even writers—should promote this assumption"? How does Hall think people ought to feel about reading?

2. In paragraph 2, what does Hall suggest is the relation between reading (or literacy) and social class? Support your answer with specific examples from the essay.

3. Explain the meaning of the statement, "Reading is an inactivity" (par. 2).

4. According to Hall, what are the four kinds of reading? Briefly outline the characteristics of each. Include examples of the types of material read for each.

5. What is the main difference between reading for information and reading literature? Why does Hall write that when we read literature, "If our lips do not actually move, it's only laziness" (par. 4)?

6. What constitutes "Careless writing" (par. 4)? Why does it become "offensive"?

7. Explain in your own words the main problem with the way "most literary intellectuals" read. Do you agree with Hall's analysis? Why? What is the result of this kind of reading activity? Why?

8. Into which category does the majority of reading fall? What is the "automated daydream"? What is the main purpose of this type of reading? What are its positive aspects? Its negative aspects? According to Hall, which outweighs the other?

9. According to the author, at what age are great readers born? When did Hall become a great reader? Was he actually suffering a "disease" at that time? Explain.

10. Throughout the essay, Hall makes various comparisons between reading and watching television. What are they? What is the main difference between the two activities? What are the similarities?

11. In your own words, state Hall's conclusion about the process of reading.

UNDERSTANDING THE WRITER'S TECHNIQUES

1. Where in this essay does Hall make his *thesis statement?* What is it? Explain it in your own words.

2. In paragraphs 1 and 2, Hall uses two very straightforward introductory phrases: "It is understandable" and "It is worth asking." What is the effect of these phrases on the

reader? Why does Hall use them? Identify other such
phrases with similar purposes throughout the essay.

3. Who is the *intended audience* (see page 2) for this essay?
How do you know?

4. *Diction* (see Glossary) refers to a writer's choice and use of
words. We classify *levels of diction*—"informal," "academic," "low-class," "snobbish," and so forth. How
would you describe the general level of diction in this essay? Does the level suit the subject matter? Why?

5. In paragraph 5, Hall includes an *extended illustration* (see
Chapter 5) based on his personal experience in taking a
course on Chaucer. Briefly outline that illustration. How
does he use it to suggest the differences between two types
of reading?

6. In paragraph 7, Hall analyzes the *process* (see Chapter 9)
through which "late adolescent narcotic reading accounts
for some of the badness of English departments." List the
various stages of this process.

7. How does Hall use *definition* (see Chapter 7) to explain the
phrase "To read literature" (par. 5)?

8. *Tone* (see Glossary) refers to the attitude a writer wants to
convey to readers about the subject. What tone does Hall
use here? Does this tone indicate a straightforward, analytical approach to the issues discussed? Explain. List three
specific examples from the text to illustrate the tone that
you perceive.

EXPLORING THE WRITER'S IDEAS

1. This article first appeared in *The New York Times*. Yet, implicit in paragraph 3 there seems to be a suggestion to the
reader not to read the *Times* too closely. Explain this seem-
ing discrepancy.

2. Hall writes, "Some readers prefer looking into the text of a

play to seeing it performed. Reading a play, it is possible to stage it oneself by an imaginative act.''

Which do you prefer—reading a play in the text or seeing it performed? Discuss some examples of plays that (a) you've only seen performed; (b) you've only read in text; (c) you've both seen performed and read in text. How were the experiences different?

3. Characterize Hall's attitudes toward television.

4. In this essay, Hall briefly discusses a relation between reading and ''the act of conversation'' (par. 2). In his essay ''Writing'' (pages 13–16), William Stafford states: ''most of what I write, like most of what I say in casual conversation, will not amount to much.'' Compare the two authors' views on the relation between conversation and their respective subjects. With whom do you tend to agree? Why?

5. Read Malcolm X's ''Prison Studies'' (pages 63–66) and compare his attitude toward the connection between reading and social status with Hall's.

IDEAS FOR WRITING

Guided Writing

Write an essay titled ''Three Ways of _____ .'' Choose one of the following activities to fill in the blank:

  a. Reading a Novel
  b. Reading a Science Textbook
  c. Reading a Weekly Magazine

Or, fill in the blank with a reading activity of your own choice.

1. Begin your essay with a discussion of the generally held opinion about this reading activity.

2. Throughout, make references to examples of the genre that are considered ''intellectual,'' and others that are considered ''pop culture.''

3. In paragraph 1, include a thesis statement that expresses your opinion about this activity.

4. Make some connection between this reading activity and the society or culture at large.

5. In successive paragraphs, name and outline three ways of doing this reading activity. Discuss the specific steps involved in each method.

6. Make comparisons between the three methods discussed in Question 5.

7. Include at least one extended illustration based on personal experience.

8. Try to invent an original term to describe part of this process.

9. Conclude your essay by comparing this reading activity with a nonreading activity.

More Writing Projects

1. In your journal, write an entry comparing Atwood's "reading for entertainment" and Hall's "narcotic reading." Are they the same? Explain your response.

2. Do you think that there are actually different ways to read (as Hall suggests), or is reading really one, integrated activity that applies to all sorts of reading matter? Explain your opinion in an extended paragraph.

3. Write an essay in which you consider whether or not it is important to be a "good" reader to succeed in life.

SUMMING UP: CHAPTER 2

1. In one way or another, all the authors in this chapter write about how reading has provided them with emotional ease or intellectual stimulation at some point in their lives. Eudora Welty describes how reading was a source of delight

in her childhood; Malcolm X explains how reading redirected his adulthood; Margaret Atwood as an adult recognizes the importance of her childhood reading habits; and Donald Hall tells how reading was an escapist technique during his adolescence.

Which of these writers, alone or in combination, best reflects your view of reading? Write an essay in which you address this question.

2. On the average, Americans are said to read less than one book per person annually. Take a survey of several people who are not students to find out how often they read, and what kind of books. In an essay, analyze the results. Indicate the types of people you interviewed and explain why your results either conformed to, or differed from, the norm. Indicate the types of books each person read.

3. List all the books you have read in the past six months. For each, write a brief two-to-three sentence reaction. Compare your list with those of your classmates. What reading trends do you notice? From these lists, what generalizations can you draw about college students' reading habits?

4. The United States ranks forty-ninth among nations in literacy. People often ask, "Why is there such a low rate of literacy in such an advanced nation?" What is your answer to this question? How do you think the writers in this chapter would respond to the question? Write an essay that explains your response by drawing on Welty, Malcolm X, Atwood, and Hall. Suggest some ways to improve the rate of literacy in this country. You might want to consider this fact: By the time the average American finishes high school, he or she has spent 18,000 hours in front of a television set as opposed to 12,000 hours in the classroom.

5. Using Welty or Atwood as an example, write an essay in which you reflect on your early memories of reading. Describe when you learned to read, when you experienced pleasure at being read to, or when you started appreciating a particular kind of reading. Call your essay "Reading When I Was Young."

CHAPTER 3

Description

Since a writer's main purpose is to explain things clearly, description is an important aid to good writing. To add liveliness to an essay, descriptive details are necessary to create a visual impression of an object or a scene. As a technique in writing, description matches the sort of details we see in vivid and effective photographs. Good descriptive writers help the reader to "see" objects, scenes, and even moods by means of language.

The essays in this section reflect key qualities in all good descriptive writing. First, description relies on a basic talent that we all have—the ability to see, touch, taste, hear, or smell various elements in the world. Talented descriptive writers refine the power of their five senses in order to recreate people, places, things, emotions, and ideas. Second, in descriptive writing, the author must select details carefully. There might be thousands of details in any given scene, but clearly a writer cannot present all of them. Instead, the writer must choose only those details most useful in painting a picture for the reader. Third, writers must organize their descriptions carefully. With description, the writer must decide on a perspective (for instance, top to bottom, left to right, front to back) and then move carefully from detail to detail. The descriptive writer has a "camera eye" that ranges over its subject in a careful, consistent way. Fourth, descriptive writing creates a "dominant impression" of its subject. This main impression arises from the author's focus on a single subject, and from the feelings that the writer brings to that subject. Finally, descriptive writing offers a thesis or main idea concerning its subject, as does all sound writing. In short, description makes a point.

Writing good descriptive papers is a challenge, because we (like the authors in this section) have to look at our world anew, to remember, to search for meaningful details, to re-create the images around us. As we write descriptive paragraphs and essays, we should keep a basic goal in mind—to permit the reader to see the world that we describe in a fresh, vivid, and concrete way. As descriptive writers, we have to be willing to look at the world, perhaps for the first time, close up.

The Shack

Margaret Laurence

In this selection from Laurence's *Heart of a Stranger* (1976), the Canadian novelist combines lush natural imagery with "portions of memory, presences in the mind" to convey to us her sense of a place to work as a writer. Notice especially how the details help create a tone of solitude and contentment. The Otonabee River described here also figures significantly in Laurence's novel, *The Diviners*.

Words to Watch

slither (par. 1)   to slide or slip along

peril (par. 1)   danger

attributes (par. 2)   characteristics

molten (par. 2)   melted; liquified by heat

drabber (par. 5)   more plain; less fancy

unwieldy (par. 6)   awkward; clumsy; not easily managed

harbinger (par. 6)   something that foreshadows what is to come

dawdle (par. 9)   to delay or spend time idly

saplings (par. 9)   young trees

homesteaded (par. 9)   claimed land by living on and cultivating it

staunch (par. 10)   substantial; steadfast

armorial (par. 10)   like military armor or protective covering

The most loved place, for me, in this country has in fact 1
been many places. It has changed throughout the years, as I
and my circumstances have changed. I haven't really lost any
of the best places from the past, though. I may no longer inhabit them, but they inhabit me, portions of memory, presences in the mind. One such place was my family's summer
cottage at Clear Lake in Riding Mountain National Park, Man-
itoba. It was known to us simply as The Lake. Before the government piers and the sturdy log staircases down to the shore
were put in, we used to slither with an exhilarating sense of
peril down the steep homemade branch and dirt shelf-steps,

through the stands of thin tall spruce and birch trees slender and graceful as girls, passing moss-hairy fallen logs and the white promise of wild strawberry blossoms, until we reached the sand and the hard bright pebbles of the beach at the edge of the cold spring-fed lake where at nights the loons still cried eerily, before too much humanshriek made them move away north.

My best place at the moment is very different, although I 2 guess it has some of the attributes of that long-ago place. It is a small cedar cabin on the Otonabee River in southern Ontario. I've lived three summers there, writing, birdwatching, river-watching. I sometimes feel sorry for the people in speedboats who spend their weekends zinging up and down the river at about a million miles an hour. For all they're able to see, the riverbanks might just as well be green concrete and the river itself flowing with molten plastic.

Before sunup, I'm wakened by birdvoices and, I may 3 say, birdfeet clattering and thumping on the cabin roof. Cursing only slightly, I get up *temporarily,* for the pre-dawn ritual of lighting a small fire in the old black woodstove (mornings are chilly here, even in summer) and looking out at the early river. The waters have a lovely spooky quality at this hour, entirely mist-covered, a secret meeting of river and sky.

By the time I get up to stay, the mist has vanished and 4 the river is a clear ale-brown, shining with sun. I drink my coffee and sit looking out to the opposite shore, where the giant maples are splendidly green now and will be trees of flame in the fall of the year. Oak and ash stand among the maples, and the grey skeletons of the dead elms, gauntly beautiful even in death. At the very edge of the river, the willows are everywhere, water-related trees, magic trees, pale green in early summer, silvergreen in late summer, greengold in autumn.

I begin work, and everytime I lift my eyes from the page 5 and glance outside, it is to see some marvel or other. The joyous dance-like flight of the swallows. The orange-black flash of the orioles who nest across the river. The amazing takeoff of a red-winged blackbird, revealing like a swiftly unfolded fan the hidden scarlet in those dark wings. The flittering of the goldfinches, who always travel in domestic pairs, he gorgeous

in black-patterned yellow feathers, she (alas) drabber in green-
ish grey-yellow.

A pair of great blue herons have their huge unwieldy nest 6
about half a mile upriver, and although they are very shy, occasionally through the open door I hear a sudden approaching
rush of air (yes, you can *hear* it) and look up quickly to see the
magnificent unhurried sweep of those powerful wings. The
only other birds which can move me so much are the Canada
geese in their autumn migration flight, their far-off wilderness
voices the harbinger of winter.

Many boats ply these waterways, and all of them are 7
given mental gradings of merit or lack of it, by me. Standing
low in the estimation of all of us along this stretch of the river
are some of the big yachts, whose ego-tripping skippers don't
have the courtesy to slow down in cottage areas and whose
violent wakes scour out our shorelines. Ranking highest in my
good books are the silent unpolluting canoes and rowboats,
and next to them, the small outboard motorboats put-putting
along and carrying patient fishermen, and the homemade house-
boats, unspeedy and somehow cosy-looking, decorated lov-
ingly with painted birds or flowers or gaudy abstract splodges.

In the quiet of afternoon, if no boats are around, I look 8
out and see the half-moon leap of a fish, carp or muskie, so
instantaneous that one has the impression of having seen not a
fish but an arc of light.

The day moves on, and about four o'clock Linda and Su- 9
san from the nearby farm arrive. I call them the Girls of the
Pony Express. Accompanied by dogs and laughter, they ride
their horses into my yard, kindly bringing my mail from the
rural route postbox up the road. For several summers it was
Old Jack who used to drive his battered Volkswagen up to
fetch the mail. He was one of the best neighbours and most
remarkable men I've ever known. As a boy of eighteen, he
had homesteaded a hundred miles north of Regina. Later, he'd
been a skilled toolmaker with Ford. He'd travelled to South
America and done many amazing things. He was a man whose
life had taught him a lot of wisdom. After his much-loved wife
died, he moved out here to the river, spending as short a winter as possible in Peterborough, and getting back into his cottage the first of anyone in the spring, when the river was still

in flood and he could only get in and out, hazardously, by boat. I used to go out in his boat with him, late afternoons, and we would dawdle along the river, looking at the forest stretches and the open rolling farmlands and vast old barns, and at the smaller things closeby, the heavy luxuriance of ferns at the water's rim, the dozens of snapping turtles with unblinking eyes, all sizes and generations of the turtle tribe, sunning themselves on the fallen logs in the river. One summer, Old Jack's eighty-fourth, he spent some time planting maple saplings on his property. A year later, when I saw him dying, it seemed to me he'd meant those trees as a kind of legacy, a declaration of faith. Those of us along the river, here, won't forget him, nor what he stood for.

After work, I go out walking and weed-inspecting. 10 Weeds and wildflowers impress me as much as any cultivated plant. I've heard that in a year when the milkweed is plentiful, the Monarch butterflies will also be plentiful. This year the light pinkish milkweed flowers stand thick and tall, and sure enough, here are the dozens of Monarch butterflies, fluttering like dusky orange-gold angels all over the place. I can't identify as many plants as I'd like, but I'm learning. Chickweed, the ragged-leafed lambs' quarters, the purple-and-white wild phlox with its expensive-smelling free perfume, the pink and mauve wild asters, the two-toned yellow of the tiny butter-and-eggs flowers, the burnt orange of devil's paintbrush, the staunch nobility of the huge purple thistles, and, almost best of all, that long stalk covered with clusters of miniature creamy blossoms which I finally tracked down in my wildflower book—this incomparable plant bears the armorial name of the Great Mullein of the Figwort Family. It may not be the absolute prettiest of our wildflowers, but it certainly has the most stunning pedigree.

It is night now, and there are no lights except those of 11 our few cottages. At sunset, an hour or so ago, I watched the sun's last flickers touching the rippling river, making it look as though some underwater world had lighted all its candles down there. Now it is dark. Dinner over, I turn out the electric lights in the cabin so I can see the stars. The black skydome (or perhaps skydom, like kingdom) is alive and alight.

Tomorrow the weekend will begin, and friends will ar- 12

rive. We'll talk all day and probably half the night, and that will be good. But for now, I'm content to be alone, because loneliness is something that doesn't exist here.

BUILDING VOCABULARY

1. In your own words, write the meaning of each italicized word or phrase taken from the selection.

   a. *exhilarating* sense of *peril* (par. 1)
   b. loons still cried *eerily* (par. 1)
   c. *pre-dawn ritual* (par. 3)
   d. *spooky* quality (par. 3)
   e. *gauntly* beautiful (par. 4)
   f. huge *unwieldy* nest (par. 6)
   g. *unhurried* sweep of those powerful wings (par. 6)
   h. boats *ply* these *waterways* (par. 7)
   i. low in *estimation* (par. 7)
   j. *gaudy, abstract splodges* (par. 7)
   k. so *instantaneous* (par. 8)
   l. heavy *luxuriance* of ferns (par. 9)
   m. as a kind of *legacy* (par. 9)
   n. this *incomparable* plan (par. 10)
   o. most *stunning pedigree* (par. 10)

2. In paragraph 10, Laurence speaks of learning to identify plants. Similarly, we must learn to identify words. Write formal, dictionary definitions for the wildflowers listed in this paragraph.

UNDERSTANDING THE WRITER'S IDEAS

1. What is "this country" mentioned in the first sentence? How do you know? What specific clues tell you which country Laurence writes about?

2. What was the author's first "most loved place"? What happened to it?

3. Briefly describe in your own words the environment of the Otonabee River where Laurence has her cabin.

4. What is the author's attitude toward speedboats on the river? Where does she express this attitude?

5. What is Laurence's "pre-dawn ritual"? Why does she curse slightly during this time? What clues does she give the reader about the climate of the place?

6. Explain the descriptions "a secret meeting of river and sky" (par. 3) and "trees of flame" (par. 4).

7. What is Laurence's "work" which she mentions in paragraph 5? Does she go into great detail about her work? Why or why not?

8. Describe the author's overall attitude toward nature. Give specific examples from the essay to support your answer.

9. Why does the author give the boats on the river "mental gradings"? Are her reactions based purely on the mechanical nature of the different boats, or are there other factors involved? Support your answer with examples.

10. What are the "gaudy abstract splodges" mentioned at the end of paragraph 7?

11. Why does Laurence call Linda and Susan "the Girls of the Pony Express"?

12. Who was Old Jack? Describe the author's feelings toward him. At the end of paragraph 9, Laurence states that no one will forget "what he stood for." What did he stand for? How are the maple saplings "a kind of legacy, a declaration of faith"?

13. What does the writer do "after work"?

14. Explain the meaning of the parenthetical expression "(or perhaps skydom, like kingdom)" in paragraph 11. How does it relate to the overall main idea of this essay?

15. In the last paragraph, Laurence writes "and that will be good" in relation to her friends visiting and talking all day and night. Does she really feel it "will be good"? Why or why not?

UNDERSTANDING THE WRITER'S TECHNIQUES

1. Do you find the first sentence self-contradictory? Why does Laurence begin with such a statement? How does it affect the rest of her description? Where else does she seem to be contradicting herself? Why?

2. What is the main idea of this essay? Writers often provide a single *thesis sentence* (see Glossary) to express the main idea. Is there a specific thesis statement in this essay? Where?

3. By what principles does Laurence organize the descriptive details in this essay? How does she use *time* as an organizing factor? List three specific examples.

4. Laurence uses figurative language throughout the essay (see Glossary). Pick out what you think are the most vivid and original figurative expressions. Defend your choices.

5. Evaluate Laurence's use of *transitions* (see Glossary). Specifically, how does she accomplish transitions between paragraphs 1 and 2? Paragraphs 4 and 5? Paragraphs 8 and 9? 9 and 10? 10 and 11?

6. Explain the description, ''the grey skeletons of the dead elms, *gauntly beautiful* even in death'' (par. 4). Why would she use images of death and suffering to express beauty? How does this description fit with her overall view of nature?

7. *Hyperbole* is the use of descriptive exaggeration to make a point. Find two instances of hyperbole in this essay. What is the purpose of these hyperbolic descriptions?

8. Most of the writing in this essay consists of long, flowing sentences. How does the author change that pattern toward the end of the essay? Why?

9. Does this essay contain a clearly defined introduction, body, and conclusion? (See Glossary.) If so, state which paragraphs make up each section.

10. Does Laurence ever really describe the shack of the title? Why? What does that tell you about her view of the relation between the shack and its environment?

EXPLORING THE WRITER'S IDEAS

1. The final sentence of this essay is somewhat puzzling: "But for now, I'm content to be alone, because loneliness is something that doesn't exist here." What do you feel is the difference between *being alone* and *loneliness?* Most people dislike or even fear loneliness. Are there times when being alone can be a good thing? Draw on your own experience to illustrate your answer. How do you deal with loneliness?

2. Throughout the essay, Laurence refers to misuse or disregard of nature by others on the river. We get the feeling that she is very critical of and annoyed by people who violate nature. Do you think her attitude is fair? Why? What have been your experiences with seeing natural beauty abused by vacationers, developers, hunters, and so on?

3. In describing Old Jack, the author states that the maple saplings he planted were meant as "a kind of legacy, a declaration of faith." Is there anything that you or someone you know has done that you would want considered as a part of your own legacy? Explain.

IDEAS FOR WRITING

Guided Writing

Write an essay in which you describe a favorite place at which you've spent a good deal of time.

1. Give your essay a short, direct title.

2. Begin with a short description of a previous, but long gone, favorite place and use a transition to associate it with the place of your essay.

3. Tell something of your connection to the place. How long have you known the place? Why do you go there? What do you do there?

4. Begin ordering your description by describing the start of a typical day at the place.

5. Order the rest of your essay by focusing on features of the environment at the place. Use supporting sensory details.

6. Use concrete sensory details—colors, sounds, smells, images of touch—to help make the place come alive.

7. In one of the body paragraphs, describe how another person has significantly affected you and the place.

8. Be sure to use clear transitions between the main paragraphs of your essay. You might want to use time as an organizing principle in your essay.

9. Make sure your essay expresses a *dominant impression* of the place.

10. End your essay at the end of a day. Indicate how you believe the next day's activities would affect your current feelings about the place.

More Writing Projects

1. Write a journal description of a familiar room from your childhood or recent past. You might describe a bedroom, a classroom, a church, a library, or a local shop.

2. In a paragraph, describe an ideal place to which you'd like to go whenever you feel nervous or upset. This place may be a room or an outdoor place, and it may be real or imaginary. Use your imagination to create a real "rest haven."

3. In her essay, Laurence clearly is describing a "ritual" that is very important to her. Write an essay describing a ritual that is significant for you. Depict the stages or components of this ritual in vivid detail.

Arizona 87

William Least Heat Moon

In this chapter from his 1982 book, *Blue Highways,* William Least Heat Moon presents a bittersweet, richly detailed description of the landscape he sees while driving his truck, Ghost Dancing, through the southwestern United States. As he drives through central Arizona, his careful eye photographs both the natural and the human landscape around him. In converting these snapshots to language, Least Heat Moon relies upon rich sensory detail and especially vivid and original comparisons.

Words to Watch

friable (par. 1)   easily crushed or pulverized

persnickety (par. 1)   fussy about small details

pollinate (par. 3)   to carry pollen to fertilize plant seeds

kamikaze (par. 3)   a member of a corps of Japanese pilots assigned to make a suicidal crash at a target

aerial (par. 3)   occurring in the air

cache (par. 4)   something hidden

marauding (par. 6)   roaming about in search of plunder

Apaches (par. 6)   a tribe of Native Americans of the southwestern United States

rodeo (par. 6)   a performance featuring cowboy stunts

badger (par. 7)   a burrowing animal with long claws

unobtrusively (par. 9)   not very obviously

escarpment (par. 9)   a long cliff

coalesced (par. 12)   came together

I don't suppose that saguaros mean to give comic relief 1 to the otherwise solemn face of the desert, but they do. Standing on the friable slopes they are quite persnickety about, saguaros mimic men as they salute, bow, dance, raise arms to wave, and grin with faces carved in by woodpeckers. Older plants, having survived odds against their reaching maturity of sixty million to one, have every right to smile.

The saguaro is ninety percent water, and a big, two- 2
hundred-year-old cactus may hold a ton of it—a two-year supply. With this weight, a plant that begins to lean is soon on the
ground; one theory now says that the arms, which begin
sprouting only after forty or fifty years when the cactus has
some height, are counterweights to keep the plant erect.

The Monday I drove northeast out of Phoenix, saguaros 3
were in bloom—comparatively small, greenish-white blossoms perched on top of the trunks like undersized Easter bon-
nets; at night, long-nosed bats came to pollinate them. But by
day, cactus wrens, birds of daring aerial skill, put on the show
as they made kamikaze dives between toothpick-size thorns
into nest cavities, where they were safe from everything except the incredible ascents over the spines by black racers in
search of eggs the snakes would swallow whole.

It was hot. The only shade along Arizona 87 lay under 4
the bottomsides of rocks; the desert gives space then closes it
up with heat. To the east, in profile, rose the Superstition
Mountains, an evil place, Pima and Maricopa Indians say,
which brings on diabolic possession to those who enter.
Somewhere among the granite and greasewood was the Lost
Dutchman gold mine, important not for whatever cache it
might hide as for providing a white dream.

North of the Sycamore River, saguaro, ocotillo, pal- 5
overde, and cholla surrendered the hills to pads of prickly
pear the size of a man's head. The road climbed and the tem-
perature dropped. At Payson, a mile high on the northern
slope of the Mazatzal Mountains, I had to pull on a jacket.

Settlers once ran into Payson for protection from ma- 6
rauding Apaches; after the Apache let things calm down, citizens tried to liven them up again by holding rodeos in the main
street. Now, streets paved, Payson lay quiet but for the whine
of sawmills releasing the sweet scent of cut timber.

I stopped at an old log hotel to quench a desert thirst. A 7
sign on the door: NO LIVE ANIMALS ALLOWED. I guess you could
bring in all the dead ones you wanted. A woman shouted,
"Ain't servin' now." Her unmoving eyes, heavy as if cast
from lead, watched suspiciously for a live badger under my
jacket or a weasel up my pantleg.

"This is a fine old hotel," I said. She ignored me. "Do 8 you mind if I look at your big map?" She shrugged and moved away, safe from any live animal attack. I was hunting a place to go next. Someone had marked the Hopi Reservation to the north in red. Why not? As I left, I asked where I could water my lizard. She ignored that too.

Highway 260, winding through the pine forests of central 9 Arizona, let the mountains be boss as it followed whatever avenues they left open, crossing ridges only when necessary, slipping unobtrusively on narrow spans over streams of rounded boulders. But when 260 reached the massive escarpment called the Mogollon Rim, it had to challenge geography and climb the face.

I shifted to low, and Ghost Dancing pulled hard. A man 10 with a dusty, leathery face creased like an old boot strained on a bicycle—the old style with fat tires. I called a hello, he said nothing. At the summit, I waited to see whether he would make the ascent. Far below lay two cars, crumpled wads. Through the clear air I could count nine ranges of mountains, each successively grayer in a way reminiscent of old Chinese woodblock prints. The Mogollon was a spectacular place; the more so because I had not been anesthetized to it by endless Kodachromes. When the cyclist passed, I called out, "Bravo!" but he acknowledged nothing. I would have liked to talk to a man who, while his contemporaries were consolidating their little empires, rides up the Mogollon Rim on a child's toy. Surely he knew something about desperate men.

The top of the great scarp, elevation sixty-five hundred 11 feet, lay flat and covered with big ponderosas standing between dirty snowdrifts and black pools of snowmelt. I began anticipating Heber, the next town. One of the best moments of any day on the road was, toward sunset, looking forward to the last stop. At Heber I hoped for an old hotel with a little bar off to the side where they would serve A-1 on draft under a stuffed moosehead; or maybe I'd find a grill dishing up steak and eggs on blue-rimmed platters. I hoped for people who had good stories, people who sometimes took you home to see their collection of carved peach pits.

That was the hope. But Heber was box houses and a 12

dingy sawmill, a couple of motels and filling stations, a glass-and-Formica cafe. Heber had no center, no focus for the eye and soul: neither a courthouse, nor high church steeple, nor hotel. Nothing has done more to take a sense of civic identity, a feeling of community, from small-town America than the loss of old hotels to the motel business. The hotel was once where things coalesced, where you could meet both towns-people and travelers. Not so in a motel. No matter how you build it, the motel remains a haunt of the quick and dirty, where the only locals are Chamber of Commerce boys every fourth Thursday. Who ever heard the returning traveler ex-claim over one of the great motels of the world he stayed in? Motels can be big, but never grand.

BUILDING VOCABULARY

1. *Compound words* are made up of two separate words joined together. They help intensify description by focusing on the connection between two words. Some compounds are formed by joining two nouns (*photograph, chairper-son*); others combine nouns with nonnoun prefixes, suf-fixes, or combining forms (*childlike, self-pity*). Some com-pounds use hyphens between the two words, although the general current trend is to omit the hyphens. For example, such words as *today* or *tomorrow* were regularly hyphen-ated just 100 years ago. However, many compound words are still acceptable in all three steps of development: two separate words, a single hyphenated word, a single non-hyphenated word (war monger, war-monger, warmonger).

   Locate at least ten compound words that in Least Heat Moon's essay are formed by joining two nouns. Use each in a sentence of your own.

2. *Denotation* refers to the dictionary definition of a word; *connotation* refers to the various shades of meaning and feeling readers bring to a word or phrase. Look up and write dictionary definitions for each of the words in italics.

Then, explain in your own words the connotative meaning of each sentence or phrase.

   a. the otherwise *solemn* face of the desert (par. 1)
   b. to *quench* a desert thirst (par. 7)
   c. it had to *challenge* geography (par. 9)
   d. I had not been *anesthetized* by endless *Kodachromes* (par. 10)
   e. glass-and-*Formica* cafe (par. 12)

3. Least Heat Moon is a careful observer of the plants, rocks, and wildlife of the Arizona landscape. List some of the words drawn from this landscape and write dictionary definitions of them.

UNDERSTANDING THE WRITER'S IDEAS

1. What are the saguaros? What are the odds of their reaching full growth? How old may saguaros become? At what age do they begin to sprout arms?

2. For what purpose do the cactus wrens use the saguaros? What is the major danger to these birds?

3. Explain the sentence: "The only shade along Arizona 87 lay under the bottom sides of rocks." (par. 4)

4. What is the American Indian legend about Superstition Mountains? Explain the "diabolic possession." What is supposedly hidden in these mountains and what is its importance? What is meant by "a white dream"?

5. How was the weather in Payson different from the weather when the writer started driving through the desert? What used to be the atmosphere in Payson? What is it like now?

6. Paragraph 9 describes the route of Highway 260. In your own words, how does the highway relate to the environment that surrounds it?

7. What is Moon's attitude toward the man on the bicycle?

What do we learn about the man's appearance? How does the man react to Moon? What does Moon describe as "a child's toy"? Why?

8. How do we know that some cars fell off the Mogollon Rim?

UNDERSTANDING THE WRITER'S TECHNIQUES

1. Writers often sharpen descriptions by making unusual comparisons. In this essay Least Heat Moon makes many such comparisons. Locate and explain the meaning of what each of the following things is compared to:

   a. The shape and look of the saguaros
   b. The saguaro blossoms
   c. The dives of the cactus wrens
   d. The appearance of the nine mountain ranges
   Locate and explain other comparisons in the essay.

2. How does Moon use elements of space and time to order details in this description? Why is this method effective? Why does he introduce himself ("I drove") in paragraph 3? Why does he wait until then to introduce himself?

3. What is the effect of the short sentence "It was hot" (par. 4) coming as it does after a number of much longer sentences in preceding paragraphs?

4. *Imagery* refers to clear, vivid description rooted in sensory detail. List several images of vivid details that employ the senses: sight (color and action), sound, smell, touch, and taste.

5. In describing the old log hotel in paragraphs 7 and 8, Moon uses *dialogue,* or accurate recordings of actual conversations (see Glossary). What is the effect of dialogue on that descriptive scene?

6. Least Heat Moon makes use of humor to make biting observations about the hotel in Payson. Explain what he

means by "I guess you could bring in all the dead ones you wanted" (par. 7) and "As I left, I asked where I could water my lizard" (par. 8). Why does the woman ignore him? Why does he use biting humor in this way?

7. Least Heat Moon does not simply present factual details of the Arizona desert. Instead, his descriptions are highly subjective, colored with personal emotions. Locate five sentences of highly subjective description. Why is he so subjective? What impression does he give you of the scenes he describes? How does his subjectivity help create the *tone* of this essay? What is that tone?

8. Do you find the ending suitable? Is it too abrupt or is it consistent with the rest of the selection? Explain. Remember, this selection is a complete chapter of a book by the author.

EXPLORING THE WRITER'S IDEAS

1. In the final paragraph Least Heat Moon writes about the disappearance of "civic identity" or "a feeling of community" from small-town America. He blames this loss on the replacement of once-bustling hotels with impersonal motels. Do you think the writer believes this is the only reason for the change? In your experience, how else have American small towns lost their unique flavors or identities?

2. In paragraph 10, in discussing the bicyclist, the author writes, "Surely he knew something about desperate men." Why do you think he feels this way about the cyclist?

IDEAS FOR WRITING

Guided Writing

Write a short essay describing a landscape you traveled through at one time. This can be a city, suburban, or country-side landscape.

1. Begin by concentrating on a particular or dominant element of the landscape.

2. Focus on the environmental conditions and the weather. Note any changes of the climate.

3. Arrange your description as you travel in time from place to place in the landscape.

4. Include at least one interaction with another person who helped you to formulate your feelings about the place.

5. Use concrete sensory detail as you write images of color, action, sound, smell, touch, and taste.

6. Use vivid and varied comparisons to describe what you saw.

7. Conclude your essay with a description and explanation of something that either greatly disappointed or excited you about your travels through this place.

More Writing Projects

1. Concentrating on both the setting and the person, enter in your journal a short description of a chance encounter with someone, as Least Heat Moon does with the bicyclist on the Mogollon Rim. End by coming to a conclusion about this person's personality.

2. Least Heat Moon writes, "Motels can be big, but never grand." Use this sentence as a thesis for a paragraph describing a specific motel you are familiar with. If you prefer to vary the lead sentence to focus on other travel facilities, feel free to do so.

3. Describe in an essay a particular place that you feel has been changed very much by modernization. Include descriptions of both the old and the new ways the place looks and feels. Also include your reactions to both the old and the new.

The Discus Thrower

Richard Selzer

Richard Selzer, a surgeon, gives his readers vivid insights into the excitement as well as the pathos of the world of medicine. His books include *Rituals of Surgery* (1974) and *Mortal Lesions* (1977). His essays are widely published in magazines, including *Esquire, Harper's,* and *Redbook.* In this essay, Selzer dramatically describes a patient's final day.

Words to Watch

furtive (par. 1)   sly
pruned (par. 2)   cut back; trimmed
facsimile (par. 2)   an exact copy
shard (par. 19)   a broken piece; fragment
forceps (par. 19)   an instrument used in operations for holding or pulling
athwart (par. 21)   leaning across
probes (par. 32)   investigates thoroughly
hefts (par. 32)   tosses; heaves

    I spy on my patients. Ought not a doctor to observe his 1
patients by any means and from any stance, that he might the
more fully assemble evidence? So I stand in the doorways of
hospital rooms and gaze. Oh, it is not all that furtive an act.
Those in bed need only look up to discover me. But they
never do.

    From the doorway of Room 542 the man in the bed 2
seems deeply tanned. Blue eyes and close-cropped white hair
give him the appearance of vigor and good health. But I know
that his skin is not brown from the sun. It is rusted, rather, in
the last stage of containing the vile repose within. And the
blue eyes are frosted, looking inward like the windows of a
snowbound cottage. This man is blind. This man is also leg-

less—the right leg missing from midthigh down, the left from just below the knee. It gives him the look of a bonsai, roots and branches pruned into the dwarfed facsimile of a great tree.

Propped on pillows, he cups his right thigh in both 3
hands. Now and then he shakes his head as though acknowledging the intensity of his suffering. In all of this he makes no sound. Is he mute as well as blind?

The room in which he dwells is empty of all posses- 4
sions—no get-well cards, small, private caches of food, day-old flowers, slippers, all the usual kick-shaws of the sickroom. There is only the bed, a chair, a nightstand, and a tray on wheels that can be swung across his lap for meals.

"What time is it?" he asks. 5

"Three o'clock." 6

"Morning or afternoon?" 7

"Afternoon." 8

He is silent. There is nothing else he wants to know. 9

"How are you?" I say. 10

"Who is it?" he asks. 11

"It's the doctor. How do you feel?" 12

He does not answer right away. 13

"Feel?" he says. 14

"I hope you feel better," I say. 15

I press the button at the side of the bed. 16

"Down you go," I say. 17

"Yes, down," he says. 18

He falls back upon the bed awkwardly. His stumps, un- 19
weighted by legs and feet, rise in the air, presenting themselves. I unwrap the bandages from the stumps, and begin to cut away the black scabs and the dead, glazed fat with scissors and forceps. A shard of white bone comes loose. I pick it away. I wash the wounds with disinfectant and redress the stumps. All this while, he does not speak. What is he thinking behind those lids that do not blink? Is he remembering a time when he was whole? Does he dream of feet? Of when his body was not a rotting log?

He lies solid and inert. In spite of everything, he remains 20
impressive, as though he were a sailor standing athwart a slanting deck.

"Anything more I can do for you?" I ask.   21

For a long moment he is silent.   22

"Yes," he says at last and without the least irony. "You   23
can bring me a pair of shoes."

In the corridor, the head nurse is waiting for me.   24

"We have to do something about him," she says. "Ev-   25
ery morning he orders scrambled eggs for breakfast, and, instead of eating them, he picks up the plate and throws it
against the wall."

"Throws his plate?"   26

"Nasty. That's what he is. No wonder his family doesn't   27
come to visit. They probably can't stand him any more than
we can."

She is waiting for me to do something.   28

"Well?"   29

"We'll see," I say.   30

The next morning I am waiting in the corridor when the   31
kitchen delivers his breakfast. I watch the aide place the tray
on the stand and swing it across his lap. She presses the button to raise the head of the bed. Then she leaves.

In time the man reaches to find the rim of the tray, then   32
on to find the dome of the covered dish. He lifts off the cover
and places it on the stand. He fingers across the plate until he
probes the eggs. He lifts the plate in both hands, sets it on the
palm of his right hand, centers it, balances it. He hefts it up
and down slightly, getting the feel of it. Abruptly, he draws
back his right arm as far as he can.

There is the crack of the plate breaking against the wall   33
at the foot of his bed and the small wet sound of the scrambled
eggs dropping to the floor.

And then he laughs. It is a sound you have never heard.   34
It is something new under the sun. It could cure cancer.

Out in the corridor, the eyes of the head nurse narrow.   35

"Laughed, did he?"   36

She writes something down on her clipboard.   37

A second aide arrives, brings a second breakfast tray,   38
puts it on the nightstand, out of his reach. She looks over at
me shaking her head and making her mouth go. I see that we
are to be accomplices.

"I've got to feed you," she says to the man.   39

"Oh, no you don't," the man says.   40

"Oh, yes I do," the aide says, "after the way you just   41
did. Nurse says so."

"Get me my shoes," the man says.   42

"Here's oatmeal," the aide says. "Open." And she   43
touches the spoon to his lower lip.

"I ordered scrambled eggs," says the man.   44

"That's right," the aide says.   45

I step forward.   46

"Is there anything I can do?" I say.   47

"Who are you?" the man asks.   48

In the evening I go once more to that ward to make my   49
rounds. The head nurse reports to me that Room 542 is de-
ceased. She has discovered this quite by accident, she says.
No, there had been no sound. Nothing. It's a blessing, she
says.

I go into his room, a spy looking for secrets. He is still   50
there in his bed. His face is relaxed, grave, dignified. After
a while, I turn to leave. My gaze sweeps the wall at the foot
of the bed, and I see the place where it has been repeatedly
washed, where the wall looks very clean and very white.

BUILDING VOCABULARY

1. In this essay, Selzer uses a few words that derive from languages other than English. Look up the following words
   and tell what language they come from. Then, write a definition for each:

   a. *bonsai*
   b. *kick-shaws*
   c. *caches*

2. Use these words from the essay in complete sentences of
   your own: *vile, repose, dwarfed, glazed, inert, accomplices.*

UNDERSTANDING THE WRITER'S IDEAS

1. What reason does Selzer give for a doctor's spying on his patients?

2. What does the man in Room 542 look like? Why is his skin brown? How does Selzer know he is blind? Why does Selzer think the patient may be mute? When do we know that he is not mute?

3. What is the author's meaning of the phrase "vile repose"?

4. How do we know that this patient does not receive many visitors?

5. Aside from wanting to know the time of day, what is the patient's one request? Do you think he is serious about his request? Why?

6. Why does the patient hurl his food tray against the wall?

7. For what reason does the head nurse complain about the patient?

8. What does Selzer feel and think about the patient? How do you know?

UNDERSTANDING THE WRITER'S TECHNIQUES

1. Throughout the essay, Selzer asks a number of questions. Locate at least three of these questions that are not a part of the dialogue. To whom do you think they are addressed? What is their effect on the reader?

2. Like William Least Heat Moon, Selzer heightens the description by making vivid and unusual comparisons. Locate and explain in your own words three comparisons that you feel are especially descriptive and intriguing.

3. Selzer uses some very short sentences interspersed among longer ones. Locate at least four very short sen-

tences. How do they draw your attention to the description?

4. Locate in Selzer's essay at least five examples of vivid description (imagery) relating to illness. What is their emotional effect on the reader?

5. How does Selzer use *dialogue* to reveal the personality of the patient? of the doctor? of the head nurse?

6. In paragraph 24, Selzer states that the patient delivers his request "without the least irony." *Irony* (see Glossary) is saying what is opposite to what one means. Why might Selzer have expected irony from the patient? Why might someone in the sick man's condition use irony? What do you think the man means by his request "You can bring me a pair of shoes"—if, in fact, the remark is not an ironical one?

7. What does the title of the essay mean? What is a discus thrower? Why has Selzer chosen an ancient image of an athlete as the title of this essay? In what way is the title ironic?

8. Why does Selzer use such an unusual word as *kick-shaws* (par. 4)?

9. *Double entendre* is a French expression that indicates that something has a double meaning, each equally valid. What might be the two meanings of the nurse's words "It's a blessing"?

10. In this essay, the author uses a *framing* device: that is, he opens and closes the essay with a similar image or idea. What is that idea? Why is it effective? What are the differences in the use of this idea in the opening and closing paragraphs?

11. The heart of this essay is the patient's insistence upon throwing his breakfast plate at the wall, and yet Selzer does not attempt to explain the man's reasons for such an act. Why do you think the man hurls his breakfast across the room each morning—and why does he laugh? Why

does Selzer not provide an analysis of the action? How does the title help us see Selzer's attitude toward the man's act?

EXPLORING THE WRITER'S IDEAS

1. In the beginning of the essay Selzer asks, "Ought not a doctor to observe his patients by any means from any stance, that he might more fully assemble evidence?" Do you feel that a doctor should have this right? Why? What rights do you believe patients should have in a hospital?

2. The head nurse in Selzer's description seems fed up with the patient in Room 542. Why do you think she feels this way? Do you think that a person in her position has the right to express this feeling on his or her job? Why or why not?

3. The patient's attitude is influenced by his physical state and his nearness to death. How have physical ailments or handicaps changed the attitudes of people you have known? How has an illness influenced your thoughts at any time?

IDEAS FOR WRITING

Guided Writing

Describe a person you have observed who was seriously ill, in danger, or under great stress.

1. Base your description upon close observation of the person during a short but concentrated span of time: a morning or afternoon, an hour or two, even a few minutes.

2. Begin with a short, direct paragraph in which you introduce the person and the critical situation he or she faces.

3. Include yourself ("I") in the description.

4. Describe the vantage point from which you are "spying" or observing, and focus on the particular subject of the scene.

5. Throughout your essay, ask key questions.

6. Use imagery and original comparisons to highlight the description of your subject.

7. Include some dialogue with either the subject or another person.

8. Describe at least one very intense action performed by your subject.

9. Tell how the subject and scene had changed when you next saw them.

More Writing Projects

1. In your journal, describe a hospital room in which you stayed or visited some other person. Focus on your sensory perceptions of the place.

2. Describe in an extended paragraph an interaction you had with a person who was blind or deaf or was disabled in some other way. In your description, focus closely on the person's features. Write about your reactions during and after the interaction.

3. Using both description and commentary, analyze the people you observe in one of the following situations: a bus or train during rush hour; breakfast at a diner or restaurant; a sports event or concert. Incorporate the description and observation into a five-paragraph essay.

A River's Route

Gretel Ehrlich

Montana resident Gretel Ehrlich celebrates nature in this highly personal, often spiritual description of her journey along a river in the Absaroka Mountains. In this essay, which was part of the introduction to the 1989 Sierra Club wilderness calendar, notice how Ehrlich not only writes strikingly clear images of the *places* she visits, but also writes of their deep effects on her. Ehrlich is also the author of *The Solace of Open Spaces*.

Words to Watch

articulation (par. 2)　interrelationship; connecting
ascent (par. 3)　rising; upward motion
verdant (par. 3)　green
archaic (par. 4)　out-of-date; antiquated
beeline (par. 4)　a straight, direct course
pitons (par. 6)　metal spikes for a rope in mountain climbing
crampons (par. 6)　spiked iron shoe plates to prevent slipping
desiccated (par. 7)　dried up
gluttony (par. 8)　excessive eating and drinking
hedonism (par. 8)　doctrine that pleasure is the highest good
cirque (par. 8)　a steep-walled basin in a mountain
vertiginous (par. 10)　causing dizziness
emanation (par. 11)　an emergence
redolent (par. 11)　full of
riffles (par. 15)　small waves

　　It's morning in the Absaroka Mountains. The word *ab-* 1
saroka means "raven" in the Crow language, though I've seen no ravens in three days. Last night I slept with my head butted against an Engelmann spruce, and on waking the limbs looked like hundreds of arms swinging in a circle. The trunk is bigger than an elephant's leg, bigger than my torso. I stick my nose against the bark. Tiny opals of sap stick to my cheeks

121

and the bark breaks up, textured: red and gray, coarse and smooth, wet and flaked.

A tree is an aerial garden, a botanical migration from the 2 sea, from those earliest plants, the seaweeds; it is a purchase on crumbled rock, on ground. The human, standing, is only a different upsweep and articulation of cells. How tree-like we are, how human the tree.

But I've come here to seek out the source of a river, and 3 as we make the daylong ascent from a verdant valley, I think about walking and wilderness. We use the word "wilderness," but perhaps we mean wildness. Isn't that why I've come here? In wilderness, I seek the wildness in myself—and in so doing, come on the wildness everywhere around me because, being part of nature, I'm cut from the same cloth.

Following the coastline of a lake, I watch how wind 4 picks up water in dark blasts and drops it again. Ducks glide in Vs away from me, out onto the fractured, darkening mirror. I stop. A hatch of mayflies powders the air and the archaic, straight-winged dragonflies hang, blunt-nosed, above me. A friend talks about aquatic bugs: water beetles, spinners, assassin bugs, and one that hatches, mates, and dies in a total lifespan of two hours. At the end of the meadow, the lake drains into a fast-moving creek. I quicken my pace and trudge upward. Walking is also an ambulation of mind. The human armor of bones rattles, fat rolls, and inside this durable, fleshy prison of mine, I make a beeline toward otherness, lightness, or, maybe like a moth, toward flame.

Somewhere along the trail I laugh out loud. How shell- 5 like the body seems suddenly—not fleshy at all, but inhuman and hard. And farther up, I step out of my body though I'm still held fast by something, but what? I don't know.

How foolish the preparations for wilderness trips seem 6 now. We pore over our maps, chart our expeditions. We "gear up" at trailheads with pitons and crampons, horsepacks and backpacks, fly rods and cameras, forgetting the meaning of simply going, of lifting thought-covers, of disburdenment. I look up from these thoughts. A blue heron rises from a gravel bar and glides behind a gray screen of dead trees, appears in an opening where an avalanche downed pines, and lands again on water.

I stop to eat lunch. Ralph Waldo Emerson wrote, "The 7
Guatama said that the first men ate the earth and found it
sweet." I eat baloney and cheese and think about eating the
earth. It's another way of framing our wonder in which the
width of the mouth stands for the generous palate of consciousness. I cleanse my palate with miner's lettuce and
stream water and try to imagine what kinds of sweetness the
earth provides: the taste of glacial flour, or the mineral taste of
basalt, the fresh and foul bouquets of rivers, the desiccated,
stinging flavor of a snowstorm—like eating red ants, my friend
says.

As I begin to walk again it occurs to me that this notion 8
of "eating the earth" is not about gluttony, hedonism, or sin,
but, rather, unconditional love. Everywhere I look I see the
possibility of love. To find wildness, I must first offer myself
up, accept all that comes before me: a bullfrog breathing hard
on a rock; moose tracks under elk scats; a cloud that looks
like a clothespin; a seep of water from a high cirque, black on
brown rock, draining down from the brain of the world.

At tree line, birdsong stops. I'm lifted into another 9
movement of music, one with no particular notes, only windsounds becoming watersounds, becoming windsounds.
Above, a cornice crowns a ridge and melts into a teal and tur-
quoise lake, like a bladder leaking its wine.

On top of Marston Pass I'm in a ruck of steep valleys 10
and gray, treeless peaks. The alpine carpet, studded with red
paintbrush and alpine buttercups, gives way to rock. Now all
the way across a vertiginous valley, I see where water oozes
from moss and mud, how, at its source, it quickly becomes
something else.

Emerson also said: "Every natural fact is an emanation, 11
and that from which it emanates is an emanation also, and
from every emanation is a new emanation." The ooze, the
source of a great river, is now a white chute tumbling over soft
folds of conglomerate rock—brown bellies. Now wind tears at
it, throwing sheets of water to another part of the mountain-
side; soft earth gives way under my feet, clouds spill upward
and spit rain. Isn't everything redolent with loss, with momen-
tary radiance, a coming to different ground? Stone basins

catch the waterfall, spill it again, like thoughts strung together, laddered down.

I see where meltwater is split by a rock—half going west 12 to the Pacific, the other going east to the Atlantic, for this is the Continental Divide. Down the other side the air I gulp feels softer. Ice spans and tunnels the creek, then, when night comes but before the full moon, falling stars have the same look as that white chute of water, falling against the rock of night.

To rise above tree line is to go above thought and after, 13 the descent back into birdsong, bog orchids, willows, and firs, is to sink into the preliterate parts of ourselves. It is to forget discontent, undisciplined needs. Here the world is only space, raw loneliness, green valleys hung vertically. Losing myself to it—if I can—I do not fall...or, if I do, I'm only another cataract of water.

Wildness has no conditions, no sure routes, no peaks or 14 goals, no source that is not instantly becoming something more than itself, then letting go of that, always becoming. It cannot be stripped of its complexity by CAT scan or telescope. Rather, it is a many-pointed truth, almost a bluntness, a sudden essence like the wild strawberries strung along the ground on scarlet runners under my feet. Wildness is source and fruition at once, as if every river circled round, the mouth eating the tail—and the tail, the source.

Now I am camped among trees again. Four yearling 15 moose, their chestnut coats shiny from a summer's diet of willow shoots, tramp past my bedroll and drink from a spring that issues sulfurous water. The ooze, the white chute, the narrow stream—now almost a river—joins this small spring and slows into skinny oxbows and deep pools before breaking again on rock, a stepladder of sequined riffles.

To trace the history of a river, or a raindrop, as John 16 Muir would have done, is also to trace the history of the soul, the history of the mind descending and arising in the body. In both, we constantly seek and stumble on divinity, which, like the cornice feeding the lake and the spring becoming a waterfall, feeds, spills, falls, and feeds itself over and over again.

BUILDING VOCABULARY

1. Determine the meaning of the words in italics from context clues—clues in the surrounding words and sentences. Do not use a dictionary until *after* you make your guess. Return to the indicated paragraph for more clues.

   a. my head *butted* against an Engelmann spruce (par. 1)
   b. The human, standing, is only a different *upsweep* and *articulation* of cells. (par. 2)
   c. Walking is also an *ambulation* of mind. (par. 4)
   d. the generous *palate* of consciousness (par. 7)
   e. a *cornice* crowns a ridge (par. 9)
   f. *studded* with red paintbrush (par. 10)
   g. folds of *conglomerate* rock (par. 11)
   h. that white *chute* of water (par. 12)
   i. the *descent* back into birdsong...is to sink into the *preliterate* parts of ourselves (par. 13)

2. This essay contains many references to nature. Look through the essay again, and list two or three nature references for each category below:

   a. vegetation
   b. water
   c. animals
   d. rock or geographic formations
   e. the sky

UNDERSTANDING THE WRITER'S IDEAS

1. Where does the name of the Absaroka Mountains come from? Who are the Crow? For what reason has Ehrlich come to the Absaroka Mountains? Does she achieve her purpose? Explain.

2. Explain the sentence, "How tree-like we are, how human the tree" (par. 2). What is its relevance to the overall message of the essay?

3. During what period of time does the author's journey take place? Outline the various stages of her journey. Where does she begin and end her journey?

4. Why does Ehrlich write, "We use the word 'wilderness,' but perhaps we mean wildness" (par. 3)? How does this statement relate to the purpose of her journey? What is the difference between *wilderness* and *wildness?*

5. Is Ehrlich alone on this journey? How do you know? Why does she not include others very much in her description?

6. Identify Ralph Waldo Emerson and John Muir. How do they relate to this essay and to Ehrlich's purpose?

7. Why does she "laugh out loud" at one point on the trip? Where is she when she does?

8. Does she go into the wilderness totally unprepared and "natural"? Explain.

9. How is the wilderness/wildness "source and fruition at once" (par. 14)?

UNDERSTANDING THE WRITER'S TECHNIQUES

1. In this essay, Ehrlich makes vivid use of imagery related to the five senses. List images related to each of these senses. On which senses does she concentrate most? Why? Which images do you find most effective? Why?

2. What is the *dominant impression* (see page 94) of this essay? Explain. What is the *tone* (see Glossary) of the essay? Give examples to support your response.

3. How does Ehrlich organize her description? How does she maintain *coherence* (see Glossary)?

4. Which paragraphs constitute the introduction? The body? The conclusion? How does Ehrlich *frame* her description?

That is, what descriptive elements are similar in the beginning and ending of the essay?

5. Is there a *thesis statement* in this essay? How would you state the thesis? Explain.

6. Identify and explain the author's use of *definition* (see Glossary and Chapter 7) in paragraphs 1, 2, and 14. Where else does she use definition? Would you characterize her definitions as *denotative* or *connotative* (see Glossary)? Explain.

7. What is the *stated purpose* of her trip? What is the *implied purpose?* Explain the difference. What is her *purpose* (see Glossary) in writing this essay?

8. This essay is part of the introduction to the 1989 Sierra Club wilderness calendar. Do you think Ehrlich's *audience* (see Glossary) is limited to like-minded environmentalists? Why? What is the intended audience?

9. In general, Ehrlich uses the first-person (''I'') *point of view* (see Glossary) throughout the essay. Yet, at a few points, she uses the plural ''we.'' Where does she change pronoun references? How do the changes affect the essay?

10. Where in the essay does the author use literary *allusions* (see Glossary)? What is their effect?

11. Ehrlich makes use of a wide range of *figurative language* in this essay, including *similes* and *metaphors* (see Glossary). Point out the most visual and original figures.

12. Explain the conclusion of the essay.

EXPLORING THE WRITER'S IDEAS

1. Clearly, this is a highly *subjective* (see Glossary) description of the author's journey through nature. In general, when you are reading about nature or travels, do you enjoy

such subjective description, or do you prefer more objective, realistic ones? Why? What are the advantages and disadvantages of each?

2. Examine a recent issue of *National Geographic* magazine. Do you feel this essay would be appropriate to appear in *National Geographic?* Why? Explain the differences or similarities in writing styles, choice of subject, and so on.

3. In the 1988 presidential campaign, George Bush's promise to be an "environmentalist president" helped focus on what is clearly a major concern of many people. Generally, where do you stand on environmental issues? What global environmental issues are of most concern to you? What local issues?

IDEAS FOR WRITING

Guided Writing

Write a subjective description of a recent experience you had in nature that took place over a period of only one day.

1. Begin your essay with the morning when you awoke. Describe the entire day.

2. Write a clear description of your starting point.

3. Continue to describe each stage and place of your experience as it occurred.

4. Clearly state the purpose of your experience.

5. Use vivid, personal imagery encompassing all five senses. Try to make your imagery include a variety of natural focuses.

6. Make your description as personal as possible. Write about what you saw, how it made you feel, and what other things it made you think about.

7. Include at least one *allusion* to a person or thing not present but somehow connected to the experience.

8. Use definition as needed in your essay. At one point, re-define a common phrase to stress your personal interpretation of it.

9. Organize your essay so that it has a clear introduction, body, and conclusion. The conclusion should sum up your experience and its meaning for you.

More Writing Projects

1. For a journal entry, select a special time of day and write about it in such a way that the description captures the moods that the scene evokes in you.

2. Describe in a paragraph a highly "un-natural" urban scene that affected you deeply.

3. Write an objective description of the same experience you wrote about in the Guided Writing exercise.

SUMMING UP: CHAPTER 3

1. As you have discovered in this chapter, one of the keys to writing effective description is the selection and creation of vivid and relevant images. How do the writers in this chapter use imagery? Which writer's images do you find most concrete, original, vivid, and creative? For each of the four essays of description in this chapter, write a paragraph in which you evaluate the writer's use of imagery.

2. In this chapter, Margaret Laurence, William Least Heat Moon, and Gretel Ehrlich all write about their solitary experience in a particular *place*—what they expected, what they found, and how it affected them emotionally.

   In *Nothing to Declare,* a book about her experiences as a woman traveling alone, novelist and essayist Mary Morris writes: "I felt ready for a change....I went in search of a place where the land and the people and the time in which they lived were somehow connected—where life would begin to make sense to me again."

Write an essay about a place you know well that reflects some of the same criteria for which Laurence, Least Heat Moon, and Ehrlich were searching.

3. Least Heat Moon and Selzer provide vivid descriptions of people. What general guidelines for describing people do you derive from these writers? Write a short essay called "How to Describe People," basing your observations on Least Heat Moon's and Selzer's techniques.

4. William Least Heat Moon's steady companion in his journey through America—a journey recorded in *Blue Highways*—was a half-ton Ford van he called Ghost Dancing. In many ways, Least Heat Moon's work is a tribute to the American automobile, not just a vehicle but also a place in which to live, a companion, a symbol of success or achievement or escape. Consider the role of the automobile in your immediate world and write an essay exploring its value as an essential (or nonessential) element of modern life.

5. Ehrlich celebrates the river in her essay, but today many waterways are threatened by man-made pollution. What problems affect the rivers and lakes in your home state or near your college? Take a trip to a water site not far from your campus or home. Read articles about local waterways in your newspaper. Write an essay called "The Fate of Our Waters."

CHAPTER 4

Narration

Narration is the telling of a story. As a technique in essay writing, it normally involves a discussion of events that are "true" or real, events that take place over a period of time. Narration helps a writer explain things and, as such, it is an important skill for the kind of writing often required of you.

Writers who use narration usually rely on descriptive details to advance their stories. Moreover, in the narrative essay, there always must be some purpose in the telling, a purpose that goes beyond mere enjoyment of the story itself. Consequently, narration in an essay advances a thesis, or main idea. For example, if you had to write an essay on the happiest event in your life, you might choose to narrate the day your team won the state championship. You would establish your thesis—your main point—quickly, and then go on to tell about the event itself. In short, you would use narration as a means to an end—to make a significant statement about an important moment in your life.

The manner in which you relate this event depends on the simplicity or complexity of the story that you want to tell. If the season before the winning game was itself filled with excitement, you certainly would want to explain that and to trace the exciting events over a period of time. If the championship itself provided most of the thrills, you would want to concentrate on a much shorter period of time, breaking your narration down to days, hours, even minutes, instead of months. Learning to present time—whether in a single personal event, a series of related events, a historical occurrence, or an aging process—is one of the key elements in narrative prose.

Normally in a narrative essay you would start at the beginning and move to the end, or from past to present, or from old to new, but there are many other ways to relate events in the narrative essay. For instance, you could begin an essay on the death of someone important to you by detailing the day of the funeral, and then moving backward in time to flesh out the events leading up to the funeral. For beginners this "flashback" technique often causes very confused writing; but skilled writers know how to "jump around" in time without confusing the reader, blurring the thesis, or destroying the progression of the essay.

As with descriptive writing, the narrative essay requires a careful selection of details. Certain moments within any time order are more important than others, and these crucial moments will be emphasized and developed fully by a good writer. Other moments, significant but less important than the main moments, will take up less space, while unimportant items will be eliminated entirely. However, the writer must connect each event in the time span to other events that come before or after. Here, transitions of time—words like "afterwards," "soon," "a day later," "suddenly"—serve as bridges to connect the various moments in the narrative pattern.

There are other aspects of narration that appear in this chapter. For example, you must select a point of view for your story—whether presenting events through your own eyes or from a more objective or detached position. You must also decide on the value of dialogue (recording of conversations). Finally, you must be aware that other techniques of prose writing (like description) can reinforce your narrative pattern. Fortunately, most individuals have a basic storytelling ability and know how to develop stories that make a point. Once you master narration as a writing pattern, you will be able to use it in a variety of situations.

The Struggle to Be an All-American Girl

Elizabeth Wong

In this poignant remembrance, Elizabeth Wong tells of the hurts and sorrows of her bicultural upbringing. Wong effectively blends concrete description and imaginative comparisons to give a vivid look into the life of a child who felt she had a Chinese exterior but an American interior.

Words to Watch

stoically (par. 1) without showing emotion
dissuade (par. 2) to talk out of doing something
ideographs (par. 7) Chinese picture symbols used to form words
disassociate (par. 8) to detach from association
vendors (par. 8) sellers of goods
gibberish (par. 9) confused, unintelligible speech or language
pidgin (par. 10) simplified speech that is usually a mixture of two or more languages

It's still there, the Chinese school on Yale Street where 1 my brother and I used to go. Despite the new coat of paint and the high wire fence, the school I knew 10 years ago remains remarkably, stoically the same.

Every day at 5 P.M., instead of playing with our fourth- 2 and fifth-grade friends or sneaking out to the empty lot to hunt ghosts and animal bones, my brother and I had to go to Chinese school. No amount of kicking, screaming, or pleading could dissuade my mother, who was solidly determined to have us learn the language of our heritage.

Forcibly, she walked us the seven long, hilly blocks from 3 our home to school, depositing our defiant tearful faces before the stern principal. My only memory of him is that he swayed on his heels like a palm tree, and he always clasped his impatient twitching hands behind his back. I recognized him as a repressed maniacal child killer, and knew that if we ever saw his hands we'd be in big trouble.

We all sat in little chairs in an empty auditorium. The 4 room smelled like Chinese medicine, an imported faraway mustiness. Like ancient mothballs or dirty closets. I hated that smell. I favored crisp new scents. Like the soft French perfume that my American teacher wore in public school.

There was a stage far to the right, flanked by an Ameri- 5 can flag and the flag of the Nationalist Republic of China, which was also red, white and blue but not as pretty.

Although the emphasis at the school was mainly lan- 6 guage—speaking, reading, writing—the lessons always began with an exercise in politeness. With the entrance of the teacher, the best student would tap a bell and everyone would get up, kowtow, and chant, "Sing san ho," the phonetic for "How are you, teacher?"

Being ten years old, I had better things to learn than 7 ideographs copied painstakingly in lines that ran right to left from the tip of a *moc but,* a real ink pen that had to be held in an awkward way if blotches were to be avoided. After all, I could do the multiplication tables, name the satellites of Mars, and write reports on "Little Women" and "Black Beauty." Nancy Drew, my favorite book heroine, never spoke Chinese.

The language was a source of embarrassment. More 8 times than not, I had tried to disassociate myself from the nagging loud voice that followed me wherever I wandered in the nearby American supermarket outside Chinatown. The voice belonged to my grandmother, a fragile woman in her seventies who could outshout the best of the street vendors. Her humor was raunchy, her Chinese rhythmless, patternless. It was quick, it was loud, it was unbeautiful. It was not like the quiet, lilting romance of French or the gentle refinement of the American South. Chinese sounded pedestrian. Public.

In Chinatown, the comings and goings of hundreds of 9 Chinese on their daily tasks sounded chaotic and frenzied. I did not want to be thought of as mad, as talking gibberish. When I spoke English, people nodded at me, smiled sweetly, said encouraging words. Even the people in my culture would cluck and say that I'd do well in life. "My, doesn't she move her lips fast," they would say, meaning that I'd be able to keep up with the world outside Chinatown.

My brother was even more fanatical than I about speak- 10 ing English. He was especially hard on my mother, criticizing her, often cruelly, for her pidgin speech—smatterings of Chinese scattered like chop suey in her conversation. "It's not 'What it is,' Mom," he'd say in exasperation. "It's 'What *is* it, what *is* it, what *is* it!" Sometimes Mom might leave out an occasional "the" or "a," or perhaps a verb of being. He would stop her in mid-sentence: "Say it again, Mom. Say it right." When he tripped over his own tongue, he'd blame it on her: "See, Mom, it's all your fault. You set a bad example."

What infuriated my mother most was when my brother 11 cornered her on her consonants, especially "r." My father had played a cruel joke on Mom by assigning her an American name that her tongue wouldn't allow her to say. No matter how hard she tried, "Ruth" always ended up "Luth" or "Roof."

After two years of writing with a *moc but* and reciting 12 words with multiples of meanings, I finally was granted a cultural divorce. I was permitted to stop Chinese school.

I thought of myself as multicultural. I preferred tacos to 13 egg rolls; I enjoyed Cinco de Mayo more than Chinese New Year.

At last, I was one of you; I wasn't one of them.   14
Sadly, I still am.   15

BUILDING VOCABULARY

For each of the words in italics, choose the letter of the word or expression that most closely matches its meaning.

1. the *stern* principal (par. 3)
   a. military   **b.** very old   **c.** immoral   **d.** strict
2. *repressed* maniacal child killer (par. 3)
   a. quiet   **b.** ugly   **c.** held back   **d.** retired
3. an imported faraway *mustiness* (par. 4)
   a. country   **b.** moth balls   **c.** chair   **d.** staleness

4. a *fragile* woman (par. 8)
    a. elderly   **b.** frail   **c.** tall   **d.** inconsistent
5. her humor was *raunchy* (par. 8)
    a. obscene   **b.** unclear   **c.** childish   **d.** very funny
6. quiet *lilting* romance of French (par. 8)
    a. musical   **b.** tilting   **c.** loving   **d.** complicated
7. thought of as *mad* (par. 9)
    a. foreign   **b.** angry   **c.** stupid   **d.** crazy
8. what *infuriated* my mother most (par. 11)
    a. angered   **b.** humiliated   **c.** made laugh   **d.** typified

UNDERSTANDING THE WRITER'S IDEAS

1. What did Elizabeth Wong and her brother do every day after school? How did that make them different from their friends? What was their attitude toward what they did? How do you know?

2. What does Wong mean when she says of the principal "I recognized him as a repressed child killer"? Why were she and her brother afraid to see his hands?

3. What was the main purpose of going to Chinese school? What did Wong feel she had learned at "regular" American school? Which did she feel was more important? What are *Little Women, Black Beauty,* and Nancy Drew?

4. In the first sentence of paragraph 8, what language is "the language"?

5. What was Wong's grandmother like? What was Wong's attitude toward her? Why?

6. When Wong spoke English in Chinatown, why did the others think it was good that she moved her lips quickly?

7. What was her brother's attitude toward speaking English? How did he treat their mother when she tried to speak English? Why was it unfortunate that the mother had the American name *Ruth?* Who gave her that name? Why?

8. Explain the expression "he tripped over his own tongue" (par. 10).

9. In paragraph 13, Wong states, "I thought of myself as multicultural." What does that mean? What are tacos, egg rolls, and Cinco de Mayo? Why is it surprising that Wong includes those items as examples of her multiculturalism?

10. Who are the "you" and "them" of paragraph 14? Explain the significance of the last sentence. What does it indicate about Wong's attitude toward Chinese school from the vantage point of being an adult?

UNDERSTANDING THE WRITER'S TECHNIQUES

1. What is Wong's purpose in writing this narrative? Is the technique of narration an appropriate one to her purpose? Why or why not?

2. Wong does not state a thesis directly in a thesis sentence. How does her title imply a thesis? If you were writing a thesis sentence of your own for this essay, what would it be?

3. This narrative contains several stories. The first one ends after paragraph 7 and tells about Wong's routine after 5 P.M. on school days. Paragraphs 8 and 9, 10 and 11, and 12 and 13 offer other related narratives. Summarize each of these briefly. How does Wong help the reader shift from story to story?

4. The writer of narration will present *time* in a way that best fulfills the purpose of the narration. This presentation may take many forms: a single, personal event; a series of related events; a historical occurrence; an aging process. Obviously Wong chose a series of related events. Why does she use such a narrative structure to make her point? Could she have chosen an alternative plan, do you think? Why or why not?

5. Writers of narration often rely upon descriptive details to flesh out their stories. Find examples of sensory language here that makes the scene come alive for the reader.

6. Writers often use figurative comparisons to enliven their writing and to make it more distinctive. A *simile* is an imaginative form of figurative comparison using "like" or "as" to connect two items. One thing is similar to another in this figure. A *metaphor* is a figure of speech in which the writer compares two items not normally thought of as similar, but unlike in a simile, the comparison is direct— that is, it does not use "like" or "as." In other words, one thing is said to be the other thing, not merely to be like it. For example, if you wanted to compare love to a rose, you might use these two comparisons:

Simile:
    My love is *like* a red, red rose.
Metaphor:
    My love *is* a red, red rose.
In Wong's essay, find the similes and metaphors in paragraphs 2, 3, 4, 10, and 12. For each, name the two items compared and explain the comparison in your own words.

7. Narratives often include lines of spoken language, that is, one person in the narrative talking alone or to another. Wong uses quoted detail sparsely here. Why did she choose to limit the dialogue? How effective is the dialogue that appears here? Where do you think she might have used more dialogue to advance the narrative?

8. The last two paragraphs are only one sentence each. Why do you think the author chose this technique?

9. What is the irony in the last sentence of the essay? (See Glossary.) How would the meaning of the last sentence change if you eliminated the word *sadly?* What is the irony in the title of the essay?

10. What is the tone (see Glossary) of this essay? How does Wong create that tone?

EXPLORING THE WRITER'S IDEAS

1. Wong and her brother deeply resented being forced to attend Chinese school. When children very clearly express displeasure or unhappiness, should parents force them to do things anyway? Why or why not?

2. On one level this essay is about a clash of cultures, here the ancient Chinese culture of Wong's ancestry and the culture of twentieth-century United States. Is it possible for someone to maintain connections to his or her ethnic or cultural backgrounds and at the same time to become an all-American girl or boy? What do people of foreign backgrounds gain when they become completely Americanized? What do they lose?

3. Because of their foreign ways, the mother and grandmother clearly embarrassed the Wong children. Under what other conditions that you can think of do parents embarrass children? Children, parents?

IDEAS FOR WRITING

Guided Writing

Write a narration in which you tell about some difficult moment that took place in grade school or high school, a moment that taught you something about yourself, your needs, or your cultural background.

1. Provide a concrete description of the school.

2. Tell in correct sequence about the event.

3. Identify people who play a part in this moment.

4. Use concrete, sensory description throughout your essay.

5. Use original similes and metaphors to make your narrative clearer and more dramatic.

6. Use dialogue (or spoken conversation) appropriately in order to advance the narrative.

7. In your conclusion, indicate what your attitude toward this moment is now that you are an adult.

8. Write a title that implies your thesis.

More Writing Projects

1. Did you have any problems in grade school or high school because of your background or ancestry? Did you know someone who had such problems? Record a specific incident in your journal.

2. Write a narrative paragraph explaining some basic insights about your heritage or culture.

3. Get together with other classmates in a small group and brainstorm or bounce ideas off one another on troubling ethnic, racial, or cultural issues on campus. Write down all the incidents. Then write a narrative essay tracing one episode or connecting a series of them.

Salvation

Langston Hughes

For more than forty years, Langston Hughes (1902–1967) was a major figure in American literature. In poetry, essays, drama, and fiction he attempted, as he said himself, "to explain and illuminate the Negro condition in America." This selection from his autobiography, *The Big Sea* (1940), tells the story of his "conversion" to Christ. Salvation was a key event in the life of his community, but Hughes tells comically how he bowed to pressure by permitting himself to be "saved from sin."

Words to Watch

dire (par. 3) terrible; disastrous

gnarled (par. 4) knotty; twisted

rounder (par. 6) watchman; policeman

deacons (par. 6) members of the clergy or laypersons who are appointed to help the minister

serenely (par. 7) calmly; tranquilly

knickerbockered (par. 11) dressed in short, loose trousers that are gathered below the knees

I was saved from sin when I was going on thirteen. But 1 not really saved. It happened like this. There was a big revival at my Auntie Reed's church. Every night for weeks there had been much preaching, singing, praying, and shouting, and some very hardened sinners had been brought to Christ, and the membership of the church had grown by leaps and bounds. Then just before the revival ended, they held a special meeting for children, "to bring the young lambs to the fold." My aunt spoke of it for days ahead. That night I was escorted to the front row and placed on the mourners' bench with all the other young sinners, who had not yet been brought to Jesus.

My aunt told me that when you were saved you saw a 2 light, and something happened to you inside! And Jesus came into your life! And God was with you from then on! She said you could see and hear and feel Jesus in your soul. I believed her. I had heard a great many old people say the same thing and it seemed to me they ought to know. So I sat there calmly in the hot, crowded church, waiting for Jesus to come to me.

The preacher preached a wonderful rhythmical sermon, 3 all moans and shouts and lonely cries and dire pictures of hell, and then he sang a song about the ninety and nine safe in the fold, but one little lamb was left out in the cold. Then he said: "Won't you come? Won't you come to Jesus? Young lambs, won't you come?" And he held out his arms to all us young sinners there on the mourners' bench. And the little girls cried. And some of them jumped up and went to Jesus right away. But most of us just sat there.

A great many old people came and knelt around us and 4 prayed, old women with jet-black faces and braided hair, old men with work-gnarled hands. And the church sang a song about the lower lights are burning, some poor sinners to be saved. And the whole building rocked with prayer and song.

Still I kept waiting to *see* Jesus. 5

Finally all the young people had gone to the altar and 6 were saved, but one boy and me. He was a rounder's son named Westley. Westley and I were surrounded by sisters and deacons praying. It was very hot in the church, and getting late now. Finally Westley said to me in a whisper: "God damn! I'm tired o' sitting here. Let's get up and be saved." So he got up and was saved.

Then I was left all alone on the mourners' bench. My 7 aunt came and knelt at my knees and cried, while prayers and songs swirled all around me in the little church. The whole congregation prayed for me alone, in a mighty wail of moans and voices. And I kept waiting serenely for Jesus, waiting, waiting—but he didn't come. I wanted to see him, but nothing happened to me. Nothing! I wanted something to happen to me, but nothing happened.

I heard the songs and the minister saying: "Why don't 8 you come? My dear child, why don't you come to Jesus? Jesus is waiting for you. He wants you. Why don't you come? Sister Reed, what is this child's name?"

"Langston," my aunt sobbed. 9

"Langston, why don't you come? Why don't you come 10 and be saved? Oh, Lamb of God! Why don't you come?''

Now it was really getting late. I began to be ashamed of 11 myself, holding everything up so long. I began to wonder what God thought about Westley, who certainly hadn't seen Jesus either, but who was now sitting proudly on the platform, swinging his knickerbockered legs and grinning down at me, surrounded by deacons and old women on their knees praying. God had not struck Westley dead for taking his name in vain or for lying in the temple. So I decided that maybe to save further trouble, I'd better lie, too, and say that Jesus had come, and get up and be saved.

So I got up.   12

Suddenly the whole room broke into a sea of shouting, 13 as they saw me rise. Waves of rejoicing swept the place. Women leaped in the air. My aunt threw her arms around me. The minister took me by the hand and led me to the platform.

When things quieted down, in a hushed silence, punctuated 14 by a few ecstatic "Amens," all the new young lambs were blessed in the name of God. Then joyous singing filled the room.

That night, for the last time in my life but one—for I was 15 a big boy twelve years old—I cried. I cried, in bed alone, and couldn't stop. I buried my head under the quilts, but my aunt heard me. She woke up and told my uncle I was crying because the Holy Ghost had come into my life, and because I had seen Jesus. But I was really crying because I couldn't bear to tell her that I had lied, that I had deceived everybody in the church, that I hadn't seen Jesus, and that now I didn't believe there was a Jesus any more, since he didn't come to help me.

BUILDING VOCABULARY

1. Throughout this essay, Hughes selects words dealing with religion to emphasize his ideas. Look the following words up in a dictionary. Then tell what *connotations* the words have for you. (See Glossary.)

   a. sin (par. 1)
   b. mourner (par. 1)

    c. lamb (par. 3)
    d. salvation (title)

2. Locate additional words that deal with religion.

3. When Hughes talks about lambs in the fold—and lambs in general—he is using a figure of speech, a comparison. What is being compared? How does religion enter into the comparison? Why is it useful as a figure of speech?

UNDERSTANDING THE WRITER'S IDEAS

1. According to Hughes's description, what is a revival meeting like? What is the effect of the "preaching, singing, praying, and shouting" on the "sinners" and the "young lambs"?

2. Why does Westley "see" Jesus? Why does Langston Hughes come to Jesus?

3. How does the author feel after his salvation? Does Hughes finally believe in Christ after his experience? How do you know?

UNDERSTANDING THE WRITER'S TECHNIQUES

1. Is there a thesis statement in the essay? Where is it located?

2. How does the first paragraph serve as an introduction to the narrative?

3. What is the value of description in this essay? List several instances of vivid description that contribute to the narrative.

4. Where does the main narration begin? How much time passes in the course of the action?

5. In narration, it is especially important to have effective *transitions*—or word bridges—from stage to stage in the

action. Transitions help the reader shift easily from idea to idea, event to event. List several transition words that Hughes uses.

6. A piece of writing has *coherence* if all its parts relate clearly and logically to each other. Each sentence grows naturally from the sentence before it; each paragraph grows naturally from the paragraph before it. Is Hughes's essay coherent? Which transitions help advance the action and relate the parts of a single paragraph to each other? Which transitions help connect paragraphs together? How does the way Hughes organized this essay help establish coherence?

7. A story (whether it is true or fiction) has to be told from the first-person ("I, we"), second-person ("you"), or third-person ("he, she, it, they") *point of view*. Point of view in narration sets up the author's position in regard to the action, making him either a part of the action or an observer of it.

   a. What is the point of view in "Salvation"—is it first, second, or third person?

   b. Why has Hughes chosen this point of view instead of any other? Can you think of any advantages to this point of view?

8. What is your opinion about the last paragraph, the conclusion of this selection? What does it suggest about the mind of a twelve-year-old boy? What does it say about adults' misunderstanding of the activities of children?

9. What does the word "conversion" mean? What conversion really takes place in this piece? How does that compare to what people usually mean when they use "conversion" in a religious sense?

EXPLORING THE WRITER'S IDEAS

1. Hughes seems to suggest that we are forced to do things because of social pressures. Do you agree with his sugges-

tion? Do people do things because their friends or families expect them to? To what extent are we part of the "herd"? Is it possible for a person to retain individuality under pressure from a group? When did you bow to group pressures? When did you resist?

2. Do you find the religious experience in Hughes's essay unusual or extreme? Why or why not? How do *you* define religion?

3. Under what circumstances might a person lie in order to satisfy others? Try to recall a specific episode in which you or someone you know was forced to lie in order to please others.

IDEAS FOR WRITING

Guided Writing

Narrate an event in your life where you (or someone you know) gave in to group pressure or were forced to lie in order to please those around you.

1. Start with a thesis statement.

2. Set the stage for your narrative in the opening paragraph by telling where and when the incident took place. Use specific names for places.

3. Try to keep the action within as brief a time period as possible. If you can write about an event that took no more than a few minutes, so much the better.

4. Use description to sketch in the characters around you. Use colors, actions, sounds, smells, sensations of touch to fill in details of the scene.

5. Use effective transitions of time to link sentences and paragraphs.

6. Use the last paragraph to explain how you felt immediately after the incident.

More Writing Projects

1. Explain in a journal entry an abstract word like "salvation," "sin," "love," or "hatred" by narrating an event that reveals the meaning of the word to you.

2. Write an extended paragraph on an important event that affected your relationship with family, friends, or your community during your childhood.

3. Make a list of all the important details that you associate with some religious occasion in your life. Then write a narrative essay on the experience.

I Became Her Target

Roger Wilkins

Roger Wilkins, who is a senior fellow at the Institute for Policy Studies in Washington, D.C., and chairperson of the Pulitzer Prize Board, here tells the story of how an understanding teacher may well have changed the course of his life. Wilkins's narration explores questions of racism as he talks about how a series of positive classroom incidents helped him renew his self-esteem. Note how the writer shifts between his childhood and adult perceptions to help weave his narrative.

Words to Watch

decade (par. 1)　a ten-year period
prevailing (par. 2)　accepted; agreed upon
pristine (par. 2)　uncorrupted; fresh and clean
deplored (par. 5)　regretted strongly on a moral level
incipient (par. 8)　in the beginning stages
derivative (par. 9)　taken or received from another source
groused (par. 13)　complained; grumbled
mortified (par. 14)　subjected to humiliation

My favorite teacher's name was "Dead-Eye" Bean. Her 1 real name was Dorothy. She taught American history to eighth graders in the junior high section of Creston, the high school that served the north end of Grand Rapids, Mich. It was the fall of 1944. Franklin D. Roosevelt was president; American troops were battling their way across France; Joe DiMaggio was still in the service; the Montgomery bus boycott was more than a decade away, and I was a 12-year-old black newcomer in a school that was otherwise all white.

My mother, who had been a widow in New York, had 2 married my stepfather, a Grand Rapids physician, the year before, and he had bought the best house he could afford for his new family. The problem for our new neighbors was that their neighborhood had previously been pristine (in their terms) and they were ignorant about black people. The prevailing wisdom in the neighborhood was that we were spoiling it and that we ought to go back where we belonged (or alternatively, ought not intrude where we were not wanted). There was a lot of angry talk among the adults, but nothing much came of it.

But some of the kids, those first few weeks, were quite 3
nasty. They threw stones at me, chased me home when I was on foot and spat on my bike seat when I was in class. For a time, I was a pretty lonely, friendless and sometimes frightened kid. I was just transplanted from Harlem, and here in Grand Rapids, the dominant culture was speaking to me insistently.

I can see now that those youngsters were bullying and 4
culturally disadvantaged. I knew then that they were bigoted, but the culture spoke to me more powerfully than my mind and I felt ashamed for being different—a nonstandard person.

I now know that Dorothy Bean understood most of that 5
and deplored it. So things began to change when I walked into her classroom. She was a pleasant-looking single woman, who looked old and wrinkled to me at the time, but who was probably about 40.

Whereas my other teachers approached the problem of 6
easing in their new black pupil by ignoring him for the first few weeks, Miss Bean went right at me. On the morning after having read our first assignment, she asked me the first question. I later came to know that in Grand Rapids, she was viewed as a very liberal person who believed, among other things, that Negroes were equal.

I gulped and answered her question and the follow-up. 7
They weren't brilliant answers, but they did establish the facts that I had read the assignment and that I could speak English. Later in the hour, when one of my classmates had bungled an answer, Miss Bean came back to me with a question that required me to clean up the girl's mess and established me as a smart person.

Thus, the teacher began to give me human dimensions, 8
though not perfect ones for an eighth grader. It was somewhat

better to be an incipient teacher's pet than merely a dark presence in the back of the room onto whose silent form my classmates could fit all the stereotypes they carried in their heads.

A few days later, Miss Bean became the first teacher 9 ever to require me to think. She asked my opinion about something Jefferson had done. In those days, all my opinions were derivative. I was for Roosevelt because my parents were and I was for the Yankees because my older buddy from Harlem was a Yankee fan. Besides, we didn't have opinions about historical figures like Jefferson. Like our high school building or old Mayor Welch, he just was.

After I had stared at her for a few seconds, she said: 10 "Well, should he have bought Louisiana or not?"

"I guess so," I replied tentatively. 11

"Why?" she shot back. 12

Why! What kind of question was that, I groused silently. 13 But I ventured an answer. Day after day, she kept doing that to me, and my answers became stronger and more confident. She was the first teacher to give me the sense that thinking was part of education and that I could form opinions that had some value.

Her final service to me came on a day when my mind 14 was wandering and I was idly digging my pencil into the writing surface on the arm of my chair. Miss Bean impulsively threw a hunk of gum eraser at me. By amazing chance, it hit my hand and sent the pencil flying. She gasped, and I crept mortified after my pencil as the class roared. That was the ice breaker.

Afterward, kids came up to me to laugh about "Old 15 Dead-Eye Bean." The incident became a legend, and I, a part of that story, became a person to talk to.

So that's how I became just another kid in school and 16 Dorothy Bean became "Old Dead-Eye."

BUILDING VOCABULARY

1. Use context clues (see Glossary) to determine the meaning of the following words in italics. Return to the appropriate

paragraph in the essay for more clues, if necessary. Write down your definitions; then check the words in a dictionary.

   a. not *intrude* where we were not wanted (par. 2)
   b. *transplanted* from Harlem (par. 3)
   c. those youngsters were *bullying* (par. 4)
   d. that they were *bigoted* (par. 4)
   e. being different—a *nonstandard* person (par. 4)
   f. I *gulped* and answered her question (par. 7)
   g. had *bungled* an answer (par. 7)
   h. I *ventured* an answer (par. 13)
   i. She *gasped* (par. 14)
   j. as the class *roared* (par. 14)

2. Wilkins uses several "*-ly*" adverbs to modify sentence meanings. Give the definition for each word below.

   a. previously (par. 2)
   b. alternatively (par. 2)
   c. culturally (par. 4)
   d. powerfully (par. 4)
   e. tentatively (par. 11)
   f. impulsively (par. 14)

UNDERSTANDING THE WRITER'S IDEAS

1. What subject, at what level, when, and where did "Dead-Eye" Bean teach? What was her real name? Why was she called "Dead-Eye"? How old was Wilkins when he was in her class?

2. Briefly explain in your own words how the author got from Harlem, New York, to Grand Rapids, Michigan.

3. What was the racial makeup of his new school? What can you assume about the racial makeup of his old school? Why?

4. Into what social class do you think Wilkins's family fit af-

ter they moved to Grand Rapids? Identify clues from the essay that support your opinion.

5. What was the attitude toward the Wilkinses in their new neighborhood? Why? How did the reactions to the Wilkinses differ among the neighborhood adults and the kids? What specific actions did each group take? Why does Wilkins say the youngsters were "culturally disadvantaged"? What was the effect of the neighbors' reactions on the young Wilkins?

6. Explain the metaphor in paragraph 3: "the dominant culture was speaking to me insistently."

7. Describe Dorothy "Dead-Eye" Bean as a person. What was her attitude on the racism that the young Wilkins was experiencing?

8. What was the result of Bean's first question to Wilkins? Why did she later ask him to answer another question? What was the result that time? How did Dorothy Bean's actions *immediately* change the young Wilkins's life?

9. How did Dorothy Bean require Wilkins *to think?* Ultimately, how did she change his life?

10. Why did Bean throw the eraser at Wilkins? Although it seems a rather hostile act, why did it turn out for the good? Explain the meaning of "That was the ice-breaker."

11. What is the main point of Wilkins's tale about "Dead-Eye" Bean?

UNDERSTANDING THE WRITER'S TECHNIQUES

1. What is the thesis of Wilkins's essay?

2. A *memoir* is a narrative composed from personal experience. On what personal experience is this memoir based?

Is using the memoir form an effective technique to communicate the author's ideas? Why?

3. *Chronological order* in narration refers to the arrangement
   of events in the order they occurred in time, beginning
   with the one in the most distant past. How does Wilkins
   use chronological order in this essay? Outline the chronology. What transitions does he use to tie together that
   chronology?

4. A writer will use *allusions* (see Glossary) to help place the
   events in an essay at a particular time in history. Identify
   the following allusions from this essay and tell how they
   help set the historical moment: Joe DiMaggio, Franklin D.
   Roosevelt, the Montgomery bus boycott.

5. Wilkins helps to structure the essay by contrasting his
   "then" and "now" views of certain incidents. Compare
   his "then" and "now" views of (a) the kids in the Grand
   Rapids neighborhood and (b) Dorothy Bean. How do
   these contrasts help structure the essay?

6. Why does Wilkins use the term "Negroes" rather than
   "blacks" in paragraph 6? How would the impact of the
   sentence have changed if he had used "blacks"?

7. Usually parenthetical expressions are used to add or further clarify information. Reread paragraph 2. For what
   other reasons might Wilkins have added the parenthetical
   expressions?

8. How many narratives do you identify here? How does
   Wilkins weave them together?

9. At two points, the author uses expressions that might
   have *double meanings* within the context of this essay.
   Explain the possible double meanings of "a dark presence" (par. 8) and "her final service" (par. 14). Could the
   title be construed as having a double meaning as well?
   How so?

10. How did you react to the final sentence? Does it ade-

quately conclude this essay? Does it fit in tone with the rest of the essay? Explain your answers.

EXPLORING THE WRITER'S IDEAS

1. Langston Hughes writes in "Salvation" (pages 141–143) of a childhood moment that occurred when he was about the same age as Wilkins in this essay. Although they come from different eras (Hughes about thirty years earlier), both boys faced important changes in their lives as reflected in the essays. What do you think was most similar about their experiences? Most different?

2. Throughout the essay, Wilkins compares his perceptions of incidents from his point of view when a child with his perceptions of them as an adult. How has the distance of years affected your views of various childhood incidents? Which viewpoint do you feel is more accurate? Which is more helpful to you in understanding your present life situation?

3. Comparing the adults' and children's responses to his family's moving into an all-white neighborhood, Wilkins indicates that in many ways the children were much nastier. It is often said that children can be very cruel to an outsider or to someone "different." Why do children react so forcefully? From where do most youngsters learn their tactics? How is it possible to bring up children who are less aggressive or nasty?

IDEAS FOR WRITING

Guided Writing

Write a narrative essay that focuses on a childhood incident with a teacher. Write your narrative about an incident that had lasting effects on you because it helped you solve a problem, face an unpleasant truth, or understand yourself better.

1. Begin by identifying the teacher, the place, and the level of your class.

2. State the year of the incident and include *allusions* to set the time period.

3. Tell what the incident was and how it also involved others (for example, your parents, your brothers and sisters).

4. Describe the teacher in more subjective terms than in your first paragraph. Use rich sensory detail. State particular qualities of the teacher that helped that teacher affect you as strongly as he or she did.

5. Use chronological order in your narration of the incident.

6. Throughout the essay, contrast your perceptions of this problem when you were a child with your perceptions in retrospect as an adult.

7. Include some dialogue between you and your teacher.

8. In your conclusion explain how this teacher changed your life.

More Writing Projects

1. In your journal, recollect in narrative and descriptive form your most memorable grade school or high school teacher.

2. Narrate in a paragraph an incident during which you felt you were the victim of bigotry, racism, sexism, or other form of prejudice.

3. Write an essay about something you did that significantly changed another person's life.

A Hanging

George Orwell

One of the masters of English prose, George Orwell (1903–1950) often used narration of personal events to explore important social issues. Notice here how he involves the reader in a simple yet fascinating and tragic story, almost as if he were writing fiction. Orwell takes a brief time span and expands that moment with specific language. At one point, as you will see, the purpose of the narrative comes into sharp focus.

Words to Watch

sodden (par. 1)   heavy with water

absurdly (par. 2)   ridiculously

desolately (par. 3)   gloomily; lifelessly; cheerlessly

prodding (par. 3)   poking or thrusting at something

Dravidian (par. 4)   any member of a group of intermixed races of southern India and Burma

pariah (par. 6)   outcast; a member of a low caste of southern India and Burma

servile (par. 11)   slavelike; lacking spirit or independence

reiterated (par. 12)   repeated

abominable (par. 13)   hateful; disagreeable; unpleasant

timorously (par. 15)   fearfully

oscillated (par. 16)   moved back and forth between two points

garrulously (par. 20)   in a talkative manner

refractory (par. 22)   stubborn

amicably (par. 24)   in a friendly way; peaceably

It was in Burma, a sodden morning of the rains. A sickly 1 light, like yellow tinfoil, was slanting over the high walls into the jail yard. We were waiting outside the condemned cells, a row of sheds fronted with double bars, like small animal cages. Each cell measured about ten feet by ten and was quite bare within except for a plank bed and a pot of drinking water. In some of them brown silent men were squatting at the inner bars, with their blankets draped round them. These were the condemned men, due to be hanged within the next week or two.

One prisoner had been brought out of his cell. He was a 2 Hindu, a puny wisp of a man, with a shaven head and vague liquid eyes. He had a thick, sprouting moustache, absurdly too big for his body, rather like the moustache of a comic man on the films. Six tall Indian warders were guarding him and getting him ready for the gallows. Two of them stood by with rifles with fixed bayonets, while the others handcuffed him, passed a chain through his handcuffs and fixed it to their belts, and lashed his arms tight to his sides. They crowded very close about him, with their hands always on him in a careful, caressing grip, as though all the while feeling him to make sure he was there. It was like men handling a fish which is still alive and may jump back into the water. But he stood quite unresisting, yielding his arms limply to the ropes, as though he hardly noticed what was happening.

Eight o'clock struck and a bugle call, desolately thin in 3 the wet air, floated from the distant barracks. The superintendent of the jail, who was standing apart from the rest of us, moodily prodding the gravel with his stick, raised his head at the sound. He was an army doctor, with a grey toothbrush moustache and a gruff voice. "For God's sake hurry up, Francis," he said irritably. "The man ought to have been dead by this time. Aren't you ready yet?"

Francis, the head jailer, a fat Dravidian in a white drill 4 suit and gold spectacles, waved his black hand. "Yes sir, yes sir," he bubbled. "All iss satisfactorily prepared. The hangman iss waiting. We shall proceed."

"Well, quick march, then. The prisoners can't get their 5 breakfast till this job's over."

We set out for the gallows. Two warders marched on ei- 6 ther side of the prisoner, with their files at the slope; two others marched close against him, gripping him by arm and shoulder, as though at once pushing and supporting him. The rest of us, magistrates and the like, followed behind. Suddenly, when we had gone ten yards, the procession stopped short without any order or warning. A dreadful thing had happened—a dog, come goodness knows whence, had appeared in the yard. It came bounding among us with a loud volley of barks, and leapt round us wagging its whole body, wild with glee at finding so many human beings together. It was a large woolly dog, half Airedale, half pariah. For a moment it pranced round us, and then, before anyone could stop it, it had made a dash for the prisoner, and jumping up tried to lick his face. Everyone stood aghast, too taken aback even to grab at the dog.

"Who let that bloody brute in here?" said the superintendent angrily. "Catch it, someone!"   7

A warder, detached from the escort, charged clumsily after the dog, but it danced and gambolled just out of his reach, taking everything as part of the game. A young Eurasian jailer picked up a handful of gravel and tried to stone the dog away, but it dodged the stones and came after us again. Its yaps echoed from the jail walls. The prisoner, in the grasp of the two warders, looked on incuriously, as though this was another formality of the hanging. It was several minutes before someone managed to catch the dog. Then we put my handkerchief through its collar and moved off once more, with the dog still straining and whimpering.   8

It was about forty yards to the gallows. I watched the bare brown back of the prisoner marching in front of me. He walked clumsily with his bound arms, but quite steadily, with that bobbing gait of the Indian who never straightens his knees. At each step his muscles slid neatly into place, the lock of hair on his scalp danced up and down, his feet printed themselves on the wet gravel. And once, in spite of the men who gripped him by each shoulder, he stepped slightly aside to avoid a puddle on the path.   9

It is curious, but till that moment I had never realised what it means to destroy a healthy, conscious man. When I saw the prisoner step aside to avoid the puddle, I saw the mystery, the unspeakable wrongness, of cutting a life short when it is in full tide. This man was not dying, he was alive just as we were alive. All the organs of his body were working—bowels digesting food, skin renewing itself, nails growing, tissues forming—all toiling away in solemn foolery. His nails would still be growing when he stood on the drop, when   10 he was falling through the air with a tenth of a second to live. His eyes saw the yellow gravel and the grey walls, and his brain still remembered, foresaw, reasoned—reasoned even about puddles. He and we were a party of men walking together, seeing, hearing, feeling, understanding the same world; and in two minutes, with a sudden snap, one of us would be gone—one mind less, one world less.

The gallows stood in a small yard, separate from the 11 main grounds of the prison, and overgrown with tall prickly weeds. It was a brick erection like three sides of a shed, with planking on top, and above that two beams and a crossbar with the rope dangling. The hangman, a grey-haired convict in the white uniform of the prison, was waiting beside his machine. He greeted us with a servile crouch as we entered. At a word from Francis the two warders, gripping the prisoner more closely than ever, half led, half pushed him to the gallows and helped him clumsily up the ladder. Then the hangman climbed up and fixed the rope round the prisoner's neck.

We stood waiting, five yards away. The warders had 12 formed in a rough circle round the gallows. And then, when the noose was fixed, the prisoner began crying out on his god. It was a high, reiterated cry of "Ram! Ram! Ram! Ram!", not urgent and fearful like a prayer or a cry for help, but steady, rhythmical, almost like the tolling of a bell. The dog answered the sound with a whine. The hangman, still standing on the gallows, produced a small cotton bag like a flour bag and drew it down over the prisoner's face. But the sound, muffled by the cloth, still persisted, over and over again: "Ram! Ram! Ram! Ram! Ram!"

The hangman climbed down and stood ready, holding 13 the lever. Minutes seemed to pass. The steady, muffled crying from the prisoner went on and on, "Ram! Ram! Ram!" never faltering for an instant. The superintendent, his head on his chest, was slowly poking the ground with his stick; perhaps he was counting the cries, allowing the prisoner a fixed number—fifty, perhaps, or a hundred. Everyone had changed colour. The Indians had gone grey like bad coffee, and one or two of the bayonets were wavering. We looked at the lashed, hooded man on the drop, and listened to his cries—each cry another

second of life; the same thought was in all our minds: oh, kill
him quickly, get it over, stop that abominable noise!

Suddenly the superintendent made up his mind. Throw- 14
ing up his head he made a swift motion with his stick.
"Chalo!" he shouted almost fiercely.

There was a clanking noise, and then dead silence. The 15
prisoner had vanished, and the rope was twisting on itself. I
let go of the dog, and it galloped immediately to the back of
the gallows; but when it got there it stopped short, barked,
and then retreated into a corner of the yard, where it stood
among the weeds, looking timorously out at us. We went
round the gallows to inspect the prisoner's body. He was dangling with his toes pointed straight downwards, very slowly
revolving, as dead as a stone.

The superintendent reached out with his stick and poked 16
the bare body; it oscillated, slightly. "*He's* all right," said the
superintendent. He backed out from under the gallows, and
blew out a deep breath. The moody look had gone out of his
face quite suddenly. He glanced at his wristwatch. "Eight
minutes past eight. Well, that's all for this morning, thank
God."

The warders unfixed bayonets and marched away. The 17
dog, sobered and conscious of having misbehaved itself,
slipped after them. We walked out of the gallows yard, past
the condemned cells with their waiting prisoners, into the big
central yard of the prison. The convicts, under the command
of warders armed with lathis, were already receiving their
breakfast. They squatted in long rows, each man holding a tin
pannikin, while two warders with buckets marched round la-
dling out rice; it seemed quite a homely, jolly scene, after the
hanging. An enormous relief had come upon us now that the
job was done. One felt an impulse to sing, to break into a run,
to snigger. All at once everyone began chattering gaily.

The Eurasian boy walking beside me nodded towards the 18
way we had come, with a knowing smile: "Do you know, sir,
our friend (he meant the dead man), when he heard his appeal
had been dismissed, he pissed on the floor of his cell. From
fright—Kindly take one of my cigarettes, sir. Do you not ad-
mire my new silver case, sir? From the boxwallah, two rupees
eight annas. Classy European style."

Several people laughed—at what, nobody seemed cer- 19
tain.

Francis was walking by the superintendent, talking gar- 20
rulously: "Well, sir, all hass passed off with the utmost satis-
factoriness. It wass all finished—flick! like that. It iss not always so—oah, no! I have known cases where the doctor wass
obliged to go beneath the gallows and pull the prisoner's legs
to ensure decease. Most disagreeable!"

"Wriggling about, eh? That's bad," said the superinten- 21
dent.

"Ach, sir, it iss worse when they become refractory! 22
One man, I recall, clung to the bars of hiss cage when we went
to take him out. You will scarcely credit, sir, that it took six
warders to dislodge him, three pulling at each leg. We reasoned with him. 'My dear fellow,' we said, 'think of all the
pain and trouble you are causing to us!' But no, he would not
listen! Ach, he wass very troublesome!"

I found that I was laughing quite loudly. Everyone was 23
laughing. Even the superintendent grinned in a tolerant way.
"You'd better all come out and have a drink," he said quite
genially. "I've got a bottle of whisky in the car. We could do
with it."

We went through the big double gates of the prison, into 24
the road. "Pulling at his legs!" exclaimed a Burmese magis-
trate suddenly, and burst into a loud chuckling. We all began
laughing again. At that moment Francis's anecdote seemed
extraordinarily funny. We all had a drink together, native and
European alike, quite amicably. The dead man was a hundred
yards away.

BUILDING VOCABULARY

1. Use context clues (see Glossary) to make an "educated
   guess" about the definitions of the following words in italics. Before you guess, look back to the paragraph for clues.
   Afterward, check your guess in a dictionary.

   a. *condemned* men (par. 1)
   b. puny *wisp* of a man (par. 2)

    c. Indian *warders* (par. 2)
    d. careful *caressing* grip (par. 2)
    e. stood *aghast* (par. 6)
    f. it danced and *gambolled* (par. 8)
    g. *solemn* foolery (par. 10)
    h. armed with *lathis* (par. 17)
    i. a tin *pannikin* (par. 17)
    j. quite *genially* (par. 23)

2. What are definitions for the words below? Look at words within them, which you may be able to recognize.

    a. moodily
    b. dreadful
    c. Eurasian
    d. incuriously
    e. formality

UNDERSTANDING THE WRITER'S IDEAS

1. What is the main point that the writer wishes to make in this essay? Which paragraph tells the author's purpose most clearly? Which sentence in that paragraph best states the main idea of the essay?

2. The events in the essay occur in Burma, a country in Asia. Describe in your own words the specific details of the action.

3. Who are the major characters in this essay? Why might you include the dog as a major character?

4. In a narrative essay the writer often tells the events in chronological order. Examine the following events from "A Hanging." Arrange them in the order in which they occurred.

    a. A large wooly dog tries to lick the prisoner's face.
    b. A Eurasian boy talks about his silver case.
    c. The superintendent signals "Chalo!" to the hangman.
    d. One prisoner, a Hindu, is brought from his cell.

   e. Francis discusses with the superintendent a prisoner who had to be pulled off the bars of his cage.

   f. The prisoner steps aside to avoid a puddle as he marches to the gallows.

5. What is the author's opinion of *capital punishment* (legally killing someone who has disobeyed the laws of society)? How does the incident with the puddle suggest that opinion, even indirectly?

UNDERSTANDING THE WRITER'S TECHNIQUES

1. In the first paragraph of the essay, we see clear images such as "brown silent men were squatting at the inner bars, with their blankets draped around them." The use of color and action make an instant appeal to our sense of sight.

   a. What images in the rest of the essay do you find most vivid?

   b. Which sentence gives the best details of sound?

   c. What word pictures suggest action and color?

   d. Where do you find words that describe a sensation of touch?

2. In order to make their images clearer, writers use *figurative language* (see Glossary). "A Hanging" is especially rich in *similes,* which are comparisons using the word *like* or *as.*

   a. What simile does Orwell use in the first paragraph in order to let us see how the light slants over the jail yard walls? How does the simile make the scene clearer?

   b. What other simile does Orwell use in the first paragraph?

   c. Discuss the similes in the paragraphs listed below. What are the things being compared? Are the similes, in your opinion, original? How do they contribute to the image the author intends to create?

     (1) It was like men handling a fish....(par. 2)

     (2) A thick sprouting moustache...rather like the moustache of a comic man on the films (par. 2)

   (3) It was a high, reiterated cry...like the tolling of a
        bell. (par. 12)
   (4) The Indians had gone grey like bad coffee....
        (par. 13)
   (5) He was dangling with his toes pointed straight
        downwards, slowly revolving, as dead as a stone.
        (par. 15)

3. You know that an important feature of narration is the writ-
    er's ability to look at a brief span of time and to expand that
    moment with specific language.

   a. How has Orwell limited the events in "A Hanging" to a
       specific moment in time and place?
   b. How does the image "a sodden morning of the rains"
       in paragraph 1 set the mood for the main event por-
       trayed in the essay? What is the effect of the image
       "brown silent men"? Why does Orwell describe the
       prisoner as "a puny wisp of a man, with a shaven head
       and vague liquid eyes" (par. 2)? Why does the author
       present him in almost a comic way?
   c. What is the effect of the image about the bugle call in
       paragraph 3? Why does Orwell create the image of the
       dog trying to lick the prisoner's face (par. 6)? How does
       it contribute to his main point? In paragraph 12, Orwell
       tells us that the dog whines. Why does he give that de-
       tail? Discuss the value of the images about the dog in
       paragraphs 15 and 17.
   d. Why does Orwell offer the image of the prisoner step-
       ping aside "to avoid a puddle on the path"? How does
       it advance the point of the essay? What is the effect of
       the image of the superintendent poking the ground with
       his stick (par. 13)?
   e. What is the importance of the superintendent's words
       in paragraph 3? What is the value of the Eurasian boy's
       conversation in paragraph 18? How does the dialogue in
       paragraphs 20 to 24 contribute to Orwell's main point?
   f. Why has Orwell left out information about the crime
       the prisoner committed? How would you feel about the
       prisoner if you knew he were, say, a rapist, a murderer,
       a molester of children, or a heroin supplier?

4. Analyze the point of view in the essay. Is the "I" narrator an observer, a participant, or both? Is he neutral or involved? Support your opinion.

5. In "A Hanging," Orwell skillfully uses several forms of *irony* to support his main ideas. Irony, in general, is the use of language to suggest the opposite of what is said. First, there is *verbal irony*, which involves a contrast between what is said and what is actually meant. Second, there is *irony of situation*, where there is a contrast between what is expected or thought appropriate and what actually happens. Then, there is *dramatic irony*, in which there is a contrast between what a character says and what the reader (or the audience) actually knows or understands.

   a. In paragraph 2, why does Orwell describe the prisoner as a *comic* type? Why does he emphasize the prisoner's *smallness?* Why does Orwell write that the prisoner "hardly noticed what was happening"? Why might this be called ironic?

   b. When the dog appears in paragraph 6, how is its behavior described? How do the dog's actions contrast with the situation?

   c. What is the major irony that Orwell analyzes in paragraph 10?

   d. In paragraph 11, how does the fact that one prisoner is being used to execute another prisoner strike you?

   e. Why is the Superintendent's remark in paragraph 11—"*He's* all right"—a good example of verbal irony?

   f. After the hanging, the men engage in seemingly normal actions. However, Orwell undercuts these actions through the use of irony. Find at least three examples of irony in paragraphs 17 to 24.

EXPLORING THE WRITER'S IDEAS

1. Orwell is clearly against capital punishment. Why might you agree or disagree with him? Are there any crimes for which capital punishment is acceptable to you? If not, what should society do with those convicted of serious crimes?

2. Do you think the method used to perform capital punishment has anything to do with the way we view it? Is death by hanging or firing squad worse than death by gas or by the electric chair? Or are they all the same? Socrates—a Greek philosopher convicted of conspiracy—was forced to drink *hemlock,* a fast-acting poison. Can you accept that?

3. Orwell shows a variety of reactions people have to an act of execution. Can you believe the way the people behave here? Why? How do you explain the large crowds that gathered to watch public executions in Europe in the sixteenth and seventeenth centuries?

IDEAS FOR WRITING

Guided Writing

Write a narrative essay in which you tell about a punishment you either saw or received. Use sensory language, selecting your details carefully. At one point in your paper—as Orwell does in paragraph 10—state your opinion or interpretation of the punishment clearly.

1. Use a number of images that name colors, sounds, smells, and actions.

2. Try to write at least three original similes. Think through your comparisons carefully. Make sure they are logical. Avoid overused comparisons like "He was white as a ghost."

3. Set your narrative in time and place. Tell the season of the year and the place in which the event occurred.

4. Fill in details of the setting. Show what the surroundings look like.

5. Name people by name. Show details of their actions. Quote some of their spoken dialogue.

6. Use the first-person point of view.

More Writing Projects

1. Narrate in your journal an event that turned out differently from what you expected—a blind date, a picnic, a holiday. Try to stress the irony of the situation.

2. Write a narrative paragraph that describes a vivid event in which you hid your true feelings about the event, such as a postelection party, the wedding of someone you disliked, a job interview, a visit to the doctor.

3. Write an editorial for your college newspaper supporting or attacking the idea of capital punishment. Communicate your position through the use of real or hypothetical narration of a relevant event.

SUMMING UP: CHAPTER 4

1. Orwell's essay has remained one of the outstanding essays of the century, widely anthologized and frequently taught in English writing classes. How do you account for its popularity? Would you consider it the best essay in this chapter? in the four chapters you have read so far? Write an essay in which you analyze and evaluate ''A Hanging.''

2. Both Wong and Wilkins present a view of schools and teachers through the eyes of young people. What conclusion can you draw about the role of educational institutions in the lives of minority children? Use ''The Struggle to Be an All-American Girl'' and ''I Was Her Target'' as a starting point for your reflections on education. Write an essay in which you consider the issue; make recommendations as you see fit.

3. You are Richard Selzer (author of ''The Discus Thrower,'' pages 113–116) and you have been asked by a local newspaper to write a short review of George Orwell's ''A Hanging.'' Basing your insights on the philosophy of ''The Discus Thrower,'' write the review. Or, if you choose, be George Orwell and write a review of Selzer's ''The Discus Thrower.''

4. What have you learned about writing strong narratives from the writers in this chapter? What generalizations can you draw? What "rules" can you derive? Write an essay called "How to Write Narratives" based on what you have learned from Wong, Hughes, Wilkins, and (or) Orwell. Make specific references to the writer(s) of your choice.

5. Hughes's essay highlights the role of religion in life. Write an essay in which you narrate an important religious experience that you remember. You might want to narrate the story of your own "conversion."

CHAPTER 5

Illustration

One convenient way for writers to present and to support a point is through *illustration*—that is, by means of several examples to back up an idea. Illustration helps a writer put general or abstract thoughts into specific examples. It also holds a reader's interest: We all respond to concrete instances when we are trying to understand a point. Certainly, you are no stranger to illustration as a way to present information. Every time you try to explain why you believe or feel something to be true, and you give more than one case to back it up, you are using this technique.

Suppose you want to share with a friend your belief that the Los Angeles Dodgers are a great baseball team. First you might point out the pitching staff; then you might bring up the quality hitters; then the fielders; then the management. Your friend would, no doubt, expect you to explain each of those illustrations by giving some details. And so you would name a couple of first-rate pitchers, perhaps describe them and state their won-lost record; you would tell which of the hitters you thought outstanding and point out their runs-batted-in and their hitting averages; you would describe a good fielder or two in action, even telling a story, perhaps, of one really first-rate play you saw when the Dodgers pounded the Reds.

When you present illustrations, it is best to have *several* reasons that lead you to a certain conclusion. A single, isolated example might not convince anyone easily, unless it is a strong, extended example. You have to make decisions, of course, about the number and kinds of details to offer for each

169

example. Sometimes each illustration will itself require a few different examples to make the point. And you have to decide which illustration to give first: No doubt you would save the most important for last.

As you have probably guessed, when you write an essay of illustration you will be using much of what you have already learned so far. Techniques of description and narration will help you support and organize your examples clearly and strongly. In fact, a number of ways to develop essays discussed later on—comparison, cause and effect, process analysis, definition, and classification—lend themselves to development by illustration. The selections you will read in this section show how four writers use illustration to advance their ideas.

Daddy Tucked the Blanket
Randall Williams

Randall Williams was a reporter for *The Alabama Journal* when he wrote this autobiographical essay. He is trying here to show how the social conditions of the poor have an ugly effect upon personal relationships. A number of examples point out how his family reacted to each other and to the environment created by poverty.

Words to Watch

humiliating (par. 5)   lowering the pride or dignity of someone
shiftless (par. 7)   incapable; inefficient; lazy
articulate (par. 7)   able to express oneself clearly
teetering (par. 9)   wavering; moving unsteadily
deteriorating (par. 12)   becoming worse
futility (par. 13)   the quality of being useless
abuse (par. 16)   mistreatment
psyche (par. 20)   the soul; the self; the mind
affluent (par. 21)   wealthy
grandeur (par. 23)   magnificence

About the time I turned 16, my folks began to wonder 1 why I didn't stay home any more. I always had an excuse for them, but what I didn't say was that I had found my freedom and I was getting out.

I went through four years of high school in semirural Al- 2 abama and became active in clubs and sports; I made a lot of friends and became a regular guy, if you know what I mean. But one thing was irregular about me: I managed those four years without ever having a friend visit at my house.

I was ashamed of where I lived. I had been ashamed for 3 as long as I had been conscious of class.

We had a big family. There were several of us sleeping in 4 one room, but that's not so bad if you get along, and we always did. As you get older, though, it gets worse.

Being poor is a humiliating experience for a young per- 5

son trying hard to be accepted. Even now—several years removed—it is hard to talk about. And I resent the weakness of
these words to make you feel what it was really like.

We lived in a lot of old houses. We moved a lot because   6
we were always looking for something just a little better than
what we had. You have to understand that my folks worked
harder than most people. My mother was always at home, but
for her that was a full-time job—and no fun, either. But my
father worked his head off from the time I can remember in
construction and shops. It was hard, physical work.

I tell you this to show that we weren't shiftless. No mat-   7
ter how much money Daddy made, we never made much
progress up the social ladder. I got out thanks to a college
scholarship and because I was a little more articulate than the
average.

I have seen my Daddy wrap copper wire through the   8
soles of his boots to keep them together in the wintertime. He
couldn't buy new boots because he had used the money for
food and shoes for us. We lived like hell, but we went to
school well-clothed and with a full stomach.

It really is hell to live in a house that was in bad shape 10   9
years before you moved in. And a big family puts a lot of wear
and tear on a new house, too, so you can imagine how one
goes downhill if it is teetering when you move in. But we lived
in houses that were sweltering in summer and freezing in winter. I woke up every morning for a year and a half with plaster
on my face where it had fallen out of the ceiling during the
night.

This wasn't during the Depression; this was in the late   10
60's and early 70's.

When we boys got old enough to learn trades in school,   11
we would try to fix up the old houses we lived in. But have
you ever tried to paint a wall that crumbled when the roller
went across it? And bright paint emphasized the holes in the
wall. You end up more frustrated than when you began, especially when you know that at best you might come up with
only enough money to improve one of the six rooms in the
house. And we might move out soon after, anyway.

The same goes for keeping a house like that clean. If you   12 have a house full of kids and the house is deteriorating, you'll never keep it clean. Daddy used to yell at Mama about that, but she couldn't do anything. I think Daddy knew it inside, but he had to have an outlet for his rage somewhere, and at least yelling isn't as bad as hitting, which they never did to each other.

But you have a kitchen which has no counter space and no hot water, and you will have dirty dishes stacked up. That sounds like an excuse, but try it. You'll go mad from the sheer sense of futility. It's the same thing in a house with no closets. You can't keep clothes clean and rooms in order if they have to be stacked up with things. 13

Living in a bad house is generally worse on girls. For one thing, they traditionally help their mother with the housework. We boys could get outside and work in the field or cut wood or even play ball and forget about living conditions. The sky was still pretty. 14

But the girls got the pressure, and as they got older it became worse. Would they accept dates knowing they had to "receive" the young man in a dirty hallway with broken windows, peeling wallpaper and a cracked ceiling? You have to live it to understand it, but it creates a shame which drives the soul of a young person inward. 15

I'm thankful none of us ever blamed our parents for this, because it would have crippled our relationships. As it worked out, only the relationship between our parents was damaged. And I think the harshness which they expressed to each other was just an outlet to get rid of their anger at the trap their lives were in. It ruined their marriage because they had no one to yell at but each other. I knew other families where the kids got the abuse, but we were too much loved for that. 16

Once I was about 16 and Mama and Daddy had had a particularly violent argument about the washing machine, which had broken down. Daddy was on the back porch— that's where the only water faucet was—trying to fix it and Mama had a washtub out there washing school clothes for the next day and they were screaming at each other. 17

Later that night everyone was in bed and I heard Daddy get up from the couch where he was reading. I looked out 18 from my bed across the hall into their room. He was standing right over Mama and she was already asleep. He pulled the blanket up and tucked it around her shoulders and just stood there and tears were dropping off his cheeks and I thought I could faintly hear them splashing against the linoleum rug.

Now they're divorced. 19

I had courses in college where housing was discussed, 20 but the sociologists never put enough emphasis on the impact living in substandard housing has on a person's psyche. Especially children's.

Small children have a hard time understanding poverty. 21 They want the same things children from more affluent families have. They want the same things they see advertised on television, and they don't understand why they can't have them.

Other children can be incredibly cruel. I was in elemen- 22 tary school in Georgia—and this is interesting because it is the only thing I remember about that particular school—when I was about eight or nine.

After Christmas vacation had ended, my teacher made 23 each student describe all his or her Christmas presents. I became more and more uncomfortable as the privilege passed around the room toward me. Other children were reciting the names of the dolls they had been given, the kinds of bicycles and the grandeur of their games and toys. Some had lists which seemed to go on and on for hours.

It took me only a few seconds to tell the class that I had 24 gotten for Christmas a belt and a pair of gloves. And then I was laughed at—because I cried—by a roomful of children and a teacher. I never forgave them, and that night I made my mother cry when I told her about it.

In retrospect, I am grateful for that moment, but I re- 25 member wanting to die at the time.

BUILDING VOCABULARY

1. For each expression in italics in Column A, select from Column B the best definition. On a separate sheet of paper, write the correct letter after each number.

Column A	*Column B*
1 one thing was *irregular* about me	**a** absolute
2 *conscious* of class	**b** object to
3 I *resent* the weakness	**c** way to express anger
4 houses that were *sweltering*	**d** are expected to
5 an *outlet for his rage*	**e** force
6 the *sheer* sense of futility	**f** not correct
7 they *traditionally* help mother	**g** very hot
8 the *impact* living in substandard housing has	**h** unbelievably
9 *incredibly* cruel	**i** aware
10 in *retrospect*	**j** looking back

UNDERSTANDING THE WRITER'S IDEAS

1. Why did the author never have a friend visit his house? How did he explain to his parents the fact that, at sixteen, he did not stay home any more?

2. Describe some of the situations Williams remembers about the houses in which he lived as a child. Why was it hard to keep the houses clean? Why was living in such a house so bad for the author's sisters? Why did the family keep moving around?

3. Why did the Williams family never "progress up the social ladder"? Why does the author stress the idea that his family was not shiftless?

4. Why, according to the author, was his parents' relationship damaged? Why were they frequently having violent arguments? How does Williams show the love his father had for his mother?

5. Why does the author believe that children can be incredibly cruel?

6. What is the meaning of the last paragraph? For which moment do you think the author is grateful, the moment in school or the moment in which his mother cried? Why would he be grateful for either of those moments?

UNDERSTANDING THE WRITER'S TECHNIQUES

1. What is Williams's main point in this essay? Which sentence expresses the writer's *thesis?*

2. What details does Williams offer to illustrate the fact that he lived in bad houses? Which details are clearest to you?

3. How does Williams illustrate how little money his father had for himself?

4. How does Williams illustrate the way his parents argued? What elements of narration do you find in that example? Where else does the author use narrative as part of an illustration?

5. In which illustrations does the writer use description? Where do you find good descriptive details in this essay? On the whole, though, the author has not used descriptive language very much. Why? Where would you have liked to see more concrete detail?

6. One way that the writer has for tying together his ideas is by frequently reminding the reader of his thesis. Review your response to question 1 above; then, find words or word groups later on in the essay that repeat the main point, either through the same words or through words that mean the same or similar things.

7. This essay is written in a very simple style. How does the writer achieve this simplicity? Is it the vocabulary? How would you describe it? Is it the sentence structure? What kinds of sentences does Williams write most of the time? What is the effect of the numerous short paragraphs? What is your reaction to the two paragraphs that have only one sentence in each of them?

8. Do the writer's illustrations support his main point success-fully? Why do you think he chose illustration as a way to develop his idea? Which illustration do you find most effec-tive? Why does he tell the story about his experience in school after Christmas one year at the *end* of the essay?

9. When a writer exaggerates emotions, he or she is often ac-cused of *sentimentality*. In sentimental writing the author plays with the reader's emotions simply for their own sake. Would you call Williams sentimental? Why? Which images deliberately convey an emotional stance? Do you feel as if he is exaggerating emotions here? Where has he *avoided* sentimentality when he might have played up the scene for its emotional content?

EXPLORING THE WRITER'S IDEAS

1. Williams says that it is hard to talk about his humiliating past experiences, and then he says, "I resent the weakness of these words to make you feel what it was really like." Do you agree that words are weak in conveying feeling to someone who might not have experienced that feeling? Williams is talking about *humiliation* and how words are not strong enough to make people feel it. What does *humil-iation* mean? Why does he find words inadequate to de-scribe it? What other feeling have you had that might be hard to convey in words? Despite the fact that the author complains about words, he writes, nonetheless, about his experiences. How do you explain that?

2. Has Williams fairly presented the condition of poverty in America? How does his own situation show some ways that a family or an individual may overcome certain fea-tures of poverty? Would you say that poverty in a rural area is the same as poverty in a large city like Atlanta, or Chicago, or New York?

3. Do you agree with Williams's analysis that his father and mother yelled at each other because they needed an outlet for their anger? Do you think the need for such an outlet

can force apart two people who love each other? Is it possible for people to fight constantly and still love each other? What instances from your own experience can you quote to demonstrate these points? How do you account for the fact that despite poverty and frequent fights, some parents stay together without divorcing?

4. The author suggests that housing plays an important part in the development of a person's psyche. Do you agree? Why? What ingredients would you list for perfect home conditions? Would you include anything other than simple physical conditions like walls that do not crumble or washing machines that work?

5. Williams's father and mother obviously sacrificed many of their own needs and comforts for their children. Do you believe that parents should make such sacrifices? Why or why not?

6. Do you agree that living in a bad house is more difficult for girls than boys? Why?

IDEAS FOR WRITING

Guided Writing

On a separate sheet of paper, fill in the blanks in this sentence and then write an essay of 350 to 500 words in which you use illustration to present your ideas:

Being _____ is a _____ experience for a young person.

1. For the blank spaces select words which reflect important aspects of your own experiences. You do not have to pick negative qualities: You might say, "Being *free* is an *essential* experience for a young person." Or, you might follow one of these other suggestions if you cannot think of one of your own. But be sure to avoid overused words like *good*, *bad*, *nice*, *fantastic*, or *interesting*.

    a. Being *lonely* is a *terrible* experience for a young person.

    b. Being *frightened* is an *unforgettable* experience for a young person.

    c. Being *loved* is a *vital* experience for a young person.

    d. Being "*different*" is a *sad* experience for a young person.

2. Use the sentence you have written as the thesis sentence of your paragraph. Build an introduction around it.

3. Illustrate your thesis with examples drawn from your own experience. Provide at least three illustrations.

4. If your illustrations require narrative, follow the techniques you learned in Chapter 4 about good narration.

5. If you have to use description, make sure you follow the suggestions in Chapter 3 about good description. Use concrete, sensory language to help your reader see your points clearly.

6. Connect the different illustrations in your essay by referring to the main point in your thesis sentence.

More Writing Projects

1. For a journal entry, consider your goals in life in light of your immediate family background. Support your general goals with specific examples drawn from family life.

2. Write a paragraph of illustration in which you show how certain conditions affected your parents' relationship. You might show the effect of *poverty* on their lives; or you might show the effect of *a city, love, religion, education, superstition, fear,* or *children* on their lives. Feel free to name any condition you choose.

3. Write an essay in which you provide illustrations to show the nature of poverty in your neighborhood, city, or state. You may want to select illustrations from your own experience or observation. Or, you might want to use other sources, like newspaper articles, books, magazines, or presentations on radio or television.

Tricks! Treats! Gangway!

Ray Bradbury

Ray Bradbury is noted for his science fiction writing—you may have read *Farenheit 451* or have seen the movie—but in this piece he is recalling a special time of year for a boy who grew up in the Midwest in the 1920s and 1930s. Illustrations drawn from his childhood show what a grand time Halloween really was in Illinois.

Words to Watch

corrupted (par. 2)   spoiled; ruined

induce (par. 2)   cause; bring about

climax (par. 6)   the highest point of interest or excitement

corn shocks (par. 7)   bunches of corn sheaves drawn together to dry

grisly renderings (par. 8)   terrifying examples

crump-backed (par. 8)   creased; humpbacked

caldron (par. 10)   a large kettle

banshee (par. 10)   a female spirit that warns of death

bereavements (par. 10)   losses of people through death

serpentines (par. 10)   coils

papier-mâché (par. 10)   a material made of paper pulp that can be molded into objects when moist

vulnerable (par. 15)   open to attack

disemboweled (par. 17)   with the bowels or entrails removed

Halloweens I have always considered wilder and richer 1
and more important than even Christmas morn. The dark and
lovely memories leap back at me as I see once again my
ghostly relatives, and the lurks and things that creaked stairs
or sang softly in the hinges when you opened a door.

For, you see, I have been most fortunate in the selection 2
of my aunts and uncles and midnight-minded cousins. My
grandma gave me her old black-velvet opera cape to cut into
batwings and fold about myself when I was eight. My aunt
gave me some white candy fangs to stick in my mouth and

make delicious and most terrible smiles. A great-aunt encouraged me in my witchcrafts by painting my face into a skull and stashing me in closets to induce cardiac arrest in passing cousins or upstairs boarders. My mother corrupted me completely by introducing me to Lon Chaney in *The Hunchback of Notre Dame* when I was three.

In sum, Halloween has always been *the* celebration for 3 me and mine. And those Halloweens in the late 1920s and early '30s come back to me now at the least scent of candle-wax or aroma of pumpkin pies.

Autumns were a combination of that dread moment 4 when you see whole windows of dime stores full of nickel pads and yellow pencils meaning School is Here—and also the bright promise of October, that stirring stuff which lurks in the blood and makes boys break out in joyful sweats, planning ahead.

For we *did* plan ahead in the Bradbury houses. We were 5 three families on one single block in Waukegan, Ill. My grandma and, until he died in 1926, grandpa, lived in the corner house; my mom and dad, and my brother Skip and I, in the house next south of that; and around the block my Uncle Bion, whose library was wise with Edgar Rice Burroughs and ancient with H. Rider Haggard.

1928 was one of the prime Halloween years. Everything 6 that was grandest came to a special climax that autumn.

My Aunt Neva was 17 and just out of high school, and 7 she had a Model-A Ford. "Okay, kiddo," she said around about October 20. "It's coming fast. Let's make plans. How do we use the attics? Where do we put the witches? How many corn shocks do we bring in from the farms? Who gets bricked up in the cellar with the Amontillado?"

"Wait, wait, wait!" I yelled—and we made a list. Neva 8 drew pictures and made paintings of the costumes we would all wear to make the holiday truly fascinating and horrible. That was Costume Painting Night. When Neva finished, there were sketches of Grandma as the nice mother in "The Monkey's Paw," paintings of my dad as Edgar Allan Poe, some fine grisly renderings of my brother as crump-backed Quasimodo, and myself playing my own xylophone skeleton as Dr. Death.

After that came, in one flying downpour, Costume Cut- 9
ting Night, Mask Painting Night, Cider Making Night, Candle
Dippling and Taffy Pulling Night, and Phonograph Playing
Night, when we picked the spookiest music. Halloween, you
see, didn't just stroll into our yards. It had to be seized and
shaped and *made* to happen!

My grandparents' home, then, was a caldron to which 10
we might bring hickory sticks that looked like witches' broken
arms and leaves from the family graveyard out where the banshee trains ran by at night souling the air with bereavements.
To their house, upstairs and down, must be fetched corn
shocks from fields just beyond the burying tombs, and pumpkins. And from Woolworth's, orange-black crepe serpentines,
and bags of black confetti which you tossed on the wind, yelling, "A witch just sneezed!" and papier-mâché masks that
smelled like a sour dog's fur after you had snuffed in and out
while running. All of it had to be fetched, carried, touched,
held, sniffed, crunched along the way.

October 29 and 30 were almost as great as October 31, 11
for those were the late afternoons, the cool, spicy dusks when
Neva and Skip and I went out for the Slaughter and final Gathering.

"Watch out, pumpkins!"   12

I stood by the Model A as the sun furnaced the western 13
sky and vanished, leaving spilled-blood and burnt-pumpkin
colors behind. "Pumpkins, if they had any brains, would hide
tonight!" said I.

"Yeah," said Skip. "Here comes the Smiler with the 14
Knife!" I beamed, feeling my Boy Scout knife in my pocket.

We reached our uncles' farms and went out to dance 15
around the corn shocks and grab great armfuls and wrestle
them like dry Indian ghosts back to the rumble seat. Then we
went back to get the harvest-moon pumpkins. They burrowed
in the cereal grass, but they could not escape the Smiler and
his friends. Then home, with the cornstalks waving their arms
wildly in the wind behind us, and the pumpkins thudding and
running around the floorboards trying to escape. Home toward a town that looked vulnerable under burning clouds,
home past real graveyards with real cold people in them, your

brother and sister, and you thinking of them suddenly and
knowing the true, deep sense of Halloween.

The whole house had to be done over in a few short,   16
wildly laughing hours. All staircases must be eliminated by
grabbing leaves out of dining-room tables and covering the
steps so you could only scrabble and slip up and then slide,
shrieking, down, down, down into night. The cellar must be
mystified with sheets hung on lines in a ghostly maze through
which giggling and screaming banshees must blunder and flee,
children suddenly searching for mothers, and finding spiders.
The icebox must be stashed with chicken viscera, beef hearts,
ox tongues, tripe, chicken legs and gizzards, so that at the
height of the party the participants, trapped in the coal cellar,
might pass around the "parts" of the dead witch: "Here's her
heart!...Here's her finger!...Here's her eyeball!"

Then, everything set and placed and ready, you run out   17
late from house to house to make certain-sure that each boy-
ghost remembers, that each girl-become-witch will be there
tomorrow night. Your gorilla fangs in your mouth, your
winged cape flapping, you come home and stand in front of
your grandparents' house and look at how great and spooky it
has become, because your sappy aunt and your loony brother
and you yourself have magicked it over, doused the lights, lit
all the disemboweled pumpkins and got it ready like a dark
beast to devour the children as they arrive through its open-
mouth door tomorrow night.

You sneak up on the porch, tiptoe down the hall, peer   18
into the dim pumpkin-lit parlor and whisper: "Boo."

And that's *it*.   19

Oh, sure, Halloween arrived. Sure, the next night was   20
wild and lovely and fine. Apples swung in doorways to be nib-
bled by two dozen hungry mice-children. Apples and gargling
kids almost drowned in water tubs while ducking for bites.

But the party was almost unimportant, wasn't it? Prepa-   21
ration was 70 percent of the lovely, mad game. As with most
holidays, the getting set, the gathering sulfur for the explosion, was sweeter, sadder, lovelier than the stampede itself.

That Halloween of 1928 came like the rusted moon up in   22
the sky—sailing, and then down like that same moon. And it

was over. I stood in the middle of my grandma's living room and wept.

On the way home across the lawn to my house, I saw the 23 pile of leaves I had made just that afternoon. I ran and dived in, and vanished. I lay there under the leaves, thinking. This is what it's like to be dead. Under grass, under dirt, under leaves. The wind blew and stirred the grand pile. Way out in farm country, a train ran past, wailing its whistle. The sound cut my soul. I felt the tears start up again. I knew if I stayed I would never get out of the grass and leaves; I would truly be dead. I jumped up, yelling, and ran in the house.

Later, I went to bed. "Darn," I said in the middle of the 24 night.

"Darn what?" asked my brother, awake in bed beside me. 25

"365 darn days until Halloween again. What if I die, 26 waiting?"

"Why, then," said my brother, after a long silence, 27 "you'll *be* Halloween. Dead people *are* Halloween."

"Hey," said I, "I never *thought* of that." 28

"Think," said my brother. 29

I thought: 365 days from now... 30

Gimme a pad, some paper. Neva, rev up that Model A! 31 Skip, hunch your back! Farmyards, grow pumpkins! Graveyards, shiver your stones! Moon, rise! Wind, hit the trees, blow up the leaves! Up, now, run! Tricks! Treats! Gangway!

And a small boy in midnight Illinois, suddenly glad to be 32 alive, felt something on his face. Between the snail-tracks of his tears...a smile.

And then he slept. 33

BUILDING VOCABULARY

1. Bradbury has often used informal expressions in this essay. First, explain the meaning of the words in italics in the following groups. Then suggest a word or phrase that an author who wished to be more formal might have used instead.

   a. *"Okay, kiddo"* (par. 7)

    b. when we picked the *spookiest* music (par. 9)
    c. your *sappy* aunt and your *loony* brother and yourself
       have *magicked* it over (par. 17)
    d. *Gangway!* (par. 31)

2. A number of figurative expressions (see Glossary) spark
this essay. In the list of examples of simile, metaphor, and
personification below, explain each figure. (Personification
is giving an object, thing, or idea lifelike or human qualities.) What is being compared to what? What other figures
can you find in the essay?

    a. Halloween, you see, didn't just stroll into our yards. It
       had to be seized and shaped and *made* to happen!
       (*personification*) (par. 9)
    b. My grandparents' home, then, was a caldron (*meta-
       phor*) to which we might bring hickory sticks that
       looked like witches' broken arms....(*simile*) (par. 10)
    c. where the *banshee* trains *ran* by at night (*metaphor*)
       (par. 10)
    d. papier-mâché masks that smelled *like* a *sour dog's fur*
       (*simile*) (par. 10)
    e. the sun *furnaced* the western sky (*personification*) and
       vanished, leaving *spilled blood* and *burnt-pumpkin col-
       ors* behind (*metaphor*) (par. 13)

UNDERSTANDING THE WRITER'S IDEAS

1. What part of the essay most clearly states the author's
purpose?

2. What two things did autumn signify to Bradbury?

3. What were some of the various activities for the Bradburys before October 29?

4. Why were October 29 and 30 almost as great as October
31? What did Bradbury and Neva and Skip do?

5. What is the "true, deep sense of Halloween"?

6. How did the young Bradburys change the house into a Halloween place?

7. How do the activities before Halloween compare with the activities after it? Which activities did the narrator prefer?

8. Why does the author say "Darn" in the middle of the night after Halloween? Why is he unhappy?

9. How does his brother ease Bradbury's unhappiness?

10. Why does the author smile just before he goes to sleep?

UNDERSTANDING THE WRITER'S TECHNIQUES

1. How is this essay an example of *illustration?* What examples does Bradbury give to show he has been lucky to have Halloween-minded relatives? How does he illustrate that "1928 was one of the prime Halloween years"?

2. The examples Bradbury offers to show the quality of the 1928 Halloween vary in their length and degree of development. Which examples are developed most fully?

3. In any essay of illustration the writer will often provide a simple listing of examples to demonstrate a point he is trying to make. Paragraph 15 offers a listing of details, but none of the examples is fully developed. Why does Bradbury use this technique here? What other paragraphs offer a listing of details to illustrate a point?

4. Check your responses to question 2 in Building Vocabulary. How do all the figurative expressions contribute to Bradbury's topic? How are most of the metaphors and similes related to the topic and to each other?

5. Underline some sentences that you think have the best sensory details. Where does the author use color? action? sound? smell?

6. Look at the last sentence in paragraph 10: "All of it had to

be fetched, carried, touched, held, sniffed, crunched along the way.'' Why has Bradbury used so many verbs? What is the effect upon the reader?

7. It is clear that the style here is simple, direct, and informal. Why has the writer chosen such a style? How is it related to the topic of the essay? to the character represented in it?

8. What is the meaning of the title? Why do you think Bradbury selected it? How does it reflect the personality of a young boy?

9. To enrich the meaning of an essay, a writer will often use *allusion,* a reference to some other work in literature (see Glossary). The statement made by Aunt Neva, ''Who gets bricked up in the cellar with the Amontillado?'' is an allusion to a short story by Edgar Allan Poe, ''The Cask of Amontillado.'' What is that brief story about? Why would Bradbury want to allude to Poe in this essay about Halloween? What other references to literature does the writer make (see paragraphs 2 and 8)? Explain them, or ask your instructor to if you are not familiar with them.

10. In what sequence has Bradbury presented the events in this essay? How has he used the order he selects to create a kind of suspense, a building up from minor events to major ones?

11. Before he states his purpose in this essay, Bradbury offers a couple of paragraphs of introduction. What information does he deal with in his introduction? How does that information set the stage for the real point of the essay?

EXPLORING THE WRITER'S IDEAS

1. It is a strong statement to make that Halloween is ''wilder and richer and more important than Christmas morn.'' Does Bradbury support his point well? In your experience, is Halloween so wild, so rich, and so important a holiday?

Why? In your family, is there a special holiday for which everyone makes grand preparations? Describe it.

2. Bradbury's wild view of Halloween was, to a large degree, encouraged by his relatives' reaction to the holiday too. How do your views about some holiday—like the Fourth of July, Thanksgiving, even Halloween—compare with or differ from the views of your relatives? In what cases do your relatives enrich your appreciation? detract from it?

3. What is the real significance of Halloween (check the dictionary or encyclopedia)? Why does that holiday still have a hold on the imagination of children today? Bradbury says that passing by a graveyard, he knew from the dead the "true deep sense of Halloween." Do you agree? Is *that* the true sense of Halloween?

4. Bradbury says in paragraph 21 that the party was less important than the preparation for it. Would you agree, in general, that the *preparation* for an event—such as a holiday, a wedding, a party—is often more important than the event itself? Explain your answer by giving a specific example from your own life.

5. How are Bradbury's feelings after Halloween is over typical of feelings any young child would have? How is he able to overcome these feelings? Are children generally able to cope with disappointment in the way young Bradbury has?

IDEAS FOR WRITING

Guided Writing

Write an essay of 500 words in which you *illustrate* the personal value of some holiday that you celebrate.

1. Write an introduction that builds up to your thesis, as Bradbury has. State in your thesis sentence just how you feel about the holiday. Is it a wild time, like Bradbury's

Halloween, or deeply religious, or just a time of nonstop fun with marvelous meals and parties?

2. Decide on an effective order for the illustrations you present. If you offer examples to support an idea about one particular holiday (the Christmas of 1986, for example) you might want to use chronology. If you present several examples (drawn over a number of years) to show why one holiday is important to you, you might again use chronology. But you might also want to tell the events according to their importance, saving the most important for last.

3. Depending upon how many examples you offer, develop your illustrations with enough details. Some of your illustrations will require expanded treatment; others will not. In any case, offer at least three examples to support your point.

4. Since you are drawing from your own experience, you will want to use sensory language—colors, smells, actions, sounds, images of touch. Try to use figurative expressions as effectively as Bradbury has.

5. After you present and develop your illustrations, discuss in your conclusion how you feel after the holiday is over.

More Writing Projects

1. Write a journal entry in which you show how one relative shared in the joys or pains of your childhood experiences. Select as illustration important moments that you can narrate clearly and in concrete, sensory language.

2. In recent years, Halloween has become a rather dangerous holiday where innocent children often come to harm by thoughtless, mean adults. Write an extended paragraph to illustrate the dangers of Halloween. Or, write an essay in which you show by means of illustration what steps your town or community takes to prevent Halloween accidents.

3. Do some research about a local festival, the preparations

for it, and the activities involved in its celebration. Or, you might choose to investigate a more remote festival in another part of the country, such as the chili contest in Texas, sausage festivals in Wisconsin, pie-eating contests associated with state fairs. After you collect your research, write a four- or five-paragraph essay illustrating different features of this festival.

Night Walker
Brent Staples

Brent Staples is a respected, experienced journalist. Yet, since his youth, he has instilled fear and suspicion in many just by taking nighttime walks to combat his insomnia. In this essay, which appeared in the *Los Angeles Times* in 1986, Staples explains how others perceive themselves as his potential victim simply because he is a black man in "urban America."

Words to Watch

affluent (par. 1)   wealthy
discreet (par. 1)   showing good judgment; careful
quarry (par. 2)   prey; object of a hunt
dismayed (par. 2)   discouraged
taut (par. 4)   tight; tense
warrenlike (par. 5)   like a crowded tenement district
bandolier (par. 5)   gun belt worn across the chest
solace (par. 5)   relief; consolation; comfort
retrospect (par. 6)   review of past event
ad hoc (par. 7)   unplanned; for the particular case at hand
labyrinthine (par. 7)   like a maze
skittish (par. 9)   nervous; jumpy
constitutionals (par. 10)   regular walks

1   My first victim was a woman—white, well dressed, probably in her early 20s. I came upon her late one evening on a deserted street in Hyde Park, a relatively affluent neighborhood in an otherwise mean, impoverished section of Chicago. As I swung onto the avenue behind her, there seemed to be a discreet, uninflammatory distance between us. Not so. She cast back a worried glance. To her, the youngish black man— a broad six feet two inches with a beard and billowing hair, both hands shoved into the pockets of a bulky military jacket—seemed menacingly close. She picked up her pace and

was soon running in earnest. Within seconds she disappeared into a cross street.

That was more than a decade ago. I was 22 years old, a 2 graduate student newly arrived at the University of Chicago. It was in the echo of that terrified woman's footfalls that I first began to know the unwieldy inheritance I'd come into—the ability to alter public space in ugly ways. It was clear that she thought herself the quarry of a mugger, a rapist, or worse. Suffering a bout of insomnia, however, I was stalking sleep, not defenseless wayfarers. As a softy who is scarcely able to take a knife to a raw chicken—let alone hold one to a person's throat—I was surprised, embarrassed, and dismayed all at once. Her flight made me feel like an accomplice in tyranny. It also made it clear that I was indistinguishable from the muggers who occasionally seeped into the area from the surrounding ghetto. I soon gathered that being perceived as dangerous is a hazard in itself: Where fear and weapons meet—and they often do in urban America—there is always the possibility of death.

In that first year, my first away from my hometown, I 3 was to become thoroughly familiar with the language of fear. At dark, shadowy intersections, I could cross in front of a car stopped at a traffic light and elicit the *thunk, thunk, thunk, thunk* of the driver—black, white, male, female—hammering down the door locks. On less traveled streets after dark, I grew accustomed to but never comfortable with people crossing to the other side of the street rather than pass me. Then there were the standard unpleasantries with policemen, doormen, bouncers, cabdrivers, and others whose business it is to screen out troublesome individuals *before* there is any nastiness.

I moved to New York nearly two years ago and I have 4 remained an avid night walker. In central Manhattan, the near-constant crowd covers the tense one-on-one street encounters. Elsewhere, things can get very taut indeed.

After dark, on the warrenlike streets of Brooklyn where 5 I live, I often see women who fear the worst from me. They seem to have set their faces on neutral, and with their purse straps strung across their chests bandolier-style, they forge ahead as though bracing themselves against being tackled. I understand, of course, that the danger they perceive is not a hallucination. Women are particularly vulnerable to street violence, and young black males are drastically overrepresented among the perpetrators of that violence. Yet these truths are no solace against the alienation that comes of being ever the suspect, an entity with whom pedestrians avoid making eye contact.

It is not altogether clear to me how I reached the ripe old 6 age of 22 without being conscious of the lethality nighttime pedestrians attributed to me. Perhaps it was because in Chester, Pa., the small, angry industrial town where I came of age in the 1960s, I was scarcely noticeable against a backdrop of gang warfare, street knifings, and murders. I grew up one of the good boys, had perhaps a half-dozen fistfights. In retrospect, my shyness of combat has clear sources. As a boy, I saw countless tough guys locked away; I have since buried several, too. They were babies, really—a teen-age cousin, a brother of 22, a childhood friend in his mid-20s—all gone down in episodes of bravado played out in the streets. I chose, perhaps unconsciously, to remain a shadow—timid, but a survivor.

The fearsomeness mistakenly attributed to me in public 7 places often has a perilous flavor. The most frightening of these confusions occurred in the late 1970s and early 1980s, when I worked as a journalist in Chicago. One day, rushing into the office of a magazine I was writing for with a deadline story in hand, I was mistaken for a burglar. The office manager called security and, with an ad hoc posse, pursued me through the labyrinthine halls, nearly to my editor's door. I had no way of proving who I was. I could only move briskly toward the company of someone who knew me.

Relatively speaking, however, I never fared as badly as 8 another black male journalist. He went to nearby Waukegan, Ill., a couple of summers ago to work on a story about a murderer who was born there. Mistaking the reporter for the killer, police officers hauled him from his car at gunpoint and but for his press credentials would probably have tried to book him. Such episodes are not uncommon. Black men trade tales like this all the time.

Over the years, I learned to smother the rage I felt at so 9 often being mistaken for a criminal. Not to do so would surely have led to madness. I now take precautions to make myself less threatening. I move about with care, particularly late in the evening. I give a wide berth to nervous people on subway platforms during the wee hours. If I happen to be entering a building behind some people who appear skittish, I may walk by, letting them clear the lobby before I return, so as not to seem to be following them. I have been calm and extremely congenial on those rare occasions when I've been pulled over by the police.

And on late-evening constitutionals I employ what has 10 proved to be an excellent tension-reducing measure: I whistle melodies from Beethoven and Vivaldi and the more popular classical composers. Even steely New Yorkers hunching toward nighttime destinations seem to relax, and occasionally they even join in the tune. Virtually everybody seems to sense that a mugger wouldn't be warbling bright, sunny selections from Vivaldi's "Four Seasons." It is my equivalent of the cowbell that hikers wear when they are in bear country.

BUILDING VOCABULARY

1. Use context clues to determine the meaning of each word in italics. Return to the appropriate paragraph in the essay for more clues. Then, if necessary, check your definitions in a dictionary and compare the dictionary meaning with the meaning you derived from the context.

   a. seemed *menacingly* close (par. 1)

      context _____

      dictionary _____

   b. I was *indistinguishable* from the muggers who occasionally *seeped* into the area (par. 2)

      context _____

      dictionary _____

   c. I have remained an *avid* night walker (par. 4)

      context _____

      dictionary _____

   d. they *forge* ahead (par. 5)

      context _____

      dictionary _____

   e. Women are particularly *vulnerable* to street violence (par. 5)

      context _____

      dictionary _____

   f. the *lethality* nighttime pedestrians attributed to me (par. 6)

      context _____

      dictionary _____

   g. episodes of *bravado* played out in the streets (par. 6)

      context _____

      dictionary _____

   h. I learned to *smother* the rage I felt...so often (par. 9)

      context _____

      dictionary _____

   i. I now take *precautions* to make myself less threatening (par. 9)

      context _____

      dictionary _____

   j. Even *steely* New Yorkers *hunching* toward nighttime destinations (par. 10)

      context _____

      dictionary _____

2. Reread paragraph 1. List all of the words suggesting action and all words involving emotion. What is the cumulative effect?

UNDERSTANDING THE WRITER'S IDEAS

1. Explain in your own words the incident Staples narrates in paragraph 1. Where does it take place? When? How old was the author at the time? What was he doing? During the incident, why did the woman "cast back a worried glance"? Was she really his "victim"? Explain. What was Staples's reaction to the incident?

2. How does Staples describe himself in paragraph 1? What point is he making by such a description?

3. What is the "unwieldy inheritance" mentioned in paragraph 2? What is Staples's definition of it? What is the implied meaning?

4. How would you describe Staples's personality? What does he mean when he describes himself as "a softy"? How does he illustrate the fact that he is "a softy"? Why did he develop this personality?

5. Explain the meaning of the statement, "I soon gathered that being perceived as dangerous is a hazard in itself" (par. 2).

6. What is "the language of fear" (par. 3)? What examples does Staples provide to illustrate this "language"?

7. Why did car drivers lock their doors when the author walked in front of their cars? How did Staples feel about that?

8. Where did Staples grow up? Did he experience the same reactions there to his nighttime walks as he did in Chicago? Why? How was Manhattan different from Chicago for the author? How was Brooklyn different from Manhattan?

9. What has been Staples's reaction to the numerous incidents of mistaken identity? How has he dealt with that reaction? What "precautions" does he take to make himself "less threatening"?

10. Summarize the example Staples narrates about the black journalist in Waukegan.

11. What has been the author's experiences with the police? Explain.

12. Does the author feel that all the danger people attribute to him when he takes night walks is unfair or unwarranted? Explain.

13. Why does his whistling selections from Beethoven and Vivaldi seem to make people less afraid of the author?

UNDERSTANDING THE WRITER'S TECHNIQUES

1. How do the title and opening statement of this essay grasp and hold the reader's interest?

2. What is Staples's thesis in this essay?

3. Reread the first paragraph. What *mood* or *tone* does Staples establish here? How? Does he sustain that mood? Is there a shift in tone? Explain.

4. How does the author use *narration* in paragraph 1 as a way to illustrate a point? What point is illustrated? Where else does he use narration?

5. What is the effect of the two-word sentence "Not so" in paragraph 1?

6. Staples uses *description* in this essay. Which descriptions serve as illustrations? Explain what ideas they support.

7. *Onomatopoeia* is the use of words whose sounds suggest their sense or action. Where in the essay does Staples use this technique? What action does the sound represent? Why does the author use this technique instead of simply describing the action?

8. What examples from Staples's childhood illustrate why he developed his particular adult personality?

9. Explain the meaning of the final sentence in the essay.

10. *Stereotypes* are oversimplified, uncritical judgments about people, races, issues, events, and so forth. Where in this essay does the author present stereotypes? For what purpose?

11. For whom was this article intended? Why do you think so? Is it written primarily for a white or black audience? Explain.

EXPLORING THE WRITER'S IDEAS

1. In this essay, Staples not only gives examples of his own experiences but also those of other black men. It is interesting, however, that he does not include examples of the experiences of black women. Why do you think he omitted these references? How do you feel about the omission? Are there any recent news stories, either in your city or in others, which might be included as such illustrations?

2. What prejudices and stereotypes about different racial and cultural groups do people in your community hold? Where do these prejudices and stereotypes come from? Do you think any are justified?

3. What everyday situations do you perceive as most dangerous? Why do you perceive them as such? How do you react to protect yourself? Do you feel your perceptions and reactions are realistic? Explain.

IDEAS FOR WRITING

Guided Writing

Write an essay that illustrates how something about your personality has been incorrectly perceived at some time or over a period of time.

1. Begin your essay by narrating a single incident that vividly illustrates the misperception. Begin this illustration with a statement that grabs and holds the reader's attention.

2. Explain the time context of this incident as it fits into your life or into a continuing misperception.

3. Describe and illustrate "who you really are" in relation to this misperception.

4. Explain how this misperception fits into a larger context outside your immediate, personal experience of it.

5. Write a series of descriptive illustrations to explain how this misperception has continued to affect you over time.

6. Explain how you first became aware of the misperception.

7. If possible, offer illustrations of others who have suffered the same or similar misperceptions of themselves.

8. Write about your emotional reaction to this overall situation.

9. Illustrate how you have learned to cope with the situation.

10. Give your essay a "catchy" title.

More Writing Projects

1. Usually stereotypes are thought of as negative. Illustrate at least three *positive* stereotypes in your latest journal entry.

2. Write a paragraph in which you illustrate your family's or friends' misconceptions about your girlfriend/boyfriend, wife/husband, or best friend.

3. Discuss in a small class group productive ways in which to solve the key problems raised by Brent Staples. Take notes, and then write an essay illustrating the problems and their possible solutions.

Death in the Open
Lewis Thomas

Dr. Lewis Thomas is president of the Memorial Sloan-Kettering Cancer Center in New York City. He has written numerous articles about science, medicine, and life structures and cycles geared for the lay reader. His observations often bring fascinating clarity to the cycles of life and death on our planet. The following essay, a brilliant inquiry into the "natural marvel" of death, appears in his book *Lives of a Cell* (1974), which won the National Book Award for Arts and Letters in 1975.

Words to Watch

voles (par. 1)   the members of any one of several species of small rodents

impropriety (par. 2)   an improper action or remark

progeny (par. 4)   descendants or offspring

mutation (par. 4)   a sudden genetic change

amebocytes (par. 4)   one-celled organisms

stipulated (par. 6)   made a special condition for

incongruity (par. 6)   something which is not consistent with its environment

conspicuous (par. 7)   very obvious

inexplicably (par. 7)   unexplainably

anomalies (par. 10)   irregularities

notion (par. 11)   an idea

detestable (par. 11)   hateful

synchrony (par. 11)   simultaneous occurrence

Most of the dead animals you see on highways near the cities are dogs, a few cats. Out in the countryside, the forms and coloring of the dead are strange; these are the wild creatures. Seen from a car window they appear as fragments, evoking memories of woodchucks, badgers, skunks, voles, snakes, sometimes the mysterious wreckage of a deer.

It is always a queer shock, part a sudden upwelling of

grief, part unaccountable amazement. It is simply astounding to see an animal dead on a highway. The outrage is more than just the location; it is the impropriety of such visible death, anywhere. You do not expect to see dead animals in the open. It is the nature of animals to die alone, off somewhere, hidden. It is wrong to see them lying out on the highway; it is wrong to see them anywhere.

Everything in the world dies, but we only know about it 3 as a kind of abstraction. If you stand in a meadow, at the edge of a hillside, and look around carefully, almost everything you can catch sight of is in the process of dying, and most things will be dead long before you are. If it were not for the constant renewal and replacement going on before your eyes, the whole place would turn to stone and sand under your feet.

There are some creatures that do not seem to die at all; 4 they simply vanish totally into their own progeny. Single cells do this. The cell becomes two, then four, and so on, and after a while the last trace is gone. It cannot be seen as death; barring mutation, the descendants are simply the first cell, living all over again. The cycles of the slime mold have episodes that seem as conclusive as death, but the withered slug, with its stalk and fruiting body, is plainly the transient tissue of a developing animal; the free-swimming amebocytes use this organ collectively in order to produce more of themselves.

There are said to be a billion billion insects on the earth 5 at any moment, most of them with very short life expectancies by our standards. Someone has estimated that there are 25 million assorted insects hanging in the air over every temperate square mile, in a column extending upward for thousands of feet, drifting through the layers of the atmosphere like plankton. They are dying steadily, some by being eaten, some just dropping in their tracks, tons of them around the earth, disintegrating as they die, invisibly.

Who ever sees dead birds, in anything like the huge num- 6 bers stipulated by the certainty of the death of all birds? A dead bird is an incongruity, more startling than an unexpected live bird, sure evidence to the human mind that something has gone wrong. Birds do their dying off somewhere, behind things, under things, never on the wing.

Animals seem to have an instinct for performing death 7
alone, hidden. Even the largest, most conspicuous ones find
ways to conceal themselves in time. If an elephant missteps
and dies in an open place, the herd will not leave him there;
the others will pick him up and carry the body from place to
place, finally putting it down in some inexplicably suitable location. When elephants encounter the skeleton of an elephant
out in the open, they methodically take up each of the bones
and distribute them, in a ponderous ceremony, over neighboring acres.

It is a natural marvel. All of the life of the earth dies, all 8
of the time, in the same volume as the new life that dazzles us
each morning, each spring. All we see of this is the odd stump,
the fly struggling on the porch floor of the summer house in
October, the fragment on the highway. I have lived all my life
with an embarrassment of squirrels in my backyard, they are
all over the place, all year long, and I have never seen, anywhere, a dead squirrel.

I suppose it is just as well. If the earth were otherwise, 9
and all the dying were done in the open, with the dead there to
be looked at, we would never have it out of our minds. We can
forget about it much of the time, or think of it as an accident to
be avoided, somehow. But it does make the process of dying
seem more exceptional than it really is, and harder to engage
in at the times when we must ourselves engage.

In our way, we conform as best we can to the rest of na- 10
ture. The obituary pages tell us of the news that we are dying
away, while the birth announcements in finer print, off at the
side of the page, inform us of our replacements, but we get no
grasp from this of the enormity of scale. There are 3 billion of
us on the earth, and all 3 billion must be dead, on a schedule,
within this lifetime. The vast mortality, involving something
over 50 million of us each year, takes place in relative secrecy.
We can only really know of the deaths in our households, or
among our friends. These, detached in our minds from all the
rest, we take to be unnatural events, anomalies, outrages. We
speak of our own dead in low voices; struck down, we say, as
though visible death can only occur for cause, by disease or
violence, avoidably. We send off for flowers, grieve, make

ceremonies, scatter bones, unaware of the rest of the 3 billion on the same schedule. All of that immense mass of flesh and bone and consciousness will disappear by absorption into the earth, without recognition by the transient survivors.

Less than a half century from now, our replacements will 11 have more than doubled the numbers. It is hard to see how we can continue to keep the secret, with such multitudes doing the dying. We will have to give up the notion that death is catastrophe, or detestable, or avoidable, or even strange. We will need to learn more about the cycling of life in the rest of the system, and about our connection to the process. Everything that comes alive seems to be in trade for something that dies, cell for cell. There might be some comfort in the recognition of synchrony, in the information that we all go down together, in the best of company.

BUILDING VOCABULARY

1. Thomas makes imaginative and often unique use of adjectival expressions. Explain the meaning of each of adjective in the phrases below:

   a. *queer* shock (par. 2)
   b. *unaccountable* amazement (par. 2)
   c. *visible* death (pars. 2 and 10)
   d. *transient* tissue (par. 4)
   e. *ponderous* ceremony (par. 7)
   f. *neighboring* acres (par. 7)
   g. *natural* marvel (par. 8)
   h. *vast* mortality (par. 10)
   i. *relative* secrecy (par. 10)
   j. *transient* survivors (par. 11)

2. An *idiom* is an expression that has a special meaning only when taken as a whole; taken separately, the words may not make sense. What are the meanings of the following idioms?

   a. upwelling of grief (par. 2)

  b. catch sight of (par. 3)
  c. on the wing (par. 6)
  d. in time (par. 7)
  e. no grasp...of (par. 10)
  f. for cause (par. 10)

UNDERSTANDING THE WRITER'S IDEAS

1. Why does Thomas feel that it is strange to see dead animals in the countryside? How are dead animals more varied in the country than in the city? According to Thomas, for what reason is it a shock to see a dead animal on the road?

2. In paragraph 3, Thomas suggests that death is often an "abstraction." What does he mean by this statement? How does he suggest we can make death something more real? In your own words, for what reasons does he suggest we accept the life-death cycle as a more concrete idea?

3. Why, according to Thomas, do single cells seem not to die?

4. What is the meaning of the question at the beginning of paragraph 6? How does it relate to the theme of the essay? To what does the author compare seeing a dead bird? Why does he call it an "incongruity"? How is it "sure evidence...that something has gone wrong"?

5. Explain the process of death among elephants as Thomas describes it.

6. Explain the meaning of "the odd stump" in paragraph 8. What two examples of "the odd stump" does Thomas offer?

7. What example from personal experience does Thomas give to show that dead animals seem "to disappear"?

8. Explain the meaning of the first sentence of paragraph 9. In your own words, tell why Thomas feels the way he does.

9. What is the "secret" in paragraph 11?

10. Thomas says, "In our own way, we conform as best we can to the rest of nature." What does he mean? What supporting examples does he offer? What is the result? What examples does Thomas give of our reactions to the death of other human beings?

11. Why does Thomas say we must change our attitude toward death? How does he suggest that we do so?

UNDERSTANDING THE WRITER'S TECHNIQUES

1. Study the introductory paragraphs. Why does the author offer several examples? Why is "the mysterious wreckage of a deer" an especially effective example?

2. What is Thomas's thesis in this essay? In what way is it reinforced by the concluding paragraph?

3. Are there any clear illustrations in paragraph 2? Why or why not? What is the effect? Explain the connection between paragraphs 2 and 3.

4. Paragraphs 4 to 8 use illustrations to support a series of generalizations or topic sentences. Put a check mark by the topic sentence in these paragraphs and identify the generalization. Then, analyze the illustrations used to support each one. Which examples are the most specific; the most visual; the most personal? Are there any extended examples?

5. How does paragraph 9 serve as a transition to the topic of paragraph 10? Why does Thomas use statistics in paragraph 10? How do they drive his point home?

6. The author's use of pronouns in this essay is interesting. First, trace the use of first-person pronouns ("I," "we," "my," "our"). Why does Thomas use such pronouns? Why is their use in paragraph 8 especially effective? Next,

consider Thomas's frequent use of the pronoun *it*. (Beginning writers are often instructed to minimize their use of such pronouns as *it, this,* and *that* because they are not specific and may leave the reader confused.) Explain what the word *it* stands for in paragraphs 2, 4, 8, and 9. Why does Thomas use a word whose meaning may be confusing?

7. Thomas uses *figurative language* (see Glossary) in this essay, particularly *similes* and *metaphors* (see Glossary). Explain in your own words the meanings of the following similes and metaphors:

    a. *the mysterious wreckage* of a deer (par. 1)
    b. episodes that seem *as conclusive as death* (par. 4)
    c. drifting through the layers of the atmosphere *like plankton* (par. 5)

8. We may say that the expression "dropping in their tracks" in paragraph 5 is a kind of pun. (A *pun* is a humorous use of a word or an expression that suggests two meanings.) What is the popular expression using the words *dropping* and *flies* that Thomas's phrase puns on?

9. Thomas makes use of a technique called "repetition with a difference," that is, saying *almost* the same thing for added emphasis. Explain how repetition with a difference adds effectiveness to the sentences in which each of the following expressions is used:

    a. alone, hidden (par. 7)
    b. each morning, each spring (par. 8)
    c. unnatural events, anomalies, outrages (par. 10)
    d. catastrophe, or detestable, or avoidable, or even strange (par. 11)

10. *Parallelism* is a type of sentence structure within a paragraph that creates a balance in the presentation of ideas and adds emphasis. It often uses a repeating pattern of subjects and verbs, prepositional phrases, questions, and so on (see Glossary). How does Thomas use parallelism in paragraph 3? paragraph 10? paragraph 11?

EXPLORING THE WRITER'S IDEAS

1. We might say that Thomas's title, "Death in the Open," is a double entendre (that is, has a double meaning; see Glossary). In what two ways may we interpret the phrase "in the open" as it relates to the contents of the essay? How do the two meanings relate to the philosophical points Thomas makes, especially in the two opening paragraphs and in the conclusion? Do you feel it is important to be more "open" about death? Why?

2. In paragraph 10, Thomas writes, "We speak of our own dead in low voices; struck down, we..." "Struck down" is used here as a *euphemism* (a word or phrase used to replace others that are upsetting or distasteful; see Glossary). What other euphemisms do we have for death? Euphemisms for dying are often used to explain death to children. Do you think it is right, or necessary, to use such "guarded language" with youngsters? Why? For what other words or expressions do we commonly use euphemisms?

3. At the end of the essay, Thomas suggests that we might be less comfortable with death if we understood it more clearly as a natural, common occurrence. What are your feelings about this philosophy?

4. According to Thomas's views in paragraph 9, because we don't often see dead animals "in the open," we are less prepared when we do encounter death. Do you think this reasoning is correct? Why or why not?

5. In paragraph 7 Thomas explains the process of death among elephants. What is your impression of the elephant herd's behavior at the death of one of its members? Why does Thomas call it "a natural marvel"? Have you ever heard the expression "the elephant dying grounds"? What does it mean?

6. Reread Gretel Ehrlich's "A River's Route." What similarities do you find between Thomas's and Ehrlich's visions of

nature? Discuss them with specific references to the essays. How are the visions different? alike? Which author's ideas most closely resemble your own view of nature?

IDEAS FOR WRITING

Guided Writing

Write an essay in which you illustrate "_____ in the open." Fill the blank with a word of your choice, a word that reflects some phenomenon, emotion, or idea that has features often hard to understand. You might write about birth in the open, concerts in the open, love in the open, fear in the open, war in the open, for example.

1. Develop an introduction with general examples that are relevant to your topic.

2. Add one or two paragraphs in which you speculate or philosophize on the phenomenon you are writing about.

3. Point out how the topic is most common throughout nature, society, or the world.

4. Give at least three extended examples that illustrate your topic.

5. Use the first-person pronouns "I" and "we" to add emphasis.

6. Illustrate ways in which we are generally unaware of certain features of the topic or tend to hide these features.

7. Try to include at least one statistic in your essay.

8. Use some idiomatic expression in your essay.

9. Conclude your essay with some examples of how and why we can become more "open" about the topic.

More Writing Projects

1. For a journal entry, use examples to tell of your first experiences with death. You may want to write about the death of a relative, a friend, an acquaintance, a celebrity, or a pet.

2. Visit a place in the countryside (or a park) for one hour. Make a written record as you walk around detailing all evidence of natural death that you come across. Then write an illustrative paragraph on natural death as you observed it.

3. In your library, explore various burial practices among different races, religions, or ethnic groups and write an essay in which you illustrate several of these practices.

SUMMING UP: CHAPTER 5

1. In this chapter, Randall Williams and Brent Staples each write richly illustrated essays that discuss very personal hardships in their lives. Write an essay of illustration about some adverse condition in your own life (either past or present) and give examples of how you have dealt with it or are dealing with it now.

2. The experiences of youth and childhood underlie the essays of Bradbury and Williams; yet these are clearly two very different essays based on dramatically different views of the world. Suppose that Bradbury could share a Halloween with the young Williams. How would the two react to the experience and to each other? Write an essay in which you explore a Bradbury-Williams Halloween.

3. From this chapter select the essay that you think best uses the mode of illustration. Write an essay in which you analyze the writer's techniques and strategies. Make specific references to the text.

4. Richard Selzer ("The Discus Thrower," pages 113–116),

Lewis Thomas ("Death in the Open," pages 200–203), and
George Orwell ("A Hanging," pages 156–161) all deal with
death and dying. Write your own essay about the issue,
drawing on points from these three authors to illustrate
your own position.

5. The world of the night, the environment of Staples's
   "Night Walker," challenges our senses and our perceptions, simply because it is so different from the typical day-
   time worlds we usually inhabit. What unusual nighttime experiences have you had? How do you feel about the night?
   Write an essay of illustration to address these questions.

CHAPTER 6

Comparison and Contrast

Comparison and contrast is a method of analyzing likenesses and differences between two or more subjects. Writers use comparison and contrast simply because it is often the best way to explain something. An object or an idea is often better understood only when its features stand next to those of another object or idea. We appreciate soccer when we compare it with football; we understand communism when we see it in the light of capitalism.

In *comparison,* the likenesses or similarities appear in a carefully organized manner. In *contrast,* the approach centers on the differences between two items. Often you will employ only comparison or only contrast in an essay, but it is also possible to combine both methods in the same paper.

You frequently make comparisons and contrasts in the course of your daily life. If you have to select an accounting course during registration, you might find out about the instructors for the various sections before making a choice. If you want to buy a new car, you might locate comparative performance ratings for models that interest you most. If you are planning to buy ten packages of hot dogs for a barbecue, you might check prices, product quality, and other details before choosing one brand over another. In all cases, you employ a thought pattern that sorts out likenesses and differences and arrives at a decision based on a comparative analysis of items.

The pattern of comparison and contrast in writing is

more carefully organized than the comparative pattern we employ in everyday situations. Yet both circumstances demand common sense. For one thing, any strong pattern of comparison and contrast treats items that are only in the same category or class. It makes little or no sense to compare an accounting teacher with a history teacher, a car with an ant, or a hot dog with a head of lettuce. Second, there always has to be a basis for your comparison; in other words, you compare or contrast two items in order to make a decision or choice about them. And third, you always try to deal with all-important aspects of the things being compared before arriving at a final determination. These common-sense characteristics of comparison and contrast apply to our pattern of thought as well as to our pattern of writing.

When you write a comparison and contrast essay, you should begin by identifying clearly the subjects of your comparison and by establishing the basis of your comparison. The thesis sentence performs this function for you ("Professor Smith is a better accounting teacher than Professor Williams because he is more experienced, more structured, and more intelligent"). There are three main ways to present your points of comparison (block, alternating, and combination); each will be dealt with in detail in this chapter. It is necessary to note here, however, that in presenting your material you should maintain a balance in the treatment of the two subjects in your comparison. In other words you do not want to devote most of your essay to subject A, and only a small fraction to subject B. Proper arrangement and balance of items in a comparative essay is a major consideration.

A Fable for Tomorrow

Rachel Carson

Rachel Carson wrote a number of books and articles in the 1950s and 1960s that alerted Americans to dangers facing our natural environment. In this section from *Silent Spring* (1962), look for the ways in which Carson establishes a series of contrasts for her imaginary American town.

Words to Watch

migrants (par. 2)   people, animals, or birds that move from one place to another

blight (par. 3)   a disease or condition that kills or checks growth

maladies (par. 3)   illnesses

moribund (par. 4)   dying

pollination (par. 5)   the transfer of pollen (male sex cells) from one part of the flower to another

granular (par. 7)   consisting of grains

specter (par. 9)   a ghost; an object of fear or dread

stark (par. 9)   bleak; barren; standing out in sharp outline

There was once a town in the heart of America where all 1 life seemed to live in harmony with its surroundings. The town lay in the midst of a checkerboard of prosperous farms, with fields of grain and hillsides of orchards where, in spring, white clouds of bloom drifted above the green fields. In autumn, oak and maple and birch set up a blaze of color that flamed and flickered across a backdrop of pines. Then foxes barked in the hills and deer silently crossed the fields, half hidden in the mists of the fall mornings.

Along the roads, laurel, viburnum and alder, great ferns 2 and wildflowers delighted the traveler's eye through much of the year. Even in winter the roadsides were places of beauty, where countless birds came to feed on the berries and on the seed heads of the dried weeds rising above the snow. The countryside was, in fact, famous for the abundance and variety of its bird life, and when the flood of migrants was pouring through in spring and fall people traveled from great distances to observe them. Others came to fish the streams, which flowed clear and cold out of the hills and contained shady pools where trout lay. So it had been from the days many years ago when the first settlers raised their houses, sank their wells, and built their barns.

Then a strange blight crept over the area and everything 3 began to change. Some evil spell had settled on the community: mysterious maladies swept the flocks of chickens; the cattle and sheep sickened and died. Everywhere was a shadow of death. The farmers spoke of much illness among their families. In the town the doctors had become more and more puzzled by new kinds of sickness appearing among their patients. There had been several sudden and unexplained deaths not only among adults but even among children, who would be stricken suddenly while at play and die within a few hours.

There was a strange stillness. The birds, for example— 4 where had they gone? Many people spoke of them, puzzled and disturbed. The feeding stations in the backyards were deserted. The few birds seen anywhere were moribund; they trembled violently and could not fly. It was a spring without voices. On the mornings that had once throbbed with the dawn chorus of robins, catbirds, doves, jays, wrens, and scores of other bird voices there was now no sound; only silence lay over the fields and woods and marsh.

On the farms the hens brooded, but no chicks hatched. 5 The farmers complained that they were unable to raise any pigs—the litters were small and the young survived only a few days. The apple trees were coming into bloom but no bees droned among the blossoms, so there was no pollination and there would be no fruit.

The roadsides, once so attractive, were now lined with 6 browned and withered vegetation as though swept by fire. These, too, were silent, deserted by all living things. Even the streams were now lifeless. Anglers no longer visited them, for all the fish had died.

In the gutters under the eaves and between the shingles 7

of the roofs, a white granular powder still showed a few patches; some weeks before it had fallen like snow upon the roofs and the lawns, the fields and streams.

No witchcraft, no enemy action had silenced the rebirth **8** of new life in this stricken world. The people had done it themselves.

This town does not actually exist, but it might easily **9** have a thousand counterparts in America or elsewhere in the world. I know of no community that has experienced all the misfortunes I describe. Yet every one of these disasters has actually happened somewhere, and many real communities have already suffered a substantial number of them. A grim specter has crept upon us almost unnoticed, and this imagined tragedy may easily become a stark reality we all shall know.

BUILDING VOCABULARY

1. In the second paragraph, find at least five concrete words that relate to trees, birds, and vegetation. How many of these objects could you identify? Look in a dictionary for the meanings of those words you do not know.

2. Try to identify the italicized words through the context clues (see Glossary) provided by the complete sentence.

   a. half-hidden in the *mists*. (par. 1)
   b. when the first settlers *raised* their houses. (par. 2)
   c. *stricken* suddenly while at play. (par. 3)
   d. the hens *brooded,* but no chicks hatched. (par. 5)
   e. *Anglers* no longer visited them, for all the fish had died. (par. 6)

UNDERSTANDING THE WRITER'S IDEAS

1. What is the quality of the world that Carson describes in her opening paragraph? If you had to describe it in just one or two words, which would you use?

2. What are some of the natural objects that Carson describes in her first two paragraphs? Why does she not focus on simply one aspect of nature—like animals, trees, or flowers?

3. How does Carson describe the "evil spell" that settles over the countryside?

4. What does Carson mean when she declares, "It was a spring without voices" (par. 4)? Why does she show that the critical action takes place in the springtime?

5. What do you think is the "white granular powder" that Carson refers to in paragraph 7? Why does she not explain what it is or where it came from?

6. In paragraph 9, the author states her basic point. What is it? Does she offer a solution to the problem that she poses?

UNDERSTANDING THE WRITER'S TECHNIQUES

1. What is the purpose of the description in this essay? Why does the writer use such vivid and precise words?

2. A *fable* is a story with a moral; in other words, a fable is a form of teaching narrative. How does Carson structure her narrative in this essay?

3. Where in this essay does Carson begin to shift from an essentially optimistic tone to a negative one?

4. Does Carson rely on comparison or contrast in this essay?

5. In this selection Carson uses what we call the *block method* of comparison and contrast. The writer presents all information about one subject, and then all information about a second subject, as in the following diagram:

```
┌─────────────┐
│             │
│      A      │
│             │
└─────────────┘
```

```
┌─────────────┐
│             │
│      B      │
│             │
└─────────────┘
```

   a. How does Carson use this pattern in her essay?

   b. Are there actually two subjects in this essay, or two different aspects of one subject? How does chronology relate to the block structure?

   c. Are the two major parts of Carson's essay equally weighted? Why or why not?

   d. In the second part of the essay, does Carson ever lose sight of the objects introduced in the first part? What new terms does she introduce?

6. How can you explain paragraphs 8 and 9—which do not involve narration, description, or comparison and contrast—in relation to the rest of the essay? What is the nature of Carson's conclusion?

EXPLORING THE WRITER'S IDEAS

1. Today chemicals are used to destroy crop insects, to color and preserve food, and to purify our water, among other things. Would Carson term this "progress"? Would you? Do you think that there are inadequate safeguards and controls in the use of chemicals? What recent examples of chemical use have made the news?

2. Why would you agree or disagree that factories and corporations should protect the environment that they use? Should a company, for example, be forced to clean up an entire river that it polluted? What about oil spills?

3. Have there been any problems with the use of chemicals and the environment in your own area? Describe them. How do local citizens feel about these problems?

4. Do you think that it will be possible in the future for Americans "to live in harmony" with their natural surroundings? Why do you believe what you do?

IDEAS FOR WRITING

Guided Writing

Write a fable (an imaginary story with a moral) in which you contrast one aspect of the life of a person, community, or nation with another.

1. Begin with a phrase similar to Carson's "There was once...." so that the reader knows you are writing a narrative fable.

2. Relate your story to an American problem.

3. Use the block method in order to establish your contrast. Write first about one aspect of the topic and then about the other.

4. Use sensory detail in order to make your narrative clear and interesting.

5. Make certain that you establish an effective transition as you move into the contrast.

6. In the second part of your essay, be sure to refer to the same points you raised in the first part.

7. Use the conclusion to establish the "moral" of your fable.

More Writing Projects

1. Contrast in a journal entry a place you know well, one that has changed for better or worse. Explain the place as it once was, and as it is now. Use concrete images that appeal to color, action, sound, smell, and touch.

2. Examine in two block paragraphs the two sides of a specific ecological issue today—for instance, acid rain, the global warming trend, or the use of nuclear energy.

3. Using the block method, compare and contrast Carson's fable with the fable you wrote in Guided Writing.

The Two Ismo's

Russell Baker

Russell Baker's witty column "The Sunday Observer" runs each week in *The New York Times* and provides readers with numerous insights into modern life. In this 1982 piece, he treats us to a tongue-in-cheek comparison between two kinds of social behavior in American cities.

Words to Watch

doctrines (par. 1)   beliefs that are taught as truths
adherents (par. 1)   believers in a particular doctrine
dogma (par. 1)   a tenet or code of beliefs
blitz (par. 2)   a fast, intensive raid or campaign
recourse (par. 5)   a source of aid or assistance
primp (par. 8)   to dress in a careful or finicky manner
Ou sont les neiges d'antan? (par. 11)   French for "Where are the snows of yesteryear?"

American city life is now torn by two violently opposed 1 doctrines of social conduct. One is machismo. Its adherents pride themselves on being "machos." The opposing dogma is quichismo (pronounced "key shizmo"), and its practitioners call themselves quiche-o's (pronounced "key shows").

A good study of a quichismo victory over machismo in 2 an urban war zone can be found in Philip Lopate's "Quiche Blitz on Columbus Avenue," included in his recent book, "Bachelorhood." Curiously, however, Mr. Lopate refers to the quichismo doctrine by its French name, *quichisme.*

In doing so he unwittingly reveals that he is himself a 3 quiche-o of the highest order, for no macho would dream of using a French word when discussing philosophy, and even the average quiche-o would avoid a word as difficult to pronounce as *quichisme* for fear of getting it wrong and being sneered at as unquiche-o.

For practitioners of quichismo there is no defense 4

219

against being sneered at, and they live in dread of it. The machismo adherent, on the other hand, positively enjoys being sneered at since it entitles him to punch the sneerer in the nose, a ritual act ceremonially confirming that he is truly macho.

When a quiche-o is sneered at, his only recourse is to jog 5 until he achieves a higher sense of total fulfillment. This is one reason behind the machismo slogan, "Machos have more fun."

Maybe so, quiche-o's say, but machos don't have 6 French dry cleaning or white bucks. Machos prefer no dry cleaning at all though they sometimes get their clothes pressed if they've slept in them all week and want to impress females during the weekend.

Machos impress females by taking them to bars after 7 opening the top four buttons on their shirts to show off the hair on their chests. Quiche-o women impress males by inviting them to dinner and serving salad from the carry-out gourmet shop, followed by a kiwi fruit. There are no macho women. If there were they would serve pigs' feet and beer because machos believe that real people don't eat salad, kiwi fruit or anything else that comes from gourmet shops.

Quiche-o people buy Swedish toothpaste at gourmet 8 drugstores, Italian loafers at gourmet shoe shops, newspapers at gourmet newsstands and dogs at gourmet pet centers. Afterwards they have them wormed by gourmet veterinarians. They also go to the islands for a month or two, especially Bermuda, St. Bart's, Barbados and Trinidad. Machos also go to the islands—Coney and Long—usually for a Sunday afternoon. To primp for these vacations, machos first go to the barber.

No quiche-o has set foot in a barber shop for the last 20 9 years. He goes to a gourmet hairdresser for a styling, then, before jetting off to the islands, goes to the gourmet luggage shop for suitcases covered with the initials of gourmet designers. The macho packs a change of underwear and a drip-dry shirt in a zippered plastic briefcase his uncle brought back from a 1977 convention of T-shirt salesmen.

Quiche-o's are always redecorating. Machos are always 10 repainting the room that has the TV set in it. When a macho's couch and chairs are finally ruined he goes to a department store and buys "a suit of furniture." Quiche-o furniture is never ruined, but it goes out of style every two years, and when it does the quiche-o goes to an environmental systems boutique and buys a new environment.

No quiche-o would ever take a walk in his undershirt un- 11 less it had something amusing printed on it, like *"Ou sont les neiges d'antan?"* No macho would ever appear on the beach in a male bikini. No quiche-o would ever wear black U.S. Keds with white soles and laces. No macho would ever walk into a hardware store and ask for a wok spatula.

Machos don't see anything funny about New Jersey. 12 Quiche-o's never laugh at people who drive Volvos, people who pay $5.50 for a hamburger or quiche jokes, unless they're told by another quiche-o. Quiche-o's like a lot of butcher block and stainless steel. Machos like a lot of children.

Machos never bake carrot cake and don't go out with 13 women who do. Quiche-o's are proud of their cholesterol levels and never belch in public and never go out with women who do since they recognize them instantly as unquiche-o and unlikely ever to serve them a salad dinner that concludes with a kiwi fruit.

BUILDING VOCABULARY

1. Baker uses a number of *geographical* references in paragraph 8. Identify the following locations:

Bermuda
St. Bart's (St. Bartholomew's Island)
Barbados
Trinidad
Coney Island
Long Island

2. Define the following foods or cooking utensils mentioned in the essay:

quiche
kiwi fruit
pig's feet

wok spatula
butcher block
carrot cake

3. Match the words in Column A (all from paragraph 4) with the correct meanings in Column B.

Column A
1 practitioner
2 sneered at
3 ritual
4 ceremonially
5 confirming

Column B
a supporting
b showed contempt
c one who engages in some technique
d praying
e system of rites
f showed great pleasure
g ritualistically

UNDERSTANDING THE WRITER'S IDEAS

1. What is quichisme? What is machismo?

2. What does Baker mean when he identifies Philip Lopate as "a quiche-o of the highest order"?

3. How do the two groups respond to sneering?

4. What is the attitude of each group toward clothing? How would you characterize the tasks of each group? Why are there no macho women?

5. For what reasons do both machos and quiche-o's avoid saying the word "quichisme"?

6. In what ways do macho men and quiche-o men try to impress women? How does each group prepare for vacations?

UNDERSTANDING THE WRITER'S TECHNIQUES

1. What is the thesis statement of this essay? What two things are identified as the subjects for treatment? Is the essay a

contrast or a *comparison?* What key words does Baker use to indicate that he is dealing primarily with similarities or differences?

2. Along with the block method (see page 216), comparison and contrast essays can also be organized according to the *alternating method.* When using the alternating method, the writer gives a point-by-point treatment of both subjects A and B. The effect looks like this:

| A |
| B |

| A |
| B |

| A |
| B |

In other words, some discussion of both subjects A and B is presented in each paragraph. Something is said about one and then about the other subject as the writer discusses some specific feature of his or her topic.

  a. How does the author use the alternating method in paragraph 1? How does he achieve *balance* between subjects A and B in the opening paragraph?
  b. How is the one-sentence paragraph 3 ("In doing so...") a good example of the alternating method?
  c. Identify sentences in paragraphs 10 and 11 that reflect Baker's use of the alternating method.
  d. For each of paragraphs 3 to 13, identify the primary focus for contrast between each of the subjects.
  e. What advantages does the alternating method have over the block method? What disadvantages does the alternating method have?

3. How does Baker use definition (see pages 244–245) in the opening paragraph of this essay? How does he use *illustration* (see pages 169–170) in the essay?

4. With the alternating method it is very important to use smooth-flowing and interesting *transitions* within and between paragraphs. In this essay, one of Baker's main transition techniques is the use of *repetition with a difference* (see page 206). How does he use this method in paragraphs 7, 8, 10, 11, and 12? What key word does he repeat to make the transition between paragraphs 8 and 9?

5. A satire (see Glossary) is a humorous treatment of a subject in order to expose the subject's vices, follies, or stupidities. Why may this essay be considered a satire on city dwellers? What follies does Baker point up for each of the two groups he is dealing with?

6. As one technique for humor, Baker uses repetition of the word "gourmet" in paragraphs 7 through 9. What does the word mean? How does the repetition achieve the humorous effects Baker wants? What other repetitions do you find here?

7. Baker plays on words as another technique to achieve humor. How does he achieve humorous effects in paragraph 8 by playing on the word "islands"? What word is he playing on within the phrase "a suit of furniture" in paragraph 10? Why does he place the phrase in quotation marks? Why does he use a question in French in paragraph 11?

8. Why does Baker refer to Philip Lopate's book? Might Baker have eliminated paragraphs 2 and 3? Why did he choose to include those paragraphs in the essay?

9. Whom do you think is the intended audience for this essay? Why?

EXPLORING THE WRITER'S IDEAS

1. Baker is implying that people's social behavior reflects the kind of status they want to achieve in society. Often that

behavior makes them affected—that is, they pretend to certain tastes and preferences just because fashion dictates them. What affected people have you met? What kind of social behavior would you expect from someone who wanted to be thought of as an intellectual, as upper class, as radical, or as a great lover, for example?

2. In the last decade gourmet shops and boutiques have grown in numbers, and more and more people are interested in purchasing items there. How do you account for the popularity of such places? Why might you choose to purchase something at a gourmet shop or a boutique? Why is Baker poking fun at those people who buy at boutiques and gourmet shops?

3. A best-selling humor book of a few years ago was *Real Men Don't Eat Quiche* by Bruce Feirstein. The author's main premise was like Baker's but with a difference. Feirstein believes that not only are quiche-o's and machos at opposite ends of the social scale but also that machos are the much more desirable group to belong to. If you had to choose, would you choose to be macho or quiche-o? Why? Is it necessary to choose between the two, or is it possible to combine features from both groups?

4. Baker as a city dweller understandably focuses his essay on urban personalities. How could you expand the idea of quiche-o's and machos to suburban areas? Rural farm areas? Small towns?

IDEAS FOR WRITING

Guided Writing

Write an essay in which you contrast two types of people in the area where you live.

1. In your first paragraph, write a clear thesis statement that uses key words to indicate the contrast your essay will make.

2. Give the two types of people special names and define those names to help the reader understand your special use of them.

3. Use the alternating method of development in your essay.

4. Base your essay on personal observation of the two types of people.

5. Make sure each paragraph has a special point of contrast around which you organize your examples.

6. Use repetition with a difference as one device to accomplish smooth transitions between subjects in your discussions.

7. Give clear-cut examples of how each group would act in certain situations.

8. Try to cite at least one other writer who has discussed the same subject.

9. If possible, aim for some humorous effects by using satire, repetition, or plays on words.

More Writing Projects

1. In your journal, develop lists for two types of college students—"jocks" and "nerds."

2. In one or two paragraphs, compare or contrast two teachers with distinctly different qualities.

3. Using the alternating method, write an essay in which your generation and your parents' generation did something such as dating, throwing a party, preparing for the future, or some such activity.

The Tapestry of Friendships

Ellen Goodman

Syndicated columnist for the *Boston Globe, Washington Post,* and other newspapers, Ellen Goodman presents a thought-provoking comparison of two categories of human relations in this selection from her book *Close to Home.* Notice especially how she blends personal experience with a clipped, direct journalistic style to examine the ways in which "friends" and "buddies" relate to one another.

Words to Watch

slight (par. 1)   not having much substance

fragility (par. 2)   condition of being easily broken or harmed

resiliency (par. 2)   condition of being able to recover easily from misfortune or change

binge (par. 4)   spree; indulgence

atavistic (par. 5)   manifesting a throwback to the past

culled (par. 5)   chosen from

palpably (par. 8)   in a way that can be touched or felt

loathsome (par. 10)   detestable; hateful

wretched (par. 13)   miserable; woeful

claustrophobic (par. 16)   uncomfortable at being confined in small places

It was, in many ways, a slight movie. Nothing actually 1 happened. There was no big-budget chase scene, no bloody shoot-out. The story ended without any cosmic conclusions.

Yet she found Claudia Weill's film *Girlfriends* gentle and 2 affecting. Slowly, it panned across the tapestry of friendship—showing its fragility, its resiliency, its role as the connecting tissue between the lives of two young women.

When it was over, she thought about the movies she'd 3 seen this year—*Julia, The Turning Point* and now *Girlfriends.* It seemed that the peculiar eye, the social lens of the cinema, had drastically shifted its focus. Suddenly the Male Buddy movies had been replaced by the Female Friendship flicks.

This wasn't just another binge of trendiness, but a kind 4 of *cinéma vérité*. For once the movies were reflecting a shift, not just from men to women but from one definition of friendship to another.

Across millions of miles of celluloid, the ideal of friend- 5 ship had always been male—a world of sidekicks and "pardners," of Butch Cassidys and Sundance Kids. There had been something almost atavistic about these visions of attachments—as if producers culled their plots from some pop anthropology book on male bonding. Movies portrayed the idea that only men, those direct descendants of hunters and Hemingways, inherited a primal capacity for friendship. In contrast, they portrayed women picking on each other, the way they once picked berries.

Well, that duality must have been mortally wounded in 6 some shoot-out at the You're OK, I'm OK Corral. Now, on the screen, they were at least aware of the subtle distinction between men and women as buddies and friends.

About 150 years ago, Coleridge had written, "A wom- 7 an's friendship borders more closely on love than man's. Men affect each other in the reflection of noble or friendly acts, whilst women ask fewer proofs and more signs and expressions of attachment."

Well, she thought, on the whole, men had buddies, while 8 women had friends. Buddies bonded, but friends loved. Buddies faced adversity together, but friends faced each other. There was something palpably different in the way they spent their time. Buddies seemed to "do" things together; friends simply "were" together.

Buddies came linked, like accessories, to one activity or 9 another. People have golf buddies and business buddies, college buddies and club buddies. Men often keep their buddies in these categories, while women keep a special category for friends.

A man once told her that men weren't real buddies until 10 they'd been "through the wars" together—corporate or athletic or military. They had to soldier together, he said.

Women, on the other hand, didn't count themselves as friends until they'd shared three loathsome confidences.

Buddies hang tough together; friends hang onto each 11 other.

It probably had something to do with pride. You don't 12 show off to a friend; you show need. Buddies try to keep the worst from each other; friends confess it.

A friend of hers once telephoned her lover, just to find 13 out if he were home. She hung up without a hello when he picked up the phone. Later, wretched with embarrassment, the friend moaned, "Can you believe me? A thirty-five-year-old lawyer, making a chicken call?" Together they laughed and made it better.

Buddies seek approval. But friends seek acceptance.   14

She knew so many men who had been trained in re- 15 straint, afraid of each other's judgment or awkward with each other's affection. She wasn't sure which. Like buddies in the movies, they would die for each other, but never hug each other.

She'd reread *Babbitt* recently, that extraordinary cata- 16 logue of male grievances. The only relationship that gave meaning to the claustrophobic life of George Babbitt had been with Paul Riesling. But not once in the tragedy of their lives had one been able to say to the other: You make a difference.

Even now men shocked her at times with their descrip- 17 tion of friendship. Does this one have a best friend? "Why, of course, we see each other every February." Does that one call his most intimate pal long distance? "Why, certainly, whenever there's a real reason." Do those two old chums ever have dinner together? "You mean alone? Without our wives?"

Yet, things were changing. The ideal of intimacy wasn't 18 this parallel playmate, this teammate, this trenchmate. Not even in Hollywood. In the double standard of friendship, for once the female version was becoming accepted as the general ideal.

After all, a buddy is a fine life-companion. But one's 19 friends, as Santayana once wrote, "are that part of the race with which one can be human."

BUILDING VOCABULARY

1. The first six paragraphs of this essay use many words and expressions related to film. Explain the meaning or connotation of each of the following such words and expressions. Pay special attention to their context in Goodman's article.

   a. big-budget chase scene (par. 1)
   b. bloody shoot-out (par. 1)
   c. it panned (par. 2)
   d. the peculiar eye (par. 3)
   e. the social lens of the cinema (par. 3)
   f. shifted its focus (par. 3)
   g. flicks (par. 3)
   h. *cinéma vérité* (par. 4)
   i. millions of miles of celluloid (par. 5)
   j. plots (par. 5)
   k. on the screen (par. 6)

2. Write *antonyms* (words with opposite meanings) for the following words in the Words to Watch section. Then use each antonym in a sentence.

   slight
   fragility
   resiliency
   atavistic
   palpably
   loathsome
   wretched

UNDERSTANDING THE WRITER'S IDEAS

1. What is the main idea of this essay? Which sentence serves as the thesis statement? What two subjects form the basis for comparison in this essay?

2. What does the author mean when she writes that the movie "ended without any cosmic conclusions" (par. 1)? Is she being critical or descriptive in this statement? Explain.

3. Who is the "she" first mentioned at the beginning of paragraph 2 and referred to throughout the essay?

4. What pattern of change does the author note in the same-year releases of the films *Julia, The Turning Point,* and *Girlfriends?* Does she feel this is a superficial or real change? How do you know?

5. What is the author's main complaint about the ways in which movies have traditionally portrayed friendships? What example does she offer? Explain the meaning of the sentence, "Movies portrayed the idea that only men, those direct descendants of hunters and Hemingway, inherited a primal capacity for friendship" (par. 5). What is "male bonding"?

6. What two allusions does Goodman combine to produce the expression "the You're OK, I'm OK Corral"? Explain the full meaning of the sentence in which that expression appears.

7. According to Goodman, what is the main difference between male and female friendships? Which type do you think she prefers? Why?

8. What quality of friendships is suggested by the title?

9. What is meant by "the double standard of friendship"?

10. How does Goodman's conclusion support her preference for male or female types of friendships?

UNDERSTANDING THE WRITER'S TECHNIQUES

1. Like most well-constructed essays, this one has three clear sections: introduction, body, conclusion. Specify which paragraphs make up each section. Does this seem a good balance? Explain.

2. How would you describe the effect of the writing in the opening paragraph? Does it give you a clear idea of the subject of this essay? Is that important in this essay? Why?

3. In the beginning, Goodman uses a number of *metaphors* (see Glossary), including the title. Explain the following metaphors in your own words:

   a. The Tapestry of Friendships (title and par. 2)
   b. the connecting tissue between the lives of two young women (par. 2)

   In what ways do the two metaphors convey similar ideas? Which do you prefer? Why?

4. What is the effect of the use of the pronoun "she" throughout the essay? Why do you suppose Goodman chose to use "she" rather than "I"?

5. Among the main purposes of a comparison or contrast essay are (a) *to explain* something unfamiliar in terms of something already familiar, (b) *to understand* better two things already known by comparing them point for point, (c) *to evaluate* the relative value of two things. Which of these objectives most closely describes Goodman's purpose? Explain.

6. Which of the three methods of writing comparison essays—block, alternating, or combination—dominates in this essay? Explain.

7. Who is the intended audience for this essay? Why?

8. There are four literary *allusions* (see Glossary) in this essay: (a) Hemingway, (b) Coleridge, (c) *Babbitt,* and (d) Santayana. Identify each and explain why Goodman chose to include them.

9. Throughout the essay, Goodman uses short, direct sentences and relatively short paragraphs. What is her purpose for that? Does it allow for adequate development of this subject matter? Why or why not?

10. At what points does Goodman make use of relatively *extended illustrations*?

11. Goodman chooses to point out the contrasts between her two subjects in short, directly contrasting sentences or

clauses, beginning with paragraph 8: "...men had buddies, while women had friends. Buddies bonded, but friends loved."

Go through the essay and list all such opposing statements. How do these statements affect your reading of the essay?

12. How does Goodman use *repetition* as a transitional device in the essay?

13. What is the effect of the series of questions that comprise paragraph 17? How is it like a dialogue? Why are some of the questions in quotation marks and others not?

14. A good conclusion for an essay of comparison or contrast will either (a) restate the main idea, (b) offer a solution, or (c) set a new frame of reference by generalizing from the thesis. Which approach or combination of approaches does Goodman use? How effective is her conclusion? Why?

EXPLORING THE WRITER'S IDEAS

1. Do you agree with Goodman's basic distinction between female and male friendships? How closely does it relate to your own experiences? Do you have any friendships that don't fit into either of the two categories she describes?

2. In the beginning of this essay, Goodman refers to the "binge of trendiness" toward pop anthropology and psychology. Such books, periodicals, and syndicated columns as *Psychology Today, Women Who Love Too Much,* and Dr. Joyce Brothers—to name just a few—are widely read. What's more, radio call-in shows offering on-the-air advice (such as *The Dr. Ruth Show* and *The Toni Grant Show*) are nationally syndicated and immensely popular.

What are your feelings about such media presentations? Do you think they are useful? Are there instances when they might be harmful? Why do you think they are so popular?

3. Why does Goodman avoid any discussion of friendship between men and women? Do you feel this omission in any way affects the forcefulness or completeness of her essay? Explain.

IDEAS FOR WRITING

Guided Writing

Write an essay that contrasts the ways in which men and women perceive or approach some aspect of interpersonal relationships. You might choose, for example, dating, parenting, expressing affection, or divorce.

1. Begin with a description of some depiction of the subject in the contemporary media (for example, a film, TV program, book, video, commercial).

2. Staying with the same medium, give other examples that illustrate how the medium is shifting away from the old, established ways of viewing the subject. Use language specific to that medium.

3. In the rest of your introductory section, use a few metaphors.

4. As a transitional device, cite a statement from a well-known authority (not necessarily on the particular subject).

5. State the main idea of your essay at the beginning of the body section.

6. Develop your contrast using short, direct, opposing statements that summarize the different approaches of men and women.

7. Develop at least two of these opposing statements through extended personal examples.

8. Make your preference for either approach *implicit* (subtle) rather than *explicit* (obvious) throughout.

9. Make the last paragraph of the body of your essay a series of questions that form an internal dialogue.

10. Conclude with a statement that generalizes the main differences and your evaluation of the two approaches.

More Writing Projects

1. Compare and contrast in a journal entry two films or books, plays, or television programs that portray contrasting views of friendship, love, or marriage.

2. Compare in one or two paragraphs the ways you relate to two close friends.

3. Write an essay that compares and/or contrasts what was considered attractive in two different time periods in America. You may either focus your essay on one sex or attempt to discuss both.

Fairy Tales and Modern Stories

Bruno Bettelheim

Bruno Bettelheim was born in Austria in 1903 and came to the United States in 1939. For many years he was one of the major child psychologists in the world. In this selection, taken from *The Uses of Enchantment* (1976), Bettelheim compares fairy tales and realistic stories, analyzing the effect that they have on both children and adults. As you read this essay, keep in mind the various stories he is comparing.

Words to Watch

realistic (par. 1)   having to do with real things

props (par. 1)   supports

elaboration (par. 1)   a thing worked out in detail

rankled (par. 1)   caused pain or resentment

idyllic (par. 2)   pleasing and simple

protracted (par. 2)   drawn out

gratifications (par. 2)   things that cause satisfaction

sustained (par. 3)   maintained; supported; comforted

effected (par. 4)   brought to pass; accomplished

consolation (par. 5)   comfort

vagaries (par. 5)   odd notions; unexpected actions

extricating (par. 5)   setting free; getting out of; releasing

prevail (par. 5)   to triumph; to gain the advantage

asocial (par. 5)   not social

The shortcomings of the realistic stories with which 1 many parents have replaced fairy tales is suggested by a comparison of two such stories—"The Little Engine That Could" and "The Swiss Family Robinson"—with the fairy tale of "Rapunzel." "The Little Engine That Could" encourages the child to believe that if he tries hard and does not give up, he will finally succeed. A young adult has recalled how much impressed she was at the age of seven when her mother read her this story. She became convinced that one's attitude indeed affects one's achievements—that if she would now approach a task with the conviction that she could conquer it, she would succeed. A few days later, this child encountered in first grade a challenging situation: she was trying to make a house out of paper, gluing various sheets together. But her house continually collapsed. Frustrated, she began to seriously doubt whether her idea of building such a paper house could be realized. But then the story of "The Little Engine That Could" came to her mind; twenty years later, she recalled how at that moment she began to sing to herself the magic formula "I think I can, I think I can, I think I can..." So she continued to work on her paper house, and it continued to collapse. The project ended in complete defeat, with this little girl convinced that she had failed where anybody else could have succeeded, as the Little Engine had. Since "The Little Engine That Could" was a story set in the present, using such common props as engines that pulled trains, this girl had tried to apply its lesson directly in her daily life, without any fantasy elaboration, and had experienced a defeat that still rankled twenty years later.

Very different was the impact of "The Swiss Family 2 Robinson" on another little girl. The story tells how a shipwrecked family manages to live an adventurous, idyllic, constructive, and pleasurable life—a life very different from this child's own existence. Her father had to be away from home a great deal, and her mother was mentally ill and spent protracted periods in institutions. So the girl was shuttled from her home to that of an aunt, then to that of a grandmother, and back home again, as the need arose. During these years, the girl read over and over again the story of this happy family who lived on a desert island, where no member could be away from the rest of the family. Many years later, she recalled what a warm, cozy feeling she had when, propped up by a few large pillows, she forgot all about her present predicament as she read this story. As soon as she had finished it, she started to read it over again. The happy hours she spent with the Family Robinson in that fantasy land permitted her not to be defeated by the difficulties that reality presented to her. She was able to counteract the impact of harsh reality by imaginary gratifications. But since the story was not a fairy tale, it merely gave her a temporary escape from her problems; it did not hold out any promise to her that her life would take a turn for the better.

Consider the effect that "Rapunzel" had on a third girl. 3 This girl's mother had died in a car accident. The girl's father, deeply upset by what had happened to his wife (he had been driving the car), withdrew entirely into himself and handed the care of his daughter over to a nursemaid, who was little interested in the girl and gave her complete freedom to do as she liked. When the girl was seven, her father remarried, and, as she recalled it, it was around that time that "Rapunzel" became so important to her. Her stepmother was clearly the witch of the story, and she was the girl locked away in the tower. The girl recalled that she felt akin to Rapunzel because the witch had "forcibly" taken possession of her, as her stepmother had forcibly worked her way into the girl's life. The girl felt imprisoned in her new home, in contrast to her life of freedom with the nursemaid. She felt as victimized as Rapunzel, who, in her tower, had so little control over her life. Rapunzel's long hair was the key to the story. The girl wanted her hair to grow long, but her stepmother cut it short; long hair in itself became the symbol of freedom and happiness to her. The story convinced her that a prince (her father) would come someday and rescue her, and this conviction sustained her. If life became too difficult, all she needed was to imagine herself as Rapunzel, her hair grown long, and the prince loving and rescuing her.

"Rapunzel" suggests why fairy tales can offer more to 4 the child than even such a very nice children's story as "The Swiss Family Robinson." In "The Swiss Family Robinson," there is no witch against whom the child can discharge her anger in fantasy and on whom she can blame the father's lack of interest. "The Swiss Family Robinson" offers escape fantasies, and it did help the girl who read it over and over to forget temporarily how difficult life was for her. But it offered no specific hope for the future. "Rapunzel," on the other hand, offered the girl a chance to see the witch of the story as so evil that by comparison even the "witch" stepmother at home was not really so bad. "Rapunzel" also promised the girl that her rescue would be effected by her own body, when her hair grew long. Most important of all, it promised that the "prince" was only temporarily blinded—that he would regain his sight and rescue his princess. This fantasy continued to sustain the girl, though to a less intense degree, until she fell in love and married, and then she no longer needed it. We can understand why at first glance the stepmother, if she had known the meaning of "Rapunzel" to her stepdaughter, would have felt that fairy tales are bad for children. What she would not have known was that unless the stepdaughter had been able to find that fantasy satisfaction through "Rapunzel," she would have tried to break up her father's marriage and that without the hope for the future which the story gave her she might have gone badly astray in life.

It seems quite understandable that when children are 5 asked to name their favorite fairy tales, hardly any modern tales are among their choices. Many of the new tales have sad endings, which fail to provide the escape and consolation that the fearsome events in the fairy tale require if the child is to be strengthened for meeting the vagaries of his life. Without such encouraging conclusions, the child, after listening to the story, feels that there is indeed no hope for extricating himself from his despairs. In the traditional fairy tale, the hero is rewarded and the evil person meets his well-deserved fate, thus satisfying the child's deep need for justice to prevail. How else can a child hope that justice will be done to him, who so often feels unfairly treated? And how else can he convince himself that he must act correctly, when he is so sorely tempted to give in to the asocial proddings of his desires?

BUILDING VOCABULARY

1. *Jargon* is specialized vocabulary that appears in a certain profession or discipline. Bettelheim uses some jargon from psychology. Try to figure out what he means by the following terms:

   a. fantasy elaboration (par. 1)
   b. imaginary gratifications (par. 2)

   c. escape fantasies (par. 4)

   d. fantasy satisfaction (par. 4)

   e. asocial proddings (par. 5)

2. Write sentences in which you use the following words correctly:

   a. impressed (par. 1)

   b. conviction (par. 1)

   c. impact (par. 2)

   d. predicament (par. 2)

   e. victimized (par. 3)

   f. astray (par. 4)

   g. sorely (par. 5)

UNDERSTANDING THE WRITER'S IDEAS

1. Check in the children's book section of your library to summarize the stories and fairy tales Bettelheim discusses. How many stories is he examining in this essay?

2. What is the most important similarity between *The Little Engine That Could* and *The Swiss Family Robinson?*

3. What is the effect on children of *The Little Engine That Could?* How does it influence the adult whom Bettelheim introduces in paragraph 1?

4. How does Bettelheim summarize the story of *The Swiss Family Robinson?* Does this story, according to the author, have a beneficial effect on adults with problems?

5. Explain why "Rapunzel" was so important to the girl who had lost her mother in the car accident.

6. Why do traditional fairy tales benefit readers more than modern fairy tales and realistic stories? What do traditional fairy tales provide?

7. What does Bettelheim mean by his last sentence, "And how else can he convince himself that he must act correctly, when he is so sorely tempted to give in to the asocial proddings of his desires"?

UNDERSTANDING THE WRITER'S TECHNIQUES

1. Where does Bettelheim state his main point? How clear is his statement of it? Does he indicate in his thesis sentence his plan of development for the essay?

2. How does Bettelheim order his essay in terms of comparison and contrast? What is interesting about the pattern he chooses?

3. Where does the writer use narration? Why does he use it? How does it support the technique of comparison and contrast?

4. What is the function of paragraph 1? of paragraph 2? of paragraph 3?

5. How does the writer organize paragraph 4?

6. Is the same amount of emphasis given to "Rapunzel" as to the two "realistic" tales? Why or why not?

7. In concluding paragraphs of comparison and contrast papers, it is common to bring the two subjects together for a final observation. Does Bettelheim follow this strategy? How does he organize his subjects in the last paragraph?

8. How does Bettelheim achieve clear transitions from paragraph to paragraph? Discuss some of the words he uses so that his ideas are connected together clearly.

EXPLORING THE WRITER'S IDEAS

1. Bettelheim suggests that certain types of fairy tales help us to cope with problems. Do you agree or disagree? What particular fairy tale do you remember that might help a child deal with his or her problems?

2. Why do most children clearly take delight from traditional fairy tales?

3. Look again at Bettelheim's psychoanalysis of the three children whom he uses as examples in his essay. Do you

accept his explanations of their behavior? How might his ideas be criticized by other psychologists?

4. Which fairy tales—traditional or modern—appealed to you as a child? Why were you so fond of them?

5. If exposure to certain types of fairy tales can affect us seriously, then what can we conclude about our exposure to stories on television, film, and other types of media? Is it fair to generalize about television from Bettelheim's argument?

IDEAS FOR WRITING

Guided Writing

Write an essay in which you compare and/or contrast two or three fairy tales or stories that you remember from early childhood. Or, do the same for two films, two television programs, two newspapers, or two subjects from another media form.

1. State the purpose of your comparison as soon as you can.

2. Decide on the best pattern of development (block, alternating, or a combination of both) for your purposes.

3. List the point of comparison or contrast that you plan to cover for each subject.

4. Be certain to support each point with substantial detail. Summarize parts of stories that bear out your point. Quote where you have to.

5. Make certain that, in the closing paragraph, you draw conclusions about all the subjects treated.

More Writing Projects

1. Compare and contrast in a journal entry the style of writing of any two writers in this section.

2. Select two heroes or heroines from popular children's stories or fairy tales; in an extended paragraph compare and contrast the two characters in regard to personality and behavior.

3. Write an essay in which you compare or contrast two newspapers or magazines. Be prepared to compare and contrast their contents, and also to indicate the type of audience at which they are aimed. Write a comparative paper on your findings.

SUMMING UP: CHAPTER 6

1. In the essays you have read thus far in this book, you have learned much about the personal lives of many of the authors. Select two whose lives seem very different, and write an essay in which you contrast their lives. In your essay, use only illustrations that you can cite or derive from the selections; that is, do not do research or use other outside information about the authors.

2. In this chapter both Bettelheim and Carson deal with two very old fictional forms, *fable* and *fairy tales*. Check definitions of the terms. Then, write an essay in which you explore the authors' use of the words.

3. Which author in this chapter do you think most successfully uses the comparison-contrast form? Write an essay in which you analyze the best comparison-contrast essay as you see it. Indicate the techniques and strategies that you feel work best. Make specific references to the essay you have chosen as a model.

4. Rachel Carson ("A Fable for Tomorrow," pages 213–215) and Gretel Ehrlich ("A River's Route," pages 121–124) both express deep environmental concerns in their essays. Write your own essay to compare and contrast these concerns. How are the two writers' treatments similar? How are they different?

5. In the manner of Rachel Carson, write your own "Fable for Tomorrow," in which you show how today's indifference to the environment will affect the future. Remember: *Silent Spring* was written in 1962 and, many scholars believe, the way people abuse the environment today is even more serious than it was then.

CHAPTER 7

Definition

Definition is a way of explaining an important word so that the reader knows, as exactly as possible, what you mean by it. You probably have written essays requiring short "dictionary definitions" of words that were not clear to the reader. However, there are terms that require longer definitions because they may be central to the writer's thought. When an entire essay focuses on the meaning of a key word or group of related words, you will need to employ "extended definition" as a method of organization.

Words requiring extended definition tend to be abstract, controversial, or complex. Terms like "freedom," "pornography," and "communism" reflect the need for extended definition. Such words depend on extended definition because they are often confused with some other word or term; because they are easily misunderstood; or because they are of special importance to the writer, who chooses to redefine the term for his or her own purposes. We can, of course, simply offer an extended definition of a word for the sake of definition itself; this is valid. But we usually have strong opinions about complex and controversial words, and, consequently, we try to provide an extended definition for the purpose of illuminating a thesis. The word "abortion" could be defined objectively, with the writer tracing its history, explaining its techniques, and describing its effects on the patient. Yet many writers asked to provide an extended definition of "abortion" would have strong personal opinions about the term. They would want to develop a thesis about it, perhaps covering much of the same ground as the objective account, but taking care that the reader understands the word as they do. It is normal for us to have our own opinions about any word, but in all instances we must make the reader understand fully what we mean by it.

Writers use several techniques to develop extended definitions. One common strategy is to define some general group to which the subject belongs (for instance, the mallard is a member of a larger group of ducks), and to show how the word differs from all other words in that general group. A second technique is to give the etymology of a word—its origin and history in the language—to help the reader. Yet another method of extended definition is to deal with what you do *not* mean by the term—a technique called "negation." Finally, many methods that you already learned can be used profitably in extended definition. You can define a word by narrating an event that reveals its meaning; you can provide specific examples, even a simple listing, to illustrate what you mean by a term; you can compare and contrast related terms; you can describe details that help to establish meaning.

Extended definition involves no single pattern of essay organization, but rather a group of available strategies that you use depending on your purpose and on the word itself. The word selected may be ordinary and relatively concrete, or it may be abstract and complex like "randomness." Often, as in the essays on "fun" and, later, on "escape," the definition is never directly stated, but is understood or put together from the information a writer gives. Because so many methods can be applied effectively in an essay of extended definition, you should be able to organize and develop this type of composition easily.

What's a Bagel?

Jack Denton Scott

Author and bagel lover Jack Denton Scott combines a variety of expository techniques, statistics, and citations from experts to define what is quickly becoming one of America's most popular foods. In the process of definition, he explains why the bagel can no longer be considered only an East-Coast ethnic food as America becomes "bagelized."

Words to Watch

aficionados (par. 1)   fans; devotees
phenomenon (par. 2)   observable fact or event
consumers (par. 2)   users of goods
croissant (par. 4)   French crescent-shaped pastry
hearth (par. 5)   brick fireplace or oven
automated (par. 6)   mechanical
quirky (par. 7)   peculiar; eccentric
tutus (par. 9)   short skirts worn by ballerinas
spirited (par. 14)   lively

If bread is the staff of life, the bagel may be the laugh of 1 life. "Brooklyn jawbreakers," "crocodile teething rings," even "doughnuts with rigor mortis" are affectionate terms invoked by bagel aficionados.

For those who haven't tried one, the flavorful bagel is a 2 shiny, hard, crisp yet chewy roll with a hole in the middle, and it is booming in popularity. Eight million are consumed daily in the United States—worth about $400 million a year. Bakery experts call the phenomenon "the Americanization of the bagel." To bagel believers it's "the bagelization of America." In the past four years retail sales of bagels have about doubled. Over 80 percent of these sales are now to non-Jewish consumers, a dramatic sociological switch. Moreover, the "bagel belt," always on the East Coast, is starting to stretch across the country. In fact, the world's largest bagel bakery is now located in Mattoon, Ill., producing over a million rolls a day.

Walter Heller of *Progressive Grocer* magazine calls the 3 bagel's rise to stardom an example of "America's current love affair with ethnic foods." Yet, unless sliced in half, toasted and eaten warm, the bagel isn't easy to handle. It may make messy sandwiches and challenge the teeth. What's more, bagels become stale and hard after 12 hours—"something you can fight wars with," as one bagel expert said.

For the health-conscious, however, the bagel has a lot 4 going for it. The plain, two-ounce toaster-size has just 150 calories and one gram of fat. (The popular buttery croissant, by comparison, contains 235 calories and 12 grams of fat.) Furthermore, the plain bagel has no cholesterol, preservatives, or artificial color.

Bagels are made with unbleached, protein-rich, high- 5 gluten flour, lightly seasoned with malt, salt and sugar, and raised with yeast. They then get a brief bath in boiling water. This results in the shiny surface after they are baked. (Most are hearth-baked to give them a crusty exterior and chewy interior.)

Some U.S. bakeries still use the Old World method of 6 rolling and shaping the stiff dough by hand. This requires about six months to learn, but one expert bagel baker can whip out about 700 an hour. (One automated machine can turn out up to 9000 an hour.)

Where did this quirky roll originate? One version has the 7 bagel created by an Austrian baker in 1683, honoring the king of Poland who had defeated Turkish invaders. It was first formed to resemble a stirrup (*beugel,* from the German *bügel,* for stirrup), because the king's favorite hobby was riding.

Another account puts the bagel in Cracow, Poland, in 8 1610, where poor Jews, who normally ate coarse black bread, considered their uncommon white-flour roll a delicacy. Bagels were officially approved as presents for women after childbirth, and mothers used them as teething rings for their children. In the 1600s in Russia, bagels were looped on strings, and were thought to bring good luck and have magical powers.

Bagels were brought to New York City and New Jersey 9
by Jewish immigrants about 1910. Among the most successful
immigrant bagel bakers was Harry Lender, who arrived from
Lublin, Poland, in 1927 and settled in New Haven, Conn. His
sons—Sam, Murray and Marvin—have almost made Lender's
Bagels household words by using humor to push sales. For
their bakery's 55th anniversary party, Murray and the executive staff attended a ballet class for two months; then, dressed
in orange leotards and yellow tutus, they gracefully tiptoed to
what was announced as "The Dance of the Bagels."

Today the baffling bagel surge to the top is even inspiring 10
bagel restaurants. They offer as many as 17 flavors, from rai-
sin and honey to zippy onion, plus bagel sandwiches, burgers,
clubs, grilled cheese, French toast, salad sandwich combos,
an egg-and-sausage bagelwich and a rancher's bagel breakfast.
Big also are bagelettes—one-inch bagels—served by the bas-
ket with dinners. Then there are hero, hoagie, pizza and taco
bagels—even Bagel Dogs. Where there's a bagel, there's a
way.

Bagel bakeries are opening in Alaska, England, Japan 11
and Israel. Ron Stieglitz, founder of the New York Bagels
bakery in London, where few people had ever seen a bagel,
had trouble raising money from banks. "A lot of them thought
we were a football team," he said. But the bakery now sup-
plies four large retail chains and many small shops and restaurants.

Lyle Fox, from Chicago, sees more potential for the ba- 12
gel in Japan than in the United States. Young Japanese view
the bagel as trendy and upscale—so much so that he easily
sells 6000 a day. Fox discovered that the Japanese associate
the bagel with New York, and New York with fashion. Thus,
a lot of his customers are young women who consider the bagel as "sort of another accessory." A long-time bagel lover,
Fox says his stomach does a sickly flip when Japanese customers ask for lox and cream cheese on a cinnamon-raisin bagel.

Cashing in on the new bagel awareness, innovators have 13
come up with some really neat twists. Three Philadelphians
started Bagels in Bed, a home-delivery business. Mike Bretz,

owner of Simon Brothers Bakery in Skokie, Ill., has borrowed an idea from Chinese fortune cookies. He stuffs slips with Yiddish wisdom into his Schlepper Simon's Yiddish Fortune Bagels. One cheerfully advises, "Smile, bubeleh, success is assured."

A spirited cookbook, *The Bagels' Bagel Book* (Acropolis 14 Books), has recipes like "Mexicali Bagel Fondue," the "Kojak Bagel" with feta cheese and Greek olives, "Tofu Bagels," and "Delhi Bagels" with whipped cream cheese, curry and chutney. The book also captures some of the laughter inspired by baking's most remarkable roll. Here's comedienne Phyllis Diller: "President Reagan was so gung-ho to get ethnic votes, he went into a deli and ordered a bagel. The waiter asked, 'How would you like that?' Ronnie said, 'On rye.'"

What's a bagel? Fun you can eat.   15

BUILDING VOCABULARY

1. Scott uses a variety of informal expressions that are fairly common in daily conversation and media talk or writing. Explain the following expressions in your own words.

   a. it is booming in popularity (par. 2)
   b. whip out (par. 6)
   c. household words (par. 9)
   d. to push sales (par. 9)
   e. trendy and upscale (par. 12)
   f. cashing in on (par. 13)
   g. gung-ho (par. 14)

2. List all the ethnic foods (other than bagels) mentioned in this essay and explain what they are.

UNDERSTANDING THE WRITER'S IDEAS

1. In paragraph 1, Scott uses a number of very colorful phrases to define bagels. Try to explain the following in

your own words: "Brooklyn jawbreakers," "crocodile teething rings," and "doughnuts with rigor mortis."

2. What ethnic group is traditionally associated with bagels? What "dramatic sociological switch" has occurred over the past few years?

3. What is meant by "the bagel belt"? Where has it traditionally been located? How is that location changing? Where is the world's largest bagel factory? Why is that surprising?

4. What are "ethnic foods"? How does the bagel figure in "America's current love affair with ethnic foods"?

5. For what reasons can a bagel be considered a food for the health conscious?

6. What is the process of making bagels? Explain the phrase "the Old World method"? What is the "Old World"?

7. In your own words, summarize the two stories concerning the origin of the bagel. What accounts for the shape of the modern bagel? Why were bagels considered delicacies among the poor Jews of Cracow? Does Scott seem to favor either story about the bagel's origins? Explain.

8. Where, when, and by whom were bagels first brought to the United States? How have these "bagel pioneers" continued to promote bagels?

9. Identify the origins of these take-offs on familiar sayings:

   a. If bread is the staff of life, the bagel may be the laugh of life. (par. 1)
   b. Where there's a bagel, there's a way. (par. 10)

10. In what other parts of the world are bagel factories operating? What was the problem in starting up a bagel business in London? Why are bagels so popular in Japan? Why does bagel manufacturer Lyle Fox get a little sick when the Japanese ask for lox and cream cheese on a cinnamon-raisin bagel?

11. Explain the meaning of the joke that concludes the essay. What serious point does it make about the bagel business?

12. Explain the meaning of the last paragraph: "What's a bagel? Fun you can eat."

UNDERSTANDING THE WRITER'S TECHNIQUES

1. Does Scott ever give a simple definition of a bagel? If so, where? Is it an objective or a subjective definition? Explain.

2. What is Scott's *purpose* in this essay? How does the title indicate that purpose? Who is his *intended audience?* Explain.

3. What is the general *tone* (see Glossary) of this essay? What is it about Scott's writing style that creates this tone? Is the tone appropriate to the subject and audience? Why?

4. Even a lighthearted essay can benefit from the use of *statistics* and *authorities* on the subject at hand. What statistics concerning bagels and their manufacture does Scott present? What authorities does he cite? What effect does the use of statistics and authorities have on the essay? Would the essay have been as effective without them? Explain.

5. Throughout the essay, Scott makes use of many of the other expository techniques discussed in this book. Explain where Scott uses each of the techniques below.

   a. Definition (Chapter 7)
   b. Process analysis (Chapter 9)
   c. Comparison and contrast (Chapter 6)
   d. Narration (Chapter 4)
   e. Illustration (Chapter 5)

What is the effect of using all these techniques in this essay?

6. Some information in this essay is contained in parentheses. Identify all the parenthetical information. Why does Scott choose to set off this material from the main text? Is it necessary to do so? Explain.

7. Scott uses various *allusions* (see Glossary). Explain or identify the origin of each allusion below:

   a. ''The Dance of the Bagels''
   b. Yiddish
   c. Kojak
   d. Delhi
   e. Phyllis Diller
   f. President Reagan

EXPLORING THE WRITER'S IDEAS

1. Over the past few years, a wide diversity of foods has become available to Americans all over the country. Most supermarkets carry a full complement of ethnic foods, and even small towns are likely to have at least one ''ethnic'' restaurant. Like Scott, some believe this is a positive trend because it allows Americans to enjoy and learn about other cultures. Others bemoan the demise of regional American foods. What is your opinion? How has the increased availability of ethnic foods affected your area?

2. Discuss with your classmates some of the most exotic foods you've ever eaten.

3. Eating habits are among the most deeply rooted of all cultural behaviors. What may be perfectly acceptable in one culture may be considered quite rude in another. Research some of the eating habits of other cultures and compare them with those of your own culture. Discuss this issue with your classmates.

4. When did you eat your first bagel? Describe the situa-

tion. What did you eat with it? Did you like it? Which of Scott's descriptions conform with your own feelings about bagels? Do you regularly eat bagels now? Why or why not?

IDEAS FOR WRITING

Guided Writing

Write a definition essay entitled "What's a _____ ?" Fill in the blank with the name of something which was once thought to belong exclusively to a particular ethnic, cultural, or social group, but now has become "Americanized" or "standardized." For example, you might choose an article of clothing, a type of music, a cooking utensil, and so forth. (You may also choose a type of food.)

1. Begin your essay with some colorful definitions of your subject. (These may be definitions you've heard or ones which you make up.)

2. Give a straightforward, objective definition of this item.

3. Explain how the item has become "Americanized." In your explanation, try to use at least three expository techniques other than definition.

4. Include some references to statistics and (or) authorities on the subject.

5. Describe the origin of this item. If possible, find out how and when it first appeared in the United States.

6. Keep an amusing tone throughout your essay.

7. Include several allusions to other cultures.

8. Conclude with a subjective definition that derives from the material presented throughout your essay.

More Writing Projects

1. Record in your journal all the associations connected with your favorite color. Then, using this list, write a definition of it.

2. Write an extended one-paragraph definition of a particular emotion.

3. Discuss with other class members all connotations related to the word "pizza." List all these associations on the chalkboard. Select the most appropriate items on the list and write an essay defining pizza.

Fun, Oh Boy. Fun. You Could Die from It.

Suzanne Britt Jordan

Most of us never really consider exactly what it means to have a good time. Suzanne Britt Jordan, a writer who claims she "tries to have fun, but often fails," offers an extended definition of the word "fun" by pointing out what it is *not*.

Words to Watch

puritan (par. 3) one who practices or preaches a more strict moral code than that which most people now follow

selfless (par. 4) unselfish; having no concern for oneself

fetish (par. 5) something regarded with extravagant trust or respect

licentiousness (par. 9) a lack of moral restraints

consumption (par. 9) act of taking in or using up a substance; eating or drinking

epitome (par. 11) an ideal; a typical representation

capacity (par. 12) the ability to hold something

damper (par. 13) something that regulates or that stops something from flowing

reverently (par. 13) respectfully; worshipfully

blaspheme (par. 13) to speak of without reverence

weary (par. 14) tired; worn-out

horizon (par. 14) the apparent line where the earth meets the sky

scan (par. 14) to examine something carefully

Fun is hard to have. 1

Fun is a rare jewel. 2

Somewhere along the line people got the modern idea 3 that fun was there for the asking, that people deserved fun, that if we didn't have a little fun every day we would turn into (sakes alive!) puritans.

"Was it fun?" became the question that overshadowed 4 all other questions: good questions like: Was it moral? Was it kind? Was it honest? Was it beneficial? Was it generous? Was it necessary? And (my favorite) was it selfless?

When the pleasure got to be the main thing, the fun fetish 5 was sure to follow. Everything was supposed to be fun. If it wasn't fun, then by Jove, we were going to make it fun, or else.

Think of all the things that got the reputation of being 6 fun. Family outings were supposed to be fun. Sex was supposed to be fun. Education was supposed to be fun. Work was supposed to be fun. Walt Disney was supposed to be fun. Church was supposed to be fun. Staying fit was supposed to be fun.

Just to make sure that everybody knew how much fun 7 we were having, we put happy faces on flunking test papers, dirty bumpers, sticky refrigerator doors, bathroom mirrors.

If a kid, looking at his very happy parents traipsing 8 through that very happy Disney World, said, "This ain't fun, ma," his ma's heart sank. She wondered where she had gone wrong. Everybody told her what fun family outings to Disney World would be. Golly gee, what was the matter?

Fun got to be such a big thing that everybody started to 9 look for more and more thrilling ways to supply it. One way was to step up the level of danger or licentiousness or alcohol or drug consumption so that you could be sure that, no matter what, you would manage to have a little fun.

Television commercials brought a lot of fun and fun- 10 loving folks into the picture. Everything that people in those commercials did looked like fun: taking Polaroid snapshots, swilling beer, buying insurance, mopping the floor, bowling, taking aspirin. We all wished, I'm sure, that we could have half as much fun as those rough-and-ready guys around the locker room, flicking each other with towels and pouring champagne. The more commercials people watched, the more they wondered when the fun would start in their own lives. It was pretty depressing.

Big occasions were supposed to be fun. Christmas, 11 Thanksgiving and Easter were obviously supposed to be fun. Your wedding day was supposed to be fun. Your wedding night was supposed to be a whole lot of fun. Your honeymoon was supposed to be the epitome of fundom. And so we ended up going through every Big Event we ever celebrated, waiting for the fun to start.

It occurred to me, while I was sitting around waiting for the fun to start, that not much is, and that I should tell you just in case you're worried about your fun capacity.   12

I don't mean to put a damper on things. I just mean we ought to treat fun reverently. It is a mystery. It cannot be caught like a virus. It cannot be trapped like an animal. The god of mirth is paying us back for all those years of thinking fun was everywhere by refusing to come to our party. I don't want to blaspheme fun anymore. When fun comes in on little dancing feet, you probably won't be expecting it. In fact, I bet it comes when you're doing your duty, your job, or your work. It may even come on a Tuesday.   13

I remember one day, long ago, on which I had an especially good time. Pam Davis and I walked to the College Village drug store one Saturday morning to buy some candy. We were about 12 years old (fun ages). She got her Bit-O-Honey. I got my malted milk balls, chocolate stars, Chunkys, and a small bag of M & M's. We started back to her house. I was going to spend the night. We had the whole day to look forward to. We had plenty of candy. It was a long way to Pam's house but every time we got weary Pam would put her hand over her eyes, scan the horizon like a sailor and say, "Oughta reach home by nightfall," at which point the two of us would laugh until we thought we couldn't stand it another minute. Then after we got calm, she'd say it again. You should have been there. It was the kind of day and friendship and occasion that made me deeply regretful that I had to grow up.   14

It was fun.   15

BUILDING VOCABULARY

1. *Trite language* refers to words and expressions that have been overused and, consequently, have lost much of their effectiveness. People do rely on trite language in their conversations, but writers usually avoid overused expressions.

However, a good writer will be able to introduce such vocabulary at strategic points. Examples of trite language in Jordan's essay appear below. Explain in your own words what they mean:

   a. a rare jewel (par. 2)
   b. by Jove (par. 5)
   c. golly gee (par. 8)
   d. his ma's heart sank (par. 8)

2. For each of the following words drawn from Jordan's essay, write a denotative definition. Then list four connotations (see Glossary) each word has for you.

   a. overshadow (par. 4)
   b. flunking (par. 7)
   c. traipsing (par. 8)
   d. swilling (par. 10)
   e. mirth (par. 13)

3. Select five words from the Words to Watch section and use them in sentences of your own.

UNDERSTANDING THE WRITER'S IDEAS

1. What are some of the things Jordan says fun is not?

2. What does Jordan suggest we did to something if it wasn't already fun? Identify some of the things she says are "supposed" to be fun.

3. In paragraph 9, Jordan lists some common things that certainly aren't any fun. How does she say people made them fun anyway?

4. What are some of the ways people make fun even more thrilling?

5. What does Jordan list as looking like fun on television commercials?

6. Discuss the relationship between big occasions and the ex-

perience of fun. Explain the meaning of the statement, "It may even come on a Tuesday."

7. Describe Jordan's attitude concerning how much in life really is fun. According to Jordan, how should we treat fun? Why? Is it something she says can only be experienced at special times?

8. How old was Jordan at the time she remembers having an especially good time with her friend Pam? Describe in your own words why she had such a good time that day. What are some of the candies she remembers buying? Why was it especially funny when Pam would say, "Oughta reach home by nightfall"?

9. For what reason does Jordan feel regretful at the end of the essay? Although she is regretful, do you think she is actually sad? Why?

UNDERSTANDING THE WRITER'S TECHNIQUES

1. Does Jordan ever offer a single-sentence definition of "fun"? Where? Is that sentence sufficient to define the concept? Why?

2. Jordan employs the technique of *negation*—defining a term through showing what it is *not*—so strongly in this essay that the writing verges on *irony*. Irony is using language to suggest the opposite of what is said (see Glossary). Explain the irony in paragraphs 9, 10, and 11.

3. Why does the author continually point out things that are supposed to be fun? What is she trying to tell us about these things?

4. Writers usually avoid vague words such as "everything" or "everybody" in their writing, yet Jordan uses these words frequently in this essay. Explain her purpose in deliberately avoiding concrete terms.

5. What is the *tone* (see Glossary) of this essay? Is it fun? How does Jordan create this tone? Much of the writing in this essay has a very conversational quality to it, as though the author were speaking directly to the reader. Locate five words or phrases that have this quality.

6. Why does Jordan use so many examples and illustrations in this essay? Which paragraphs use multiple illustrations with special effectiveness?

7. There is a definite turning point in this essay where Jordan switches from an ironic to an affirmative point of view in which she begins to explain what fun *can be* rather than what it *is not*. One paragraph in particular serves as the transition between the two attitudes. Which one is it? Which is the first paragraph to be mostly affirmative? What is the result of this switch?

8. Jordan uses specific brand names in the essay. Locate at least four of them. Why do you think she uses these brand names instead of names that simply identify the object?

9. What is the function of narration in the development of this essay? Where does the author *narrate* an imagined incident? Where does she use a real incident? Why does Jordan use narration in this paper?

10. Compare the effects of the two simple, direct statements that begin and end the essay. Why does Jordan not develop a more elaborate introduction and conclusion?

EXPLORING THE WRITER'S IDEAS

1. Jordan begins her essay by stating, "Fun is hard to have." At one point she indicates that "Fun got to be such a big thing that everybody started looking for more and more thrilling ways to supply it" (par. 9). Do you think that fun is hard to have? Why or why not? What relationship does the epidemic use of drugs and alcohol have to our difficulties in having fun today?

2. The author raises the question of how at big events we are
   sometimes left "waiting for the fun to start" (par. 11).
   What functions do events or occasions such as holidays,
   weddings, or birthdays play in our society? Why is there an
   emphasis placed on having fun at those events? Do you
   think there should be such an emphasis? Why?

3. This essay appeared as a guest editorial in *The New York
   Times*. We do not usually think of *The New York Times* as
   a "fun" newspaper, but rather as one that deals with serious issues of international significance. Jordan's article
   might be considered popular writing or light reading. Do
   you feel there is a place in the media—newspapers, magazines, radio, television—for a mixture of "heavy" and
   "light" attitudes? What well-respected newspapers or
   magazines that you know include articles on popular topics? What subjects do you think would currently be most
   appealing to popular audiences?

4. At the end of the essay, Jordan seems to imply that it is
   easier for children to have fun than it is for grownups. Do
   you agree? Is the basic experience of fun any different for
   kids or for adults? Do you feel it was any easier for people
   to have fun in days past than it is now? Why?

IDEAS FOR WRITING

Guided Writing

Select one of the following highly connotative terms for various types of experiences and write an extended definition
about it: love, creativity, alienation, prejudice, fidelity.

1. Prepare for your essay by consulting a good dictionary for
   the lexical definition of the term. However, instead of beginning with this definition, start with some catchy, interesting opening statements related to the definition.

2. Write a thesis sentence that names the word you will define

and that tells the special opinion, attitude, or point of view you have about the word.

3. Attempt to establish the importance of your subject by considering it in terms of our current understanding of fun.

4. Use the technique of negation (see page 245) by providing various examples and illustrations of what your topic *is not* in order to establish your own viewpoint of what it *is*.

5. Use other strategies—description, narration, comparison and contrast, and so forth—to aid in clearly establishing an extended definition of your topic.

6. At the end of your essay dramatize through narration at least one personal experience that relates the importance of the topic to your life.

More Writing Projects

1. Sit someplace on campus and observe people having fun. Record in your journal their behavior—actions, gestures, noises, and so forth. Then turn these notes into a definition of ''campus fun.''

2. Write a brief one-paragraph definition of a ''funny person.'' Use vivid details to create this portrait.

3. From a book of popular quotations (*Bartlett's Familiar Quotations*, the *Oxford Dictionary of Quotations*) check under the heading ''fun'' and select a number of statements about fun by professional writers. Then write an essay in which you expand one of those definitions. Draw upon your own experiences or readings to support the definition you choose to expand.

Escape Valve

Gregg Easterbrook

A contemporary journalist, Gregg Easterbrook tries here to define a phrase that he has coined to identify a phenomenon of modern life. Take note of the way he develops his definition by means of personal anecdote, history, and causal analysis. As you read, think about whether or not you know anyone guilty of "automatic-out."

Words to Watch

deep-rooted (par. 3)   firmly planted

foundations (par. 4)   underlying supports

stints (par. 5)   fixed shares of work to be performed within a given time period

truism (par. 5)   statement of a very obvious truth

hierarchies (par. 6)   bodies of people organized or classified according to rank

integrity (par. 7)   adherence to a code of behavior: honesty; uprightness

perpetuate (par. 9)   prolong the existence of

A man and woman I know moved in together recently. It 1 was, as such occasions are, a moment of sentiment and celebration. It was also a limited engagement. Before moving in, they had already set a fixed date when they would break up.

They explained their reasons to one and all. In a year, 2 the woman planned to change jobs and cities; the man did not plan to follow. An eventual split is unfortunate, they said, but also inevitable, so why not plan on it? Yet, far from being a sad twist of fate, my woman friend's scheduled departure, I fear, was a liberating force, making possible whatever short-term romance the couple will enjoy. Without the escape clause of a pre-set termination of their affair, they might never have lived together at all.

This situation is not unique. More and more, people are 3 ordering their lives along a principle I call the "automatic-out." In love, friendship, work, and the community, people increasingly prefer arrangements that automatically end at some pre-set date. Automatic-out is not a phenomenon confined to my still-unsettled generation (the late 20's), with its flair for "flexible" styles of life. It is a force in society as a whole, as more of us hunger for lives that appear stable and deep-rooted but lack the complications of commitment.

Automatic-out may have its foundations in the pre-set 4 cycles of academic life. In recent decades, an ever-higher percentage of the population has been able to attend college and postgraduate schools. That's a good thing for the cause of education but perhaps not so good for society's spirit. Longtime students learn to view institutions as places where people briefly come to rest, and from which they will be automatically removed on a date known years in advance. They also tend to see institutions as a means by which to take things for themselves, instead of adding things for others.

So it may be no surprise that professionals—usually the 5 beneficiaries of advanced schooling—seem increasingly uninterested in staying put. Or, if they remain with one organization, lean toward fellowships, temporary assignments, and other stints with automatic-outs. For some time, this has been a troubling truism of Washington. A Brookings Institution study shows that Government-agency managers immediately below the rank of Presidential appointees turn over, on average, every 21 months. Now it is becoming true of private enterprise as well. According to the Conference Board, a business research organization, top corporate executives now switch jobs every 4.5 years on average—an all-time high.

The job-switching mania, it is sometimes suggested, 6 stems from a combination of boredom and expectations of promotion. But most switches among Government agencies and corporate hierarchies do not involve dramatic changes of life; they are changes from one job to another fairly similar to it, in a fairly similar organization. The number of top-level positions available doesn't increase just because the switching rate is increasing.

The switch mania is, I think, motivated by the desire for 7 automatic-outs. When you know in advance that you will soon be changing jobs, you are relieved of concern for the overall integrity of your institution—whether the quality of its products, the fairness of its service, the odds of its survival. You have a built-in excuse for selfishness (''I'll be leaving in a year anyway'') and can concentrate on advancing yourself, secure in the knowledge that if you fail to improve your organization—or, as in the case of so many business and Government managers, actively damage it—you personally won't suffer. You'll be one step ahead of the crumbling walls.

It seems to be the same way in love. If a romance oper- 8 ates under some pre-set restriction, neither partner feels obliged to sacrifice his interests for joint interests. Why sacrifice for something not expected to last anyway? Thus, the short-term benefits of marriage and living together (companionship, warmth, convenience) remain popular. But long-term obligation to the institution of marriage has fallen into disrepute among many young people. Children and family life are especially in disrepute today, for whenever children are present there is no easy out, emotionally or legally. The weekend romance is especially desirable today, not because ''people move around more now'' but because distance guarantees an automatic-out. Just step back on the plane Sunday night.

Many troublesome aspects of life perpetuate themselves 9 through downward-drawing spirals. As corporate and public institutions fall deeper into disrepair, as men and women become increasingly small-minded and cool to the touch, there seems all the more reason to opt for automatic-outs. Who wants to be committed to the kinds of people and organizations at loose in the world today? This, of course, helps only to accelerate the decay. Many people capable of helping right what's wrong with society seek instead mainly to exempt themselves from responsibility for its condition. Why should I care? I'll be leaving in a year anyway.

BUILDING VOCABULARY

Match each term in Column A with an appropriate definition from Column B. There are two more definitions than you need.

Column A	*Column B*
1 inevitable (par. 2)	**a** disgrace
2 stable (par. 3)	**b** attractive
3 beneficiaries (par. 5)	**c** stimulated to action
4 mania (par. 6)	**d** speed up
5 motivated (par. 7)	**e** intense, abnormal desire
6 disrepute (par. 8)	for something
7 disrepair (par. 9)	**f** automatic
8 opt (par. 9)	**g** resistant to change
9 accelerate (par. 9)	**h** free from obligation
10 exempt (par. 9)	**i** choose
	j unavoidable
	k state of neglect
	l those who receive
	advantages

UNDERSTANDING THE WRITER'S IDEAS

1. What arrangement does the couple the author knows make? What reasons do they offer for this arrangement?

2. What is the "automatic-out" principle? Why does the author believe that it appeals to society as a whole and not just to his own generation of men and women in their late twenties?

3. What, according to Easterbrook, are the foundations for automatic-out?

4. What does the Brookings Institution study demonstrate? How does the Conference Board reinforce that study in a business setting?

5. What are the reasons generally offered for what Easterbrook calls "the job-switching mania"? Why are top-level positions not increasing in number? How does Easterbrook explain the switch mania?

6. For what reason does the desire to switch operate for love as well as for jobs? What are the short-term benefits of marriage and living together? Why, according to the au-

thor, has the long-term obligation to marriage fallen into
disrepute? Why is the weekend romance attractive?

7. How does the automatic-out serve to accelerate the decay
of people and institutions today?

UNDERSTANDING THE WRITER'S TECHNIQUES

1. Which sentence of this essay is the thesis sentence? Why
does Easterbrook not place it in the opening paragraph?

2. What is your opinion of the introduction in paragraphs 1
and 2? What is the value to the essay of the incident about
the author's acquaintances? What rhetorical technique appears?

3. Where does the writer use negation (see page 245)?

4. In paragraph 4 why does he give backgrounds to the concept "automatic-out"?

5. Why does Easterbrook present findings of the Brookings
Institution and the Conference Board? How do the findings enhance his point?

6. Where does the writer use causal analysis (see Glossary)?
Why does he use it?

7. What transitions serve to connect one paragraph to the
next? Look especially at the first sentence in paragraphs
3, 4, 5, 6, 7, and 8.

8. In paragraphs 3, 7, and 8 Easterbrook uses parenthetical
expressions. Why does he choose to place information in
parentheses?

9. The writer frames a number of questions in the essay. For
example, in paragraph 8, he says, "Why sacrifice for
something not expected to last anyway?" What is the
value of the question? Why doesn't Easterbrook answer
it? What other unanswered questions appear?

10. What is your opinion of the conclusion? How does East-
    erbrook establish a new, broader context for the term
    "automatic-out"? Why does he choose that context to
    close the essay?

11. Why do you think that the essay is called "Escape Valve"
    instead of "Automatic-Out"? What is an escape valve?
    Used here, of course, the title is metaphorical (see Glos-
    sary). What value is there in using the metaphorical title in
    this case?

12. What is your reaction to the conclusion? Why does East-
    erbrook end by condemning the automatic-out philoso-
    phy? Do you find the last two sentences effective? Why?

EXPLORING THE WRITER'S IDEAS

1. Has Easterbrook defined clearly a recognizable principle in
   today's society as you view it? Why do you feel as you do?
   What evidence of the automatic-out do you find among
   your family, friends, or acquaintances? Have you yourself
   ever entered into a relationship based upon automatic-out?

2. Easterbrook blames in part the academic institution—our
   public and private schools and colleges—for our acceptance of the value in short-term commitments. Why might
   you agree or disagree with him? What other forces or institutions may encourage short-term commitments?

3. Do you agree that the high level of job switching apparent
   today is related more to the desire for escaping commitments than to "boredom and expectations of promotion"?
   Defend your answer.

4. Why might you agree or disagree that "marriage has fallen
   into disrepute among many young people"? Is automatic-
   out a real threat to marriage as a basic institution of our
   culture? Why? (Look ahead to the essay "I Want a Wife"
   by Judy Syfers for another perspective on marriage.)

5. Answer the question in paragraph 9: "Who wants to be

committed to the kinds of people and organizations at loose in the world today?''

6. The writer states that ''many people capable of helping right what's wrong with society'' try ''to exempt themselves from responsibility for its condition.'' What are some of the things wrong with society today? How might people right those wrongs?

IDEAS FOR WRITING

Guided Writing

Choose a word or term that you think is opposite in meaning to ''automatic-out'' and write an essay of 500 to 750 words in which you define that term. You may choose a word or term like *commitment, staying in, holding on, hanging in,* or some such expression. You may even want to coin your own phrase.

1. Start with an anecdote about friends or acquaintances and explain it. Your anecdote should demonstrate the word or phrase that you are trying to define.

2. In your thesis statement name the term and give an expanded definition of it in a paragraph or two.

3. Explain the foundations or the history of the situation your term is naming as Easterbrook does in paragraph 4 of his essay.

4. If possible, present data to support your interpretation of the term.

5. Give examples to expand your meanings further. Draw your examples from people at work or from personal relationships with other people.

6. Use an occasional unanswered question to challenge the reader.

7. If you can, use negation to help you define the term.

8. Connect your paragraphs with transitions that relate one idea thoughtfully to the next.

9. In your conclusion, place the term in a broader perspective, one that goes beyond the specific conditions you are explaining.

10. Try to give your essay a metaphorical title.

More Writing Projects

1. Easterbrook uses the term "switch mania" when he writes about jobs. Think about the term and then in your journal write a definition of it as it pertains to our culture today.

2. Write a one-paragraph definition of the phrase "short-term commitment." Make certain that you establish a sharp thesis for your definition.

3. An "escapist" is someone who looks to break loose from unpleasant realities through self-deceiving fantasy or entertainment. In an essay write an extended definition of the word "escapist." Draw upon your own experiences and (or) your readings to support your definition.

To the Victor Belongs the Language
Rita Mae Brown

Rita Mae Brown is a novelist whose works include *High Hearts* and *Southern Discomfort*. This essay is taken from her *Starting from Scratch: A Writer's Manual* (1988), a fascinating look at language and the creative process that goes far beyond the usual cut-and-dried rules and references. Notice how she uses definition not only to inform and explain, but also to entertain the reader and to illustrate strong sociopolitical opinions.

Words to Watch

pendulum (par. 2) a mechanism that swings freely back and forth under the force of gravity

via (par. 3) by way of

yield (par. 4) give way to

lingers (par. 4) stays on

vibrant (par. 6) alive; healthy

tarot deck (par. 6) a deck of illustrated cards thought to be able to predict the future

dangle (par. 6) hang loosely and so as to be able to swing freely

potent (par. 7) strong; forceful

benign (par. 7) not harmful

subversion (par. 8) an attempt to undermine the established way

bloodbath (par. 8) massacre

tyrant (par. 8) absolute, oppressive ruler

indiscriminately (par. 9) without any plan or order

attendant (par. 9) accompanying; following as a consequence

Language is the road map of a culture. It tells you where 1 its people come from and where they are going. A study of the English language reveals a dramatic history and astonishing versatility. It is the language of survivors, of conquerors, of laughter.

A word is more like a pendulum than a fixed entity. It 2 can sweep by your ear and through its very sound suggest hid-

271

den meanings, preconscious associations. Listen to these words: "blood," "tranquil," "democracy." Besides their literal meanings, they carry associations that are cultural as well as personal.

One word can illustrate this idea of meaning in flux: 3 "revolution." The word enters English in the 14th century from the Latin via French. (At least that's when it was first written; it may have been spoken earlier.) "Revolution" means a turning around; that was how it was used. Most often "revolution" was applied to astronomy to describe a planet revolving in space. The word carried no political meaning.

"Rebellion" was the loaded political word. It too comes 4 from Latin (as does about 60 percent of our word pool), and it means a renewal of war. In the 14th century "rebellion" was used to indicate a resistance to lawful authority. This can yield amusing results. Whichever side won called the losers rebels—they, the winners, being the repositories of virtue and more gunpowder. This meaning lingers today. The Confederate fighters are called rebels. Since the North won that war, it can be dismissed as a rebellion and not called a revolution. Whoever wins the war redefines the language.

"Revolution" did not acquire a political meaning in English until at least the 16th century. Its meaning—a circular movement—was still tied to its origin but had spilled over into politics. It could now mean a turnaround in power. This is more complicated than you might think.

The 16th century, vibrant, cruel, progressive, held as a 6 persistent popular image the wheel of fortune—an image familiar to anyone who has played with a tarot deck. Human beings dangle on a giant wheel. Some are on the bottom turning upward, some are on the top, and some are hurtling toward the ground. It's as good an image as any for the sudden twists and turns of Fate, Life or the Human Condition. This idea was so dominant at the time that the word "revolution" absorbed its meaning. Instead of a card or a complicated explanation of the wheel of fortune, that one word captured the concept. It's a concept we would do well to remember.

Politically, "rebellion" was still the more potent word. 7 Cromwell's seizure of state power in the mid-17th century

came to be called the Great Rebellion, because Charles II followed Cromwell in the restoration of monarchy. Cromwell
didn't call his own actions rebellious. In 1689 when William
and Mary took over the throne of England, the event was
tagged the Glorious Revolution. "Revolution" is benign here
and politically inferior in intensity to "rebellion."

By 1796 a shift occurred and "revolution" had come to   8
mean the subversion or overthrow of tyrants. Rebellion, specifically, was a subversion of the laws. Revolution was personal.
So we had the American Revolution, which dumped George III
out of the Colonies, and the French Revolution, which gave us
the murder of Louis XVI and the spectacle of a nation devouring
itself. If you're a Marxist you can recast that to mean one
class destroying another. At any rate, the French Revolution
was a bloodbath and "revolution" began to get a bad name as
far as monarchists were concerned and holy significance as
far as Jacobins were concerned. By that time "revolution"
was developing into the word we know today—not just the
overthrow of a tyrant but action based on belief in a new
principle. Revolution became a political idea, not just a political act.

The Russian Revolution, the Chinese Revolution, the   9
Cuban Revolution—by now "revolution" is the powerful
word, not "rebellion." In the late 1960's and early 1970's
young Americans used the word "revolution" indiscriminately. True, they wanted political power, they were opposed
to tyrants and believed in a new political principle (or an old
one, depending on your outlook) called participatory democracy. However, that period of unrest, with its attendant creativity, did not produce a revolution. The word quickly became corrupted until by the 80's "revolution" was a word
used to sell running shoes.

Whither goest thou, Revolution?   10

BUILDING VOCABULARY

1. Explain the meaning of the terms and phrases in italics.
   Look up any words you don't recognize.

    a. A study of the English language *reveals a dramatic history and astonishing versatility.* (par. 1)

    b. *a fixed entity* (par. 2)

    c. suggest hidden meanings, *preconscious associations* (par. 2)

    d. this idea of meaning *in flux* (par. 3)

    e. 60 percent of our *word pool* (par. 4)

    f. being *the repositories of virtue* and more gunpowder (par. 4)

    g. Its meaning—*a circular movement*—was still *tied to* its origin but had *spilled over* into politics. (par. 5)

    h. when William and Mary took over *the throne of England* (par. 7)

    i. *the spectacle of a nation devouring itself* (par. 8)

    j. ''revolution'' began *to get a bad name* as far as monarchists were concerned and *holy significance* as far as Jacobins were concerned (par. 8)

2. Throughout the essay, Brown makes extensive use of historical *allusions* (see Glossary) including allusions to historical figures and groups, sociopolitical movements, and places. There are fifteen allusions in all. See if you can find and list all fifteen; then choose ten to identify in depth.

UNDERSTANDING THE WRITER'S IDEAS

1. What is the meaning of the opening sentence?

2. According to the author, is English a language that has followed a fixed and steady course in its development? Explain.

3. Explain in your own words what the author means when she writes of words such as ''blood,'' ''tranquil,'' or ''democracy'' that ''besides their literal meanings, they carry associations that are cultural as well as personal'' (par. 1). Write the literal meanings of those words; then write three cultural and personal associations for each.

4. From what language does the English word ''revolution''

come? When did it enter the English language? What was
its earliest recorded meaning in English? From where did
the word "rebellion" come? When? What was its original
meaning?

5. Why does Brown write: "Whoever wins the war redefines
the language" (par. 4)? How does she illustrate this statement?

6. With reference to this essay, outline the changes in cultural associations for the words "revolution" and "rebellion" over the centuries. How were they different? Similar? How did they help to define each other?

7. Briefly describe the sixteenth-century concept of the
"wheel of fortune." How did its meaning change from a
literal image to an abstract concept?

8. At what point in history did "revolution" become a more
politically powerful word than "rebellion"? Why?

9. What is Brown's attitude toward the French Revolution?
If one accepts her opinion, how did the French Revolution
significantly alter the meaning of the word "revolution"?

10. According to Brown, what was the attitude of young
Americans in the 1960s and 1970s? By what events was
this attitude shaped? Does Brown feel this attitude was
positive or negative? Explain.

11. What is Brown's opinion about the use of the word "revolution" in the 1980s?

12. Explain the meaning of the final sentence.

UNDERSTANDING THE WRITER'S TECHNIQUES

1. Writers can use one of several techniques to develop an
extended definition. They include (a) showing how a particular term differs from others that belong to the same
general category, (b) developing the etymology of a term

(its origin and history in the language), and (c) using negation to show what the term does *not* mean.

Which of these three techniques best describes Brown's predominant method in this essay? Does she also make use of the other two techniques? If so, where?

Write a paragraph-by-paragraph outline that traces the development of the predominant technique throughout the essay.

2. How does Brown use the principle of *chronological order* (see Glossary) in this essay?

3. Is there a single thesis statement in the essay? If so, what is it?

4. How does Brown use a *metaphor* in paragraph 1 and a *simile* in paragraph 2 to increase the reader's understanding of language and words?

5. Where is *negation* used in this essay?

6. Who was Brown's intended audience for this essay? How does her choice of subject help you to understand her intended audience? Name three other factors that made you decide that this was Brown's audience.

7. Most essays of definition focus on a single term or concept. Why does Brown choose to define two terms in this essay? In what ways do the two definitions complement each other? Which is the primary term being defined? How do you know?

8. Describe the author's overall purpose in writing this essay. (Refer, if you like, to the introduction to this chapter.)

9. Describe the overall *tone* of this essay. Does the tone befit the subject? How does Brown use *irony* and *sarcasm* (see Glossary) in the essay? Give examples of each. How do the irony and sarcasm influence your reading of this piece?

10. One might say that the last line is written in such a way as

to give it an almost biblical tone. Why would Brown choose this tone? What stylistic elements contribute to that tone?

11. Where does the author use *illustration* in this essay? Comparison and contrast?

12. Would you characterize this definition as primarily *objective* or *subjective* (see Glossary)? Why?

13. Brown clearly indicates the depth of her research and grasp of history through the many historical *allusions* (see Glossary and the Building Vocabulary section) included here. What is their value to the essay? Is it essential that the reader be able to identify each of the allusions? Why or why not?

14. Describe at least two methods by which Brown achieves smooth *transitions* and maintains *coherence* throughout the essay. Give examples.

EXPLORING THE WRITER'S IDEAS

1. The *Oxford English Dictionary*, which you can find in the reference section of the library, traces the etymology of nearly all words in the English language. It includes the historical development of words, with examples of recorded usage, and makes fascinating reading. Select five words from this essay and read their etymologies in the *OED*.

2. In paragraph 1, Brown writes of the "astonishing versatility" of the English language. Later in the book from which this selection is excerpted, she writes: "Fortunately for writers of English we possess the largest vocabulary in the world." Do you feel English is a particularly versatile and expressive language? If so, in what areas of communication is it most versatile or expressive?

   Do you speak or write a language other than English? If so, which do you feel is the best suited for your self-expression? Why? If you don't speak another language, are there any languages you enjoy listening to or looking at even if you can't understand? What makes you feel this way?

3. Americans are sometimes criticized for being essentially monolingual (able to speak only one language). By comparison, many other cultures are multilingual (able to speak more than one language), with the second language often being English. Do you feel people miss anything by being monolingual? For what reasons do you believe the majority of Americans do not learn languages other than English? For what reasons do you feel people all over the world are trying to learn English?

4. In paragraph 3, Brown alludes to the differences between the spoken and the written language—that most often words enter a language's oral communication before they become part of the written language. Give some examples of the differences between oral and written language usage today.

IDEAS FOR WRITING

Guided Writing

Write an extended definition of a term that you feel is critical to the understanding of a particular field of study or skilled activity. For example, if you choose the field-of-study approach, you might consider defining *dig* in archeology, *memory* in computer science, or *comic strip* in pop culture. If you choose a skilled activity, you might consider defining *pas de deux* in ballet, *space* in architecture, or *focal point* in painting.

1. Begin with an original metaphor.

2. Isolate the most important element of the study or activity. Introduce it in paragraph 2 with an original simile expressing the need for illustrating and defining a particular term.

3. Give examples of other terms that also need definition.

4. Write a clear thesis statement that categorizes two sub-topics to help organize your definition.

5. Introduce a secondary, closely related term that can be compared or contrasted with the first in order to produce a clearer definition.

6. Chronologically discuss the etymology of the two terms, continually illustrating the way they relate to each other.

7. Try to include interesting historical allusions.

8. Make use of negation.

9. Don't shy away from making the essay subjective—that is, interjecting your opinions.

10. End your essay with an observation about recent developments in your field of study or activity.

More Writing Projects

1. In your journal, write your own definition of the word "revolution."

2. Select a word that has always intrigued you. Gather information on it from standard sources. Then write an extended one-paragraph definition of it.

3. Write an extended definition of a term that describes a current, serious social issue—for example, homelessness, financial uncertainty, unemployment, substance abuse.

SUMMING UP: CHAPTER 7

1. In her essay on fun in this chapter, Suzanne Britt Jordan defines a term we all understand but might have difficulty explaining. One way she approaches this definition is through negation, that is, explaining what fun *is not*. Write an essay that defines by negation a similar, understood but

difficult-to-explain term—for example "privacy," "the blues," "class," "happiness," or "success."

2. Working with another class member, make a comparative analysis of the Jordan and Scott pieces. Give consideration to theme, subject matter, tone, and language. Then decide how both essays would help a visitor to the United States understand something about American culture. After you have discussed your findings, write your own essay on how the Jordan and Scott selections help to define American culture.

3. Except for Jack Denton Scott's definition of a bagel, the essays in this chapter attempt to define abstractions: *fun, escape* or "*automatic-out,*" and *revolution.* In an essay based on your understanding of the selections by Jordan, Easterbrook, and Brown, explore the nature of successful extended definitions that tend to be abstract. You might pose for yourself the following questions: What examples do the writers offer to support their definitions? How do they limit their approach to the abstract term they are defining? Are their definitions purely personal, and, if so, why?

4. At the beginning of her essay "To the Victor Belongs the Language," Rita Mae Brown declares, "Language is the road map of a culture." For one week, keep a journal in which you list the words, phrases, and expressions that seem to be the most popular among your peers on campus. At the end of the week, compare notes with other members of the class or discuss your findings in a collaborative group of three or four members. Then write an essay defining your campus environment through the language that the students use.

5. Look back over the titles of all the essays in previous chapters of this book. Choose one term from any title (for example, "All-American Girl," "Survival," "Salvation," "Night Walker," "Shack,") and write an essay defining that term *subjectively* (from a personal viewpoint).

CHAPTER 8

Classification

Classification is the arrangement of information into groups or categories in order to make clear the relationships among members of the group. Writers need to classify, because it helps them present a mass of material by means of some orderly system. Related bits of information seem clearer when presented together as parts of a group. We are always classifying things in our daily lives: We put all our textbooks on one shelf or in one corner of the desk; we count on similar items in the supermarket being grouped together so we can buy all our canned vegetables or snacks in a single area; we make categories in our minds of the teachers we like, of the relatives who annoy us, and of the cars that look sleekest on the road. In classifying, we show how things within a large body of information relate to each other; we organize those things into groups so that they make sense to us and to anybody else who is interested in what we are thinking, or saying, or doing.

Classification helps writers explain relationships to their readers. First, a writer will *analyze* a body of material in order to divide some large subject into categories. Called *division* or *analysis,* this first task helps split an idea or an object into parts. Then, some of the parts can serve as categories into which the writer can fit individual pieces that share some common qualities. So, if you wanted to write about sports, for example, you might first break the topic down—*divide* it—into *team sports* and *individual sports* (although there are many other ways you might have made the division). Then you

281

could group together (*classify*) baseball, soccer, and football in the first category; and, perhaps, boxing, wrestling and tennis in the second. Your purpose in dividing or analyzing is to determine the parts of a whole (team sports and individual sports *are* very different).

Division does not always require that classification follow it. Your purpose in classifying, however, is to show how things in a group are similar. (Baseball, soccer, and football have interesting similarities as team sports; boxing, wrestling, and tennis—stressing individual achievement—are related too.) Yet division and classification do work together. If you emptied the contents of a pocketbook onto a table, you would begin to divide those contents into groups. Through division, you would identify objects relating to finances, objects relating to personal care, objects relating to school work. Once you had the divisions clear, you would place objects in each category: money, checks, and credit cards in the first; cosmetics, a comb, perfume in the second; pens, pencils, a notebook in the third.

When you divide and classify for writing, you have to keep several things in mind. You have to think carefully about the division of the topic so that you limit the overlap from group to group. That is best achieved by creating categories different enough from each other so there is no blending. Since you, the writer, have to establish the groups (and sometimes there are many different ways to set up groups for the same topic), you need to use a principle of classification that is sensible, accurate, and complete. Do not force categories just for the sake of making groups. You have to show how things in a group relate to each other, and this you must do without ignoring their differences and without making them stereotypes. If you stereotype objects in a group (whether the objects are people, things, or ideas), you will be oversimplifying them, taking away their individuality, and forcing them to fit your categories.

Classification resembles outlining. It provides the writer with a plan of organization. Whether the subject is personal, technical, simple, complex, or abstract, the writer can organize material about it into categories, and can move carefully from one category to another in developing an essay.

Friends, Good Friends—And Such Good Friends

Judith Viorst

In this essay Judith Viorst, who writes for numerous popular magazines, examines types of friends in her life. Her pattern of development is easy to follow, because she tends to stay on one level in the
process of classification. As you read this essay, try to keep in mind
the similarities and distinctions that Viorst makes among types of
friends, as well as the principles of classification that she uses.

Words to Watch

nonchalant (par. 3)   showing an easy unconcern or disinterest

endodontist (par. 14)   a dentist specializing in diseases of dental
pulp and root canals

sibling (par. 16)   brother or sister

dormant (par. 19)   as if asleep; inactive

self-revelation (par. 22)   self-discovery; self-disclosure

calibrated (par. 29)   measured; fixed; checked carefully

Women are friends, I once would have said, when they 1
totally love and support and trust each other, and bare to each
other the secrets of their souls, and run—no questions
asked—to help each other, and tell harsh truths to each other
(no, you can't wear that dress unless you lose ten pounds first)
when harsh truths must be told.

Women are friends, I once would have said, when they 2
share the same affection for Ingmar Bergman, plus train rides,
cats, warm rain, charades, Camus, and hate with equal ardor
Newark and Brussels sprouts and Lawrence Welk and camping.

In other words, I once would have said that a friend is a 3
friend all the way, but now I believe that's a narrow point of
view. For the friendships I have and the friendships I see are
conducted at many levels of intensity, serve many different
functions, meet different needs and range from those as all-

the-way as the friendship of the soul sisters mentioned above
to that of the most nonchalant and casual playmates.

Consider these varieties of friendship: 4

1. Convenience friends. These are the women with   5
whom, if our paths weren't crossing all the time, we'd have no
particular reason to be friends: a next-door neighbor, a woman
in our car pool, the mother of one of our children's closest
friends or maybe some mommy with whom we serve juice and
cookies each week at the Glenwood Co-op Nursery.

Convenience friends are convenient indeed. They'll lend   6
us their cups and silverware for a party. They'll drive our kids
to soccer when we're sick. They'll take us to pick up our car
when we need a lift to the garage. They'll even take our cats
when we go on vacation. As we will for them.

But we don't, with convenience friends, ever come too   7
close or tell too much; we maintain our public face and emotional distance. "Which means," says Elaine, "that I'll talk
about being overweight but not about being depressed. Which
means I'll admit being mad but not blind with rage. Which
means I might say that we're pinched this month but never
that I'm worried sick over money."

But which doesn't mean that there isn't sufficient value   8
to be found in these friendships of mutual aid, in convenience
friends.

2. Special-interest friends. These friendships aren't inti-   9
mate, and they needn't involve kids or silverware or cats.
Their value lies in some interest jointly shared. And so we
may have an office friend or a yoga friend or a tennis friend or
a friend from the Women's Democratic Club.

"I've got one woman friend," says Joyce, "who likes, as   10
I do, to take psychology courses. Which makes it nice for me—
and nice for her. It's fun to go with someone you know and it's
fun to discuss what you've learned, driving back from the classes." And for the most part, she says, that's all they discuss.

"I'd say that what we're doing is *doing* together, not be-   11
ing together," Suzanne says of her Tuesday-doubles friends.
"It's mainly a tennis relationship, but we play together well.
And I guess we all need to have a couple of playmates."

I agree.   12

My playmate is a shopping friend, a woman of marvelous 13
taste, a woman who knows exactly *where* to buy *what,* and
furthermore is a woman who always knows beyond a doubt
what one ought to be buying. I don't have the time to keep up
with what's new in eyeshadow, hemlines and shoes and
whether the smock look is in or finished already. But since
(oh, shame!) I care a lot about eyeshadow, hemlines and
shoes, and since I don't *want* to wear smocks if the smock
look is finished, I'm very glad to have a shopping friend.

3. Historical friends. We all have a friend who knew us 14
when...maybe way back in Miss Meltzer's second grade,
when our family lived in that three-room flat in Brooklyn,
when our dad was out of work for seven months, when our
brother Allie got in that fight where they had to call the police,
when our sister married the endodontist from Yonkers and
when, the morning after we lost our virginity, she was the
first, the only, friend we told.

The years have gone by and we've gone separate ways 15
and we've little in common now, but we're still an intimate
part of each other's past. And so whenever we go to Detroit
we always go to visit this friend of our girlhood. Who knows
how we looked before our teeth were straightened. Who
knows how we talked before our voice got unBrooklyned.
Who knows what we ate before we learned about artichokes.
And who, by her presence, puts us in touch with an earlier
part of ourself, a part of ourself it's important never to lose.

"What this friend means to me and what I mean to her," 16
says Grace, "is having a sister without sibling rivalry. We
know the texture of each other's lives. She remembers my
grandmother's cabbage soup. I remember the way her uncle
played the piano. There's simply no other friend who remembers those things."

4. Crossroads friends. Like historical friends, our cross- 17
roads friends are important for *what was*—for the friendship
we shared at a crucial, now past, time of life. A time, perhaps,
when we roomed in college together; or worked as eager
young singles in the Big City together; or went together, as my
friend Elizabeth and I did through pregnancy, birth and that
scary first year of new motherhood.

Crossroads friends forge powerful links, links strong 18
enough to endure with not much more contact than once-a-
year letters at Christmas. And out of respect for those crossroads years, for those dramas and dreams we once shared, we
will always be friends.

5. Cross-generational friends. Historical friends and 19
crossroads friends seem to maintain a special kind of intimacy—dormant but always ready to be revived—and though
we may rarely meet, whenever we do connect, it's personal
and intense. Another kind of intimacy exists in the friendships
that form across generations in what one woman calls her
daughter-mother and her mother-daughter relationships.

Evelyn's friend is her mother's age—"but I share so 20
much more than I ever could with my mother"—a woman she
talks to of music, of books and of life. "What I get from her is
the benefit of her experience. What she gets—and enjoys—
from me is a youthful perspective. It's a pleasure for both of
us."

I have in my own life a precious friend, a woman of 65 21
who has lived very hard, who is wise, who listens well; who
has been where I am and can help me understand it; and who
represents not only an ultimate ideal mother to me but also the
person I'd like to be when I grow up.

In our daughter role we tend to do more than our share 22
of self-revelation; in our mother role we tend to receive what's
revealed. It's another kind of pleasure—playing wise mother
to a questing younger person. It's another very lovely kind of
friendship.

6. Part-of-a-couple friends. Some of the women we call 23
our friends we never see alone—we see them as part of a couple at couples' parties. And though we share interests in many
things and respect each other's views, we aren't moved to
deepen the relationship. Whatever the reason, a lack of time
or—and this is more likely—a lack of chemistry, our friendship remains in the context of a group. But the fact that our
feeling on seeing each other is always, "I'm *so* glad she's
here" and the fact that we spend half the evening talking together says that this too, in its own way, counts as a friendship.

(Other part-of-a-couple friends are the friends that came 24

with the marriage, and some of these are friends we could live
without. But sometimes, alas, she married our husband's best
friend; and sometimes, alas, she *is* our husband's best friend.
And so we find ourself dealing with her, somewhat against our
will, in a spirit of what I'll call *reluctant* friendship.)

7. Men who are friends. I wanted to write just of women 25
friends, but the women I've talked to won't let me—they say
I must mention man-woman friendships too. For these friendships can be just as close and as dear as those that we form with
women. Listen to Lucy's description of one such friendship:

"We've found we have things to talk about that are dif- 26
ferent from what he talks about with my husband and different
from what I talk about with his wife. So sometimes we call on
the phone or meet for lunch. There are similar intellectual interests—we always pass on to each other the books that we
love—but there's also something tender and caring too."

In a couple of crises, Lucy says, "he offered himself, for 27
talking and for helping. And when someone died in his family
he wanted me there. The sexual, flirty part of our friendship is
very small, but *some*—just enough to make it fun and different." She thinks—and I agree—that the sexual part, though
small is always *some,* is always there when a man and a
woman are friends.

It's only in the past few years that I've made friends with 28
men, in the sense of a friendship that's *mine,* not just part of
two couples. And achieving with them the ease and the trust
I've found with women friends has value indeed. Under the
dryer at home last week, putting on mascara and rouge, I comfortably sat and talked with a fellow named Peter. Peter, I finally decided, could handle the shock of me minus mascara
under the dryer. Because we care for each other. Because
we're friends.

8. There are medium friends, and pretty good friends, 29
and very good friends indeed, and these friendships are defined by their level of intimacy. And what we'll reveal at each
of these levels of intimacy is calibrated with care. We might
tell a medium friend, for example, that yesterday we had a
fight with our husband. And we might tell a pretty good friend
that this fight with our husband made us so mad that we slept

on the couch. And we might tell a very good friend that the reason we got so mad in that fight that we slept on the couch had something to do with that girl who works in his office. But it's only to our very best friends that we're willing to tell all, to tell what's going on with that girl in his office.

The best of friends, I still believe, totally love and sup- 30
port and trust each other, and bare to each other the secrets of their souls, and run—no questions asked—to help each other, and tell harsh truths to each other when they must be told.

But we needn't agree about everything (only 12-year-old 31
girl friends agree about *everything*) to tolerate each other's point of view. To accept without judgment. To give and to take without ever keeping score. And to *be* there, as I am for them and as they are for me, to comfort our sorrows, to celebrate our joys.

BUILDING VOCABULARY

1. Find *antonyms* (words that mean the opposite of given words) for the following entries:

   a. harsh (par. 1)
   b. mutual (par. 8)
   c. crucial (par. 17)
   d. intimacy (par. 29)
   e. tolerate (par. 31)

2. The *derivation* of a word—how it originated and where it came from—can make you more aware of meanings. Your dictionary normally lists abbreviations (for instance, L. for Latin, Fr. for French) for word origins, and sometimes explains fully the way a word came into use. Look up the following words to determine their origins:

   a. psychology (par. 10)
   b. historical (par. 14)
   c. sibling (par. 16)
   d. Christmas (par. 18)
   e. sexual (par. 27)

UNDERSTANDING THE WRITER'S IDEAS

1. What is Viorst's definition of friendship in the first two paragraphs? Does she accept this definition? Why or why not?

2. Name and describe in your own words the types of friends that Viorst mentions in her essay.

3. In what way are "convenience friends" and "special interest friends" alike? How are "historical friends" and "crossroads friends" alike?

4. What does Viorst mean when she writes, "In our daughter role we tend to do more than our share of self-revelation; in our mother role we tend to receive what's revealed" (par. 22)?

5. How do part-of-a-couple friends who came with the marriage differ from primary part-of-a-couple friends?

6. Does Viorst think that men can be friends for women? Why or why not? What complicates such friendships?

7. For Viorst, who are the best friends?

UNDERSTANDING THE WRITER'S TECHNIQUES

1. Which paragraphs make up the introduction in this essay? How does Viorst organize these paragraphs? Where does she place her thesis sentence?

2. How does the thesis sentence reveal the principles of classification (the questions Viorst asks to produce the various categories) that the author employs in the essay?

3. Does Viorst seem to emphasize each of her categories equally? Is she effective in handling each category? Why or why not? Do you think that men belong in the article as a category? For what reasons?

4. Analyze the importance of illustration in this essay. From what sources does Viorst tend to draw her examples?

5. How do definition and comparison and contrast operate in the essay? Cite specific examples of these techniques.

6. The level of language in this essay tends to be informal at times, reflecting patterns that are as close to conversation as to formal writing. Identify some sentences that seem to resemble informal speech. Why does Viorst try to achieve a conversational style?

7. Which main group in the essay is further broken down into categories?

8. Analyze Viorst's conclusion. How many paragraphs are involved? What strategies does she use? How does she achieve balanced sentence structure (parallelism) in her last lines?

EXPLORING THE WRITER'S IDEAS

1. Do you accept all of Viorst's categories of friendship? Which categories seem the most meaningful to you?

2. Try to think of people you know who fit into the various categories established by Viorst. Can you think of people who might exist in more than one category? How do you explain this fact? What are the dangers in trying to stereotype people in terms of categories, roles, backgrounds, or functions?

3. Viorst maintains that you can define friends in terms of functions and needs (see paragraph 3 and paragraphs 29 to 31). Would you agree? Why or why not? What principle or principles do you use to classify friends? In fact, *do* you classify friends? For what reasons?

IDEAS FOR WRITING

Guided Writing

Using the classification method, write an essay on a specific group of individuals—for instance, *types of friends, types of enemies, types of students, types of teachers, types of politicians, types of dates*—and so forth.

1. Establish your subject in the first paragraph. Also indicate to the reader the principle(s) of classification that you plan to use. (For guidelines look again at the second sentence in paragraph 3 of Viorst's essay.)

2. Start the body of the essay with a single short sentence that introduces categories (see paragraph 4). In the body, use numbers and category headings (''Convenience friends''... ''Special interest friends'') to separate groups.

3. Try to achieve a balance in the presentation of information on each category. Define each type and provide appropriate examples.

4. If helpful, use comparison and contrast to indicate from time to time the similarities and differences among groups. Try to avoid too much overlapping of groups, since this is harmful to the classification process.

5. Employ the personal ''I'' and other conversational techniques to achieve an informal style.

6. Return to your principle(s) of classification and amplify this feature in your conclusion. If you want, make a value judgment, as Viorst does, about which type of person in your classification scheme is the most significant.

More Writing Projects

1. As journal practice, classify varieties of show business comedians, singers, talk show hosts, star athletes, or the like.

2. In a paragraph, use division and(or) classification to explain the various roles that you must play as a friend.

3. Ask each student in your class to explain what he or she means by the term "friendship." List all responses and then divide the list into at least three categories. Using your notes, write a classification essay reporting your findings.

The Three New Yorks

E. B. White

E. B. White, whose frequently used book *The Elements of Style* is well known to college composition students, here classifies "The Three New Yorks." Although the selection is an excerpt from his book *Here is New York* (1949), the descriptive illustrations remain remarkably fresh after more than forty years. Look closely at the way White clearly defines his categories of classification, then skillfully blends them to create a vivid sense of the whole city.

Words to Watch

locusts (par. 1)   migratory grasshoppers that travel in swarms, stripping vegetation as they pass over the land

disposition (par. 1)   temperament; way of acting

deportment (par. 1)   the way in which a person carries himself or herself

tidal (par. 1)   coming in wave-like motions

continuity (par. 1)   uninterrupted flow of events

slum (par. 1)   a highly congested residential area marked by unsanitary buildings, poverty, and social disorder

indignity (par. 1)   humiliating treatment

vitality (par. 2)   lively and animated character

gloaming (par. 2)   a poetic term for "twilight"

ramparts (par. 2)   high broad structures guarding a building

negligently (par. 2)   nonchalantly; neglectfully

loiterer (par. 2)   a person who hangs around aimlessly

spewing (par. 2)   coming in a flood or gush

rover (par. 2)   wanderer; roamer

There are roughly three New Yorks. There is, first, the 1 New York of the man or woman who was born here, who takes the city for granted and accepts its size and its turbulence as natural and inevitable. Second, there is the New York of the commuter—the city that is devoured by locusts each day and spat out each night. Third, there is the New York of the person who was born somewhere else and came to New York in quest of something. Of these three trembling cities the greatest is the last—the city of final destination, the city that is a goal. It is this third city that accounts for New York's high-strung disposition, its poetical deportment, its dedication to the arts, and its incomparable achievements. Commuters give the city its tidal restlessness; natives give it solidity and continuity; but the settlers give it passion. And whether it is a farmer arriving from Italy to set up a small grocery store in a slum, or a young girl arriving from a small town in Mississippi to escape the indignity of being observed by her neighbors, or a boy arriving from the Corn Belt with a manuscript in his suitcase and a pain in his heart, it makes no difference; each embraces New York with the intense excitement of first love, each absorbs New York with the fresh eyes of an adventurer, each generates heat and light to dwarf the Consolidated Edison Company.

 The commuter is the queerest bird of all. The suburb he 2 inhabits has no essential vitality of its own and is a mere roost where he comes at day's end to go to sleep. Except in rare cases, the man who lives in Mamaroneck or Little Neck or Teaneck, and works in New York, discovers nothing much about the city except the time of arrival and departure of trains and buses, and the path to a quick lunch. He is deskbound, and has never, idly roaming in the gloaming, stumbled suddenly on Belvedere Tower in the Park, seen the ramparts rise sheer from the water of the pond, and the boys along the shore fishing for minnows, girls stretched out negligently on the shelves of the rocks; he has never come suddenly on anything at all in New York as a loiterer, because he has had no time between trains. He has fished in Manhattan's wallet and dug out coins, but has never listened to Manhattan's breathing, never awakened to its morning, never dropped off to sleep in its night. About 400,000 men and women come charging onto the Island each week-day morning, out of the mouths of tubes and tunnels. Not many among them have ever spent a drowsy afternoon in the great rustling oaken silence of the reading room of the Public Library, with the book elevator (like an old water wheel) spewing out books onto the trays. They tend their fur-

naces in Westchester and in Jersey, but have never seen the
furnaces of the Bowery, the fires that burn in oil drums on
zero winter nights. They may work in the financial district
downtown and never see the extravagant plantings of Rock-
efeller Center—the daffodils and grape hyacinths and birches
of the flags trimmed to the wind on a fine morning in spring.
Or they may work in a midtown office and may let a whole
year swing round without sighting Governor's Island from the
sea wall. The commuter dies with tremendous mileage to his
credit, but he is no rover. His entrances and exits are more
devious than those in a prairie-dog village; and he calmly
plays bridge while his train is buried in the mud at the bottom
of the East River. The Long Island Rail Road alone carried
forty million commuters last year; but many of them were the
same fellow retracing his steps.

The terrain of New York is such that a resident some-   3
times travels farther, in the end, than a commuter. The journey of the composer Irving Berlin from Cherry Street in the
lower East Side to an apartment uptown was through an alley
and was only three or four miles in length; but it was like going
three times around the world.

BUILDING VOCABULARY

1. Underline the numerous references in this essay to buildings, people, and areas in and around New York City and
   identify them. If necessary, consult a guidebook, map, or
   history of New York City for help.

2. Write *synonyms* (words that mean the same) for each of
   these words in the essay. Use a dictionary if necessary.

   a. turbulence (par. 1)
   b. inevitable (par. 1)
   c. quest (par. 1)
   d. high-strung (par. 1)
   e. incomparable (par. 1)
   f. essential (par. 2)

g. deskbound (par. 2)

h. drowsy (par. 2)

i. extravagant (par. 2)

j. devious (par. 2)

UNDERSTANDING THE WRITER'S IDEAS

1. What are the three New Yorks?

2. What single-word designation does E. B. White assign to each of the three types of New Yorkers? Match up each of the three New Yorks you identified in the first question with each of the three types of New Yorkers.

3. For what reasons do people born elsewhere come to New York to live? What three illustrations of such people does White describe? What is the young girl's indignity? What is the occupation or hope of the boy from the Corn Belt? Why might he have "a pain in his heart"?

4. What does each type of New Yorker give to the city?

5. What is White's attitude toward the suburbs? What key phrases reveal this attitude?

6. What are some of the things commuters miss about New York by dashing in and out of the city? What does White ironically suggest will be the commuter's final fate?

7. Are we to take literally White's conclusion that "many of them are the same fellow retracing his steps"? Why or why not?

8. Explain the sentence "The terrain of New York is such that a resident sometimes travels farther, in the end, than a commuter." Be aware that White is using language figuratively.

9. The author tells of composer Irving Berlin's journey through an alley. He is referring to "Tin Pan Alley." Identify this place.

UNDERSTANDING THE WRITER'S TECHNIQUES

1. In this essay what is the thesis? Where is it? Is it developed fully?

2. What is the purpose of classification in this essay? What is the basis of the classification White uses? What key words at the beginning of paragraph 1 direct your attention to each category discussed? How do these key words contrast in tone with the descriptions in the first few sentences? What sort of rhythm is established?

3. White vividly *personifies* (see Glossary) New York City in paragraph 1. List and explain the effects of these personifications. Where else does he personify?

4. Refer to your answer to question 2 in the Building Vocabulary section. Are the literal meanings of those words appropriate to White's three types of New Yorkers? Defend your answer. Figuratively, what does each term make you think of? How do the figurative meanings enhance the essay?

5. How does White use *illustration* in this essay? Where does he use it most effectively?

6. What is the function of *negation* (see page 245) in the first part of paragraph 2? What is the *implied contrast* in this paragraph?

7. How is White's attitude toward New York reflected in the tone of this essay?

8. White makes widespread use of *metaphor* (see Glossary) in this essay. How does his use of metaphor affect the *tone* of the essay? State in your own words the meaning of each of the following metaphors:

   a. ...the city that is devoured by locusts each day and spat out each night. (par. 1)
   b. The commuter is the queerest bird of all. (par. 2)
   c. a mere roost (par. 2)
   d. idly roaming in the gloaming (par. 2)

   e. He has fished in Manhattan's wallet and dug out coins,
   but he has never listened to Manhattan's breathing.
   (par. 2)
   f. the great rustling oaken silence (par. 2)

9. Among all the metaphors, White uses just one *simile* (see
Glossary). What is it? What is the effect of placing it where
he did?

EXPLORING THE WRITER'S IDEAS

1. At the beginning of the essay, E. B. White states that New
York's "turbulence" is considered "natural and inevitable" by its native residents. But such a condition is true for
any large city. If you live in a large city, or if you have ever
visited one, what are some examples of its turbulence? Do
you think it is always a good idea to accept the disorder of
the place where you live? How can such acceptance be a
positive attitude? How can it be negative? How do you
deal with disruptions in your environment?

2. White writes of "a young girl arriving from a small town in
Mississippi to escape the indignity of being observed by her
neighbors." Tell in your own words what might cause her indignity. How can neighbors bring about such a condition?

3. Some people feel the anonymity of a big city like New
York makes it easier just to "be yourself" without having
to worry about what others might say. Others feel such anonymity creates a terrible feeling of impersonality. Discuss
the advantages and disadvantages of each attitude.

4. Do you agree that the suburbs have "no essential vitality"?
Explain your response by referring to suburbs you have
visited, have read about, or have inhabited.

5. White claims that those who choose to leave their homes
and who come to live in New York give the place a special
vitality. Do you know any people who chose to leave their
places of birth to live in a large city like New York? Why
did they move? How have things gone for them since they

began living in the city? Have you noticed any changes? For what reasons do people leave one place to live in another? When have you moved from place to place? Why?

IDEAS FOR WRITING

Guided Writing

Organize a classification essay around the city or town in which you live.

1. Begin with a simple direct thesis statement that tells the reader how many categories of classification you will consider.

2. Briefly outline the different categories. Indicate each with a key organizational word or phrase.

3. Indicate which category is the most important. Tell why.

4. Develop this category with at least three vivid illustrations.

5. Define one of the categories through both negation and an implied contrast to another category.

6. Use figurative language (metaphors, similes, personification) throughout your essay.

7. Use specific name or place references.

8. End your essay with a brief factual narrative that gives the reader a feel for your town or city.

More Writing Projects

1. Use classification in a journal entry to capture at least three ways of viewing your college.

2. Write a classification paragraph on the suburbs or the country.

3. Select a cultural group and classify in an essay various characteristics common to that group. Be careful to avoid stereotyping.

How Do We Find the Student in a World of Academic Gymnasts and Worker Ants?

James T. Baker

As you look around your classrooms, school cafeteria, lecture halls, or gymnasium, perhaps you will recognize representatives of the types of students that James Baker classifies in this witty, wry essay. The author's unique categories are enhanced by his use of description, definition, and colloquial language, which help make his deliberate stereotypes "come alive."

Words to Watch

musings (par. 3)   dreamy, abstract thoughts

sabbatical (par. 3)   a paid leave from a job earned after a certain period of time

malaise (par. 3)   uneasiness; feelings of restlessness

impaired (par. 3)   made less effective

clones (par. 4)   exact biological replicas, asexually produced

recuperate (par. 5)   to undergo recovery from an illness

esoteric (par. 7)   understood by a limited group with special knowledge

primeval (par. 7)   primitive; relating to the earliest ages

mundane (par. 8)   ordinary

jaded (par. 20)   exhausted; bored by something from overexposure to it

Anatole France once wrote that "the whole art of teaching is only the art of awakening the natural curiosity of young minds." I fully agree, except I have to wonder if, by using the word "only," he thought that the art of awakening such natural curiosity was an easy job. For me, it never has been— sometimes exciting, always challenging, but definitely not easy. 1

Robert M. Hutchins used to say that a good education prepares students to go on educating themselves throughout 2

299

their lives. A fine definition, to be sure, but it has at times made me doubt that my own students, who seem only too eager to graduate so they can lay down their books forever, are receiving a good education.

But then maybe these are merely the pessimistic musings ₃ of someone suffering from battle fatigue. I have almost qualified for my second sabbatical leave, and I am scratching a severe case of the seven-year itch. About the only power my malaise has not impaired is my eye for spotting certain "types" of students. In fact, as the rest of me declines, my eye seems to grow more acute.

Has anyone else noticed that the very same students ₄ people college classrooms year after year? Has anyone else found the same bodies, faces, personalities returning semester after semester? Forgive me for violating my students' individual "personhoods," but reality makes it so tempting to see them as types. Doubtless you will recognize at least some of them. They have twins, or perhaps clones, on your campus, too.

There is the eternal Good Time Charlie (or Charlene), ₅ who makes every party on and off the campus, who by November of his freshman year has worked his face into a case of terminal acne, who misses every set of examinations because of "mono," who finally burns himself out physically and mentally by the age of 19 and drops out to go home and recuperate, and who returns at 20 after a long talk with Dad to major in accounting.

There is the Young General Patton, the one who comes ₆ to college on an R.O.T.C. scholarship and for a year twirls his rifle at basketball games while loudly sniffing out pinko professors, who at midpoint takes a sudden but predictable, radical swing from far right to far left, who grows a beard and moves in with a girl who refuses to shave her legs, who then makes the just as predictable, radical swing back to the right and ends up preaching fundamentalist sermons on the steps of the student union while the Good Time Charlies and Charlenes jeer.

There is the Egghead, the campus intellectual who ₇ shakes up his fellow students—and even a professor or two—

with references to esoteric formulas and obscure Bulgarian poets, who is recognized by friend and foe alike as a promising young academic, someday to be a professional scholar, who disappears every summer for six weeks ostensibly to search for primeval human remains in Colorado caves, and who at 37 is shot dead by Arab terrorists while on a mission for the c.i.a.

There is the Performer—the music or theater major, the rock or folk singer—who spends all of his or her time working up an act, who gives barely a nod to mundane subjects like history, sociology, or physics, who dreams only of the day he or she will be on stage full time, praised by critics, cheered by audiences, who ends up either pregnant or responsible for a pregnancy and at 30 is either an insurance salesman or a housewife with a very lush garden. **8**

There is the Jock, of course—the every-afternoon intra- mural champ, smelling of liniment and Brut, with bulging calves and a blue-eyed twinkle, the subject of untold numbers of female fantasies, the walking personification of he-man- ism—who upon graduation is granted managerial rank by a California bank because of his golden tan and low golf score, who is seen five years later buying the drinks at a San Fran- cisco gay bar. **9**

There is the Academic Gymnast—the guy or gal who sees college as an obstacle course, as so many stumbling blocks in the way of a great career or a perfect marriage—who strains every moment to finish and be done with "this place" forever, who toward the end of the junior year begins to slow down, to grow quieter and less eager to leave, who attends summer school, but never quite finishes those last six hours, who never leaves "this place," and who at 40 is still working at the campus laundry, still here, still a student. **10**

There is the Medal Hound, the student who comes to college not to learn or expand any intellectual horizons but simply to win honors—medals, cups, plates, ribbons, scrolls— who is here because this is the best place to win the most the fastest, who plasticizes and mounts on his wall every certifi- cate of excellence he wins, who at 39 will be a colonel in the U.S. Army and at 55 Secretary of something or other in a con- servative Administration in Washington. **11**

There is the Worker Ant, the student (loosely rendered) 12
who takes 21 hours a semester and works 49 hours a week at
the local car wash, who sleeps only on Sundays and during
classes, who will somehow graduate on time and be the owner
of his own vending-machine company at 30 and be dead of a
heart attack at 40, and who will be remembered for the words
chiseled on his tombstone:

All This Was Accomplished Without Ever Having So 13
Much as Darkened The Door Of A Library

There is the Lost Soul, the sad kid who is in college only 14
because teachers, parents, and society at large said so, who
hasn't a career in mind or a dream to follow, who hasn't a
clue, who heads home every Friday afternoon to spend the
weekend cruising the local Dairee-Freeze, who at 50 will have
done all his teachers, parents, and society said to do, still
without a career in mind or a dream to follow or a clue.

There is also the Saved Soul—the young woman who has 15
received, through the ministry of one Gospel freak or another,
a Holy Calling to save the world, or at least some special part
of it—who majors in Russian studies so that she can be caught
smuggling Bibles into the Soviet Union and be sent to Siberia
where she can preach to souls imprisoned by the Agents of Satan in the Gulag Archipelago.

Then, finally, there is the Happy Child, who comes to 16
college to find a husband or wife—and finds one—and there is
the Determined Child, who comes to get a degree—and gets
one.

Enough said.   17

All of which, I suppose, should make me throw up my 18
hands in despair and say that education, like youth and love,
is wasted on the young. Not quite.

For there does come along, on occasion, that one of a 19
hundred or so who is maybe at first a bit lost, certainly puzzled; who may well start out a Good Timer, an Egghead, a
Performer, a Jock, a Medal Hound, a Gymnast, a Worker
Ant; who may indeed have trouble settling on a major, who
will be distressed by what sometimes passes for education,
who might even be a temporary dropout; but who has a vital
capacity for growth and is able to fall in love with learning,

who acquires a taste for intellectual pleasure, who becomes in the finest sense of the word a Student.

This is the one who keeps the most jaded of us going 20 back to class after class, and he or she must be oh-so-carefully cultivated. He or she must be artfully awakened, given the tools needed to continue learning for a lifetime, and let grow at whatever pace and in whatever direction nature dictates.

For I try always to remember that this student is me, my 21 continuing self, my immortality. This person is my only hope that my own search for Truth will continue after me, on and on, forever.

BUILDING VOCABULARY

1. Explain these *colloquialisms* (see Glossary) in Baker's essay:

   a. I am scratching a severe case of the seven-year itch (par. 3)
   b. someone suffering from battle fatigue (par. 3)
   c. worked his face into a case of terminal acne (par. 5)
   d. burns himself out physically and mentally (par. 5)
   e. loudly sniffing out pinko professors (par. 6)
   f. working up an act (par. 8)
   g. gives barely a nod (par. 8)
   h. the walking personification of he-man-ism (par. 9)
   i. to spend the weekend cruising the local Dairee-Freeze (par. 14)
   j. he or she must be oh-so-carefully cultivated (par. 20)

2. Identify these references:

   a. R.O.T.C. (par. 6)
   b. C.I.A. (par. 7)
   c. Brut (par. 9)
   d. Dairee-Freeze (par. 14)
   e. Gospel freak (par. 15)
   f. Agents of Satan (par. 15)
   g. Gulag Archipelago (par. 15)

UNDERSTANDING THE WRITER'S IDEAS

1. In common language, describe the various categories of college students that Baker names.

2. Who is Anatole France? What process is described in the quotation from him? Why does Baker cite it at the beginning of the essay? What is his attitude toward France's idea?

3. For how long has Baker been teaching? What is his attitude toward his work?

4. About what age do you think Baker is? Why? Explain the meaning of the sentence: "In fact, as the rest of me declines, my eye seems to grow more acute" (par. 3).

5. Choose three of Baker's categories and paraphrase each description and meaning in a serious way.

6. What does Baker feel, overall, is the contemporary college student's attitude toward studying and receiving an education? How does it differ from Baker's own attitude toward these things?

7. Although Baker's classification may seem a bit pessimistic, he refuses to "throw up...[his] hands in despair" (par. 18). Why?

8. Describe the characteristics that are embodied in the category of *Student*. To whom does Baker compare the "true" Student? Why?

UNDERSTANDING THE WRITER'S TECHNIQUES

1. In this essay Baker deliberately creates, rather than avoids, stereotypes (see Introduction to Chapter 8, page 282). He does so to establish exaggerated representatives of types. Why?

   For paragraphs 5 to 16, prepare a paragraph-by-

paragraph outline of the main groups of students classified. For each, include the following information:

 a. type represented by the stereotype
 b. motivation of type for being a student
 c. main activity as a student
 d. condition in which the type ends up

2. What is Baker's thesis in this essay? Does he state it directly or not? What, in your own words, is his purpose?

3. This article was published in "The Chronicle of Higher
Education," a weekly newspaper for college and university educators and administrators. How do you think this
audience influenced Baker's analysis of types of students?
His tone and language?

4. What is Baker's tone in the essay? Give specific examples. In general, how would you characterize his attitude
toward the contemporary college student? Why? Does his
attitude or tone undergo any shifts in the essay? Explain.

5. Why does Baker use the term "personhoods" in paragraph 4? What attitude, about what subject, does he convey in his use of that word?

6. Why does the author capitalize the names he gives to the
various categories of students? Why does he capitalize the
word "Truth" in the last sentence?

7. How does Baker use *definition* in this essay? What purpose does it serve?

8. How does Baker use *description* to enhance his analysis
in this essay?

9. In this essay, what is the role of *process analysis? (Process analysis,* discussed in the next chapter, is telling how
something is done or proceeds; see pages 322–323.) Look
especially at Baker's descriptions of each type of student.
How does process analysis figure into the title of the essay?

10. What is the purpose of the one-sentence paragraph 13?

Why does Baker set it aside from paragraph 12, since it is a logical conclusion to that paragraph? Why does he use a two-word sentence as the complete paragraph 17? In what ways do these words signal the beginning of the essay's conclusion?

EXPLORING THE WRITER'S IDEAS

1. Do you think Baker's classifications in this essay are fair? Are they representative of the whole spectrum of students? How closely do they mirror the student population at your school? The article was written in 1982; how well have Baker's classifications held up to the present conditions?

2. Into which category (or categories) would you place yourself? Why?

3. Based on your reaction to and understanding of this article, would you like to have Baker as your professor? Why or why not?

IDEAS FOR WRITING

Guided Writing

Write a classification of at least three "types" in a situation with which you are familiar, other than school—a certain job, social event, sport, or some such situation.

1. Begin your essay with a reference, direct or indirect, to what some well-known writer or expert said about this situation.

2. Identify your role in relation to the situation described.

3. Write about your attitude toward the particular situation and why you are less than thrilled about it at present.

4. Make sure you involve the reader as someone who would be familiar with the situation and activities described.

5. Divide your essay into exaggerated or stereotyped categories which you feel represent almost the complete range of types in these situations. In your categorization, be sure to include motivations, activities, and results for each type.

6. Use description to make your categories vivid.

7. Use satire and a bit of gentle cynicism as part of your description.

8. Select a lively title.

9. In the conclusion, identify another type that you consider the "purest" or "most truthful" representative of persons in this situation. Either by comparison with yourself, or by some other means, explain why you like this type best.

More Writing Projects

1. In your journal, write your own classification of three college "types." Your entry can be serious or humorous.

2. In a 250-word paragraph, classify types of college dates.

3. Look in current magazines for advertisements directed at men or women, or both. Write an essay in which you classify current advertisements according to some logical scheme. Limit your essay to three to five categories.

What to Listen for in Music

Aaron Copland

Aaron Copland, born at the turn of the century, is among America's most renowned composers and commentators on music. His musical compositions include symphonies, chamber music, film scores, and perhaps best known, his scores for the ballets *Rodeo, Billy the Kid,* and *Appalachian Spring.* In this essay, he classifies three "planes" of the process of listening to music, and he develops his concept of each one through a skillful blending of description, comparison, illustration, and direct appeals to the reader. Ultimately, it is Copland's wish that the reader become more actively involved in the listening process.

Words to Watch

engendered (par. 2)　　caused to exist

belittle (par. 3)　　ridicule

consolation (par. 4)　　comfort; relief

apropos (par. 4)　　pertinent to

disproportionate (par. 5)　　unbalanced

constitute (par. 5)　　to make up or contribute to something

commensurate (par. 6)　　proportionate; corresponding

fury (par. 10)　　rage; anger

pessimistically (par. 12)　　without hope

inherent (par. 14)　　involved in the essential character of something

engrossed (par. 17)　　mentally absorbed in something

layman (par. 17)　　nonprofessional; amateur

correlate (par. 20)　　relate to; correspond to

We all listen to music according to our separate capacities. But, for the sake of analysis, the whole listening process may become clearer if we break it up into its component parts, so to speak. In a certain sense we all listen to music on three separate planes. For lack of a better terminology, one might name these: (1) the sensuous plane, (2) the expressive plane, (3) the sheerly musical plane. The only advantage to be gained from mechanically splitting up the listening process into these hypothetical planes is the clearer view to be had of the way in which we listen.

The simplest way of listening to music is to listen for the 2 sheer pleasure of the musical sound itself. That is the sensuous plane. It is the plane on which we hear music without thinking, without considering it in any way. One turns on the radio while doing something else and absentmindedly bathes in the sound. A kind of brainless but attractive state of mind is engendered by the mere sound appeal of the music.

You may be sitting in a room reading this book. Imagine 3 one note struck on the piano. Immediately that one note is enough to change the atmosphere of the room—proving that the sound element in music is a powerful and mysterious agent, which it would be foolish to deride or belittle.

The surprising thing is that many people who consider 4 themselves qualified music lovers abuse that plane in listening. They go to concerts in order to lose themselves. They use music as a consolation or an escape. They enter an ideal world where one doesn't have to think of the realities of everyday life. Of course they aren't thinking about the music either. Music allows them to leave it, and they go off to a place to dream, dreaming because of and apropos of the music yet never quite listening to it.

Yes, the sound appeal of music is a potent and primitive 5 force, but you must not allow it to usurp a disproportionate share of your interest. The sensuous plane is an important one in music, a very important one, but it does not constitute the whole story.

There is no need to digress further on the sensuous 6 plane. Its appeal to every normal human being is self-evident. There is, however, such a thing as becoming more sensitive to the different kinds of sound stuff as used by various composers. For all composers do not use that sound stuff in the same way. Don't get the idea that the value of music is commensurate with its sensuous appeal or that the loveliest sounding music is made by the greatest composer. If that were so, Ravel would be a greater creator than Beethoven. The point is that the sound element varies with each composer, that his usage of sound forms an integral part of his style and must be taken into account when listening. The reader can see, therefore, that a more conscious approach is valuable even on this primary plane of music listening.

The second plane on which music exists is what I have called the expressive one. Here, immediately, we tread on controversial ground. Composers have a way of shying away from any discussion of music's expressive side. Did not Stravinsky himself proclaim that his music was an "object," a "thing," with a life of its own, and with no other meaning than its own purely musical existence? This intransigent attitude of Stravinsky's may be due to the fact that so many people have tried to read different meanings into so many pieces. Heaven knows it is difficult enough to say precisely what it is that a piece of music means, to say it definitely, to say it finally so that everyone is satisfied with your explanation. But that should not lead one to the other extreme of denying to music the right to be "expressive." 7

My own belief is that all music has an expressive power, some more and some less, but that all music has a certain meaning behind the notes and that that meaning behind the note constitutes, after all, what the piece is saying, what the piece is about. This whole problem can be stated quite simply by asking, "Is there a meaning to music?" My answer to that would be "Yes." And "Can you state in so many words what the meaning is?" My answer to that would be, "No." Therein lies the difficulty. 8

Simple-minded souls will never be satisfied with the answer to the second of these questions. They always want music to have a meaning, and the more concrete it is the better they like it. The more the music reminds them of a train, a storm, a funeral, or any other familiar conception the more expressive it appears to be to them. This popular idea of music's meaning—stimulated and abetted by the usual run of musical commentator—should be discouraged wherever and whenever it is met. One timid lady once confessed to me that she suspected something seriously lacking in her appreciation of music because of her inability to connect it with anything definite. That is getting the whole thing backward, of course. 9

Still, the question remains, How close should the intelli- 10
gent music lover wish to come to pinning a definite meaning to
any particular work? No closer than a general concept, I
should say. Music expresses, at different moments, serenity
or exuberance, regret or triumph, fury or delight. It expresses
each of these moods, and many others, in a numberless variety of subtle shadings and differences. It may even express a
state of meaning for which there exists no adequate word in
any language. In that case, musicians often like to say that it
has only a purely musical meaning. They sometimes go farther
and say that *all* music has only a purely musical meaning.
What they really mean is that no appropriate word can be
found to express the music's meaning and that, even if it
could, they do not feel the need of finding it.

But whatever the professional musician may hold, most 11
musical novices still search for specific words with which to
pin down their musical reactions. That is why they always find
Tchaikovsky easier to "understand" than Beethoven. In the
first place, it is easier to pin a meaning-word on a Tchaikovsky
piece than on a Beethoven one. Much easier. Moreover, with
the Russian composer, every time you come back to a piece of
his it almost always says the same thing to you, whereas with
Beethoven it is often quite difficult to put your finger right on
what he is saying. And any musician will tell you that that is
why Beethoven is the greater composer. Because music
which always says the same thing to you will necessarily
soon become dull music, but music whose meaning is slightly different with each hearing has a greater chance of remaining alive.

Listen, if you can, to the forty-eight fugue themes of 12
Bach's *Well Tempered Clavichord*. Listen to each theme, one
after another. You will soon realize that each theme mirrors a
different world of feeling. You will also soon realize that the
more beautiful a theme seems to you the harder it is to find
any word that will describe it to your complete satisfaction.
Yes, you will certainly know whether it is a gay theme or a sad
one. You will be able, in other words, in your own mind, to
draw a frame of emotional feeling around your theme. Now
study the sad one a little closer. Try to pin down the exact

quality of its sadness. Is it pessimistically sad or resignedly sad; is it fatefully sad or smilingly sad?

Let us suppose that you are fortunate and can describe 13 to your own satisfaction in so many words the exact meaning of your chosen theme. There is still no guarantee that anyone else will be satisfied. Nor need they be. The important thing is that each one feel for himself the specific expressive quality of a theme or, similarly, an entire piece of music. And if it is a great work of art, don't expect it to mean exactly the same thing to you each time you return to it.

Themes or pieces need not express only one emotion, of 14 course. Take such a theme as the first main one of the *Ninth Symphony*, for example. It is clearly made up of different elements. It does not say only one thing. Yet anyone hearing it immediately gets a feeling of strength, a feeling of power. It isn't a power that comes simply because the theme is played loudly. It is a power inherent in the theme itself. The extraordinary strength and vigor of the theme results in the listener's receiving an impression that a forceful statement has been made. But one should never try to boil it down to "the fateful hammer of life," etc. That is where the trouble begins. The musician, in his exasperation, says it means nothing but the notes themselves, whereas the nonprofessional is only too anxious to hang on to any explanation that gives him the illusion of getting closer to the music's meaning.

Now, perhaps, the reader will know better what I mean 15 when I say that music does have an expressive meaning but that we cannot say in so many words what that meaning is.

The third plane on which music exists is the sheerly mu- 16 sical plane. Besides the pleasurable sound of music and the expressive feeling that it gives off, music does exist in terms of the notes themselves and of their manipulation. Most listeners are not sufficiently conscious of this third plane....

Professional musicians, on the other hand, are, if any- 17 thing, too conscious of the mere notes themselves. They often fall into the error of becoming so engrossed with their arpeggios and staccatos that they forget the deeper aspects of the music they are performing. But from the layman's standpoint, it is not so much a matter of getting over bad habits on the sheerly musical plane as of increasing one's awareness of what is going on, in so far as the notes are concerned.

When the man in the street listens to the "notes themselves" with any degree of concentration, he is most likely to make some mention of the melody. Either he hears a pretty melody or he does not, and he generally lets it go at that. Rhythm is likely to gain his attention next, particularly if it seems exciting. But harmony and tone color are generally taken for granted, if they are thought of consciously at all. As for music's having a definite form of some kind, that idea seems never to have occurred to him. 18

It is very important for all of us to become more alive to music on its sheerly musical plane. After all, an actual musical material is being used. The intelligent listener must be prepared to increase his awareness of the musical material and what happens to it. He must hear the melodies, the rhythms, the harmonies, the tone colors in a more conscious fashion. But above all he must, in order to follow the line of the composer's thought, know something of the principles of musical form. Listening to all of these elements is listening on the sheerly musical plane. 19

Let me repeat that I have split up mechanically the three separate planes on which we listen merely for the sake of greater clarity. Actually, we never listen on one or the other of these planes. What we do is to correlate them—listening in all three ways at the same time. It takes no mental effort, for we do it instinctively. 20

Perhaps an analogy with what happens to us when we visit the theater will make this instinctive correlation clearer. In the theater, you are aware of the actors and actresses, costumes and sets, sounds and movements. All these give one the sense that the theater is a pleasant place to be in. They constitute the sensuous plane in our theatrical reactions. 21

The expressive plane in the theater would be derived from the feeling that you get from what is happening on the stage. You are moved to pity, excitement, or gayety. It is this general feeling, generated aside from the particular words being spoken, a certain emotional something which exists on the stage, that is analogous to the expressive quality in music. 22

The plot and plot development is equivalent to our 23
sheerly musical plane. The playwright creates and develops a
character in just the same way that a composer creates and
develops a theme. According to the degree of your awareness
of the way in which the artist in either field handles his material will you become a more intelligent listener.

It is easy enough to see that the theatergoer never is con- 24
scious of any of these elements separately. He is aware of
them all at the same time. The same is true of music listening.
We simultaneously and without thinking listen on all three
planes.

In a sense, the ideal listener is both inside and outside 25
the music at the same moment, judging it and enjoying it,
wishing it would go one way and watching it go another—almost like the composer at the moment he composes it; because in order to write his music, the composer must also be
inside and outside his music, carried away by it and yet coldly
critical of it. A subjective and objective attitude is implied in
both creating and listening to music.

What the reader should strive for, then, is a more *active* 26
kind of listening. Whether you listen to Mozart or Duke Ellington, you can deepen your understanding of music only
by being a more conscious and aware listener—not someone
who is just listening, but someone who is listening *for* something.

BUILDING VOCABULARY

1. Identify the following composers mentioned in this essay:

   Ravel
   Beethoven
   Stravinsky
   Tchaikovsky
   Bach
   Duke Ellington

2. Match the words in Column A with their *synonyms* in Column B.

Column A	Column B
1 hypothetical	**a** irritation
2 deride	**b** essential
3 potent	**c** strength
4 usurp	**d** ridicule
5 integral	**e** strong
6 intransigent	**f** idea
7 conception	**g** calm
8 abetted	**h** assisted
9 serenity	**i** artful
10 exuberance	**j** uncompromising
11 subtle	**k** conjectural
12 novices	**l** seize
13 exasperation	**m** enthusiasm
14 vigor	**n** beginners

UNDERSTANDING THE WRITER'S IDEAS

1. According to Copland, what are the three separate "planes" of the process of listening to music? Does Copland feel that these classifications correspond to real divisions? How do you know? What is his purpose in describing and explaining these planes? Which is most important? Least important?

2. Outline in some detail the elements of each plane of listening.

3. Does the author believe that we all listen to music in the same way? Explain your answer.

4. What is Copland's opinion of those who listen to music primarily on the sensuous plane? How does he involve the reader in his discussion of that plane? What are the main uses of the sensuous plane?

5. What is "sound stuff" (par. 6)?

6. What is Copland's opinion of the composer Igor Stravinsky? How do you know?

7. According to the author, what is the difficulty in trying to assign a meaning to music? To which plane does the attempt to assign meaning belong? What does he call those listeners who insist on trying to assign concrete meaning to a piece of music?

8. Copland states that musical novices "always find Tchaikovsky easier to 'understand' than Beethoven" but that "any musician will tell you that...Beethoven is the greater composer." Why?

9. How would you summarize Copland's attitude toward the majority of music listeners? Support your opinion with examples from the essay. Compare Copland's assessment of the layperson and the professional musician in the purely musical plane.

10. What, in the author's opinion, are the characteristics of "the ideal listener"? What is the ideal condition for a composer at the moment of composition?

11. Summarize the main purpose of this essay.

UNDERSTANDING THE WRITER'S TECHNIQUES

1. How would you characterize Copland's *tone* and *style* (see Glossary)? Give at least five examples from the essay to support your answer.

2. *Jargon* is the use of special, technical words associated with a specific activity or profession (see Glossary). Does Copland use much jargon in this essay? Why? What does that say about his intended *audience?*

3. Which paragraphs does the author devote to each of the three planes? Which paragraphs serve as transitions? How does he order his transition paragraphs? Compare the use of the word "yes" at the beginning of paragraph 5 and "now" at the beginning of paragraph 15 as transition devices.

4. What *extended analogy* (see Glossary) forms the basis of

paragraphs 21 to 24? What is the purpose of this analogy? Do you find it useful in understanding Copland's discussion of how to listen to music? Why?

5. Evaluate the following sentence both as a transitional device and as a means to involve the reader more directly in the discussion: "The reader can see, therefore, that a more conscious approach is valuable even on this primary plane of music listening" (par. 6).

6. In paragraph 8, why does Copland use a series of questions in quotation marks? To whom are those questions addressed?

7. Where does the author use the techniques of *comparison* and *contrast?* For what purposes?

8. Note uses of *description* and *illustration* in this essay.

9. How does Copland use *summation* in paragraph 16?

10. Why does Copland use the word "must" three times in paragraph 19? What is the topic sentence of that paragraph? How does the repetition help formulate the topic sentence?

11. What purpose is made clear in the final paragraph? Compare the purpose stated there with the purpose stated in the opening paragraph. How are they related?

12. Repetition, return to thesis, and summary of major points are all techniques used in writing conclusions. Where does Copland use each in the conclusion to this essay?

EXPLORING THE WRITER'S IDEAS

1. In his opening sentence, Copland states: "We all listen to music according to our separate capacities." Do you agree? Why?

2. Toward the end of this essay, Copland writes an extended analogy relating the experience of listening to music to that of seeing a play in the theater; he says he does this in order

to "make this instinctive correlation clearer." Why do you suppose he feels it is easier for most readers to understand the theater experience than it is for them to understand the musical experience? Do you personally find this to be true? Why? In what ways?

3. In paragraph 25, the author states that "in order to write his music, the composer must also be inside and outside his music, carried away by it yet coldly critical of it." This sounds like a very difficult creative process. What is Copland's meaning? What other creative processes are similar? What experiences have you had to which similar descriptions could apply?

4. What is your favorite type of music? What is it that you enjoy most about this music? Do you think your enjoyment fits into any of Copland's "hypothetical planes"? Explain.

5. Copland uses a fairly tightly constructed framework on which to develop his discussion of the subject of music appreciation in general. Yet, he seems to focus almost entirely on classical music. Do you feel that his discussion can apply just as well to other musical forms—rock, jazz, rap, blues, soul, heavy metal, pop, folk? Why or why not?

6. Between the widespread use of Walkmans and portable "boxes," it seems as though people listen to music all the time. What do you feel are the positive and negative sides to this trend?

7. Copland delineates three planes in order to classify his ideas concerning music appreciation, but readily admits that they are artificial creations and that the most important thing to strive for is a "more *active* kind of listening."

Some critics of music videos claim that they encourage *passive* responses to music. That is, instead of listeners feeling their own sensations or creating their own images to accompany what they listen to, these images and sensations have become fixed and externalized according to what the video shows. What is your opinion of music videos? Of this criticism of them?

IDEAS FOR WRITING

Guided Writing

Write a classification essay that deals with what to look for in
_____ (films, television, sculpture, paintings).
Choose one of these four, or another visual medium.

1. Begin with a generalization about the common "looking experience."

2. Divide the "looking experience" into three categories.

3. Devote at least two paragraphs to each category. Arrange your essay in order of ascending importance of the categories.

4. Throughout the essay, express your opinions about the "common looker."

5. Use full-paragraph transitions between sections devoted to each category.

6. Compare two well-known creators in the medium you've chosen. Explain why one is more popular among "novice lookers" while the other is more respected among experts.

7. Describe a particular piece of work in the medium as a way to illustrate your main point.

8. At the end of your essay, describe the attributes of an "ideal looker" and state what your readers should strive for in order to better appreciate and observe the medium.

More Writing Projects

1. For a journal entry, characterize the ways in which you listen to music. Generate your ideas through classification and division.

2. The next time you go to the movies, pay attention to the different ways in which the audience reacts. Then, write a paragraph classifying the different types of moviegoers.

3. Write an essay in which you classify the different types of music in a particular musical genre: jazz, soul, pop, rock, and so forth. For example, for an essay on the blues, you might deal with delta blues, Chicago blues, and piano blues.

SUMMING UP: CHAPTER 8

1. Write an essay that classifies the readings in this book by a method other than *exposition* (detailed explanation). As you discuss each category, be sure to give examples that explain why particular readings fall into that classification.

2. Reread Judith Viorst's "Friends, Good Friends—And Such Good Friends" in this chapter. Then, write down the names of several of your closest friends. Keep a journal for one week in which you list what you did, how you felt, and what you talked about with each of these friends. Write an essay that classifies these friends into three categories. Use entries from your journal to support your method of classification.

3. With the class divided into four groups, assemble a guide to the city, town, or neighborhood surrounding your campus. Each group should be responsible for one category of information: Types of People; Types of Places; Types of Entertainment; Types of Services, and so on. Be sure that each category is covered in detail; you may refer to E. B. White's essay on "The Three New Yorks" as a model. After each group has completed its work, choose someone to present findings to the class. Now write your own guide to the areas based on the classifications discussed.

4. Although both Viorst's and Copland's essays are classifications, they are also prescriptions for how to do something: Viorst's essay has an underlying message about how to choose friends, while Copland's instructs us on listening to music. Write an essay on classification entitled "What to Avoid When _____ ." Fill in the blank with an

activity that would involve a decision-making process on the part of the reader.

5. Many of the essays in this book deal with crucial experiences in the various authors' lives. Among others, Hughes, Wong, and Atwood tell us of coming-of-age experiences; Selzer and Wilkins write of their special insights into human nature; and Ehrlich and Thomas describe their relationships to the world of nature. Try writing an essay that classifies the personal essays that you have read in this anthology.

CHAPTER 9

Process Analysis

Process analysis concentrates on *how* something is done, how something works, or how something occurs. If writing aims essentially to explain things, you can see why writers need to use process analysis. Often, the major point that will impress a reader depends on his or her ability to understand the logical steps in some plan of procedure. As a method of paragraph or essay development, process analysis traces all important steps, from beginning to end, in an activity or event. The amount of detail provided for each step in the process will depend on how much the audience knows about the subject.

Whether you are dealing with such subjects as how Columbus discovered America, how a carburetor works, how to deliver a good speech, or how to can fruit at home, you must present all essential information to your audience. Frequently, other methods of essay development help reinforce your analysis of process. (For example, writers often use *definition* to explain terms in a technical process that might not be familiar to readers; and to relate in clear order the steps in a process, an essay might require *narrative* techniques.) These methods will serve your main objective of explaining the process from beginning to end.

Although the purpose of process analysis is to provide your audience with a step-by-step explanation of a procedure, process analysis can also inform readers about the *significance* of the process; that is, it will instruct and inform. A typical problem in explanations of process is that a writer often assumes that readers know more than they do. You can avoid this problem by defining your audience carefully. Certainly, you would use one approach to explain how to make a perfect cheese omelet to newlyweds; and you would use a completely different approach to explain it to students in advanced cooking class. Although both groups might have to follow the same sequence of steps, the kind of information you provide and the range of your explanations would be significantly different. No matter what approach you take to process analysis, remember to present material in a clear and lively manner. In reading about how something is done, or how something works, no reader wants to be bored; make an effort to keep your writing interesting.

How to Write a Personal Letter

Garrison Keillor

Garrison Keillor is well known for his creation of the mythical town of Lake Wobegon, Minnesota. For years, he delighted radio audiences with stories of the town's goings-on as host of the program *A Prairie Home Companion. Leaving Home: Lake Wobegon Stories,* published in 1987, made these tales available in print. In this essay, Keillor maintains his folksy, whimsical tone to tell us how to "Take it easy" when faced with a task that many of us find alternately guilt-inspiring and immobilizing—writing a personal letter! Keillor blends step-by-step technical advice with emotional reassurance to guide us through the process.

Words to Watch

immortal (par. 2)   eternal; undying

sincere (par. 2)   truthful; faithful

vague (par. 3)   unclear; uncertain

anonymity (par. 4)   the condition of being unknown or nameless

obligatory (par. 6)   required

sensuous (par. 8)   voluptuous; sexy

episode (par. 12)   occasion; circumstance

sibling (par. 12)   brother or sister

1   We shy persons need to write a letter now and then, or else we'll dry up and blow away. It's true. And I speak as one who loves to reach for the phone and talk. The telephone is to shyness what Hawaii is to February, it's a way out of the woods. *And yet:* a letter is better.

2   Such a sweet gift—a piece of handmade writing, in an envelope that is not a bill, sitting in our friend's path when she trudges home from a long day spent among wahoos and savages, a day our words will help repair. They don't need to be immortal, just sincere. She can read them twice and again tomorrow: *You're someone I care about, Corinne, and think of often, and every time I do, you make me smile.*

3   We need to write, otherwise nobody will know who we

are. They will have only a vague impression of us as A Nice Person, because, frankly, we don't shine at conversation, we lack the confidence to thrust our faces forward and say, "Hi, I'm Heather Hooten, let me tell you about my week." Mostly we say "Uh-huh" and "Oh really." People smile and look over our shoulder, looking for someone else to talk to.

So a shy person sits down and writes a letter. To be known 4 by another person—to meet and talk freely on the page—to be close despite distance. To escape from anonymity and be our own sweet selves and express the music of our souls.

We want our dear Aunt Eleanor to know that we have 5 fallen in love, that we quit our job, that we're moving to New York, and we want to say a few things that might not get said in casual conversation: *Thank you for what you've meant to me. I am very happy right now.*

The first step in writing letters is to get over the guilt of 6 *not* writing. You don't "owe" anybody a letter. Letters are a gift. The burning shame you feel when you see unanswered mail makes it harder to pick up a pen and makes for a cheerless letter when you finally do. *I feel bad about not writing, but I've been so busy,* etc. Skip this. Few letters are obligatory, and they are *Thanks for the wonderful gift* and *I am terribly sorry to hear about George's death.* Write these promptly if you want to keep your friends. Don't worry about the others, except love letters, of course. When your true love writes *Dear Light of My Life, Joy of My Heart,* some response is called for.

Some of the best letters are tossed off in a burst of inspi- 7 ration, so keep your writing stuff in one place where you can sit down for a few minutes and—*Dear Roy, I am in the middle of an essay but thought I'd drop you a line. Hi to your sweetie too*—dash off a note to a pal. Envelopes, stamps, address book, everything in a drawer so you can write fast when the pen is hot.

A blank white 8″ × 11″ sheet can look as big as Mon- 8 tana if the pen's not so hot—try a smaller page and write boldly. Get a pen that makes a sensuous line, get a comfortable typewriter, a friendly word processor—whichever feels easy to the hand.

Sit for a few minutes with the blank sheet of paper in ⁹
front of you, and let your friend come to mind. Remember the
last time you saw each other and how your friend looked and
what you said and what perhaps was unsaid between you;
when your friend becomes real to you, start to write.

Write the salutation—*Dear You*—and take a deep breath ¹⁰
and plunge in. A simple declarative sentence will do, followed
by another and another. As if you were talking to us. Don't
think about grammar, don't think about style, just give us
your news. Where did you go, who did you see, what did they
say, what do you think?

If you don't know where to begin, start with the present: ¹¹
I'm sitting at the kitchen table on a rainy Saturday morning.
Everyone is gone and the house is quiet. Let the letter drift
along. The toughest letter to crank out is one that is meant to
impress, as we all know from writing job applications; if it's
hard work to slip off a letter to a friend, maybe you're trying
too hard to be terrific. A letter is only a report to someone
who already likes you for reasons other than your brilliance.
Take it easy.

Don't worry about form. It's not a term paper. When ¹²
you come to the end of one episode, just start a new paragraph. You can go from a few lines about the sad state of rock
'n' roll to the fight with your mother to your fond memories of
Mexico to the kitchen sink and what's in it. The more you
write, the easier it gets, and when you have a True True
Friend to write to, a soul sibling, then it's like driving a car;
you just press on the gas.

Don't tear up the page and start over when you write a ¹³
bad line—try to write your way out of it. Make mistakes and
plunge on. Let the letter cook along and let yourself be bold.
Outrage, confusion, love—whatever is in your mind, let it find
a way to the page. Writing is a means of discovery, always,
and when you come to the end and write *Yours ever* or *Hugs*
and Kisses, you'll know something you didn't when you wrote
Dear Pal.

Probably your friend will put your letter away, and it'll ¹⁴
be read again a few years from now—and it will improve with
age.

And forty years from now, your friend's grandkids will ₁₅ dig it out of the attic and read it, a sweet and precious relic of the ancient Eighties that gives them a sudden clear glimpse of the world we old-timers knew. You will have then created an object of art. Your simple lines about where you went, who you saw, what they said, will speak to those children and they will feel in their hearts the humanity of our times.

You can't pick up a phone and call the future and tell ₁₆ them about our times. You have to pick up a piece of paper.

BUILDING VOCABULARY

1. Throughout the essay, Keillor uses numerous *idioms* that are fairly *colloquial* (see Glossary); that is, they are informal conversational expressions. For each excerpt below, rewrite the *whole* sentence, replacing just the italicized idiomatic expression with your own words.

   a. Some of the best letters are *tossed off* in a burst of inspiration. (par. 7)
   b. *dash off* a note to a pal (par. 7)
   c. take a deep breath and *plunge in* (par. 10)
   d. Let the letter *drift along* (par. 11)
   e. The toughest letter to *crank out* is the one that is meant to impress (par. 11)
   f. if it's hard work to *slip off* a letter to a friend (par. 11)
   g. Don't *tear up* the page and *start over* (par. 13)
   h. Make mistakes and *plunge on* (par. 13)
   i. Let the letter *cook along* (par. 13)
   j. You can't *pick up* a phone and call the future (par. 16)

2. Write sentences for any five of the words in the Words to Watch section, page 322.

UNDERSTANDING THE WRITER'S IDEAS

1. Explain in your own words why, according to Keillor, people need to write letters.

2. An *analogy* is a figurative comparison that illustrates an idea by relating subjects from different categories. Explain Keillor's statement that "The telephone is to shyness what Hawaii is to February" (par. 1). What does he mean by "it's a way out of the woods"?

3. In what ways is a letter "a small gift"? Why does it not "need to be immortal, just sincere"?

4. Who are "wahoos and savages" (par. 2)?

5. Who is "A Nice Person" (par. 3)? Why is the phrase capitalized?

6. Throughout the essay, Keillor uses direct address and specific names. Who are "Corinne" (par. 2) and "Aunt Eleanor" (par. 5)? Find and list other names. Who are these people? Why does he use their names?

7. In paragraph 5, Keillor suggests that we might not say "Thank you for what you've meant to me. I am very happy right now" in casual conversation, but we could in a letter. Why might this be true? What other comparisons does he make between letter writing and conversation? What is his general feeling about the similarities or differences between the two activities?

8. What types of letters are obligatory? How does Keillor suggest we handle them? Why?

9. Explain the meaning of the following:
   a. the pen is hot (par. 7)
   b. A blank 8″ × 11″ sheet can look as big as Montana if the pen's not so hot (par. 8)
   c. Get a pen that makes a sensuous line (par. 8)

10. Why does Keillor make the following suggestion: "Don't think about grammar, don't think about style" (par. 10)?

11. In general, does Keillor think personal letter writing need be a very serious endeavor? Support your response with specific references to the essay.

12. Explain the "message" of paragraph 15 in your own words. Explain the "message" of paragraph 16.

UNDERSTANDING THE WRITER'S TECHNIQUES

1. Which paragraphs constitute the introduction, body, and conclusion of this essay? What *transitions* does Keillor use between the sections? Are they effective?

2. Is there a single *thesis statement* in this essay? Explain.

3. In a process analysis, it is important to tailor the depth and range of your explanations to your audience. For what *audience* (see Glossary) do you think Keillor wrote this essay? Does he highlight any one particular group? How does his language and *tone* (see Glossary) reflect his audience?

4. A process analysis often provides a step-by-step explanation of how to do something. Try to write a step-by-step outline of Keillor's *procedure* for writing personal letters. Would this procedure be easy to follow for someone who had trouble writing letters? Explain.

5. In the first five paragraphs of this essay, Keillor uses the first-person plural pronoun form (we, our, us) instead of the more common first-person singular (I, me) or second person (you). Why does he do this? To whom is he referring? What clues in the text lead you to believe this? What is the effect of using this particular *point of view?* Where does he shift the point of view? To what? How does this change affect the essay?

6. Evaluate the author's use of infinitive verb constructions in paragraph 4 ("to be known"; "to meet"; "to escape"). What *tone* is created by these constructions?

7. How would you describe the *level of diction* (see Glossary) in this essay? Is the diction appropriate to the subject? To the intended audience?

8. How does Keillor use *definition* in paragraphs 11 and 13?

9. Where does Keillor use *classification* in this essay?

10. Throughout the essay, Keillor uses *italics*. Identify each use of italics, then explain its particular purpose.

11. Discuss in what ways Keillor uses *negation* (see page 245) in this essay.

12. Reread your answer to Question 12 in the Understanding the Writer's Ideas section. What is the *tone* of paragraph 15? How does it differ from the rest of the essay? Is it appropriate to the message of that paragraph? What is the tone of paragraph 16? How does the tone change between paragraphs 15 and 16? Do you feel this transition is smooth? Explain.

EXPLORING THE WRITER'S IDEAS

1. How closely does Keillor's essay relate to your own letter-writing experiences? Do you enjoy letter writing? Why or why not? When do you feel most inspired to write a letter? What special procedure, if any, do you follow?

2. In this essay, Keillor offers various suggestions on how to approach letter writing from both a technical and an emotional standpoint. Look back over the essays in Chapter 1, "On Writing." Which of the four writers in this chapter do you think Garrison Keillor is most in tune with concerning his ideas about the *writing process* (not just letter writing). Explain your answer with specific references to the essays.

3. Look over some old letters or postcards. How does it make you feel to read them? Are your impressions of the writer and(or) subject different now than they were when you first received the card or letter? Why?

4. In general, do you prefer face-to-face conversations, telephone conversations, or letter writing? In what *specific in-*

stances would you prefer each means of communication? Which method do you find most effective?

IDEAS FOR WRITING

Guided Writing

Write an essay in which you explain how to call someone for a first date.

1. Begin the essay by explaining how this is an activity that we all share in at one time or another. Do this by:

   a. Using the first-person plural point of view
   b. Explaining why it is a difficult process in general

2. Explain what is pleasurable about the process despite its difficulties.

3. Compare calling for a first date to a similar but easier process, and use that process in an imaginative analogy.

4. Throughout your essay, use italics to highlight special examples of what to say or do to make the process go more smoothly.

5. Write a step-by-step process analysis. Begin with how to overcome normal fear and trepidation.

6. Maintain a lighthearted, personal, conversational tone throughout. Use colloquialisms to help create this tone.

7. Reassure your reader by explaining what he or she does *not* have to do or say during this process.

8. In your conclusion, shift to a somewhat more serious tone to discuss the possible outcome of the call. Explain the effects of making the call.

More Writing Projects

1. What guidelines do you follow when you write a letter?

What characteristics do you think a letter should have? Respond to these quesions in your journal.

2. Write a paragraph directed to a friend explaining how he or she can get the most out of an upcoming special event: a party; a reunion; a concert; a wedding; a football game; and so forth.

3. Write a personal letter. Keep Keillor's essay next to you as you write this letter. Reread each paragraph closely and follow his process step-by-step.

Eating Alone in Restaurants

Bruce Jay Friedman

In this selection from his book, *The Lonely Guy's Book of Life,*
Bruce Jay Friedman touches a nerve in all of us as he explains the
process of dining out alone. He may not tell us exactly what to order,
but through his use of ironic narration, vivid description, and thorough illustration, he creates a delightful essay that gives us a consum-
mate personal lesson.

Words to Watch

inconspicuous (par. 1)   not easily noticeable

hors d'oeuvre (par. 7)   appetizer

scenario (par. 8)   script or outline of a plot

foreboding (par. 10)   a feeling of something bad to come

suffice (par. 10)   to be adequate for the purpose

promenade (par. 13)   leisurely walk

imperiously (par. 14)   haughtily; arrogantly

conviviality (par. 17)   condition of enjoyment of good food and
drink and good company

pervade (par. 17)   to spread through every part of something

audacious (par. 24)   daring

Hunched over, trying to be as inconspicuous as possible, 1
a solitary diner slips into a midtown Manhattan steakhouse.
No sooner does he check his coat than the voice of the headwaiter comes booming across the restaurant.

"Alone again, eh?" 2

As all eyes are raised, the bartender, with enormous 3
good cheer, chimes in: "That's because they all left him high
and dry."

And then, just in case there is a customer in the restau- 4
rant who isn't yet aware of his situation, a waiter shouts out
from the buffet table: "Well, we'll take care of him anyway,
won't we fellas!"

Haw, haw, haw, and a lot of sly winks and pokes in the ⁵ ribs.

Eating alone in a restaurant is one of the most terrifying ⁶ experiences in America.

Sniffed at by headwaiters, an object of scorn and amuse- ⁷ ment to couples, the solitary diner is the unwanted and unloved child of Restaurant Row. No sooner does he make his appearance than he is whisked out of sight and seated at a thin sliver of a table with barely enough room on it for an hors d'oeuvre. Wedged between busboy stations, a hair's breadth from the men's room, there he sits, feet lodged in a railing as if he were in Pilgrim stocks, wondering where he went wrong in life.

Rather than face this grim scenario, most Lonely Guys ⁸ would prefer to nibble away at a tuna fish sandwich in the relative safety of their high-rise apartments.

What can be done to ease the pain of this not only starv- ⁹ ing but silent minority—to make dining alone in restaurants a rewarding experience? Absolutely nothing. But some small strategies *do* exist for making the experience bearable.

Before You Get There

Once the Lonely Guy has decided to dine alone at a res- ¹⁰ taurant, a sense of terror and foreboding will begin to build throughout the day. All the more reason for him to get there as quickly as possible so that the experience can soon be forgotten and he can resume his normal life. Clothing should be light and loose-fitting, especially around the neck—on the off chance of a fainting attack during the appetizer. It is best to dress modestly, avoiding both the funeral-director-style suit as well as the bold, eye-arresting costume of the gaucho. A single cocktail should suffice; little sympathy will be given to the Lonely Guy who tumbles in, stewed to the gills. (The fellow who stoops to putting morphine in his toes for courage does not belong in this discussion.) En route to the restaurant, it is best to play down dramatics, such as swinging the arms pluckily and humming the theme from *The Bridge on the River Kwai.*

Once You Arrive

The way your entrance comes off is of critical impor- 11
tance. Do not skulk in, slipping along the walls as if you are
carrying some dirty little secret. There is no need, on the other
hand, to fling your coat arrogantly at the hatcheck girl, slap
the headwaiter across the cheeks with your gloves and demand to be seated immediately. Simply walk in with a brisk
rubbing of the hands and approach the headwaiter. When
asked how many are in your party, avoid cute responses such
as "Jes lil ol' me." Tell him you are a party of one; the Lonely
Guy who does not trust his voice can simply lift a finger. Do
not launch into a story about how tired you are of taking out
fashion models, night after night, and what a pleasure it is going to be to dine alone.

It is best to arrive with no reservation. Asked to set aside 12
a table for one, the restaurant owner will suspect either a
prank on the part of an ex-waiter, or a terrorist plot, in which
case windows will be boarded up and the kitchen bombswept.
An advantage of the "no reservation" approach is that you
will appear to have just stepped off the plane from Des
Moines, your first night in years away from Marge and the
kids.

All eyes will be upon you when you make the promenade 13
to your table. Stay as close as possible to the headwaiter, trying to match him step for step. This will reduce your visibility
and fool some diners into thinking you are a member of the
staff. If you hear a generalized snickering throughout the restaurant, do not assume automatically that you are being
laughed at. The other diners may all have just recalled an
amusing moment in a Feydeau farce.

If your table is unsatisfactory, do not demand imperi- 14
ously that one for eight people be cleared immediately so that
you can dine in solitary grandeur. Glance around discreetly
and see if there are other possibilities. The ideal table will allow you to keep your back to the wall so that you can see if
anyone is laughing at you. Try to get one close to another couple so that if you lean over at a 45-degree angle it will appear
that you are a swinging member of their group. Sitting oppo-

site a mirror can be useful; after a drink or two, you will begin
to feel that there are a few of you.

   Once you have been seated, and it becomes clear to the 15
staff that you are alone, there will follow The Single Most
Heartbreaking Moment in Dining Out Alone—when the second setting is whisked away and yours is spread out a bit to
make the table look busier. This will be done with great ceremony by the waiter—angered in advance at being tipped for
only one dinner. At this point, you may be tempted to smack
your forehead against the table and curse the fates that
brought you to this desolate position in life. A wiser course is
to grit your teeth, order a drink and use this opportunity to
make contact with other Lonely Guys sprinkled about the
room. A menu or a leafy stalk of celery can be used as a shield
for peering out at them. Do not expect a hearty greeting or a
cry of "huzzah" from these frightened and browbeaten people. Too much excitement may cause them to slump over, cur-
tains. Smile gently and be content if you receive a pale wave
of the hand in return. It is unfair to imply that you have come
to help them throw off their chains.

   When the headwaiter arrives to take your order, do not 16
be bullied into ordering the last of the gazelle haunches unless
you really want them. Thrilled to be offered anything at all,
many Lonely Guys will say "Get them right out here" and
wolf them down. Restaurants take unfair advantage of Lonely
Guys, using them to get rid of anything from withered liver to
old heels of roast beef. Order anything you like, although it is
good to keep to the light and simple in case of a sudden attack
of violent stomach cramps.

Some Proven Strategies

   Once the meal is under way, a certain pressure will begin 17
to build as couples snuggle together, the women clucking sym-
pathetically in your direction. Warmth and conviviality will
pervade the room, none of it encompassing you. At this point,
many Lonely Guys will keep their eyes riveted to the restaurant paintings of early Milan or bury themselves in a paper-
back anthology they have no wish to read.

Here are some ploys designed to confuse other diners 18 and make them feel less sorry for you.

- After each bite of food, lift your head, smack your lips 19 thoughtfully, swallow and make a notation in a pad. Diners will assume you are a restaurant critic.
- Between courses, pull out a walkie-talkie and whisper a 20 message into it. This will lead everyone to believe you are part of a police stake-out team, about to bust the salad man as an international dope dealer.
- Pretend you are a foreigner. This is done by pointing to 21 items on the menu with an alert smile and saying to the headwaiter: "Is good, no?"
- When the main course arrives, brush the restaurant silver- 22 ware off the table and pull some of your own out of a breastpocket. People will think you are a wealthy eccentric.
- Keep glancing at the door, and make occasional trips to 23 look out at the street, as if you are waiting for a beautiful woman. Half-way through the meal, shrug in a world-weary manner and begin to eat with gusto. The world is full of women! Why tolerate bad manners! Life is too short.

The Right Way

One other course is open to the Lonely Guy, an auda- 24 cious one, full of perils, but all the more satisfying if you can bring it off. That is to take off your dark glasses, sit erectly, smile broadly at anyone who looks in your direction, wave off inferior wines, and begin to eat with heartiness and enormous confidence. As outrageous as the thought may be—enjoy your own company. Suddenly, titters and sly winks will tail off, the headwaiter's disdain will fade, and friction will build among couples who will turn out to be not as tightly cemented as they appear. The heads of other Lonely Guys will lift with hope as you become the attractive center of the room.

If that doesn't work, you still have your fainting option. 25

BUILDING VOCABULARY

1. *Colloquial language* (see Glossary) is the language used in most conversation and in some informal writing. Clearly, Friedman uses a good deal of such language in this essay. Explain in your own words the following colloquialisms, then list and explain five others derived from the essay:

    a. chimes in (par. 3)
    b. stewed to the gills (par. 10)
    c. launch into a story (par. 11)
    d. grit your teeth (par. 15)
    e. wolf them down (par. 16)

2. Identify:

    Restaurant Row (par. 7)
    Pilgrim stocks (par. 7)
    The Bridge on the River Kwai (par. 10)
    gaucho (par. 10)
    Feydeau (par. 13)

UNDERSTANDING THE WRITER'S IDEAS

1. In the opening paragraphs, what is the author's main point about eating alone in restaurants? What does he say people who work in restaurants think about those eating alone? What does paragraph 5 indicate about this attitude?

2. Who are the "Lonely Guys"?

3. According to the author, how should a Lonely Guy prepare himself to eat alone?

4. Make a step-by-step outline of Friedman's instructions for what to do once you arrive at a restaurant to eat alone.

5. Why is it best *not* to make an advance reservation?

6. What is the "ideal table" for a diner alone? What makes it so?

7. Explain "The Single Most Heartbreaking Moment in Dining Out Alone." What makes it such a terrible moment?

8. In what ways do restaurants attempt to take advantage of solitary diners?

9. According to Friedman, what is the attitude of other diners toward the person eating alone? What are some of the best ways to combat this attitude?

10. Ultimately, what is the "Right Way" to dine alone? What do the author's ideas about the Right Way suggest about the real meaning and purpose of this essay? Explain your answer.

11. If all the author's suggestions fail, what last resort is available to the Lonely Guy? In the context of this essay, would this be an effective tactic?

UNDERSTANDING THE WRITER'S TECHNIQUES

1. What is the *thesis* statement of this essay?

2. An *anecdote* is a brief narration of an incident, often personal. How does Friedman use an anecdote in the introduction to this essay? Is it effective? Why?

3. *Hyperbole* in writing is the use of extreme exaggeration either to make a particular point or to achieve a special effect. Friedman makes liberal use of hyperbole throughout the essay. What is the main point of the author's hyperbole? What effects are achieved by it? List at least ten examples of hyperbolic writing in this essay.

4. How would you characterize the *tone* of this essay? Look up the definition of *irony, cynicism,* and *sarcasm.* Which term do you think most closely describes Friedman's tone? Does his tone fit the subject matter? Explain.

   Go back to your list of hyperboles and note for each whether you think it is intended to be ironic, cynical, or sarcastic.

5. Friedman also makes liberal use of capitalization throughout the essay. Why? List a few examples of the use of capitalization other than at the beginning of sentences or for proper nouns.

6. Evaluate the use of *classification* (see Chapter 8, pages 281–282) in this essay. How does it affect the process analysis? What are the main categories of classification? How are they organized?

7. Indicate those paragraphs that constitute the introduction, body, and conclusion of this essay.

8. Which sentence in the introduction alerts us that this is a process-analysis essay? Write an outline of the process steps discussed.

9. How does Friedman use a list in this essay? Is it effective in terms of suiting the overall tone and fitting the context of this essay? Explain.

10. Writing teachers often tell their students: "Show. Don't tell." In other words, use gestures and actions to characterize someone or make a point rather than just give the reader an explanation. How does Friedman use gestures and actions to express characters' feelings in this essay? Give five examples.

11. Who is the intended audience for this essay? How do you know?

12. How does Friedman use *narration* in this essay? *Description? Definition? Illustration?*

13. Evaluate the conclusion of this essay. How does it relate to the rest of the essay? Do you feel the last sentence enhances or detracts from the conclusion? Why?

EXPLORING THE WRITER'S IDEAS

1. Do you think Friedman has written this essay from personal experience? Why do you think so?

2. Friedman focuses his essay on a species he calls Lonely Guys. Why do you think he doesn't write about women dining out alone—Lonely Gals? What are your reactions when you see a woman dining alone in a restaurant? How do these reactions differ from your responses when you see a man dining alone?

3. How do you feel about eating out alone? For what reasons might you choose to take yourself out to eat? Do you enjoy it, or do you feel uncomfortable as the author suggests? What preparations do you make in order to make the experience more enjoyable? Do they usually work?

4. Friedman writes here of big city experiences—specifically, midtown Manhattan. Do you feel his analysis and suggestions apply just as well to other environments? How so?

IDEAS FOR WRITING

Guided Writing

Write an essay in which you explain how to do something that is generally thought of as an uncomfortable activity. For example, you might write about asking for a first date, interviewing for a job, meeting a boyfriend's or girlfriend's family for the first time.

1. Begin with an anecdote illustrating the most embarrassing "worst case scenario" that might occur during this activity.

2. Invent a name for the type of person most likely to feel uncomfortable in this situation.

3. Include a direct thesis statement.

4. Make the body of your essay instructions for how to make this process less uncomfortable. Arrange your suggestions into three categories following the chronology of the process. Title your categories.

5. Identify the "Most Uncomfortable Moment" that is likely to occur during the activity's process.

6. Make frequent use of colloquialisms throughout the essay.

7. Use irony and occasional sarcasm and cynicism to add humor to the essay.

8. Include a list of hyperbolic strategies for relieving the pressure once one is fully absorbed in the process.

9. Use your conclusion to make a serious point about human nature and the deeper meaning of overcoming the uncomfortableness of this situation.

10. Leave your reader with a humorous statement that undercuts the seriousness of your conclusion.

More Writing Projects

1. In your journal write about the process you recently used to deal with an extremely embarrassing moment. Make sure to tell what led up to the moment and what happened during and after the incident.

2. Write a paragraph about the process you use when you're out with one person and meet someone else whose name you don't remember.

3. Write a process-analysis essay telling how to get satisfaction when you've bought a defective product or gotten bad service in a store.

Coors Beer

Grace Lichtenstein

Process analysis often deals with mechanical or technical procedures. In this short selection by Grace Lichtenstein, who is a correspondent for *The New York Times,* the author examines a mechanical process—the brewing of beer. As you read this piece, look for the methods that the author uses to make this technical process interesting and understandable to the general reader.

Words to Watch

palate (par. 1)   taste or sense of taste

mystique (par. 2)   special, almost mysterious attitudes and feelings surrounding a person, place, or thing

Spartan (par. 3)   simple and severe

rancid (par. 3)   not fresh; having a bad smell

permeate (par. 3)   to spread through everything

nondescript (par. 3)   lacking any recognizable character or quality

cellulose (par. 4)   the main substance in woody parts of plants, used in many manufacturing processes

Coors is a light-bodied beer, meaning it is brewed with 1 less malt, fewer hops and more rice than beers with a tangy taste. Compared with Heineken's or other more full-bodied foreign beers, Coors does seem almost flavorless and it is this quality that could account for its popularity among young people just starting to get acquainted with the pleasures of beer drinking. A few locals scoff at Coors, calling it "Colorado Kool-Aid." But the fact is that, according to Ernest Pyler, "if you conducted a blindfold test of the four leading beers, the chances of picking our Coors would be minimal." Indeed, one national newspaper conducted an informal test among eight beer drinkers, finding that only three could correctly identify Coors. My own admittedly uneducated palate detects no difference between Coors and Schaefer. In short, the difference between Coors and any other decent beer could be 1,800 miles. Maybe, if Paul Newman suddenly switched to Schaefer, Denverites would pay $15 a case for it.

There is one aspect to the Coors mystique that does have 2 measurable validity. Company officials make much of the fact that Coors has good mountain water and the most expensive brewing process in the country. Several elements are unusual, though not unique.

Thousands of visitors have learned about the process on 3 guided tours through the antiseptic, Spartan plant. (For out-of-towners, the tour is often a pilgrimage—but for local students of the Colorado School of Mines, it's usually more in the line of a quick belt before classes. The tour lasts 30 minutes, at the end of which visitors are invited to quaff to their heart's content in the hospitality lounge. "I've come here 50 times," boasted one student as he polished off a glass at 11:30 one morning in the lounge.) Situated in the center of town, between two high, flat mesas in the foothills of the Rockies, the plant dominates the community just as the somewhat rancid smell of malt seems to permeate the air; one-fourth of the town's families are said to owe their jobs to the factory's operations. Anyone expecting to see in Golden the foaming white waterfall amid mountain pines that is pictured on every yellow can of Coors will be disappointed. The water used in the brewing comes from nondescript wells hidden in concrete blockhouses. The brewery now puts out about 12 million barrels of beer a year, but construction sites throughout the grounds bear witness to the company's hopes for doubling that capacity by 1984.

Like other beers, Coors is produced from barley. Most 4 of the big Midwestern brewers use barley grown in North Dakota and Minnesota. Coors is the single American brewer to use a Moravian strain, grown under company supervision, on farms in Colorado, Idaho, Wyoming and Montana. At the brewery, the barley is turned into malt by being soaked in water—which must be biologically pure and of a known mineral content—for several days, causing it to sprout and producing a chemical change—breaking down starch into sugar. The malt is toasted, a process that halts the sprouting and determines the color and sweetness (the more the roasting, the darker, more bitter the beer). It is ground into flour and brewed, with more pure water, in huge copper-domed kettles until it is the consistency of oatmeal. Rice and refined starch are added to make mash; solids are strained out, leaving an amber liquid malt extract, which is boiled with hops—the dried cones from the hop vine which add to the bitterness, or tang. The hops are strained, yeast is added, turning the sugar to alcohol, and the beer is aged in huge red vats at near-freezing temperatures for almost two months, during which the second fermentation takes place and the liquid becomes carbonated, or bubbly. (Many breweries chemically age their beer to speed up production; Coors people say only naturally aged brew can be called a true "lager.") Next, the beer is filtered through cellulose filters to remove bacteria, and finally is pumped into cans, bottles or kegs for shipping.

The most unusual aspect of the Coors process is that the beer is not pasteurized, as all but a half-dozen of the 90 or so American beers are. In the pasteurization process, bottles or cans of beer are passed through a heating unit and then cooled. This destroys the yeast in the brew which could cause spoilage, if the cans or bottles or barrels are unrefrigerated for any long period. However, pasteurization also changes the flavor of beer. Coors stopped pasteurizing its product 18 years ago because it decided that "heat is an enemy of beer," according to a company spokesman.

Unpasteurized beer must be kept under constant refrigeration. Thus, Coors does not warehouse any of its finished product, as many other brewers do, but ships everything out cold, immediately. In effect, my tour guide, a young management trainee wearing a beer-can tie clip, explained as we wandered through the packaging area, watching workers in surgical masks feed aluminum lids into machines that sealed cans whirling by on conveyor belts, the six-pack you buy in a store contains not only a very fresh beer but also a beer that could be considered draft, since it has been kept cold from vat to home refrigerator.

BUILDING VOCABULARY

1. For the italicized word in each example in Column A below
   select a definition from Column B.

Column A
  1 locals *scoff* (par. 1)
  2 *informal* test (par. 1)
  3 measurable *validity*
    (par. 2)
  4 the *antiseptic* Spartan
    plant (par. 3)
  5 to *quaff* to their heart's
    content (par. 3)
  6 flat *mesas* (par. 3)
  7 construction *sites* (par. 3)
  8 a Moravian *strain* (par. 4)
  9 the *consistency* of
    oatmeal (par. 4)
 10 liquid malt *extract* (par. 4)

Column B
  a drink heartily
  b locations
  c thickness
  d not according to fixed
    rules
  e a line of certain species
  f a concentrated form of
    something
  g soundness
  h make fun of
  i free from infection
  j hills

2. Use five of the italicized words in the first exercise in sentences of your own.

UNDERSTANDING THE WRITER'S IDEAS

1. What is a "light-bodied" beer?

2. What does the author mean when she states, "In short, the
   difference between Coors and any other decent beer could
   be 1,800 miles"?

3. What *is* special about Coors beer?

4. Why do college students like to visit the Coors plant?

5. Describe the setting of the Coors brewery. How does it
   contrast with the picture on the Coors can?

6. Explain in your own words the process by which Coors is
   produced.

7. Why is the pasteurization process important to the final flavor of any beer?

8. Why can Coors almost be considered a draft beer?

UNDERSTANDING THE WRITER'S TECHNIQUES

1. How do comparison and contrast operate in the first paragraph? Does the author also use definition in this paragraph? Where? For what purpose?

2. What is the function of paragraph 2? What is the purpose of paragraph 3? How does the author develop paragraph 3?

3. Analyze the author's use of transitional devices (see Glossary) between paragraphs 2 and 3.

4. Which paragraphs analyze the process of brewing Coors? Make a list of the steps on a sheet of paper. Is the process clear and complete? Does the author use process analysis simply to inform? Does she also provide commentary? Where?

5. Where does the author introduce personal or subjective elements into this essay? Why, at these points, does she provide personal rather than technical details?

EXPLORING THE WRITER'S IDEAS

1. Suppose that three unidentified brands of beer, cola, or cigarettes were placed before you. Would you be able to identify them by taste? What is the importance of ''mystique'' (or image) or ''brand loyalty'' to a product's success?

2. Can you think of other products that have a mystique associated with them? What are they, and what accounts for the mystique?

3. Would the fact that Paul Newman drinks Coors affect people's attitudes toward the brand? Why do manufacturers attempt to have certain celebrities associated with their products? Why should consumers be influenced by these associations?

4. Based on this essay, what are some ways to make a technical analysis of process interesting to the reader?

IDEAS FOR WRITING

Guided Writing

Explain how to make or to assemble a particular item or product. For example, you might want to explain how to prepare a certain dish; how to assemble a piece of equipment; how to produce something in a factory. You might want to follow Lichtenstein's example: Explain how a popular drink is made.

1. Start by introducing the reader to your "perfect product," indicating how it is possible to achieve high-quality results in its preparation.

2. Use as examples of the quality of the product, positive statements made by other individuals. These may be the ideas of friends, relatives, or experts.

3. Explain the "mystique," if there is one, surrounding the product.

4. After arousing reader interest sufficiently, describe the actual process involved, concentrating on all important details in the sequence.

5. In your last paragraph, try to capture the taste, look, or feel of the final product.

More Writing Projects

1. Many television commercials aim at selling beer to viewers. In your journal reflect on these commercials. What do

they reveal about the manufacturers? the viewers? American society in general?

2. Set up an actual testing situation in your class. Have various members test three types of a particular item, such as chocolate, diet soda, a kitchen cleanser. Then write a paragraph report describing either the process involved in the testing or the process by which results were obtained.

3. Consult an encyclopedia or other reference book to learn about the making of some product—steel, automobiles, plywood, and so forth. Then explain this process in your own words.

Camping Out

Ernest Hemingway

In this essay by Ernest Hemingway (1899–1961), the author uses the pattern of process analysis to order his materials on the art of camping. Hemingway wrote this piece for the *Toronto Star* in the early 1920s, before he gained worldwide recognition as a major American writer. In it, we see his lifelong interest in the outdoors and in his desire to do things well.

Words to Watch

relief map (par. 2)   a map that shows by lines and colors the various heights and forms of the land

Caucasus (par. 2)   a mountain range in southeastern Europe

proprietary (par. 7)   held under patent or trademark

rhapsodize (par. 9)   to speak enthusiastically

browse bed (par. 9)   a portable cot

tyro (par. 11)   an amateur; a beginner in learning something

dyspepsia (par. 13)   indigestion

mulligan (par. 18)   a stew made from odds and ends of meats and vegetables

Thousands of people will go into the bush this summer to cut the high cost of living. A man who gets his two weeks' salary while he is on vacation should be able to put those two weeks in fishing and camping and be able to save one week's salary clear. He ought to be able to sleep comfortably every night, to eat well every day and to return to the city rested and in good condition. 1

But if he goes into the woods with a frying pan, an ignorance of black flies and mosquitoes, and a great and abiding lack of knowledge about cookery the chances are that his return will be very different. He will come back with enough mosquito bites to make the back of his neck look like a relief map of the Caucasus. His digestion will be wrecked after a valiant battle to assimilate half-cooked or charred grub. And he won't have had a decent night's sleep while he has been gone. 2

350

He will solemnly raise his right hand and inform you that ₃ he has joined the grand army of never-agains. The call of the wild may be all right, but it's a dog's life. He's heard the call of the tame with both ears. Waiter, bring him an order of milk toast.

In the first place he overlooked the insects. Black flies, ₄ no-see-ums, deer flies, gnats and mosquitoes were instituted by the devil to force people to live in cities where he could get at them better. If it weren't for them everybody would live in the bush and he would be out of work. It was a rather successful invention.

But there are lots of dopes that will counteract the pests. ₅ The simplest perhaps is oil of citronella. Two bits' worth of this purchased at any pharmacist's will be enough to last for two weeks in the worst fly and mosquito-ridden country.

Rub a little on the back of your neck, your forehead and ₆ your wrists before you start fishing, and the blacks and skeeters will shun you. The odor of citronella is not offensive to people. It smells like gun oil. But the bugs do hate it.

Oil of pennyroyal and eucalyptol are also much hated by ₇ mosquitoes, and with citronella they form the basis for many proprietary preparations. But it is cheaper and better to buy the straight citronella. Put a little on the mosquito netting that covers the front of your pup tent or canoe tent at night, and you won't be bothered.

To be really rested and get any benefit out of a vacation ₈ a man must get a good night's sleep every night. The first requisite for this is to have plenty of cover. It is twice as cold as you expect it will be in the bush four nights out of five, and a good plan is to take just double the bedding that you think you will need. An old quilt that you can wrap up in is as warm as two blankets.

Nearly all outdoor writers rhapsodize over the browse ₉ bed. It is all right for the man who knows how to make one and has plenty of time. But in a succession of one-night camps on a canoe trip all you need is level ground for your tent floor and you will sleep all right if you have plenty of covers under you. Take twice as much cover as you think that you will need, and then put two-thirds of it under you. You will sleep warm and get your rest.

When it is clear weather you don't need to pitch your tent 10 if you are only stopping for the night. Drive four stakes at the head of your made-up bed and drape your mosquito bar over that, then you can sleep like a log and laugh at the mosquitoes.

Outside of insects and bum sleeping the rock that wrecks most camping trips is cooking. The average tyro's idea of 11 cooking is to fry everything and fry it good and plenty. Now, a frying pan is a most necessary thing to any trip, but you also need the old stew kettle and the folding reflector baker.

A pan of fried trout can't be bettered and they don't cost any more than ever. But there is a good and bad way of frying 12 them.

The beginner puts his trout and his bacon in and over a 13 brightly burning fire the bacon curls up and dries into a dry tasteless cinder and the trout is burned outside while it is still raw inside. He eats them and it is all right if he is only out for the day and going home to a good meal at night. But if he is going to face more trout and bacon the next morning and other equally well-cooked dishes for the remainder of two weeks he is on the pathway to nervous dyspepsia.

The proper way is to cook over coals. Have several cans 14 of Crisco or Cotosuet or one of the vegetable shortenings along that are as good as lard and excellent for all kinds of shortening. Put the bacon in and when it is about half cooked lay the trout in the hot grease, dipping them in corn meal first. Then put the bacon on top of the trout and it will baste them as it slowly cooks.

The coffee can be boiling at the same time and in a 15 smaller skillet pancakes being made that are satisfying the other campers while they are waiting for the trout.

With the prepared pancake flours you take a cupful of 16 pancake flour and add a cup of water. Mix the water and flour and as soon as the lumps are out it is ready for cooking. Have the skillet hot and keep it well greased. Drop the batter in and as soon as it is done on one side loosen it in the skillet and flip it over. Apple butter, syrup or cinnamon and sugar go well with the cakes.

While the crowd have taken the edge from their appetites 17 with flapjacks the trout have been cooked and they and the bacon are ready to serve. The trout are crisp outside and firm and pink inside and the bacon is well done—but not too done. If there is anything better than that combination the writer has yet to taste it in a lifetime devoted largely and studiously to eating.

18 The stew kettle will cook you dried apricots when they have resumed their predried plumpness after a night of soaking, it will serve to concoct a mulligan in, and it will cook macaroni. When you are not using it, it should be boiling water for the dishes.

19 In the baker, mere man comes into his own, for he can make a pie that to his bush appetite will have it all over the product that mother used to make, like a tent. Men have always believed that there was something mysterious and difficult about making a pie. Here is a great secret. There is nothing to it. We've been kidded for years. Any man of average office intelligence can make at least as good a pie as his wife.

20 All there is to a pie is a cup and a half of flour, one-half teaspoonful of salt, one-half cup of lard and cold water. That will make pie crust that will bring tears of joy into your camping partner's eyes.

21 Mix the salt with the flour, work the lard into the flour, make it up into a good workmanlike dough with cold water. Spread some flour on the back of a box or something flat, and pat the dough around a while. Then roll it out with whatever kind of round bottle you prefer. Put a little more lard on the surface of the sheet of dough and then slosh a little flour on and roll it up and then roll it out again with the bottle.

22 Cut out a piece of the rolled out dough big enough to line a pie tin. I like the kind with holes in the bottom. Then put in your dried apples that have soaked all night and been sweetened, or your apricots, or your blueberries, and then take another sheet of the dough and drape it gracefully over the top, soldering it down at the edges with your fingers. Cut a couple of slits in the top dough sheet and prick it a few times with a fork in an artistic manner.

23 Put it in the baker with a good slow fire for forty-five minutes and then take it out and if your pals are Frenchmen they will kiss you. The penalty for knowing how to cook is that the others will make you do all the cooking.

It is all right to talk about roughing it in the woods. But   24
the real woodsman is the man who can be really comfortable
in the bush.

BUILDING VOCABULARY

1. For each word below write your own definition, based on
   how the word is used in the selection. Check back to the
   appropriate paragraph in the essay for more help, if necessary.

   a. abiding (par. 2)
   b. assimilate (par. 2)
   c. valiant (par. 2)
   d. charred (par. 2)
   e. solemnly (par. 3)
   f. requisite (par. 8)
   g. succession (par. 9)
   h. studiously (par. 17)
   i. concoct (par. 18)
   j. soldering (par. 22)

UNDERSTANDING THE WRITER'S IDEAS

1. What is Hemingway's main purpose in this essay? Does he
   simply want to explain how to set up camp and how to
   cook outdoors?

2. What, according to the writer, are the two possible results
   of camping out on your vacation?

3. Why is oil of citronella the one insecticide that Hemingway
   recommends over all others?

4. Is it always necessary to pitch a tent when camping out?
   What are alternatives to it? How can you sleep warmly and
   comfortably?

5. Explain the author's process for cooking trout. Also explain his process for baking a pie.

6. Is it enough for Hemingway simply to enjoy "roughing it" while camping out?

UNDERSTANDING THE WRITER'S TECHNIQUES

1. Identify those paragraphs in the essay that involve process analysis, and explain how Hemingway develops his subject in each.

2. What is the main writing pattern in paragraphs 1 and 2? How does this method serve as an organizing principle throughout the essay?

3. How would you characterize the author's style of writing? Is it appropriate to a newspaper audience? Is it more apt for professional fishermen?

4. In what way does Hemingway employ classification in this essay?

5. Analyze the tone of Hemingway's essay.

6. The concluding paragraph is short. Is it effective, nevertheless, and why? How does it reinforce the opening paragraph?

EXPLORING THE WRITER'S IDEAS

1. Camping out was popular in the 1920s, as it is in the 1990s. What are some of the reasons that it remains so attractive today?

2. Hemingway's essay describes many basic strategies for successful camping. He does not rely on "gadgets," or modern inventions to make camping easier. Do such gadgets make camping more fun today than it might have been in the 1920s?

3. The author suggests that there is a right way and a wrong

way to do things. Does it matter if you perform a recreational activity right as long as you enjoy doing it? Why?

IDEAS FOR WRITING

Guided Writing

Write an essay on how to do something wrong, and how to do it right—going on vacation, looking for a job, fishing, or whatever.

1. Reexamine the author's first three paragraphs and imitate his method of introducing the right and wrong ways about the subject, and the possible results.

2. Adopt a simple, informal, "chatty" style. Feel free to use a few well-placed clichés and other forms of spoken English. Use several similes.

3. Divide your subject into useful categories. Just as Hemingway treated insects, sleeping, and cooking, try to cover the main aspects of your subject.

4. Explain the process involved for each aspect of your subject. Make certain that you compare and contrast the right and wrong ways of your activity.

5. Write a short, crisp conclusion that reinforces your longer introduction.

More Writing Projects

1. How do you explain the fascination that camping out holds for many people? Reflect on this question in your journal.

2. In a paragraph describe how to get to your favorite vacation spot, and what to do when you get there.

3. If you have ever camped out, write a process paper explaining one important feature of setting up camp.

SUMMING UP: CHAPTER 9

1. Divide the class into groups and choose one Guided Writing essay per group on either the Keillor, Friedman, or Hemingway selection. Collaboratively discuss, evaluate, correct, edit, and rewrite the Guided Writing process essay. By consensus, establish grades for the original and the revised essay. Present your findings to the class.

2. On the basis of your experience reading the four essays in the section, write about the *types* of processes the authors deal with (you may want to read the introduction to the previous chapter on classification) and *how* they manage these processes. Clarify the main steps that you consider to be important in the writing of any process analysis.

3. Grace Lichtenstein in her essay reveals the brewing process behind the ''Coors mystique.'' Everyone has a favorite food. For this exercise, contribute a recipe for your favorite food to be included in a class cookbook. In addition to describing step-by-step the process for preparing the food, you should also tell something about the tradition behind the food, special occasions for eating it, the first time you ate it, and so forth. In other words, establish your own ''mystique'' for it.

4. Three of the essays in this chapter tell us how to do things that can have direct and immediate effects on our lives—writing letters, eating out, camping—while the fourth illuminates a process that produces a product that may also directly affect our lives—beer. Try to write an essay that describes a process with much less immediate effect.

5. Interview a classmate about something that he or she does very well. Make sure the questions you ask don't omit any important steps or materials used in the process. Take careful notes during the interview, then try to replicate the process on your own. If there were any difficulties in accomplishing the process, reinterview your classmate. After you are satisfied that no steps or materials were left out, write up the procedure in such a way that someone else could easily follow it.

CHAPTER 10

Cause-and-Effect Analysis

The analysis of cause and effect—often called *causal analysis*—seeks to explain why events occur, or what the outcome or *expected* results of a chain of happenings might be. Basically, cause-and-effect analysis looks for connections between things and reasons behind them. It involves a way of thinking that identifies conditions (the causes) and establishes results or consequences (the effects). In order to discuss an idea intelligently a writer needs to explore causes and effects. The strength of an explanation may lie simply in his or her ability to point out *why* something is so.

Like all the other writing patterns discussed in this text, cause-and-effect analysis reflects a kind of thinking we do every day. If someone were to ask you why you selected the college that you are now attending, you would offer reasons to explain your choice: the cost, the geographic location, the reputation of the institution, and so forth. These would be the *causes* that you have identified. On the other hand, someone might ask you if and why you like the college now that you are there. You could discuss your satisfaction (or lack of it) with the teachers, the course offerings, the opportunity to work part time, the availability of scholarship money and loans, the beauty of the campus, the variety in your social life. Those are the consequences or results—in other words, the *effects*—of your decision. Of course, basic reasoning and common sense are involved in the way that you identify causes and effects.

How do you determine causal relationships? First, you look at the *immediate* causes that gave rise to a situation—that is, you look at the causes most directly related to it, the ones you discover closest at hand. (Here you must be careful not to assume that because one event simply preceded another it also caused it.) But for most events a good analyst looks beyond immediate causes to more fundamental ones. These are the *ultimate* causes of a situation, the basic conditions that stimulated the more obvious ones.

For example, if you looked for causes to explain why your supervisor dismissed you from your job, your first response might be that you and she did not get along well. That could be an *immediate cause*. (Because one of your coworkers left your supervisor's office after a private conference with her just before you were fired, you could *not* assume safely that that coworker necessarily caused your dismissal.) But the immediate cause you uncovered could certainly be influenced by other underlying conditions. Perhaps your attendance record on the job was poor. Perhaps you did not get your work done quickly enough. Or, on the other hand, perhaps you worked so quickly and efficiently that your supervisor saw you as a threat to her own position. One or more of those and others like them might be the *ultimate* causes to explain why you lost the job.

Of course, as in the above example, causes you name for many situations may be thought of only as possibilities. It's often impossible to *prove* causes and effects absolutely. Yet in evaluating the causal relationships you present in an essay, readers expect you to offer evidence. Therefore, you do have to support the causes and effects you present with specific details drawn from personal experiences, from statistics, or from statements by experts, for example. The more details and evidence you offer, the better your paper will be.

When writers use causal analysis as a pattern, they can concentrate either on causes or effects, or they can attempt to balance the two. Moreover, in longer and more complicated papers, a writer can show how one cause produces an effect that, in turn, creates *another* set of causes leading to a second effect. Wherever the pattern takes you, remember to be thorough in presenting all links in your chain of analysis; to consider all possible factors; to avoid oversimplification; and to emphasize all important major and minor causes and effects.

Why Marriages Fail

Anne Roiphe

Anne Roiphe is the author of the well-known novel about relation-ships, *Up the Sandbox!,* which was later made into a popular film. In this essay, notice how she presents a series of interconnected reasons for the currently high divorce rate.

Words to Watch

obsolete (par. 1)   out-of-date; no longer in use

perils (par. 2)   dangers

infertility (par. 2)   the lack of ability to have children

turbulent (par. 2)   very chaotic or uneasy

stupefying (par. 2)   bewildering

obese (par. 3)   very fat, overweight

entrapment (par. 4)   the act of trapping, sometimes by devious methods

yearning (par. 4)   a strong desire

euphoric (par. 7)   characterized by a feeling of well-being

proverbial (par. 13)   relating to a proverb or accepted truth

infidelity (par. 13)   sexual unfaithfulness

These days so many marriages end in divorce that our 1 most sacred vows no longer ring with truth. "Happily ever af-ter" and "Till death do us part" are expressions that seem on the way to becoming obsolete. Why has it become so hard for couples to stay together? What goes wrong? What has hap-pened to us that close to one-half of all marriages are destined for the divorce courts? How could we have created a society in which 42 percent of our children will grow up in single-parent homes? If statistics could only measure loneliness, re-gret, pain, loss of self-confidence and fear of the future, the numbers would be beyond quantifying.

Even though each broken marriage is unique, we can still 2 find the common perils, the common causes for marital de-spair. Each marriage has crisis points and each marriage tests endurance, the capacity for both intimacy and change. Out-side pressures such as job loss, illness, infertility, trouble with a child, care of aging parents and all the other plagues of life hit marriage the way hurricanes blast our shores. Some marriages survive these storms and others don't. Marriages fail, however, not simply because of the outside weather but because the inner climate becomes too hot or too cold, too turbulent or too stupefying.

When we look at how we choose our partners and what 3 expectations exist at the tender beginnings of romance, some of the reasons for disaster become quite clear. We all select with unconscious accuracy a mate who will recreate with us the emotional patterns of our first homes. Dr. Carl A. Whitaker, a marital therapist and emeritus professor of psychiatry at the University of Wisconsin explains, "From early childhood on, each of us carried models for marriage, femininity, masculinity, motherhood, fatherhood and all the other family roles." Each of us falls in love with a mate who has qualities of our parents, who will help us rediscover both the psychological happiness and miseries of our past lives. We may think we have found a man unlike Dad, but then he turns to drink or drugs, or loses his job over and over again or sits silently in front of the T.V. just the way Dad did. A man may choose a woman who doesn't like kids just like his mother or who gambles away the family savings just like his mother. Or he may choose a slender wife who seems unlike his obese mother but then turns out to have other addictions that destroy their mutual happiness.

A man and a woman bring to their marriage bed a 4 blended concoction of conscious and unconscious memories of their parents' lives together. The human way is to compulsively repeat and recreate the patterns of the past. Sigmund Freud so well described the unhappy design that many of us get trapped in: the unmet needs of childhood, the angry feelings left over from frustrations of long ago, the limits of trust and the recurrence of old fears. Once an individual senses this entrapment, there may follow a yearning to escape, and the result could be a broken, splintered marriage.

Of course people can overcome the habits and attitudes 5

that developed in childhood. We all have hidden strengths and amazing capacities for growth and creative change. Change, however, requires work—observing your part in a rotten pattern, bringing difficulties out into the open—and work runs counter to the basic myth of marriage: "When I wed this person all my problems will be over. I will have achieved success and I will become the center of life for this other person and this person will be my center, and we will mean everything to each other forever." This myth, which every marriage relies on, is soon exposed. The coming of children, the pulls and tugs of their demands on affection and time, place a considerable strain on that basic myth of meaning everything to each other, of merging together and solving all of life's problems.

Concern and tension about money take each partner away from the other. Obligations to demanding parents or still-depended-upon parents create further strain. Couples today must also deal with all the cultural changes brought on in recent years by the women's movement and the sexual revolution. The altering of roles and the shifting of responsibilities have been extremely trying for many marriages. 6

These and other realities of life erode the visions of marital bliss the way sandstorms eat at rock and the ocean nibbles away at the dunes. Those euphoric, grand feelings that accompany romantic love are really self-delusions, self-hypnotic dreams that enable us to forge a relationship. Real life, failure at work, disappointments, exhaustion, bad smells, bad colds and hard times all puncture the dream and leave us stranded with our mate, with our childhood patterns pushing us this way and that, with our unfulfilled expectations. 7

The struggle to survive in marriage requires adaptability, flexibility, genuine love and kindness and an imagination strong enough to feel what the other is feeling. Many marriages fall apart because either partner cannot imagine what the other wants or cannot communicate what he or she needs or feels. Anger builds until it erupts into a volcanic burst that buries the marriage in ash. 8

It is not hard to see, therefore, how essential communication is for a good marriage. A man and a woman must be able to tell each other how they feel and why they feel the way 9 they do; otherwise they will impose on each other roles and actions that lead to further unhappiness. In some cases, the communication patterns of childhood—of not talking, of talking too much, of not listening, of distrust and anger, of withdrawal—spill into the marriage and prevent a healthy exchange of thoughts and feelings. The answer is to set up new patterns of communication and intimacy.

At the same time, however, we must see each other as 10 individuals. "To achieve a balance between separateness and closeness is one of the major psychological tasks of all human beings at every stage of life," says Dr. Stuart Bartle, a psychiatrist at the New York University Medical Center.

If we sense from our mate a need for too much intimacy, 11 we tend to push him or her away, fearing that we may lose our identities in the merging of marriage. One partner may suffocate the other partner in a childlike dependency.

A good marriage means growing as a couple but also 12 growing as individuals. This isn't easy. Richard gives up his interest in carpentry because his wife, Helen, is jealous of the time he spends away from her. Karen quits her choir group because her husband dislikes the friends she makes there. Each pair clings to each other and are angry with each other as life closes in on them. This kind of marital balance is easily thrown as one or the other pulls away and divorce follows.

Sometimes people pretend that a new partner will solve 13 the old problems. Most often extramarital sex destroys a marriage because it allows an artificial split between the good and the bad—the good is projected on the new partner and the bad is dumped on the head of the old. Dishonesty, hiding and cheating create walls between men and women. Infidelity is just a symptom of trouble. It is a symbolic complaint, a weapon of revenge, as well as an unraveler of closeness. Infidelity is often that proverbial last straw that sinks the camel to the ground.

All right—marriage has always been difficult. Why then 14 are we seeing so many divorces at this time? Yes, our modern social fabric is thin, and yes the permissiveness of society has created unrealistic expectations and thrown the family into chaos. But divorce is so common because people today are unwilling to exercise the self-discipline that marriage requires. They expect easy joy, like the entertainment on TV, the thrill of a good party.

Marriage takes some kind of sacrifice, not dreadful self- 15 sacrifice of the soul, but some level of compromise. Some of one's fantasies, some of one's legitimate desires have to be given up for the value of the marriage itself. "While all marital partners feel shackled at times, it is they who really choose to make the marital ties into confining chains or supporting bonds," says Dr. Whitaker. Marriage requires sexual, financial and emotional discipline. A man and a woman cannot follow every impulse, cannot allow themselves to stop growing or changing.

Divorce is not an evil act. Sometimes it provides salva- 16 tion for people who have grown hopelessly apart or were frozen in patterns of pain or mutual unhappiness. Divorce can be, despite its initial devastation, like the first cut of the surgeon's knife, a step toward new health and a good life. On the other hand, if the partners can stay past the breaking up of the romantic myths into the development of real love and intimacy, they have achieved a work as amazing as the greatest cathedrals of the world. Marriages that do not fail but improve, that persist despite imperfections, are not only rare these days but offer a wondrous shelter in which the face of our mutual humanity can safely show itself.

BUILDING VOCABULARY

1. Roiphe loads her essay with some very common expressions to make the discussion more easily understandable to the reader. Below is a list of ten such expressions. Use each in a sentence of your own.

   a. ring with truth (par. 1)
   b. crisis points (par. 2)
   c. tender beginnings (par. 3)
   d. mutual happiness (par. 3)
   e. marriage bed (par. 4)

    f. hidden strengths (par. 5)
    g. marital bliss (par. 7)
    h. healthy exchange (par. 9)
    i. childlike dependency (par. 11)
    j. social fabric (par. 14)

2. Locate and explain five terms that the author draws from psychology.

UNDERSTANDING THE WRITER'S IDEAS

1. What are the "sacred vows" the author mentions in paragraph 1? Identify the source of the expressions "happily ever after" and "till death do us part." What does she mean when she says that these expressions "seem on the way to becoming obsolete"?

2. What is a "single-parent home"?

3. How does Roiphe define "endurance" in a marriage? What does she mean by "outside pressures" in paragraph 2? What are some of these pressures? Does Roiphe feel they are the primary causes for marriages failing? Why?

4. According to the essay, how do we choose husbands and wives? What is the meaning of "our first home" in paragraph 3? According to Roiphe, for what reasons is the way we choose mates a possible cause for marriages failing?

5. What is the "basic myth" of marriage? How does it create a possibly bad marriage?

6. How have the women's movement and the sexual revolution created strains on modern marriages?

7. Explain what the writer means by "Real life, failure at work, disappointments, exhaustion, bad smells, bad colds, and hard times" in paragraph 7. How do they affect marriages?

8. What is the role of communication between husband and

wife in a marriage? What are the results of poor communication? What solutions to this problem does Roiphe suggest?

9. What two types of "growth" does Roiphe suggest as necessary to a good marriage? Who are Richard, Helen, and Karen, named in paragraph 12?

10. According to Roiphe, what is the common cause for extramarital sexual affairs? What are her projected results of infidelity?

11. What does Roiphe identify as the primary cause of divorce? What does she propose as a solution to this problem?

12. According to the last paragraph, do you think Roiphe is in favor of each divorce? Why? In this paragraph, she presents both the positive and negative effects of divorce. What are the positive effects? the negative effects?

UNDERSTANDING THE WRITER'S TECHNIQUES

1. How does the title almost predict for the reader that the writer's main technique of development will be cause-and-effect analysis?

2. One strategy for developing an introductory paragraph is to ask a question. What is the purpose of the questions that the author asks in the opening paragraph? What is the relationship among the questions? How do the questions themselves dictate a cause-effect pattern of development? How do they immediately involve the reader in the topic?

3. In which paragraph does Roiphe list the immediate or common causes of marital failure? Why is this placement effective?

4. The use of clear *topic sentences* for each paragraph can often be an important technique in writing a clear causal

analysis because they usually identify main causes for the effect under discussion. Identify the topic sentences for paragraphs 3, 4, and 6. What causes for marriage failure does each identify?

5. What causal chain of behavior does Roiphe build in paragraphs 8 to 13?

6. Why does Roiphe begin paragraph 14 with the words "All right"? Whom is she addressing? How does this address compare with the technique used in her introduction?

7. What two authorities does Roiphe quote in this essay? How are their citations useful? How are they identified? In what ways do their identifications add to their credibility as sources of opinions or information on Roiphe's topic?

8. Where does Roiphe use statistics in this essay? Why is it especially important to the development of the article?

9. Roiphe makes use of *definition* (see pages 244–245) in a number of places in this essay. What are her definitions of the following:

   a. "work" in a marriage (par. 5)
   b. "A good marriage" (par. 12)
   c. "divorce" (par. 16)
   d. "marriages that do not fail but improve" (par. 16)

   Locate other places where she uses definition.

10. In some essays, the introduction and conclusion are each simply the first and last paragraphs. In this essay, the writer uses more than one paragraph for each. Which paragraphs make up her introduction? Which make up the conclusion? Why might she have structured her introduction and conclusion in this way? How does the structure affect the essay?

11. You have learned that two of the most common types of comparisons used by writers to enliven their essays are *similes* and *metaphors*. Look up the definition of these terms in the Glossary to refresh your memory. In addi-

tion, writers may use *extended metaphors*. This technique relies upon a number of metaphoric comparisons which revolve around a main idea rather than a single comparison. Roiphe uses comparisons in a number of paragraphs in this essay. In each of the following cases identify and explain the comparisons indicated:

   a. extended metaphor (par. 2)
   b. metaphor (par. 7)
   c. metaphor (par. 8)
   d. metaphor (par. 9)
   e. simile (par. 14)
   f. metaphor (par. 15)
   g. similes, metaphors (par. 16)

   How does Roiphe's frequent use of metaphors and similes affect the tone of the essay?

12. Why does Roiphe end her essay with references to successful marriages? Would you consider that as being off the topic? Why or why not?

EXPLORING THE WRITER'S IDEAS

1. Roiphe discusses quite a few causes for marriages failing. Discuss with the class some additional causes. Why are they also important?

2. Paragraph 6 states that "Couples today must also deal with all the cultural changes brought on in recent years by the women's movement and the sexual revolution." Identify these two social phenomena. Among the people you know, have these cultural changes affected their marriages? How? If you are not married, and plan to marry, do you feel that the changes will present any foreseeable problems? If you are not married, and do not plan to marry, have they influenced your decision in any ways? What other effects have these two movements had in American society? Do you think these influences have been positive or negative? Why?

3. If you are married or in a close relationship, how did you choose your mate? If you are not married or in a relationship, what qualities would you look for in a mate? Why?

4. In paragraphs 6 and 7, Roiphe mentions "realities of life" that destroy romantic notions of "marital bliss." What other realities can you add to her list?

5. Paragraph 15 discusses the idea of self-sacrifice in marriage. Roiphe writes, "Some of one's fantasies, some of one's legitimate desires have to be given up for the value of the marriage itself." However, some people insist that for a marriage to survive, each partner must maintain complete integrity, that is, must not be forced into major sacrifices of values or life-styles. What is your opinion of these two opposing viewpoints?

6. Both Gregg Easterbrook in "Escape Valve" (pages 263–265) and Judy Syfers in "I Want a Wife" (pages 407–409) provide some insights into marriage that complement Roiphe's. How do their positions compare with hers? How, for example, could the principle of "automatic-out" explain to some degree why marriages fail?

IDEAS FOR WRITING

Guided Writing

Using cause-and-effect analysis, write an essay in which you explain *why marriages succeed.*

1. Limit your topic sufficiently so that you can concentrate your discussion on closely interrelated cause-and-effect patterns.

2. In the introduction, involve your reader with a series of pertinent questions.

3. Identify what many people think are common or immediate

causes of successful marriages; then show how other causes are perhaps even more important.

4. In the course of your essay, cite at least one relevant statistic that will add extra importance to your topic.

5. Try to use at least one quotation from a reputable authority. Consult your library for books and articles that deal with marriage. Be sure to include full identification of your source.

6. Use clear topic sentences in each paragraph as you present analysis of the various causes for successful marriages.

7. Make use of metaphors, similes, and extended metaphors.

8. In your essay, offer necessary definitions of terms that are especially important to your topic. Try for at least one definition by negation.

9. Write a conclusion in which you make some commentary upon divorce. Make your comment as an outgrowth of your discussion of a successful marriage.

More Writing Projects

1. What is the "ideal marriage"? In your journal, speculate on those qualities that you think would make a perfect marriage. Share observations with others in the class.

2. In a paragraph, explain some of the reasons why you ever ended a relationship (a marriage, a close friendship, a relationship with a girlfriend or boyfriend).

3. Write an essay in which you explain the effects of divorce on the lives of the couple involved. Here, do not concern yourself with causes; look only at the results of the failed marriage.

Rite of Spring

Arthur Miller

The renowned author of such modern dramatic classics as *Death of a Salesman, The Crucible,* and *A View from the Bridge* reveals the causes behind his thirty-six-year mixed relationship with his vegetable gardens. Miller's facility with descriptions and transitions allows him to move deftly between the realities of dirt between his fingers and the abstractions of God's purposes for the universe.

Words to Watch

atavism (par. 1)   a throwback to past patterns
bountiful (par. 6)   plentiful; in great supply
paternal (par. 7)   relating to fatherhood
maternal (par. 7)   relating to motherhood
botanist (par. 9)   a scientist concerned with plant life
toddles (par. 9)   walks with short, tottering steps
compensations (par. 10)   rewards; payments for services
metamorphose (par. 10)   to change significantly from one form to another
mason (par. 12)   a skilled worker in stone
perpetual (par. 12)   everlasting
unregenerate (par. 12)   not reformed from past ways

I have never understood why we keep a garden and why, over 36 years ago when I bought my first house in the country, I started digging up a patch for vegetables before doing anything else. When you think how easy and cheap, relatively, it is to buy a bunch of carrots or beets, why raise them? And root crops especially are hard to tell apart, when store-bought, from our own. There is an atavism at work here, a kind of back-breaking make-believe that has no reality. Besides, I don't particularly like eating vegetables. I'd much rather eat something juicy and fat. Like hot dogs.

Now, hot dogs and mustard with some warm sauerkraut—if you could raise *them* outside your window, you'd really have something you could justify without a second's hesitation. Or a hot pastrami vine.

As it is, though, I can't deny that come April I find myself going out to lean on the fence and look at that cursed rectangle, resolving with all my rational powers not to plant it again. But inevitably a morning arrives when, just as I am awakening, a scent wafts through the window, something like earth-as-air, a scent that seems to come up from the very center of this planet. And the sun means business, suddenly, and has a different, deeper yellow in its beams on the carpet. The birds begin screaming hysterically, thinking what I am thinking—the worms are deliciously worming their way through the melting soil.

It is not only pleasure sending me back to stare at that plot of soil, it is really conflict. The question is the same each year—what method should we use? The last few years we unrolled 36-inch-wide black plastic between the rows, and it worked perfectly, keeping the soil moist in dry times and weed-free.

But black plastic looks so industrial, so unromantic, that I have gradually moved over to hay mulch. We cut a lot of hay and, as it rots, it does improve the soil's composition. Besides, it looks lovely, and comes to us free.

Keeping a garden makes you aware of how delicate, bountiful, and easily ruined the surface of this little planet is. In that 50-by-70-foot patch there must be a dozen different types of soil. Parsley won't grow in one part but loves another, and the same goes for the other crops. I suppose if you loaded the soil with chemical fertilizer these differences would be less noticeable, but I use it sparingly and only in rows right where seeds are planted rather than broadcast over the whole area. I'm not sure why I do this beyond the saving in fertilizer and my unwillingness to aid the weeds.

The attractions of gardening, I think, at least for a certain number of gardeners, are neurotic and moral. Whenever life seems pointless and difficult to grasp, you can always get out in the garden and *get something done*. Also, your paternal or maternal instincts come into play because helpless living things are depending on you, require training and encouragement and protection from enemies. In some cases, as with squash and cucumbers, your offspring—as it were—begin to turn upon you in massive numbers, proliferating more and more each morning and threatening to follow you into the house to strangle you in their vines.

Gardening is a moral occupation, as well, because you always start in spring resolved to keep it looking neat this year, just like the pictures in the catalogues. But by July, you once again face the chaos of unthinned carrots, lettuce and beets. This is when my wife becomes—openly now—mistress of the garden. A consumer of vast quantities of vegetables, she does the thinning and hand-cultivating of the tiny plants. Squatting, she patiently moves down each row selecting which plants shall live and which she will cast aside. 8

At about this time, my wife's 86-year-old mother, a botanist, makes her first visit to the garden. She looks about skeptically. Her favorite task is binding the tomato plants to stakes. She is an outspoken, truthful woman, or she was until she learned better. Now, instead of saying, "You have planted the tomatoes in the damp part of the garden," she waits until October when she makes her annual trip to her home in Europe; then she gives me my good-by kiss and says offhandedly, "Tomatoes in damp soil tend more to get fungi," and toddles away to her plane. But by October nothing in the garden matters, so sure am I that I will never plant it again. 9

I garden, I suppose, because I must. It would be intolerable to have to pass an unplanted fenced garden a few times a day. There are also certain compensations, and these must be what annually tilt my mind toward all that work. There are few sights quite as gratifyingly beautiful as a vegetable garden glistening in the sun, all dewy and glittering with a dozen shades of green at seven in the morning. Far lovelier, in fact, than rows of hot dogs. In some pocket of the mind there may even be a tendency to metamorphose this vision into a personal reassurance that all this healthy growth, this orderliness and thrusting life must somehow reflect similar movements in one's own spirit. Without a garden to till and plant I would not know what April was for. 10

As it is, April is for getting irritated all over again at this 11 pointless, time-consuming hobby. I do not understand people who claim to "love" gardening. A garden is an extension of oneself—or selves—and so it has to be an arena where striving does not cease, but continues by other means. As an example: you simply have to face the moment when you must admit that the lettuce was planted too deep or was not watered enough, cease hoping it will show itself tomorrow, and dig up the row again. But you will feel better for not standing on your dignity. And that's what gardening is all about—character building. Which is why Adam was a gardener. (And we all know where it got him, too.)

But is it conceivable that the father of us all should have 12 been a mason, weaver, shoemaker, or anything but a gardener? Of course not. Only the gardener is capable of endlessly reviving so much hope that this year, regardless of drought, flood, typhoon, or his own stupidity, this year he is going to do it *right!* Leave it to God to have picked the proper occupation for his only creature capable of such perpetual and unregenerate self-delusion.

I suppose it should be added, for honesty's sake, that the 13 above was written on one of the coldest days in December.

BUILDING VOCABULARY

1. Use context clues to determine meanings of the words in italics below. Select the letter of the appropriate choice.

   1. *justify* without a second's hesitation (par. 2)

      a support
      b achieve
      c dig up
      d cook

   2. *resolving* with all my rational powers (par. 3)

      a looking at
      b showing strongly
      c digging up
      d declaring formally

3. a scent *wafts* through the window (par. 3)

   a smells bad
   b drifts dreamily
   c escapes noisily
   d moves tiredly

4. use it *sparingly* (par. 6)

   a heavily
   b wisely
   c in small amounts
   d without much thought

5. rather than *broadcast* over the whole area (par. 6)

   a planted
   b delivered on the radio
   c scattered in all directions
   d distributed one-by-one

6. in *massive* numbers (par. 7)

   a very small
   b very weak
   c very large
   d very strange

7. *proliferating* more and more each morning (par. 7)

   a dying
   b reproducing rapidly
   c going away
   d eating again

8. as *gratifyingly* beautiful (par. 10)

   a making unhappy
   b strikingly
   c surprisingly
   d giving pleasure

9. *glistening* in the sun (par. 10)

   a burning

    b fading

    c glittering

    d lazing

10. endlessly *reviving* (par. 12)

    a bringing to life

    b dreaming about

    c working up

    d losing out

2. Miller uses a number of hyphenated compound words. Write meanings for each word below. Then use each word in an original sentence.

    a. back-breaking (par. 1)

    b. make-believe (par. 1)

    c. earth-as-air (par. 3)

    d. weed-free (par. 4)

    e. hand-cultivating (par. 8)

    f. self-delusion (par. 12)

UNDERSTANDING THE WRITER'S IDEAS

1. Who is the "we" of paragraph 1? The "you"? Why does Miller use these pronouns in the very beginning?

2. What are "root crops" (par. 1)?

3. What is a "rite"? Explain the meaning of the title.

4. What is "that cursed rectangle" (par. 3)? Why is it "cursed"?

5. Why do they cover the garden with black plastic? What is *mulch?* Why do they switch to it from using the plastic?

6. Name the main reasons why Miller *does* garden. Name the reasons why he would consider *not* gardening. How does he relate the two in the essay?

7. What are the "helpless living things" mentioned in paragraph 7?

8. How does Miller's mother-in-law figure in his gardening rites? Does he appreciate her role or not?

9. Why does Miller "not understand people who claim to 'love' gardening"?

10. What is the meaning of the sentence, "Which is why Adam was a gardener" (par. 11)? What attitude or tone is expressed in the parenthetical sentence that follows?

UNDERSTANDING THE WRITER'S TECHNIQUES

1. How does the repetition of the word "why" in paragraph 1 give us clues to the rhetorical nature of this essay?

2. In paragraph 1, Miller seems to make contradictory statements. He calls gardening "back-breaking," yet he also says it is "make-believe" and "has no reality." How can something unreal be back-breaking? Why does he link these elements?

3. Among his categories of reasons for gardening, Miller includes pleasure, conflict, neurosis, and morality. Summarize in your own words Miller's development of each of those categories of causes. How does he organize these categories within the essay? Which does he consider most important? Explain your answer with references to Miller's technique: placement in essay, key words, rhetorical strategies, and so on.

4. Paragraph 3 is particularly descriptive (see Chapter 3). How does Miller use various sensory imagery—olfactory, aural, visual—in this paragraph? How does he use *simile, metaphor,* and *personification* (see Glossary)?

5. Analyze the cause-and-effect development of paragraphs 4 and 5, and of paragraph 6.

6. Miller's use of transitions between paragraphs is highly effective, but not too obvious on first reading. Comment on

the various transitions that connect the paragraphs in this piece.

7. How and where does Miller use *personification* (see Glossary) in this essay? Is it effective? Why?

8. Although Miller focuses quite well on specifics, he also makes some broad generalizations, some of them even spiritual in nature. Identify a few such generalizations and explain their meanings.

9. In this essay, does Miller concentrate more on causes or effects? Explain.

10. What would you say is Miller's overall attitude toward vegetable gardening? Does he maintain one attitude throughout the essay? If not, why does he change?

11. Does this essay have a thesis? If so, where is it placed? Why?

12. What is the meaning of Miller's last-paragraph "confession"? What is its purpose?

EXPLORING THE WRITER'S IDEAS

1. Arthur Miller is a world-famous, Pulitzer Prize–winning playwright whose plays have become an integral part of social and political thought from Providence to Peking. How does he qualify to write about vegetable gardening? Do you feel his essay is accurate? Do you feel that Miller is a "city boy" writing about "country things"? How well do you trust Miller's information in this essay? Explain.

2. Miller writes about both the satisfaction and hardship of growing things. What have been your experiences with planting or growing things—from houseplants to farm crops? How does it make you feel?

3. Generally, when you create things, do you get the most sat-

isfaction from the process or the product? From tangible results or from spiritual and emotional uplifts? Explain with examples.

IDEAS FOR WRITING

Guided Writing

Write an essay in which you explain why for years you have pursued a certain hobby or activity about which you have mixed feelings.

1. Begin your essay with a series of questions about your motives for pursuing this activity.

2. State how long you've been involved in it.

3. Use contradictory statements to describe your mixed feelings.

4. Offer some absurd alternative to doing this activity.

5. Organize your essay into broad categories of reasons why you continue.

6. To explain the categories of reasons, use combinations of rhetorical modes that help you make your point.

7. Use some sensory imagery and figurative language.

8. Use clear, yet subtle, transitions between paragraphs.

9. Try to connect your activity—and your reasons for pursuing it—with some result that goes beyond the immediate or obvious ones.

10. Near the end of your essay, identify the main reason why you and others pursue this hobby or activity.

11. Relate your reasoning to more abstract or spiritual reasons.

12. End with a tongue-in-cheek confession about how or why you wrote this essay.

More Writing Projects

1. In your journal write about why you recently did something you didn't really want to do. Then, try to explain why you did it.

2. Write a paragraph in which you explain the effects of a certain requirement at your school.

3. In an essay explain how and why you recently became interested in some new activity or philosophy.

The Ambivalence of Abortion
Linda Bird Francke

In this autobiographical narrative, author Linda Bird Francke tells about her mixed feelings toward the issue of abortion. Although she has strong political convictions on the subject, her ambivalence surfaces when she must confront abortion personally. Notice how she blends descriptive details with personal insights to explain the reasons for her uncertainty.

Words to Watch

dwell (par. 1)   keep attention directed on something

heralded (par. 1)   announced in a joyous manner

rationalize (par. 2)   to justify one's behavior (especially to oneself)

freelance (par. 3)   working without long-range contractual agreements

cycled (par. 5)   moved through a complete series of operations or steps

common denominator (par. 10)   similar traits or themes

rhetoric (par. 13)   ways of speaking or writing effectively

fetus (par. 13)   an unborn child still in the mother's womb

neurotic (par. 14)   emotionally unstable

vaccinated (par. 14)   injected with a harmless virus to produce immunity to a disease

inoculated (par. 14)   treated with a serum or antibody to prevent disease

uterus (par. 16)   the womb; the place within the mother where the fetus develops

sensation (par. 18)   feeling

Novocain (par. 18)   a drug used to numb the feeling of pain

quivered (par. 18)   shook

We were sitting in a bar on Lexington Avenue when I 1 told my husband I was pregnant. It is not a memory I like to dwell on. Instead of the champagne and hope which had heralded the impending births of the first, second and third child, the news of this one was greeted with shocked silence and Scotch. "Jesus," my husband kept saying to himself, stirring the ice cubes around and around. "Oh, Jesus."

Oh, how we tried to rationalize it that night as the starting time for the movie came and went. My husband talked about his plans for a career change in the next year, to stem the staleness that fourteen years with the same investment-banking firm had brought him. A new baby would preclude that option.

The timing wasn't right for me either. Having juggled pregnancies and child care with what freelance jobs I could fit in between feedings, I had just taken on a full-time job. A new baby would put me right back in the nursery just when our youngest child was finally school age. It was time for *us,* we tried to rationalize. There just wasn't room in our lives now for another baby. We both agreed. And agreed. And agreed.

How very considerate they are at the Women's Services, known formally as the Center for Reproductive and Sexual Health. Yes, indeed, I could have an abortion that very Saturday morning and be out in time to drive to the country that afternoon. Bring a first morning urine specimen, a sanitary belt and napkins, a money order or $125 cash—and a friend.

My friend turned out to be my husband, standing awkwardly and ill at ease as men always do in places that are exclusively for women, as I checked in at nine A.M. Other men hovered around just as anxiously, knowing they had to be there, wishing they weren't. No one spoke to each other. When I would be cycled out of there four hours later, the same men would be slumped in their same seats, locked downcast in their cells of embarrassment.

The Saturday morning women's group was more dispirited than the men in the waiting room. There were around fifteen of us, a mixture of races, ages and backgrounds. Three didn't speak English at all and a fourth, a pregnant Puerto Rican girl around eighteen, translated for them.

There were six black women and a hodgepodge of whites, among them a T-shirted teenager who kept leaving the room to throw up and a puzzled middle-aged woman from Queens with three grown children.

"What form of birth control were you using?" the vol- 8
unteer asked each one of us. The answer was inevitably
"none." She then went on to describe the various forms of birth
control available at the clinic, and offered them to each of us.

The youngest Puerto Rican girl was asked through the in- 9
terpreter which she'd like to use: the loop, diaphragm, or pill.
She shook her head "no" three times. "You don't want to
come back here again, do you?" the volunteer pressed. The
girl's head was so low her chin rested on her breastbone. "*Sí,*"
she whispered.

We had been there two hours by that time, filling out 10
endless forms, giving blood and urine, receiving lectures. But
unlike any other group of women I've been in, we didn't talk.
Our common denominator, the one which usually floods
across language and economic barriers into familiarity, today
was one of shame. We were losing life that day, not giving it.

The group kept getting cut back to smaller, more work- 11
able units, and finally I was put in a small waiting room with
just two other women. We changed into paper bathrobes and
paper slippers, and we rustled whenever we moved. One of
the women in my room was shivering and an aide brought her
a blanket.

"What's the matter?" the aide asked her. "I'm scared," 12
the woman said. "How much will it hurt?" The aide smiled.
"Oh, nothing worse than a couple of bad cramps," she said.
"This afternoon you'll be dancing a jig."

I began to panic. Suddenly the rhetoric, the abortion 13
marches I'd walked in, the telegrams sent to Albany to counteract the Friends of the Fetus, the Zero Population Growth
buttons I'd worn, peeled away, and I was all alone with my
microscopic baby. There were just the two of us there, and
soon, because it was more convenient for me and my husband, there would be one again.

How could it be that I, who am so neurotic about life 14
that I step over bugs rather than on them, who spend hours
planting flowers and vegetables in the spring even though we
rent out the house and never see them, who make sure the
children are vaccinated and inoculated and filled with vitamin
C, could so arbitrarily decide that this life shouldn't be?

"It's not a life," my husband had argued, more to convince himself than me. "It's a bunch of cells smaller than my fingernail." 15

But any woman who has had children knows that certain feeling in her taut, swollen breasts, and the slight but constant ache in her uterus that signals the arrival of a life. Though I would march myself into blisters for a woman's right to exercise the option of motherhood, I discovered there in the waiting room that I was not the modern woman I thought I was. 16

When my name was called, my body felt so heavy the nurse had to help me into the examining room. I waited for my husband to burst through the door and yell "stop," but of course he didn't. I concentrated on three black spots in the acoustic ceiling until they grew in size to the shape of saucers, while the doctor swabbed my insides with antiseptic. 17

"You're going to feel a burning sensation now," he said, injecting Novocain into the neck of the womb. The pain was swift and severe, and I twisted to get away from him. He was hurting my baby, I reasoned, and the black saucers quivered in the air. "Stop," I cried. "Please stop." He shook his head, busy with his equipment. "It's too late to stop now," he said. "It'll just take a few more seconds." 18

What good sports we women are. And how obedient. Physically the pain passed even before the hum of the machine signaled that the vacuuming of my uterus was completed, my baby sucked up like ashes after a cocktail party. Ten minutes start to finish. And I was back on the arm of the nurse. 19

There were twelve beds in the recovery room. Each one had a gaily flowered draw sheet and a soft green or blue thermal blanket. It was all very feminine. Lying on these beds for an hour or more were the shocked victims of their sex, their full wombs now stripped clean, their futures less encumbered. 20

It was very quiet in that room. The only voice was that of the nurse, locating the new women who had just come in so she could monitor their blood pressure, and checking out the recovered women who were free to leave. 21

Juice was being passed about, and I found myself sipping a Dixie cup of Hawaiian Punch. An older woman with tightly 22

curled bleached hair was just getting up from the next bed.
"That was no goddamn snap," she said, resting before putting
on her miniskirt and high white boots. Other women came and
went, some walking out as dazed as they had entered, others
with a bounce that signaled they were going right back to
Bloomingdale's.

Finally then, it was time for me to leave. I checked out, 23
making an appointment to return in two weeks for an IUD in-
sertion. My husband was slumped in the waiting room, clutch-
ing a single yellow rose wrapped in a wet paper towel and
stuffed into a Baggie.

We didn't talk the whole way home, but just held hands 24
very tightly. At home there were more yellow roses and a tray
in bed for me and the children's curiosity to divert.

It had certainly been a successful operation. I didn't 25
bleed at all for two days just as they had predicted, and then I
bled only moderately for another four days. Within a week my
breasts had subsided and the tenderness vanished, and my
body felt mine again instead of the eggshell it becomes when
it's protecting someone else.

My husband and I are back to planning our summer va- 26
cation and his career switch.

And it certainly does make more sense not to be having 27
a baby right now—we say that to each other all the time. But
I have this ghost now. A very little ghost that only appears
when I'm seeing something beautiful, like the full moon on the
ocean last weekend. And the baby waves at me. And I wave
at the baby. "Of course, we have room," I cry to the ghost.
"Of course, we do."

BUILDING VOCABULARY

1. Develop definitions of your own for the italicized words by
   relying on context clues, that is, clues from surrounding
   words and sentences. Then check your definition against a
   dictionary definition.

   a. "My husband talked about his plans for a career

change in the next year, *to stem* the staleness that four-teen years with the same investment-banking firm had brought him. A new baby would *preclude* that *option*." (par. 2)

b. "Though I would march myself into blisters for a wom-an's right to *exercise* the *option* of motherhood, I dis-covered there in the waiting room that I was not the modern woman I thought I was." (par. 16)

c. "The pain was *swift* and *severe,* and I twisted to get away from him." (par. 18)

d. "Lying on these beds for an hour or more were the shocked victims of their sex, their full wombs now stripped clean, their futures less *encumbered*." (par. 20)

e. "It had certainly been a successful operation. I didn't bleed at all for two days just as they had predicted, and then I bled only *moderately* for another four days." (par. 25)

2. For each italicized word in Column A, write the correct *synonym* (a word of similar meaning) from Column B. Look up unfamiliar words in a dictionary.

Column A

1 *impending* birth (par. 1)
2 *hovered* around (par. 5)
3 locked *downcast* (par. 5)
4 more *dispirited* (par. 6)
5 *puzzled* middle-aged woman (par. 7)
6 *inevitably* "none" (par. 8)
7 *taut*, swollen breasts (par. 16)
8 how *obedient* (par. 19)
9 curiosity to *divert* (par. 24)
10 had *subsided* (par. 25)

Column B

a decreased
b complying
c confused
d lingered
e about to happen
f tight
g distract
h dejected
i unavoidable
j discouraged

UNDERSTANDING THE WRITER'S IDEAS

1. What is the setting in which Francke breaks the news to her husband that she is pregnant? How does he receive the news?

2. What reasons does the husband give for not wanting another child? Why does Francke feel it is a bad time for herself as well?

3. What is the attitude of the men waiting at the abortion clinic? Explain.

4. Why is there a women's group meeting before Francke actually gets her abortion? Are all the women pretty much alike at this meeting? How so? What is Francke's attitude toward these other women? Give specific examples to support your answer.

5. What common reason do all the women in the group share for being pregnant?

6. In the past, what was the author's viewpoint concerning women's rights to have abortions? What specific examples does she give to illustrate this point of view? Do you assume that she still holds this opinion? Why?

7. What examples does Francke give to illustrate that she supports life? Are they convincing?

8. Explain what the author means by the statement "Though I would march myself into blisters for a woman's right to exercise the option of motherhood, I discovered there in the waiting room that I was not the modern woman I thought I was" (par. 16).

9. When she is in the examining room, what does the author do to deal with her anxieties about the abortion?

10. Explain what the woman means when she says to Francke, "'That was no goddamn snap.'"

11. How does Francke know the operation has been successful?

UNDERSTANDING THE WRITER'S TECHNIQUES

1. What rhetorical strategy does the word "ambivalence" in the title suggest? How does Francke use that strategy in the very first paragraph? Where does she use it elsewhere in the essay?

2. Does Francke successfully explain the ambivalence named in the title? Why or why not?

3. Which does this analysis concentrate on more—causes, effects, or a combination of the two? What evidence can you offer to support your answer? What specifically is the relationship between cause and effect in paragraphs 6 to 10? Analyze the pattern of cause and effect in paragraphs 19 to 22.

4. What is the use of narration in this essay? What is the narrative *point of view* (see Glossary) in this selection? How is it used to enhance the essay?

5. What would you say is the overall tone of the selection? The author uses repetition in this essay to help set that tone. How does the repetition in "We both agreed. And agreed. And agreed" (par. 3) contribute to it?

6. *Paradox* is a special variety of irony (see Glossary) in which there is a clear contradiction in a situation. A paradox is a statement or attitude which, on the surface, seems unlikely, and yet, on analysis, can indeed be true. For example, it is paradoxical that the author should have such ambivalent feelings about abortion while she is sitting in an abortion clinic. Why is that situation considered paradoxical? What other paradoxes do you find in this essay?

7. What is the function of description in this essay? Select passages in which you feel the descriptions are especially vivid. How is description used by the author to characterize the women mentioned in paragraph 22? Are the women stereotyped in this description? Explain.

8. Only toward the last part of the essay does Francke use any metaphors or similes—some of them quite startling. Identify the metaphors or similes in paragraph 19, paragraph 25, and paragraph 27. Why do you think she saved this figurative language for the end?

9. Analyze the last paragraph. What causes and effects discussed throughout the essay are echoed here? What new ones are suggested? Compare the effect of the statement "'Of course, we have room'" to the statement in paragraph 3, "There just wasn't room...." How does this repetition affect the conclusion?

10. Writers who write about highly charged emotional issues must take special care to avoid *sentimentality*—the excessive display of emotion (see Glossary). Has Francke been successful in avoiding it everywhere in the essay? How has she used concrete descriptions to avoid being sentimental? Does the conclusion strike you as being excessively emotional or does it strike you simply as a dramatic but effective closing? Explain your responses.

EXPLORING THE WRITER'S IDEAS

1. When this article was originally published in 1976, it appeared under the *pseudonym* (a fictitious name) "Jane Doe." What reason might Linda Francke have had for not using her real name? Why do you think that a few years later she admitted to the authorship of the article? In general, what do you think about a writer publishing his or her work under an assumed name? Explain. What historical examples can you offer for the use of pseudonyms?

2. Francke describes some very intimate personal emotions and experiences in her attempt to explain what causes her ambivalence toward abortion. On the basis of the material presented, do you think she is justified in feeling ambivalent? Do you feel she should have been more definite one way or the other? Why?

3. In her description of the Saturday morning women's group (pars. 6 to 10), Francke shows that the women present were of all types—"a mixture of races, ages, and backgrounds." This suggests, of course, that abortion is a subject affecting all women. Does it, in fact, affect all women equally? Explain your answer.

4. In paragraph 5, the author describes her husband as "standing awkwardly and ill at ease as men always do in places that are exclusively for women." What sorts of places are exclusively for persons of one sex? Discuss how you felt and acted if you were ever in a place which was really more for persons of the opposite sex.

5. Much controversy about abortion revolves around modern definitions of life and death. Some people argue that life begins at conception; others argue that life begins at birth. With which group do you agree? Why? How has modern science complicated our concepts of life and death?

6. Abortion and antiabortion forces have increased their attacks against each other dramatically in recent years. How does Francke's essay crystallize both sides of the complex, emotionally charged issue?

IDEAS FOR WRITING

Guided Writing

Select an important issue facing society, an issue with which you have had personal experience and about which you have mixed feelings. After you fill in the blank, write an essay titled "Two Sides of _____ ." In your essay explore the reasons for your ambivalence. You can select from a wide range of social, moral, health, or education topics. For example, you might want to consider ambivalence toward interracial dating or marriages, a compulsory draft, legalization of drugs, cigarette smoking, a liberal arts education—but feel free to select any issue that is especially important to you.

1. Write the essay as a first-person narrative. Begin with an incident when you first clearly realized the ambivalent nature of the issue, and explain why or how this particular incident focused your attention on the subject.

2. Tell about how and for what reasons you came to a decision to take a certain action despite your mixed feelings. What rationalizations did you or others use to help you feel you were doing the right thing?

3. Narrate in detail the sequence of events that followed your decision. Make the narrative come to life with concrete sensory detail. As you tell your story, analyze the various causes and effects of your decision and actions.

4. Discuss how the same event you experienced affects others. Explain how the causes and effects of the action are different or similar for you and for others.

5. Explain how you felt immediately before, during, and after the crucial experience.

6. In your conclusion, express your deepest feelings about the consequences of your decision and experiences. Use similes, metaphors, and an echo of your original attempts to rationalize your ambivalence.

More Writing Projects

1. In your journal reflect on the issue of abortion. Analyze your reasons for your attitudes.

2. Write a brief paragraph in which you explain the causes and (or) effects of a political standpoint you feel very strongly about.

3. In an essay of analysis, propose the effects on children if elementary schools throughout the country offered compulsory sex education programs.

When Bright Girls Decide That Math Is "a Waste of Time"

Susan Jacoby

In this article, Susan Jacoby explains how cultural expectations and societal stereotyping are overshadowed by women's own decisions to keep themselves away from scientific and technological studies. Notice how she uses narrative and process analysis to reinforce the causes and effects she is exploring here.

Words to Watch

sanguine (par. 3)   cheerful, hopeful
vulnerable (par. 6)   open to attack or suggestion
syndrome (par. 7)   a group of symptoms that characterize a condition
akin to (par. 7)   similar to
phobia (par. 7)   an excessive fear of something
constitute (par. 7)   to make up; compose
epitomize (par. 8)   to be a prime example of
prone (par. 15)   disposed to; susceptible
accede to (par. 16)   give in to

1   Susannah, a 16-year-old who has always been an A student in every subject from algebra to English, recently informed her parents that she intended to drop physics and calculus in her senior year of high school and replace them with a drama seminar and a work-study program. She expects a major in art or history in college, she explained, and "any more science or math will just be a waste of my time."

2   Her parents were neither concerned by nor opposed to her decision. "Fine, dear," they said. Their daughter is, after all, an outstanding student. What does it matter if, at age 16, she has taken a step that may limit her understanding of both machines and the natural world for the rest of her life?

3   This kind of decision, in which girls turn away from studies that would give them a sure footing in the world of sci-

ence and technology, is a self-inflicted female disability that is, regrettably, almost as common today as it was when I was in high school. If Susannah had announced that she had decided to stop taking English in her senior year, her mother and father would have been horrified. I also think they would have been a good deal less sanguine about her decision if she were a boy.

In saying that scientific and mathematical ignorance is a   4 self-inflicted female wound, I do not, obviously, mean that cultural expectations play no role in the process. But the world does not conspire to deprive modern women of access to science as it did in the 1930's, when Rosalyn S. Yalow, the Nobel Prize-winning physicist, graduated from Hunter College and was advised to go to work as a secretary because no graduate school would admit her to its physics department. The current generation of adolescent girls—and their parents, bred on old expectations about women's interests—are active conspirators in limiting their own intellectual development.

It is true that the proportion of young women in science-   5 related graduate and professional schools, most notably medical schools, has increased significantly in the past decade. It is also true that so few women were studying advanced science and mathematics before the early 1970's that the percentage increase in female enrollment does not yet translate into large numbers of women actually working in science.

The real problem is that so many girls eliminate them-   6 selves from any serious possibility of studying science as a result of decisions made during the vulnerable period of midadolescence, when they are most likely to be influenced—on both conscious and subconscious levels—by the traditional belief that math and science are "masculine" subjects.

During the teen-age years the well-documented phenom-   7 enon of "math anxiety" strikes girls who never had any problem handling numbers during earlier schooling. Some men, too, experience this syndrome—a form of panic, akin to a phobia, at any task involving numbers—but women constitute the overwhelming majority of sufferers. The onset of acute math anxiety during the teen-age years is, as Stalin was fond of saying, "not by accident."

In adolescence girls begin to fear that they will be unat- 8
tractive to boys if they are typed as "brains." Science and
math epitomize unfeminine braininess in a way that, say, foreign languages do not. High-school girls who pursue an advanced interest in science and math (unless they are students
at special institutions like the Bronx High School of Science
where everyone is a brain) usually find that they are greatly
outnumbered by boys in their classes. They are, therefore, in-
truding on male turf at a time when their sexual confidence, as
well as that of the boys, is most fragile.

A 1981 assessment of female achievement in mathemat- 9
ics, based on research conducted under a National Institute
for Education grant, found significant differences in the mathematical achievements of 9th and 12th graders. At age 13 girls
were equal to or slightly better than boys in tests involving algebra, problem solving and spatial ability; four years later the
boys had outstripped the girls.

It is not mysterious that some very bright high-school 10
girls suddenly decide that math is "too hard" and "a waste of
time." In my experience, self-sabotage of mathematical and
scientific ability is often a conscious process. I remember deliberately pretending to be puzzled by geometry problems in
my sophomore year in high school. A male teacher called me
in after class and said, in a baffled tone, "I don't see how you
can be having so much trouble when you got straight A's last
year in my algebra class."

The decision to avoid advanced biology, chemistry, 11
physics and calculus in high school automatically restricts academic and professional choices that ought to be wide open to
anyone beginning college. At all coeducational universities
women are overwhelmingly concentrated in the fine arts, social sciences and traditionally female departments like education. Courses leading to degrees in science- and technology-
related fields are filled mainly by men.

In my generation, the practical consequences of mathe- 12
matical and scientific illiteracy are visible in the large number
of special programs to help professional women overcome the
anxiety they feel when they are promoted into jobs that require them to handle statistics.

The consequences of this syndrome should not, how- 13
ever, be viewed in narrowly professional terms. Competence
in science and math does not mean one is going to become a
scientist or mathematician any more than competence in writing English means one is going to become a professional
writer. Scientific and mathematical illiteracy—which has been
cited in several recent critiques by panels studying American
education from kindergarten through college—produces an incalculably impoverished vision of human experience.

Scientific illiteracy is not, of course, the exclusive prov- 14
ince of women. In certain intellectual circles it has become
fashionable to proclaim a willed, aggressive ignorance about
science and technology. Some female writers specialize in ominous, uninformed diatribes against genetic research as a plot
to remove control of childbearing from women, while some
well-known men of letters proudly announce that they understand absolutely nothing about computers, or, for that matter,
about electricity. This lack of understanding is nothing in
which women or men ought to take pride.

Failure to comprehend either computers or chromo- 15
somes leads to a terrible sense of helplessness, because the
profound impact of science on everyday life is evident even to
those who insist they don't, won't, can't understand why the
changes are taking place. At this stage of history women are
more prone to such feelings of helplessness than men because
the culture judges their ignorance less harshly and because
women themselves acquiesce in that indulgence.

Since there is ample evidence of such feelings in adoles- 16
cence, it is up to parents to see that their daughters do not
accede to the old stereotypes about "masculine" and "feminine" knowledge. Unless we want our daughters to share
our intellectual handicaps, we had better tell them no, they
can't stop taking mathematics and science at the ripe old
age of 16.

BUILDING VOCABULARY

1. Use a dictionary to look up any unfamiliar words in the phrases below from Jacoby's essay. Then, write a short explanation of each expression.

  a. sure footing (par. 3)
  b. cultural expectations (par. 4)
  c. overwhelming majority (par. 7)
  d. male turf (par. 8)
  e. spatial ability (par. 9)
  f. the exclusive province (par. 14)
  g. ominous, uninformed diatribes (par. 14)
  h. acquiesce in that indulgence (par. 15)
  i. ample evidence (par. 16)
  j. our intellectual handicaps (par. 16)

2. Explain the connotations (see Glossary) that the following words have for you: "disability" (par. 3), "conspire" (par. 4), "adolescent" (par. 4), "vulnerable" (par. 6), "acute" (par. 8). Use each of these words correctly in sentences of your own.

UNDERSTANDING THE WRITER'S IDEAS

  1. What condition is Jacoby trying to analyze? Is the main *effect* analyzed in this cause-and-effect analysis? On what primary cause does she blame women's "scientific and mathematical ignorance"? What exactly does she mean by that term? How is society to blame? What is the "process" mentioned in paragraph 4? What point does the example of Rosalyn S. Yalow illustrate?

  2. Why does Jacoby think that the greater proportion of women students now in science and medical graduate and professional schools does not really mean that there are many women working in these areas?

  3. According to Jacoby, when do most girls decide not to study the sciences? Why does this happen?

  4. What is "math anxiety"? Who suffers more from it—boys or girls? Why? What does the author mean by "brains" (par. 8)?

5. Who was Joseph Stalin (par. 7)?

6. What subjects does Jacoby identify as "feminine"? Which are "unfeminine"?

7. According to the research evidence discussed in paragraph 9, how do the math abilities of girls and boys change between ninth and tenth grades? What does Jacoby say is the *cause* for this change? What are the *results?*

8. Explain what Jacoby means by the expression "self-inflicted female wound" (par. 4) and "self-sabotage" (par. 10). How are these expressions similar? How are they different?

9. What is the difference between what men and women study at coeducational universities?

10. What does Jacoby mean by "mathematical and scientific illiteracy" (par. 12)? Do only women suffer from this syndrome? According to Jacoby, why does it lead to "an incalculably impoverished vision of human experience"? What does she mean by this phrase? What examples of scientific illiteracy does Jacoby offer?

11. Why does the author think women feel more helpless than men do about scientific changes?

12. What suggestion does Jacoby offer in her conclusion?

UNDERSTANDING THE WRITER'S TECHNIQUES

1. Which paragraphs make up the introductory section of this essay? What cause-and-effect relation does Jacoby establish and how does she present it? How does Jacoby use narration in her introduction? How does she use illustration?

2. What is the thesis statement of this essay? Why is it placed where it is? Find another statement before it that expresses a similar cause-and-effect relation. How are the two different?

3. Both sentences of paragraph 5 begin with the phrase "It is true," yet the sentences contradict each other. How and why does the author set up this contradiction? What is the effect on Jacoby's analysis of beginning paragraph 6 with the words "The real problem is..."?

4. How does she use *process analysis* (see pages 322–323) from paragraph 6 to paragraph 8?

5. Where does the author use definition in this essay?

6. Trace the cause-and-effect developments in paragraphs 7 and 8.

7. In paragraph 9, Jacoby mentions a study conducted under "a National Institute for Education grant." How does the evidence she presents support her position in the essay?

8. What is the effect of the phrase "in my experience" in paragraph 10? What expository technique does she use there?

9. Trace the cause-and-effect patterns in paragraphs 11 through 13. Be sure to show the interrelationship between the causes and the effects (that is, how can the effect of something also be the cause of something else?).

10. How is the first sentence of paragraph 15 ("Failure to comprehend....") a good example in itself of cause-and-effect development?

11. Why does Jacoby use quotation marks around the words "masculine" and "feminine" in the phrase "'masculine' and 'feminine' knowledge" (par. 16)?

12. What is the overall tone of this essay? At three points, Jacoby switches tone and uses irony (see Glossary). Explain the irony in the following sentences:

   a. "What does it matter if, at age 16, she has taken a step that may limit her understanding of both machines and the natural world for the rest of her life?" (par. 2)
   b. "The onset of acute math anxiety during the teen-age years is, as Stalin was fond of saying, 'not by accident.'" (par. 7)

c. "Unless we want our daughters to share our intellectual handicaps, we had better tell them no, they can't stop taking mathematics and science at the ripe old age of 16." (par. 16)

Compare the irony in paragraph 16 with that in paragraph 2. How is the impact the same or different?

13. Who do you think is the intended *audience* for this essay? Cite evidence for your answer.

14. Jacoby uses a variety of transitional devices to connect smoothly the ideas expressed in the various paragraphs of this essay. Look especially at paragraphs 1 to 4. How does the writer achieve coherence between paragraphs? What transitional elements do you find in the opening sentences of each of those paragraphs? What other transitions do you find throughout the essay?

EXPLORING THE WRITER'S IDEAS

1. One of the underlying suggestions in this essay is that society has long considered there to be "masculine" and "feminine" subjects to study. What is your opinion on this issue? Do you feel that any subjects are particularly more suited to men or women? Which? Why? Are there any other school activities that you feel are exclusively masculine or feminine? Why? Are there any jobs that are more suited to men or women?

2. In paragraph 4, Jacoby mentions the "old expectations about women's interests." What do you think these expectations are? What do you consider *new* expectations for women?

3. A *stereotype* is an opinion of a category of people that is unoriginal and often based on strong prejudices. For example, some prejudicial stereotypes include "All immigrants are lazy"; "All Republicans are rich"; "All women are terrible drivers." What other stereotypes do you know? Where do you think they originate?

4. The general implication of paragraph 8 is that people minimize their skills in order to be socially acceptable. In your
   experience, where have you seen this principle operating?
   Do people sometimes pretend to be unable to achieve
   something? What motivates them, do you think?

5. A recent study shows that among major nations in the
   world America's students—boys and girls—are the worst
   mathematics students. How do you account for the poor
   showing of Americans as mathematicians? How would you
   remedy this situation?

IDEAS FOR WRITING

Guided Writing

Select a job or profession that is usually male-dominated.
Write a cause-and-effect analysis explaining how and why
women both have been excluded from this profession *and* (or)
have self-selected themselves from the job. (Some examples
may include fire fighters, physicians, marines, bank executives, carpenters, and so on.)

1. Begin with an anecdote to illustrate the condition that you
   are analyzing.

2. Present and analyze the partial causes of this condition that
   arise from society's expectations and norms.

3. State your main point clearly in a thesis statement.

4. Clearly identify what you consider "the real problem."

5. If you believe that women have deliberately excluded
   themselves, explain when and how the process of self-
   selection begins for women.

6. Analyze the consequences of this process of self-selection
   and give examples of the results of it.

7. Provide evidence that supports your analysis.

8. Link paragraphs with appropriate transitions.

9. In your conclusion offer a suggestion to change or improve this situation.

More Writing Projects

1. In your journal, make a list of everything that comes into your mind about this word "mathematics." Do not edit your writing. When you are finished, share your list with other people in the class. How do your impressions compare? contrast?

2. In a paragraph, analyze why you think boys and men exclude themselves from a certain field or profession—nursing, cooking, grammar-school teaching, and so on.

3. Margaret Mead, the famous anthropologist, once wrote, "Women in our society complain of the lack of stimulation, of the loneliness, of the dullness of staying at home." In an essay write a causal analysis of this situation.

SUMMING UP: CHAPTER 10

1. In her essay, Susan Jacoby analyzes a kind of "self-destructive behavior" on the part of many young women. Write an essay about a friend, relative, or someone else close to you who is doing something that you feel will have a very negative effect on him or her. Analyze *why* he or she is doing this and what effects, both short- and long-term, these actions are likely to have.

2. In this section, we hear female voices analyzing some of the experiences of women in American life today. Using their approaches to causal analysis, examine these experiences and the impact that they have had on your own thinking and activities. Clarify the connections between what you have read and how your sense of self has deepened or been sharpened.

3. Working in small groups, develop a questionnaire focusing on male/female roles in our society. After the questionnaire has been prepared, each group member should interview at least three people. When all the interviews have been completed, each group should write a collective analysis of the results and present the analysis to the class.

4. In this chapter, both Roiphe and Francke deal with various aspects of married life. If you are currently married, write an essay analyzing why you did (or did not) want to get married. If you are unmarried, analyze why you do (or do not) plan to get married.

5. For the next week, keep a journal about something that is currently causing you to have mixed emotions. (Note: This should not be the same issue you've written about in the Guided Writing exercise following Linda Bird Francke's essay; it should be a *current* issue.) Try to write five reasons each day (or expand upon previous ones). At the end of the week, write an essay that analyzes how the issue is affecting your life or how you plan to deal with it in the future.

CHAPTER 11

Argumentation and Persuasion

Argumentation in prose is an attempt to convince the reader to have the opinion *you* have on a subject; frequently, it also involves an effort to persuade the reader to act in a particular manner. In many ways, argumentation is a good end point for a course in writing. In a formal argument, you can use, according to your purpose, all the prose strategies and principles of sound composition practiced until now.

You can see how important it is to state your thesis very clearly in argumentation, and to support your main point with convincing minor points. You have to make these points according to reason, and you need to arrange them so they have the greatest effect on your reader. Moreover, as in any prose, writers of argument must offer the reader particulars of details, whether sensory, quoted, statistical, or based upon historical evidence. Finally, techniques of comparison, process analysis, description, narration, cause and effect, definition, all can help strengthen an argument.

Although argumentation reflects all these earlier prose techniques, it is important for you to understand the special characteristics of this method. To begin with, although argumentation as a written form is often emotional, it differs sharply from those little battles and those major disagreements with friends over coffee or in hallways outside class. Perhaps that last shouting match between you and your friend about who would win the World Series is, no doubt, one that you would call an argument: There is a disagreement there for which each of you tries to make your own point of view stick. Yet often these argumentative conversations deteriorate into loss of temper, angry personal comments about your friend's judgment or character, departures from the argument itself, and inability to reason.

In written arguments, writers always should keep clearly in mind the point they wish to make, and should not lose sight of it. They may try to convince readers that some issue requires action ("Colleges and businesses should follow special admissions procedures for minority applicants"). Or, they may try to convince readers that something is true ("Wives are taken for granted"). Whatever the point, writers always offer their reasons for their beliefs in a logical way, without losing command of their subject and without attacking anyone personally; they may, though, attack someone's ideas or attitudes.

The main point in an argument—often termed the *major proposition*—is an idea which is debatable or can be disputed. As such it differs from theses in ordinary essays, which state main ideas without necessarily taking sides. The major proposition gives an essay its "argumentative edge." Frequently this argumentative edge appears in the very title of the essay, and it should form the basis of a crisp introductory paragraph laying out the terms of the position that you plan to take.

Once you state clearly and carefully your major proposition at the outset of the essay, you must then proceed to *convince* readers about the position that you have taken. There are basic strategies to succeed in this goal, beginning with the ordered presentation of reasons to defend the major proposition. We term these reasons *minor propositions*—in other words, assertions designed to support your main argument. To support each minor proposition, the writer must offer *evidence* in the form of facts, statistics, testimony from authorities, and personal experience. Here, a variety of writing methods, ranging from comparison and contrast to definition to causal analysis, can serve to develop minor propositions effectively.

In addition to presenting your own argument logically

and convincingly, you must also recognize and deal with opposing arguments, a technique called *refutation*. Obviously, there has to be more than one side to any debatable issue, and you have to take this fact into account. For one thing, acknowledgment of the opposition indicates fairness on your part—a willingness to recognize that there *are* two sides to the argument. More significantly, your refutation of rival propositions, both major and minor, makes your own case more convincing. Whether at the outset of your argumentative essay or in the body as you are developing your own minor propositions, you should take care to indicate opposing views and to refute them effectively.

An argumentative essay ultimately is only as strong as the logic that a writer brings to it. Such logical errors as hasty generalizations (main ideas unsupported by sufficient evidence), attacks on the opposition's character, faulty conclusions that do not follow from the facts, faulty analogies, and excessive appeals to emotion damage your argument. In short, any convincing argument requires clear, orderly thinking. By learning how to present ideas logically through the preparation of convincing argumentative essays, you will strengthen your overall reasoning ability. You will also learn how to deal with those arguments, many of which are important, that occur in your daily life.

I Want a Wife

Judy Syfers

Judy Syfers, a wife and mother of two children, argues in this essay for a wife of her own. Although her argument might seem strange, her position will become apparent once you move into the essay. She presents many points to support her position, so you want to keep in mind those you think are the strongest.

Words to Watch

nurturant (par. 3)   giving affectionate care and attention

hors d'oeuvres (par. 6)   food served before the regular courses of the meal

monogamy (par. 8)   the habit of having only one mate; the practice of marrying only once during life

1   I belong to that classification of people known as wives. I am A Wife. And, not altogether incidentally, I am a mother.

2   Not too long ago a male friend of mine appeared on the scene fresh from a recent divorce. He had one child, who is, of course, with his ex-wife. He is obviously looking for another wife. As I thought about him while I was ironing one evening, it suddenly occurred to me that I, too, would like to have a wife. Why do I want a wife?

3   I would like to go back to school so that I can become economically independent, support myself, and, if need be, support those dependent upon me. I want a wife who will work and send me to school. And while I am going to school I want a wife to keep track of the children's doctor and dentist appointments. And to keep track of mine, too. I want a wife to make sure my children eat properly and are kept clean. I want a wife who will wash the children's clothes and keep them mended. I want a wife who is a good nurturant attendant to my children, who arranges for their schooling, makes sure that they have an adequate social life with their peers, takes them to the park, the zoo, etc. I want a wife who takes care of the children when they are sick, a wife who arranges to be around

when the children need special care, because, of course, I cannot miss classes at school. My wife must arrange to lose time at work and not lose the job. It may mean a small cut in my wife's income from time to time, but I guess I can tolerate that. Needless to say, my wife will arrange and pay for the care of the children while my wife is working.

I want a wife who will take care of *my* physical needs. I want a wife who will keep my house clean. A wife who will pick up after me. I want a wife who will keep my clothes clean, ironed, mended, replaced when need be, and who will see to it that my personal things are kept in their proper place so that I can find what I need the minute I need it. I want a wife who cooks the meals, a wife who is a *good* cook. I want a wife who will plan the menus, do the necessary grocery shopping, prepare the meals, serve them pleasantly, and then do the cleaning up while I do my studying. I want a wife who will care for me when I am sick and sympathize with my pain and loss of time from school. I want a wife to go along when our family takes a vacation so that someone can continue to care for me and my children when I need a rest and change of scene.

I want a wife who will not bother me with rambling complaints about a wife's duties. But I want a wife who will listen to me when I feel the need to explain a rather difficult point I have come across in my course of studies. And I want a wife who will type my papers for me when I have written them.

I want a wife who will take care of the details of my social life. When my wife and I are invited out by my friends, I want a wife who will take care of the babysitting arrangements. When I meet people at school that I like and want to entertain, I want a wife who will have the house clean, will prepare a special meal, serve it to me and my friends, and not interrupt when I talk about the things that interest me and my friends. I want a wife who will have arranged that the children are fed and ready for bed before my guests arrive so that the children do not bother us. I want a wife who takes care of the needs of my guests so that they feel comfortable, who makes sure that they have an ashtray, that they are passed the hors d'oeuvres, that they are offered a second helping of the food, that their wine glasses are replenished when necessary, that their coffee is served to them as they like it.

And I want a wife who knows that sometimes I need a 7 night out by myself.

I want a wife who is sensitive to my sexual needs, a wife 8 who makes love passionately and eagerly when I feel like it, a wife who makes sure that I am satisfied. And, of course, I want a wife who will not demand sexual attention when I am not in the mood for it. I want a wife who assumes the complete responsibility for birth control, because I do not want more children. I want a wife who will remain sexually faithful to me so that I do not have to clutter up my intellectual life with jealousies. And I want a wife who understands that *my* sexual needs may entail more than strict adherence to monogamy. I must, after all, be able to relate to people as fully as possible.

If, by chance, I find another person more suitable as a 9 wife than the wife I already have, I want the liberty to replace my present wife with another one. Naturally, I will expect a fresh, new life; my wife will take the children and be solely-responsible for them so that I am left free.

When I am through with school and have a job, I want 10 my wife to quit working and remain at home so that my wife can more fully and completely take care of a wife's duties.

My God, who *wouldn't* want a wife?   11

BUILDING VOCABULARY

1. After checking a dictionary write definitions of each of these words:

   a. attendant (par. 3)
   b. adequate (par. 3)
   c. peers (par. 3)
   d. tolerate (par. 3)
   e. rambling (par. 5)
   f. replenished (par. 6)
   g. adherence (par. 8)

2. Write an original sentence for each word above.

UNDERSTANDING THE WRITER'S IDEAS

1. What incident made Syfers think about wanting a wife?

2. How would a wife help the writer achieve economic independence?

3. In what ways would a wife take care of the writer's children? Why would the writer like someone to assume those responsibilities?

4. What physical needs would Syfers's "wife" take care of?

5. How would a wife deal with the writer's social life? Her sex life?

UNDERSTANDING THE WRITER'S TECHNIQUES

1. In formal argumentation, we often call the writer's main point the *major* or *main proposition*. What is Syfers's major proposition? Is it simply what she says in paragraph 2, or is the proposition more complex than that? State it in your own words.

2. What is the value of the question Syfers asks in paragraph 2? Where else does she ask a question? What value does this other question have in its place in the essay? What impact does it have on the reader?

3. The points a writer offers to support the major proposition are called *minor propositions*. What minor propositions does Syfers present to show why she wants a wife? In which instance do they serve as topic sentences within paragraphs? What details does she offer to illustrate those minor propositions?

4. What order has the writer chosen to arrange the minor propositions? Why has she chosen such an order? Do you think she builds from the least to the most important rea-

sons for having a wife? What changes would you urge in the order of the minor propositions?

5. Most of the paragraphs here develop through illustration. Where has Syfers used a *simple listing* of details? Why has she chosen that format?

6. Syfers's style is obviously straightforward, her sentences for the most part simple and often brief. Why has she chosen such a style? What is the effect of the repetition of ''I want'' at the start of so many sentences? Why has Syfers used several short paragraphs (5, 7, 9, 10, 11) in addition to longer ones?

7. What is the author's *tone* (see Glossary)? Point out the uses of *irony* (see Glossary) in the essay. How does irony contribute to Syfers's main intent in this essay? How does the fact that Syfers is a woman contribute to this sense of irony?

EXPLORING THE WRITER'S IDEAS

1. By claiming she wants a wife, Syfers is showing us all the duties and responsibilities of the woman in a contemporary household. Has Syfers represented these duties fairly? Do husbands generally expect their wives to do all these things?

2. To what degree do wives today fit Syfers's description? How could a wife avoid many of the responsibilities spelled out in the essay? How does the ''modern husband'' figure in the way many couples meet household responsibilities now?

3. Syfers has characterized all the traditional and stereotyped roles usually assigned to wives. What ''wifely responsibilities'' has she left out?

4. Has Syfers presented a balanced picture of the issues or is her argument one-sided? Support your opinion with spe-

cific references to the essay. Could the author have dealt effectively with opposing arguments? Why or why not? What might these opposing arguments be?

5. Answer the question in the last line of the essay.

6. Read the essays "Night Walker" by Brent Staples (pages 191-194), "The Two Ismo's" by Russell Baker (219-221), and "How Do We Find the Student in a World of Academic Gymnasts and Worker Ants" by James T. Baker (pages 299-303). Compare the use of stereotyping in these essays. How is it different from Syfers's stereotypes?

IDEAS FOR WRITING

Guided Writing

Write an essay of 750 to 1,000 words, which you call, "I Want a Husband."

1. Write the essay from the point of view of a *man*. As Syfers wrote as a woman who wanted a wife, you write this essay as a man who wants a *husband*.

2. Start your essay with a brief personal story as in paragraph 2 in "I Want a Wife."

3. Support your main point with a number of minor points. Expand each minor point with details that explain your premises.

4. Arrange your minor premises carefully so that you build to the most convincing point at the end.

5. Use a simple and straightforward style. Connect your points with transitions; use repetition as one transitional device.

6. Balance your longer paragraphs with occasional shorter ones.

7. End your essay with a crisp, one-sentence question of your own.

More Writing Projects

1. In your journal, copy any three sentences from Syfers's essay that you find particularly provocative, challenging, strange, or unbelievable. Explain why you chose them.

2. Write a paragraph in which you argue *for* or *against* this issue: "A married woman belongs at home."

3. Write an essay in which you argue about whose role you think harder to play effectively in today's society: the role of the mother or the role of the father.

Are the Homeless Crazy?

Jonathan Kozol

Jonathan Kozol is an educator and writer on social issues who, until recently, was perhaps best-known for his book-length study, *Why Children Fail*. In the past few years, he has turned his attention to America's ever-increasing problem of homelessness. In 1988, he published the book *Rachel and Her Children* on the subject, along with this essay, which derives from "Distancing the Homeless," published in the *Yale Review*. In this essay, Kozol effectively challenges the common assumption that much of today's homelessness has resulted from release of patients from mental hospitals in the 1970s. Instead, he presents a convincing argument that the "deinstitutionalizing" explanation is a self-serving myth, and that the reality is much simpler: Homelessness is caused by insufficient and overly expensive housing.

Words to Watch

deinstitutionalize (par. 1)   to let inmates out of hospitals, prisons, and so forth

conceding (par. 2)   acknowledging; admitting to

arson (par. 4)   the crime of deliberately setting a fire

subsidized (par. 5)   aided with public money

destitute (par. 6)   very poor

afflictions (par. 7)   ills; problems

stigma (par. 7)   a mark of shame or discredit

complacence (par. 7)   self-satisfaction

bulk (par. 10)   the main part

de facto (par. 11)   actually; in reality

resilience (par. 12)   ability to recover easily from misfortune

paranoids (par. 13)   psychotic people who experience persecution delusions

vengeance (par. 14)   retribution; retaliation

It is commonly believed by many journalists and politi-   1
cians that the homeless of America are, in large part, former
patients of large mental hospitals who were deinstitutionalized

414

in the 1970s—the consequence, it is sometimes said, of misguided liberal opinion that favored the treatment of such persons in community-based centers. It is argued that this policy, and the subsequent failure of society to build such centers or to provide them in sufficient number, is the primary cause of homelessness in the United States.

Those who work among the homeless do not find that explanation satisfactory. While conceding that a certain number of the homeless are or have been mentally unwell, they believe that, in the case of most unsheltered people, the primary reason is economic rather than clinical. The cause of homelessness, they say with disarming logic, is the lack of homes and of income with which to rent or acquire them. 2

They point to the loss of traditional jobs in industry (2 million every year since 1980) and to the fact that half of those who are laid off end up in work that pays a poverty-level wage. They point out that since 1968 the number of children living in poverty has grown by 3 million, while welfare benefits to families with children have declined by 35 percent. 3

And they note, too, that these developments have occurred during a time in which the shortage of low-income housing has intensified as the gentrification of our major cities has accelerated. Half a million units of low-income housing are lost each year to condominium conversion as well as to arson, demolition, or abandonment. Between 1978 and 1980, median rents climbed 30 percent for people in the lowest income sector, driving many of these families into the streets. Since 1980, rents have risen at even faster rates. 4

Hard numbers, in this instance, would appear to be of greater help than psychiatric labels in telling us why so many people become homeless. Eight million American families now use half or more of their income to pay their rent or mortgage. At the same time, federal support for low-income housing dropped from $30 billion (1980) to $7.5 billion (1988). Under Presidents Ford and Carter, 500,000 subsidized private housing units were constructed. By President Reagan's second term, the number had dropped to 25,000. 5

In our rush to explain the homeless as a psychiatric problem even the words of medical practitioners who care for 6

homeless people have been curiously ignored. A study published by the Massachusetts Medical Society, for instance,
has noted that, with the exceptions of alcohol and drug use,
the most frequent illnesses among a sample of the homeless
population were trauma (31 percent), upper-respiratory disorders (28 percent), limb disorders (19 percent), mental illness
(16 percent), skin diseases (15 percent), hypertension (14 percent), and neurological illnesses (12 percent). Why, we may
ask, of all these calamities, does mental illness command so
much political and press attention? The answer may be that
the label of mental illness places the destitute outside the
sphere of ordinary life. It personalizes an anguish that is public in its genesis; it individualizes a misery that is both general
in cause and general in application.

There is another reason to assign labels to the destitute   7
and single out mental illness from among their many afflictions. All these other problems—tuberculosis, asthma, sca-
bies, diarrhea, bleeding gums, impacted teeth, etc.—bear no
stigma, and mental illness does. It conveys a stigma in the
United States. It conveys a stigma in the Soviet Union as well.
In both nations the label is used, whether as a matter of deliberate policy or not, to isolate and treat as special cases those
who, by deed or word or by sheer presence, represent a threat
to national complacence. The two situations are obviously not
identical, but they are enough alike to give Americans reason
for concern.

The notion that the homeless are largely psychotics who   8
belong in institutions, rather than victims of displacement at
the hands of enterprising realtors, spares us from the need to
offer realistic solutions to the deep and widening extremes of
wealth and poverty in the United States. It also enables us to
tell ourselves that the despair of homeless people bears no intimate connection to the privileged existence we enjoy—
when, for example, we rent or purchase one of those restored
town houses that once provided shelter for people now hud-
dled in the street.

What is to be made, then, of the supposition that the   9

homeless are primarily the former residents of mental hospitals, persons who were carelessly released during the 1970s?
Many of them are, to be sure. Among the older men and
women in the streets and shelters, as many as one-third (some
believe as many as one-half) may be chronically disturbed,
and a number of these people were deinstitutionalized during
the 1970s. But to operate on that assumption in a city such as
New York—where nearly half the homeless are small children
whose average age is six—makes no sense. Their parents,
with an average age of twenty-seven, are not likely to have
been hospitalized in the 1970s, either.

A frequently cited set of figures tells us that in 1955 the   10
average daily census of non-federal psychiatric institutions
was 677,000, and that by 1984 the number had dropped to
151,000. But these people didn't go directly from a hospital
room to the street. The bulk of those who had been psychiatric patients and were released from hospitals during the 1960s
and early 1970s had been living in low-income housing, many
in skid-row hotels or boardinghouses. Such housing—commonly known as SRO (single-room occupancy) units—was
drastically diminished by the gentrification of our cities that
began in the early '70s. Almost 50 percent of SRO housing
was replaced by luxury apartments or office buildings between
1970 and 1980, and the remaining units have been disappearing
even more rapidly.

Even for those persons who are ill and were deinstitu-   11
tionalized during the decades before 1980, the precipitating
cause of homelessness in 1987 is not illness but loss of housing. SRO housing offered low-cost sanctuaries for the homeless, providing a degree of safety and mutual support for those
who lived within them. They were a demeaning version of the
community health centers that society had promised; they
were the de facto "halfway houses" of the 1970s. For these
people too—at most half of the homeless single persons in
America—the cause of homelessness is lack of housing.

Even in those cases where mental instability is apparent,   12
homelessness itself is often the precipitating factor. For example, many pregnant women without homes are denied prenatal
care because they constantly travel from one shelter to an-

other. Many are anemic. Many are denied essential dietary supplements by recent federal cuts. As a consequence, some of their children do not live to see their second year of life. Do these mothers sometimes show signs of stress? Do they appear disorganized, depressed, disordered? Frequently. They are immobilized by pain, traumatized by fear. So it is no surprise that when researchers enter the scene to ask them how they "feel," the resulting reports tell us that the homeless are emotionally unwell. The reports do not tell us that we have *made* these people ill. They do not tell us that illness is a natural response to intolerable conditions. Nor do they tell us of the strength and the resilience that so many of these people retain despite the miseries they must endure.

A writer in the *New York Times* describes a homeless 13 woman standing on a traffic island in Manhattan. "She was evicted from her small room in the hotel just across the street," and she is determined to get revenge. Until she does, "nothing will move her from that spot.... Her argumentativeness and her angry fixation on revenge, along with the apparent absence of hallucinations, mark her as a paranoid." Most physicians, I imagine, would be more reserved in passing judgment with so little evidence, but this reporter makes his diagnosis without hesitation. "The paranoids of the street," he says, "are among the most difficult to help."

Perhaps so. But does it depend on who is offering the 14 help? Is anyone offering to help this woman get back her home? Is it crazy to seek vengeance for being thrown into the street? The absence of anger, some psychiatrists believe, might indicate much greater illness.

"No one will be turned away," says the mayor of New 15 York City, as hundreds of young mothers with their infants are turned from the doors of shelters season after season. That may sound to some like a denial of reality. "Now you're hearing all kinds of horror stories," says the President of the United States as he denies that anyone is cold or hungry or unhoused. On another occasion he says that the unsheltered "are homeless, you might say, by choice." That sounds every bit as self-deceiving.

The woman standing on the traffic island screaming for 16

revenge until her room has been restored to her sounds relatively healthy by comparison. If 3 million homeless people did the same, and all at the same time, we might finally be forced to listen.

BUILDING VOCABULARY

1. Throughout this essay, Kozol uses medical and psychiatric *jargon* (see Glossary). List the medical or psychiatric terms or references that you find here. Then look up any five in the dictionary and write definitions for them.

2. Explain in your own words the meanings of the following phrases. Use clues from the surrounding text to help you understand.

   a. sufficient number (par. 1)
   b. primary cause (par. 1)
   c. poverty-level wage (par. 3)
   d. median rents (par. 4)
   e. low-income housing (par. 5)
   f. sheer presence (par. 7)
   g. intimate connection (par. 8)
   h. chronically disturbed (par. 9)
   i. skid-row hotels (par. 10)
   j. precipitating cause (par. 11)
   k. low-cost sanctuaries (par. 11)
   l. mutual support (par. 11)
   m. demeaning version (par. 11)
   n. natural response (par. 12)
   o. intolerable conditions (par. 12)
   p. angry fixation (par. 13)

UNDERSTANDING THE WRITER'S IDEAS

1. According to Kozol, who has suggested that the deinstitutionalizing of mental-hospital patients is the major cause

of homelessness? Does he agree? If not, what does he identify as the major causes?

2. In the opening paragraph, what two groups does Kozol link together? Why? What relation between them does he suggest?

3. In New York City today, what percentage of the homeless are children? What is the average age of their parents? In the past twenty years, has the number of children living in poverty increased or decreased? What about welfare payments to families with children? How has this affected the homelessness situation?

4. What are "gentrification" and "condominium conversion" (par. 4)? How have they affected homelessness?

5. Explain the meaning of the statement: "Hard numbers, in this instance, would appear to be of greater help than psychiatric labels in telling us why so many people become homeless" (par. 5).

6. List in descending order the most common illnesses among the homeless. From what does Kozol draw these statistics? What is his conclusion about them?

7. In your own words, summarize why Kozol feels that journalists and politicians concentrate so heavily on the problems of mental illness among the homeless.

8. What are SRO's? Explain how they figure in the homeless situation.

9. What is meant by the "press" (par. 6)? What are "halfway houses" (par. 11)?

10. What is Kozol's attitude toward former President Reagan? toward former New York City Mayor Ed Koch? Explain your answers with specific references to the beginning and ending of the essay.

11. Summarize in your own words *The New York Times* story to which Kozol refers. According to the *Times* reporter, why did the homeless woman mentioned refuse to move

from the traffic island? Does Kozol agree with the reporter's interpretation? Explain.

12. In one sentence, state in your own words the opinion Kozol expresses in the last paragraph.

UNDERSTANDING THE WRITER'S TECHNIQUES

1. Describe Kozol's argumentative *purpose* in this essay. Is it primarily to *convince* or to *persuade?* Explain.

2. Which sentence states the *major proposition* of the essay?

3. In paragraph 1, the author uses a particular verbal construction that he doesn't repeat elsewhere in the essay. He writes: "It is commonly believed..."; "it is sometimes said..."; and "It is argued...." Why does he use the "it is" construction? What effect does it have? How does he change that pattern in paragraph 2? Why?

4. In paragraph 2, Kozol uses the phrase "mentally unwell" instead of the more common "mentally ill," and he uses "unsheltered people" instead of "homeless people." Why does he use these less-expected phrases? Does he use them again in the essay? Why?

5. *Cynicism* adds an edge of pessimism or anger to a statement that might otherwise be perceived as *irony* (see Glossary). In the sentence, "The cause of homelessness, they say with disarming logic, is the lack of homes and of income with which to rent or acquire them" (par. 2), the clause set off by commas might be considered cynical. Why? Find and explain several other examples of cynicism in this essay. Are they effective? Are they justified?

6. Identify the *minor-proposition* statements in this essay. How do they add *coherence* (see Glossary) to the essay?

7. How important is Kozol's use of *statistics* in this essay? Which are the most effective? Why?

8. What is the difference between *refutation* (see Glossary) and *negation* (see page 245)? Kozol uses refutation as a major technique in this essay. Analyze his use of refutation in paragraphs 1 and 2. List and discuss at least three other instances where he uses refutation. Where in the essay does he specifically use negation?

9. Evaluate Kozol's use of *cause-and-effect analysis* in paragraphs 1 through 6. In paragraph 12, how does Kozol revise the more commonly cited causal relationship between homelessness and mental illness?

10. Discuss Kozol's use of *comparison* in paragraph 7?

11. In what ways does he use *illustration?* How is his use of illustration in the last paragraph different from his other uses of it?

12. Characterize the overall *tone* of the essay. *How* does Kozol develop this tone? *Why* does he develop it?

13. Who is the intended *audience* for this essay? What is the *level of diction?* How are the two connected? What assumption about the audience is implied in the last sentence of paragraph 8?

14. Writers often use *rhetorical questions* in order to prompt the reader to pay special attention to an issue, but rhetorical questions are usually not meant to be answered. Evaluate Kozol's use of rhetorical questions in paragraph 12. What is the effect of the one-word answer, "Frequently"? Where else does he use rhetorical questions? What message does he attempt to convey with them?

15. Returning to the thesis in the course of an essay is often an effective technique to refocus the reader's attention before beginning a new analysis or a conclusion. Explain how Kozol uses this technique in paragraph 11 to make it a key turning point in the essay.

16. Although Kozol cites various studies and authorities, he makes little use of *direct quotations*. Why? Identify and analyze the three instances where he *does* use direct quo-

tations. How does it help to convey his attitude toward the material he's quoting?

17. Evaluate Kozol's conclusion. How does he establish an aura of unreality in paragraphs 15 and 16? Why does he do so? Does he effectively answer the title question? Explain.

EXPLORING THE WRITER'S IDEAS

1. In small groups, discuss your own experiences, both positive and negative, with homeless people.

2. If possible, conduct an interview with one or more homeless people. Try to find out:

   a. how they became homeless
   b. how long they've been homeless
   c. what they do to survive
   d. whether they feel there may be an end to their homelessness

   Write a report based on your interviews and share it with your classmates.

3. This essay is an excerpt from a much longer essay entitled "Distancing the Homeless" published in the 1988 *Yale Review*. How is the theme of the title expressed in this essay?

4. In this essay, Kozol presents an impressive array of statistics. Working in small groups, compile as many other statistics about homelessness as possible. Each group should then draw a subjective conclusion from the data and be prepared to present and defend it to the class as a whole.

5. Read the following description of New York City's Bowery district:

   > Walk under the El at night and all you feel is a sort of cold guilt. Touched for a dime, you try to drop the coin and not touch the hand, because the hand is dirty; you try to avoid the glance, because the glance accuses.

> This is not so much personal menace as universal—the
> cold menace of unresolved human suffering and poverty
> and the advanced stages of the disease alcoholism. On
> a summer night the drunks sleep in the open. The
> sidewalk is a free bed, and there are no lice.
> Pedestrians step along and over and around the still
> forms as though walking on a battlefield among the
> dead. In doorways, on the steps of the savings bank,
> the bums lie sleeping it off. Standing sentinel at each
> sleeper's head is the empty bottle from which he
> drained his release. Wedged in the crook of his arm is
> the paper bag containing his things.

This description is from E. B. White's 1949 essay, "Here Is New York," the same essay from which the selection "The Three New Yorks" (pages 292–294) in this book is drawn. It is but one small indication that the current problem of homelessness is nothing new. Try to find other examples, either written or visual, that indicate that homelessness is a long-standing social issue. (You may want to contact such organizations as the Coalition for the Homeless or the Salvation Army.)

In your own experience, how have the conditions of homelessness changed in your own environment over the past five years? The past one year?

IDEAS FOR WRITING

Guided Writing

Choose a controversial local issue about which you hold a strong opinion that is not the generally accepted one. (For example, you might write about a decision by the town council to build a new shopping mall on an old vacant lot; the limiting of public library hours in order to save money; a decision to open a halfway house in your neighborhood; and so forth.) Write an essay that will convince the reader of the validity of your stance on the issue.

1. Begin your essay with a discussion of the commonly held

opinion on this issue. Use the verbal construction "it is" to help distance you from that opinion.

2. In the next section, strongly refute the commonly held opinion by stating your major proposition clearly and directly.

3. Develop your opinion by the use of comparative statistics.

4. While trying to remain as objective as possible, establish a slightly cynical edge to your tone.

5. If appropriate, include some jargon related to the issue.

6. Explain and refute the causal logic (cause-and-effect analysis) of the common opinion.

7. About midway through the essay, return to the thesis in a paragraph that serves as a "pivot" for your essay.

8. Link ideas, statistics, and opinions by means of well-placed minor proposition statements.

9. Continue to refute the common opinion by

   a. using rhetorical questions;
   b. citing and showing the invalidity of a recent media item on the issue;
   c. lightly ridiculing some of the "big names" associated with the common opinion on the issue.

10. Conclude your essay with a somewhat unrealistic, exaggerated image that both reinforces your opinion and invokes the reader to reexamine the issue more closely.

More Writing Projects

1. In your journal write freely about this topic: the homeless. Do not edit your writing. Write nonstop for at least fifteen minutes. When you finish, exchange journal entries with another student in the class. How do your responses compare? contrast?

2. Do you think it is correct to give money to panhandlers? Write a paragraph in which you state and defend your opinion.

3. Write an essay in the form of a letter to your local chief executive (mayor, town supervisor, and so forth) in which you express your opinion about the local homeless situation. Include some specific measures that you feel need to be enacted. Draw freely on your journal entry in Question 1 of this exercise.

The Vandal and the Sportsman
Joseph Wood Krutch

Joseph Wood Krutch is a renowned author, scholar, and social commentator. Here he argues forcefully—sometimes even righteously—against sports hunting. He uses language for its fullest impact, telling us of "pure evil," "a fathomless abyss," and "wicked ideas." This essay, from *The Best Nature Writing of Joseph Wood Krutch*, is a model of both logical and emotional appeal in argumentative writing.

Words to Watch

impediment (par. 3)   obstacle
vitality (par. 3)   the quality distinguishing the living from the dead
wantonly (par. 3)   without moral restraint
unassailable (par. 5)   unquestionable
compassion (par. 6)   deep understanding of others' feelings
quail (par. 7)   a stout-bodied game bird
delinquency (par. 7)   living immorally
cultivate (par. 7)   develop

It would not be quite true to say that "some of my best 1 friends are hunters." Nevertheless, I do number among my respected acquaintances some who not only kill for the sake of killing but count it among their keenest pleasures. I can think of no better illustration of the fact that men may be separated at some point by a fathomless abyss yet share elsewhere much common ground.

To me it is inconceivable how anyone should think an 2 animal more interesting dead than alive. I can also easily prove to my own satisfaction that killing "for sport" is the perfect type of that pure evil for which metaphysicians have sometimes sought.

Most wicked deeds are done because the doer proposes 3 some good to himself. The liar lies to gain some end; the swindler and thief want things which, if honestly got, might be good in themselves. Even the murderer may be removing an impediment to normal desires or gaining possession of something which his victim keeps from him. None of these usually does evil for evil's sake. They are selfish or unscrupulous, but their deeds are not gratuitously evil. The killer for sport has no such comprehensible motive. He prefers death to life, darkness to light. He gets nothing except the satisfaction of saying, "Something which wanted to live is dead. There is that much less vitality, consciousness, and, perhaps, joy in the universe. I am the Spirit that Denies." When a man wantonly destroys one of the works of man we call him Vandal. When he wantonly destroys one of the works of God we call him Sportsman.

The hunter-for-food may be as wicked and as misguided   4
as vegetarians sometimes say; but he does not kill for the sake of killing. The rancher and the farmer who exterminate all living things not immediately profitable to them may sometimes be working against their own best interests; but whether they are or are not, they hope to achieve some supposed good by their exterminations. If to do evil not in the hope of gain but for evil's sake involves the deepest guilt by which man can be stained, then killing for killing's sake is a terrifying phenomenon and as strong a proof as we could have of that "reality of evil" with which present-day theologians are again concerned.

Despite all this I know that sportsmen are not necessar-   5
ily monsters. Even if the logic of my position is unassailable, the fact still remains that men are not logical creatures; that most if not all are blind to much they might be expected to see and are habitually inconsistent; that both the blind spots and the inconsistencies vary from person to person.

To say as we all do: "Any man who would do A would   6
do B," is to state a proposition mercifully proved false almost as often as it is stated. The murderer is not necessarily a liar any more than the liar is necessarily a murderer, and few men feel that if they break one commandment there is little use in keeping the others. Many have been known to say that they considered adultery worse than homicide but not all adulterers are potential murderers and there are even murderers to whom incontinence would be unthinkable. So the sportsman may exhibit any of the virtues—including compassion and re-

spect for life—everywhere except in connection with his "sporting" activities. It may even be often enough true that, as "antisentimentalists" are fond of pointing out, those tenderest toward animals are not necessarily most philanthropic. They no more than sportsmen are always consistent.

When the Winchester gun company makes a propaganda 7 movie concluding with a scene in which a "typical American boy" shoots a number of quail and when it then ends with the slogan "Go hunting with your boy and you'll never have to go hunting for him," I may suspect that the gun company is moved by a desire to sell more guns at least as much as by a determination to do what it can toward reducing the incidence of delinquency. I will certainly add also my belief that there are even better ways of diminishing the likelihood that a boy will grow up to do even worse things. Though it seems to me that he is being taught a pure evil I know that he will not necessarily cultivate a taste for all or, for that matter, any one of the innumerable other forms under which evil may be loved.

BUILDING VOCABULARY

1. Match each word or phrase in Column A with the word or phrase in Column B which most closely matches its meaning.

Column A
1 keenest (par. 1)
2 fathomless abyss (par. 1)
3 pure evil (par. 2)
4 gratuitously evil (par. 3)
5 unscrupulous (par. 3)
6 comprehensible motive (par. 3)
7 habitually inconsistent (par. 5)
8 incontinence (par. 6)
9 philanthropic (par. 6)
10 propaganda (par. 7)

Column B
a immeasurable depths
b ideas used to damage an opposing cause
c understandable reason
d dishonest
e absolute immorality
f lack of self-restraint
g most special
h with great generosity
i usually changeable
j vicious without cause

2. Both "metaphysicians" (par. 2) and "theologians" (par. 4) deal with questions of virtues (par. 6). Look up each word and write a definition.

3. What are the crimes of "adultery" and "homicide" (par. 6)?

UNDERSTANDING THE WRITER'S IDEAS

1. Does Krutch have many close friends who are hunters? How do you know? What does he think of his acquaintances that do enjoy hunting? Explain the sentence that tells you this information.

2. What is Krutch's opinion of hunting as a sport?

3. According to Krutch, what is the major motivation for which people do bad things? What examples does he offer to support his opinion? What does Krutch say is the primary motivation for sports hunters? How does this motivation differ from that of other "evil doers"?

4. For what does the author substitute the phrase "killer for sport" (par. 3)? Why?

5. Explain the difference between a Vandal and a Sportsman in your own words.

6. How are the hunters-for-food different from sports hunters? How are the ranchers and farmers different?

7. Try to explain the meaning of the sentence at the end of paragraph 4 which begins, "If to do evil...."

8. Explain the statement "men are not logical creatures" (par. 5) as it is used by Krutch in this essay.

9. What excuses does the author offer for sports hunters? Do you feel he believes these excuses? Why? In paragraph 6 what does he say about the ethics of sports hunting?

10. What does the phrase "if they break one commandment" refer to?

11. What is the Winchester gun company? What is Krutch's opinion of the film made by that company?

UNDERSTANDING THE WRITER'S TECHNIQUES

1. In your own words, what is Krutch's *major proposition* in this essay? Does he ever state it as a single-thesis statement? Why?

2. How does Krutch use logical explanation and appeals to intelligence in this essay? What is he trying to "prove"?

3. A special type of argumentative strategy is *ethical* appeal, in which the writer addresses the moral standards of his or her audience. What is the nature of Krutch's ethical appeal? How is it presented?

4. Throughout this essay Krutch uses very emotionally charged language to describe or explain things. One of the techniques of argumentation is to use such language subtly to influence your readers' opinions. For example, in paragraph 3, Krutch helps the reader to make unconscious connections between a sports hunter and "wicked deeds," a "liar," a "swindler," a "thief," and a "murderer." How and why does he do this?

Read through the essay once again and find as many other examples of emotionally charged language as you can. How do these emotional or nonlogical appeals affect Krutch's intended audience?

5. One of the techniques the author uses is to put quotation marks (" ") around words or groups of words other than for the purpose of quotation or citation. What does the quotation mark indicate about the enclosed words? Find all the places Krutch uses this technique and explain the meaning of each word or phrase.

6. Krutch also uses exaggeration to influence his readers. *Hyperbole* is a type of very extravagant exaggeration—

heightened exaggeration, so to speak. Explain the hyperbole of the last part of paragraph 3, from ''The killer for sport has....'' to the end. How does this section influence your opinion? Why?

7. A good argumentative essay will in some way deal with the opposition's argument to show that the writer has at least recognized that differing opinions exist. Usually, however, a writer will rebut (disprove) the opposition argument to enhance the correctness of his or her own opinions. Where in this essay does Krutch present the opposition argument? How does he deal with it? How does he feel about the correctness of his own opinions? What one sentence tells us so?

8. What is the tone of this essay? Give at least three examples to support your answer, at least one of which should come from the introductory paragraph.

9. What is the purpose of the discussion of the film made by the Winchester gun company? How does it connect to the rest of the essay? How does Krutch use extended example in this discussion?

10. Explain the significance of the title.

EXPLORING THE WRITER'S IDEAS

1. In paragraph 3, Krutch compares sports hunters to liars, thieves, even murderers. Do you think they are comparable? Why?

   Krutch also says sports hunters enjoy killing and death. Do you agree or disagree? Why?

2. Krutch makes a distinction between hunters-for-food and sports hunters. What do you think are the differences between the two? Do you feel either is more or less justified in his or her activity? Why?

3. The expression in quotations in the first paragraph (''some of my best friends are hunters'') is a parody of an expres-

sion often used by people attempting to hide or defend their prejudices. For example, a person might say, "But some of my best friends are Jewish (or black, or Irish, or Chinese, or...)" after making an ethnic slur or offensive remark. What is the purpose of Krutch's parody here? What does it tell us about the author?

4. Are there degrees of humaneness in sports hunting? For example, is it more humane to use a rifle, a shotgun, or a bow and arrow? Why?

   If you have ever gone sports hunting, describe how you felt when you pulled the trigger or let the arrow fly. Explain what made you feel this way.

5. Research the sports hunting laws in your state. What are they? Do you think they are fair? If possible, find out on what basis some of the laws, quotas, and restrictions were made.

6. Krutch is very forceful and dogmatic in this essay, perhaps even a bit self-righteous at times. For instance, in paragraph 5 he says, "...the logic of my position is unassailable." How did the tone of this essay affect you? Were you ever put off by it or did it draw you nearer to the writer's position?

IDEAS FOR WRITING

Guided Writing

Write an argumentative essay in which you support or oppose hunting.

1. Acknowledge your opposition in the first paragraph of the essay. Explain your possible closeness to such individuals, but take a critical attitude toward their position regarding hunting.

2. Tell why it is "inconceivable" to you that anyone would support or oppose hunting.

3. Logically refute the propositions of those who oppose your position. After explaining your opposition's viewpoint, you can *deny* that their point is right or true; or you can *admit* that what they say seems reasonable, but that they have left out important ideas; or you can try to find a *shortcoming* in the way they reason about the topic.

4. Make your essay strong in *emotional* appeals. Lace your essay generously with emotionally charged terms and comparisons.

5. Introduce *ethical* appeals in support of your argument.

6. Carefully draw distinctions between different types of opponents.

7. End your essay with an extended example from an outside source that substantiates your proposition, that is, that puts your opponents in an unfavorable position.

More Writing Projects

1. People more and more are opposing the use of animals in what formerly were accepted ways—for food, clothing, or medical research, for example. These people oppose eating meat, wearing fur, or doing laboratory experiments using animals. What are your views on this issue? What should be humanity's relation to lower animal forms? Write a journal entry to answer these questions.

2. Write a paragraph-length letter to the editor in which you argue for or against handgun controls.

3. Write an argumentative essay that responds to the following quotation from the American novelist and screenplay writer Nathaniel West: "In America violence is daily."

America Needs Its Nerds

Leonid Fridman

Leonid Fridman studies mathematics at Harvard University and is in the doctoral program there. He claims with pride that he is a founding member of the Society of Nerds and Geeks. Fridman uses terms often thought of as negative to argue in favor of a change in America's values.

Words to Watch

derogatory (par. 1) detracting; belittling
rampant (par. 3) running wild
ostracized (par. 3) banished; excluded
haunt (par. 6) be continually present
deride (par. 10) treat with mirthful contempt
debase (par. 10) lower in character, quality, or value

There is something very wrong with the system of values 1
in a society that has only derogatory terms like nerd and geek
for the intellectually curious and academically serious.

A geek, according to "Webster's New World Dictio- 2
nary," is a street performer who shocks the public by biting
off heads of live chickens. It is a telling fact about our language and our culture that someone dedicated to pursuit of
knowledge is compared to a freak biting the head off a live
chicken.

Even at a prestigious academic institution like Harvard, 3
anti-intellectualism is rampant: Many students are ashamed to
admit, even to their friends, how much they study. Although
most students try to keep up their grades, there is but a minority of undergraduates for whom pursuing knowledge is the
top priority during their years at Harvard. Nerds are ostracized while athletes are idolized.

The same thing happens in U.S. elementary and high 4
schools. Children who prefer to read books rather than play
football, prefer to build model airplanes rather than get wasted

at parties with their classmates, become social outcasts. Ostracized for their intelligence and refusal to conform to society's anti-intellectual values, many are deprived of a chance to learn adequate social skills and acquire good communication tools.

Enough is enough. 5

Nerds and geeks must stop being ashamed of who they 6 are. It is high time to face the persecutors who haunt the bright kid with thick glasses from kindergarten to the grave. For America's sake, the anti-intellectual values that pervade our society must be fought.

There are very few countries in the world where anti- 7 intellectualism runs as high in popular culture as it does in the U.S. In most industrialized nations, not least of all our economic rivals in East Asia, a kid who studies hard is lauded and held up as an example to other students.

In many parts of the world, university professorships are 8 the most prestigious and materially rewarding positions. But not in America, where average professional ballplayers are much more respected and better paid than faculty members of the best universities.

How can a country where typical parents are ashamed of 9 their daughter studying mathematics instead of going dancing, or of their son reading Weber while his friends play baseball, be expected to compete in the technology race with Japan or remain a leading political and cultural force in Europe? How long can America remain a world-class power if we constantly emphasize social skills and physical prowess over academic achievement and intellectual ability?

Do we really expect to stay afloat largely by importing 10 our scientists and intellectuals from abroad, as we have done for a major portion of this century, without making an effort to also cultivate a pro-intellectual culture at home? Even if we have the political will to spend substantially more money on education than we do now, do we think we can improve our schools if we deride our studious pupils and debase their impoverished teachers?

Our fault lies not so much with our economy or with our 11 politics as within ourselves, our values and our image of a good life. America's culture has not adapted to the demands of our times, to the economic realities that demand a highly educated workforce and innovative intelligent leadership.

If we are to succeed as a society in the 21st century, we 12 had better shed our anti-intellectualism and imbue in our children the vision that a good life is impossible without stretching one's mind and pursuing knowledge to the full extent of one's abilities.

And until the words "nerd" and "geek" become terms 13 of approbation and not derision, we do not stand a chance.

BUILDING VOCABULARY

1. How does knowledge of prefixes, suffixes, or roots contribute to your understanding the meaning of the words below? Identify and explain the key word parts and provide definitions for the words themselves. Use a dictionary if you need one.

   a. prestigious (par. 3)
   b. anti-intellectualism (par. 3)
   c. undergraduates (par. 3)
   d. outcasts (par. 4)
   e. professorships (par. 8)
   f. world-class (par. 9)
   g. afloat (par. 10)
   h. pro-intellectual (par. 10)
   i. workforce (par. 11)
   j. leadership (par. 11)

2. Use context clues to determine meanings of the following words in italics. Then, choose the letter of the word or expression that most closely matches the meaning of the italicized word.

   1. face the *persecutors* (par. 6)
   a. those who relax
   b. those who support or defend
   c. those who oppress or annoy
   d. those who complain

2. values that *pervade* our society (par. 6)
    a. are present throughout
    b. persecute
    c. weaken
    d. are important in

3. *lauded* and held up as an example (par. 7)
    a. laughed at
    b. praised
    c. condemned
    d. ignored

4. physical *prowess* (par. 9)
    a. weakness
    b. undeserved privilege
    c. attractiveness
    d. superior ability

5. *cultivate* a pro-intellectual culture at home (par. 10)
    a. study in school
    b. develop by farming in
    c. trap
    d. promote the growth of

6. their *impoverished* teachers (par. 10)
    a. hard-working
    b. poor
    c. long-suffering
    d. thoughtful

7. *innovative* intelligent leadership (par. 11)
    a. bold and dramatic
    b. weak and tedious
    c. new and creative
    d. lost and hopeless

8. *imbue* in our children (par. 12)
    a. inspire
    b. deny
    c. demonstrate
    d. avoid

9. terms of *approbation* (par. 13)
    a. endearment
    b. weakness
    c. approval
    d. appreciation

10. and not *derision* (par. 13)
   a. sorrow
   b. love
   c. support
   d. scorn

UNDERSTANDING THE WRITER'S IDEAS

1. What, according to Fridman, is the denotation of the word "geek"? In what way is the word metaphorical as we use it?

2. According to the writer, how are intellectuals viewed on American campuses? What about athletes? How is the situation similar in elementary and high schools?

3. What does Fridman see as a consequence of our making outcasts of school children who prefer to read or build models? In what societies does he think this situation is different?

4. What point does the writer make about professors and ballplayers?

5. What, according to Fridman, is the relation between our view of intellectuals and America's economic and political future?

UNDERSTANDING THE WRITER'S TECHNIQUES

1. What is the thesis of this essay? Would you consider it the major proposition? Why or why not? What sentence do you think best expresses the thesis? What would you point to as minor propositions?

2. How do the introduction and conclusion support each other in this essay?

3. How does Fridman use definition? How does he use comparison and contrast? Causal analysis? In what ways do those strategies contribute to the argument?

4. What specific examples does Fridman provide to support his propositions?

5. What is the purpose of using the short fragment alone in paragraph 5? What other short paragraphs do you find? Why does Fridman use them?

6. Who is the audience for this piece? It was first published on the Op-Ed page of *The New York Times*. Does that surprise you? Why or why not?

7. What is the tone of this selection? Would you call it *serious, angry, relaxed, annoyed,* or *humorous?* Defend your choice.

8. Comment on the writer's vocabulary and word choice. Is the language well-suited to the intent of the essay? What do the slang words "nerd" and "geek" contribute here? In other instances would you say that the vocabulary was more difficult than necessary? Comment particularly on the appropriateness of words like "derogatory," "prestigious," "ostracized," "anti-intellectualism," and "approbation."

9. What transitional devices has the writer used to advantage here?

10. Comment on the strengths and weaknesses, if any, in the title. Why has Fridman chosen it instead of a title like "On Intellectualism" or "Opposing Anti-Intellectualism"?

UNDERSTANDING THE WRITER'S IDEAS

1. Do you agree that most students are ashamed to admit, even to their friends, how much they study? Why do you think this is so? How much do you study? Would you be reluctant to share your response with others in the class? Why or why not?

2. Do you agree that "For America's sake, the anti-intellectual values that pervade our society must be fought"?

Why or why not? Has Fridman made the point satisfactorily that our future economy depends on our academic
achievement and intellectual ability?

3. Fridman separates intellectuals and athletes. Must the two
   be split? Is it possible that both groups make important
   contributions to American society? Can any person represent the values inherent both in athletics and academics?
   Explain your position.

4. Fridman raises the issue of comparative worth in considering salaries for different jobs. Do you agree that athletes
   are paid much more than they are worth in our society?
   That teachers are paid less than they are worth? If so, how
   would you propose remedying the situation? Would you
   support government-set limits on how much people in certain job categories could earn?

5. The writer questions the value of accenting social skills
   over other skills that he feels are more important. What social skills do you think Fridman means? Do you see any
   value in emphasizing the development of social skills?
   Which social skills should we emphasize? Why?

IDEAS FOR WRITING

Guided Writing

Write an essay called "America Needs Its _____."
Fill in the blank with a word or term—preferably a slang or colloquial word—that names a group you feel has been ignored,
overlooked, undervalued, or unsupported in our society. You
might want to use a word like "jocks," "loners," "kooks,"
"rednecks," "airheads," "losers," "showoffs," "boneheads,"
"con-artists," or the like.

1. Write a short introduction to set the stage for your argument. Develop a major proposition and state it in a thesis
   sentence. Place your thesis strategically—either in the in-

troduction or in some other key position in the essay. State minor propositions clearly.

2. Briefly define the term you've used to fill the blank in the title. Use a dictionary to develop your definition; then comment on it.

3. Develop a clear sense of who your audience is, and direct your argument to that group. Be sure that your word choice reflects your sense of audience.

4. Use specific examples to support your propositions.

5. Draw on other rhetorical strategies as needed—comparison, causal analysis, exemplification, and so forth.

6. Include one short paragraph—a fragment, perhaps, or a single sentence.

7. Develop a conclusion that logically extends your introduction and thesis.

More Writing Projects

1. In your journal make a list of everything that comes to mind when you think of the word "nerd." Don't edit your thoughts.

2. Using the journal entry above, write a one-paragraph argument for defining "nerd" as you have used the word. You may use a dictionary to get started, but essentially you should draw on your own perceptions to flesh out your definition and argument. To support your point provide examples where necessary.

3. Write an essay in which you argue *against* the need for a particular group. You might want to call your essay "America Does Not Need Its _____." (Use the word "nerd" in the blank.)

SUMMING UP: CHAPTER 11

1. Keep a journal in which you record your thoughts on, and

observations of, homelessness in your part of the country. Try to gather specific data from reading, viewing television, or observation. Ask such questions as:

How many are male? How many female?
How many are children?
How many are elderly
How many appear to be mentally ill?
What symptoms or signs do they exhibit?

Use this data, along with your observations, to present your position on homelessness in a letter to the editor of your campus or local newspaper.

2. Invite a local expert to class to speak on a current, controversial issue. Write an essay of support for, or opposition to, the speaker's opinions.

3. Justify the inclusion of the essays by Kozol, Krutch, Syfers, and Fridman under the category "Argumentation and Persuasion." Treat the major issues that they raise, their positions on these issues, their minor propositions and use of evidence, and the tone of their language. Finally, establish the degree to which you are persuaded by these arguments.

4. Exchange with a classmate essays you've each written for a Guided Writing exercise in Chapter 11. Even if you agree with your partner's opinion, write a strongly worded response opposing it. Be sure you touch on the same or similar, major and minor propositions.

5. Fill in the blanks in the following essay topic as you please, and use it as the major proposition for a well-developed argumentation-persuasion paper. Draw on the expository writing skills you have studied throughout the book.

"I am very concerned about _____ , and I believe it's necessary to _____ ."

CHAPTER 12

Prose for
Further Reading

In Deep

Maxine Kumin

Early winter. Foliage gone, the woods reveal their inner architecture. In a strong wind, oak and maple branches creak and rub against each other, cranky as old door hinges. I can see in deep now, deep into this second-growth forest where pastures once were, and farms prospered. I can spot the occasional apple tree and lilac sprawl, the tumbled stone walls and caved-in foundations at a considerable distance.

The deerflies, those scourges of midsummer shaped like tiny deltoid planes, have vanished. Ground wasps that lurked in rotten logs waiting to pounce on the unwary traveler are now in hibernation. Only the deer hunters are left for us to contend with.

Weekends we ride out in threes and fours, horses and people bedecked in extremely orange pinnies—Ten Mile Cloth, the manufacturer calls it, claiming it can be seen at that remove. Each of us has a cowbell tied to one stirrup. I carry a folding saw across the cantle of my saddle. Aurally and visually we make a fearsome procession. Of course the hunters hate us, but these are *our* woods too, and this is our only season for bushwhacking.

Midweek, theorizing that the Sunday shooters have gone home, I risk my neck alone. Riding along old rangeways between vanished settlements I peer down every track. All those roads not taken! Bending low under overhanging branches, sometimes stopping to saw my way clear, I take them one by one. And one by one they peter out like rambling thoughts, glimmering ideas unrealized.

Somehow I am never cured of my fantasy; surely one will carry me through? One day, riding in deep, the perfect trail will materialize, a leafy carpet underfoot, and overhead just room enough—a tunnel for my chestnut horse and me. We will trot for miles this way, admiring the crackle we make in late November, admiring the configurations of hummocks and rivulets underfoot with glistens of ice between, and bits of bright blue sky visible over the next rise. Eventually we will come out on the other side.

What is waiting on the other side? Maybe nothing special, maybe only more of the same, dear enough for this watcher. But the quest is real. To get there you have to go in deep.

An American Childhood

Annie Dillard

When everything else has gone from my brain—the President's name, the state capitals, the neighborhoods where I lived, and then my own name and what it was on earth I sought, and then at length the faces of my friends, and finally the faces of my family—when all this has dissolved, what will be left, I believe, is topology: the dreaming memory of land as it lay this way and that.

I will see the city poured rolling down the mountain valleys like slag, and see the city lights sprinkled and curved around the hills' curves, rows of bonfires winding. At sunset a red light like housefires shines from the narrow hillside windows; the houses' bricks burn like glowing coals.

The three wide rivers divide and cool the mountains. Calm old bridges span the banks and link the hills. The Allegheny River flows in brawling from the north, from near the shore of Lake Erie, and from Lake Chautauqua in New York and eastward. The Monongahela River flows in shallow and slow from the south, from West Virginia. The Allegheny and the Monongahela meet and form the westward-wending Ohio.

Where the two rivers join lies an acute point of flat land from which rises the city. The tall buildings rise lighted to their tips. Their lights illumine other buildings' clean sides, and illumine the narrow city canyons below, where people move, and shine reflected red and white at night from the black waters.

When the shining city, too, fades, I will see only those forested mountains and hills, and the way the rivers lie flat and moving among them, and the way the low land lies wooded among them, and the blunt mountains rise in darkness from the rivers' banks, steep from the rugged south and rolling from the north, and from farther, from the inclined eastward plateau where the high ridges begin to run so long north and south unbroken that to get around them you practically have to navigate Cape Horn.

In those first days, people said, a squirrel could run the long length of Pennsylvania without ever touching the ground.

447

In those first days, the woods were white oak and chestnut, hickory, maple, sycamore, walnut, wild ash, wild plum, and white pine. The pine grew on the ridgetops where the mountains' lumpy spines stuck up and their skin was thinnest.

The wilderness was uncanny, unknown. Benjamin Franklin had already invented his stove in Philadelphia by 1753, and Thomas Jefferson was a schoolboy in Virginia; French soldiers had been living in forts along Lake Erie for two generations. But west of the Alleghenies in western Pennsylvania, there was not even a settlement, not even a cabin. No Indians lived there, or even near there.

Wild grapevines tangled the treetops and shut out the sun. Few songbirds lived in the deep woods. Bright Carolina parakeets—red, green, and yellow—nested in the dark forest. There were ravens then, too. Woodpeckers rattled the big trees' trunks, ruffed grouse whirred their tail feathers in the fall, and every long once in a while a nervous gang of empty-headed turkeys came hustling and kicking through the leaves—but no one heard any of this, no one at all.

In 1753, young George Washington surveyed for the English this point of land where rivers met. To see the forest-blurred lay of the land, he rode his horse to a ridgetop and climbed a tree. He judged it would make a good spot for a fort. And an English fort it became, and a depot for Indian traders to the Ohio country, and later a French fort and way station to New Orleans.

But it would be another ten years before any settlers lived there on that land where the rivers met, lived to draw in the flowery scent of June rhododendrons with every breath. It would be another ten years before, for the first time on earth, tall men and women lay exhausted in their cabins, sleeping in the sweetness, worn out from planting corn.

If Black English Isn't a Language, Then Tell Me, What Is?

James Baldwin

The argument concerning the use, or the status, or the reality, of black English is rooted in American history and has absolutely nothing to do with the question the argument supposes itself to be posing. The argument has nothing to do with language itself but with the *role* of language. Language, incontestably, reveals the speaker. Language, also, far more dubiously, is meant to define the other—and, in this case, the other is refusing to be defined by a language that has never been able to recognize him.

People evolve a language in order to describe and thus control their circumstances, or in order not to be submerged by a reality that they cannot articulate. (And, if they cannot articulate it, they *are* submerged.) A Frenchman living in Paris speaks a subtly and crucially different language from that of the man living in Marseilles; neither sounds very much like a man living in Quebec; and they would all have great difficulty in apprehending what the man from Guadeloupe, or Martinique, is saying, to say nothing of the man from Senegal—although the "common" language of all these areas is French. But each has paid, and is paying, a different price for this "common" language, in which, as it turns out, they are not saying, and cannot be saying, the same things: They each have very different realities to articulate or control.

What joins all languages, and all men, is the necessity to confront life, in order, not inconceivably, to outwit death: The price for this is the acceptance, and achievement, of one's temporal identity. So that, for example, though it is not taught in the schools (and this has the potential of becoming a political issue) the south of France still clings to its ancient and musical Provençal, which resists being described as a "dialect." And much of the tension in the Basque countries, and in Wales, is due to the Basque and Welsh determination not to allow their languages to be destroyed. This determination also feeds the flames in Ireland for among the many indignities the

449

Irish have been forced to undergo at English hands is the English contempt for their language.

It goes without saying, then, that language is also a political instrument, means, and proof of power. It is the most vivid and crucial key to identity: It reveals the private identity, and connects one with, or divorces one from, the larger public, or communal identity. There have been, and are, times, and places, when to speak a certain language could be dangerous, even fatal. Or, one may speak the same language, but in such a way that one's antecedents are revealed, or (one hopes) hidden. This is true in France, and is absolutely true in England: The range (and reign) of accents on that damp little island make England coherent for the English and totally incomprehensible for everyone else. To open your mouth in England is (if I may use black English) to "put your business in the street": You have confessed your parents, your youth, your school, your salary, your self-esteem, and, alas, your future.

Now, I do not know what white Americans would sound like if there had never been any black people in the United States, but they would not sound the way they sound. *Jazz,* for example, is a very specific sexual term, as in *jazz me, baby,* but white people purified it into the Jazz Age. *Sock it to me,* which means, roughly, the same thing, has been adopted by Nathaniel Hawthorne's descendants with no qualms or hesitations at all, along with *let it all hang out* and *right on! Beat to his socks,* which was once the black's most total and despairing image of poverty, was transformed into a thing called the Beat Generation, which phenomenon was, largely, composed of *uptight,* middle-class white people, imitating poverty, trying to *get down,* to get *with it,* doing their *thing,* doing their despairing best to be *funky,* which we, the blacks, never dreamed of doing—we *were* funky, baby, like *funk* was going out of style.

Now, no one can eat his cake, and have it, too, and it is late in the day to attempt to penalize black people for having created a language that permits the nation its only glimpse of reality, a language without which the nation would be even more *whipped* than it is.

I say that this present skirmish is rooted in American history, and it is. Black English is the creation of the black diaspora. Blacks came to the United States chained to each other, but from different tribes: Neither could speak the other's language. If two black people, at that bitter hour of the world's history, had been able to speak to each other, the institution of chattel slavery could never have lasted as long as it did. Subsequently, the slave was given, under the eye, and the gun, of his master, Congo Square, and the Bible—or, in other words, and under these conditions, the slave began the formation of the black church, and it is within this unprecedented tabernacle that black English began to be formed. This was not, merely, as in the European example, the adoption of a foreign tongue, but an alchemy that transformed ancient elements into new language: *A language comes into existence by means of brutal necessity, and the rules of the language are dictated by what the language must convey.*

There was a moment, in time, and in this place, when my brother, or my mother, or my father, or my sister, had to convey to me, for example, the danger in which I was standing from the white man standing just behind me, and to convey this with a speed, and in a language, that the white man could not possibly understand, and that, indeed, he cannot understand, until today. He cannot afford to understand it. This understanding would reveal to him too much about himself, and smash that mirror before which he has been frozen for so long.

Now, if this passion, this skill, this (to quote Toni Morrison) "sheer intelligence," this incredible music, the mighty achievement of having brought a people utterly unknown to, or despised by "history"—to have brought this people to their present, troubled, troubling, and unassailable and unanswerable place—if this absolutely unprecedented journey does not indicate that black English is a language, I am curious to know what definition of language is to be trusted.

A people at the center of the Western world, and in the midst of so hostile a population, has not endured and transcended by means of what is patronizingly called a "dialect." We, the blacks, are in trouble, certainly, but we are not doomed, and we are not inarticulate because we are not compelled to defend a morality that we know to be a lie.

The brutal truth is that the bulk of the white people in America never had any interest in educating black people, except as this could serve white purposes. It is not the black child's language that is in question, it is not his language that is despised: It is his experience. A child cannot be taught by anyone who despises him, and a child cannot afford to be fooled. A child cannot be taught by anyone whose demand, essentially, is that the child repudiate his experience, and all that gives him sustenance, and enter a limbo in which he will no longer be black, and in which he knows that he can never become white. Black people have lost too many black children that way.

And, after all, finally, in a country with standards so untrustworthy, a country that makes heroes of so many criminal mediocrities, a country unable to face why so many of the non-white are in prison, or on the needle, or standing, futureless, in the streets—it may very well be that both the child, and his elder, have concluded that they have nothing whatever to learn from the people of a country that has managed to learn so little.

The Fight

Maya Angelou

The last inch of space was filled, yet people continued to wedge themselves along the walls of the Store. Uncle Willie had turned the radio up to its last notch so that youngsters on the porch wouldn't miss a word. Women sat on kitchen chairs, dining-room chairs, stools and upturned wooden boxes. Small children and babies perched on every lap available and men leaned on the shelves or on each other.

The apprehensive mood was shot through with shafts of gaiety, as a black sky is streaked with lightning.

"I ain't worried 'bout this fight. Joe's gonna whip that cracker like it's open season."

"He gone whip him till that white boy call him Momma."

At last the talking was finished and the string-along songs about razor blades were over and the fight began.

"A quick jab to the head." In the Store the crowd grunted. "A left to the head and a right and another left." One of the listeners cackled like a hen and was quieted.

"They're in a clench, Louis is trying to fight his way out."

Some bitter comedian on the porch said, "That white man don't mind hugging that niggah now, I betcha."

"The referee is moving in to break them up, but Louis finally pushed the contender away and it's an uppercut to the chin. The contender is hanging on, now he's backing away. Louis catches him with a short left to the jaw."

A tide of murmuring assent poured out the doors and into the yard.

"Another left and another left. Louis is saving that mighty right..." The mutter in the Store had grown into a baby roar and it was pierced by the clang of a bell and the announcer's "That's the bell for round three, ladies and gentlemen."

As I pushed my way into the Store I wondered if the announcer gave any thought to the fact that he was addressing as "ladies and gentlemen" all the Negroes around the world who sat sweating and praying, glued to their "master's voice."

There were only a few calls for R. C. Colas, Dr. Peppers, and Hire's root beer. The real festivities would begin after the fight. Then even the old Christian ladies who taught their children and tried themselves to practice turning the other cheek would buy soft drinks, and if the Brown Bomber's victory was a particularly bloody one they would order peanut patties and Baby Ruths also.

Bailey and I lay the coins on top of the cash register. Uncle Willie didn't allow us to ring up sales during a fight. It was too noisy and might shake up the atmosphere. When the gong rang for the next round we pushed through the near-sacred quiet to the herd of children outside.

"He's got Louis against the ropes and now it's a left to the body and a right to the ribs. Another right to the body, it looks like it was low... Yes, ladies and gentlemen, the referee is signaling but the contender keeps raining the blows on Louis. It's another to the body, and it looks like Louis is going down."

My race groaned. It was our people falling. It was another lynching, yet another Black man hanging on a tree. One more woman ambushed and raped. A Black boy whipped and maimed. It was hounds on the trail of a man running through slimy swamps. It was a white woman slapping her maid for being forgetful.

The men in the Store stood away from the walls and at attention. Women greedily clutched the babes on their laps while on the porch the shufflings and smiles, flirtings and pinching of a few minutes before were gone. This might be the end of the world. If Joe lost we were back in slavery and beyond help. It would all be true, the accusations that we were lower types of human beings. Only a little higher than the apes. True that we were stupid and ugly and lazy and dirty and, unlucky and worst of all, that God Himself hated us and ordained us to be hewers of wood and drawers of water, forever and ever, world without end.

We didn't breathe. We didn't hope. We waited.

"He's off the ropes, ladies and gentlemen. He's moving

towards the center of the ring." There was no time to be relieved. The worst might still happen.

"And now it looks like Joe is mad. He's caught Carnera
with a left hook to the head and a right to the head. It's a left
jab to the body and another left to the head. There's a left
cross and a right to the head. The contender's right eye is
bleeding and he can't seem to keep his block up. Louis is pen-
etrating every block. The referee is moving in, but Louis
sends a left to the body and it's the uppercut to the chin and
the contender is dropping. He's on the canvas, ladies and gentlemen."

Babies slid to the floor as women stood up and men
leaned toward the radio.

"Here's the referee. He's counting. One, two, three, four,
five, six, seven...Is the contender trying to get up again?"

All the men in the store shouted, "NO."

"—eight, nine, ten." There were a few sounds from the
audience, but they seemed to be holding themselves in against
tremendous pressure.

"The fight is all over, ladies and gentlemen. Let's get the
microphone over to the referee...Here he is. He's got the
Brown Bomber's hand, he's holding it up...Here he is..."

Then the voice, husky and familiar, came to wash over
us—"The winnah, and still heavyweight champeen of the
world...Joe Louis."

Champion of the world. A Black boy. Some Black mother's son. He was the strongest man in the world. People drank
Coca-Colas like ambrosia and ate candy bars like Christmas.
Some of the men went behind the Store and poured white
lightning in their soft-drink bottles, and a few of the bigger
boys followed them. Those who were not chased away came
back blowing their breath in front of themselves like proud
smokers.

It would take an hour or more before the people would
leave the Store and head for home. Those who lived too far
had made arrangements to stay in town. It wouldn't do for a
Black man and his family to be caught on a lonely country
road on a night when Joe Louis had proved that we were the
strongest people in the world.

The Ugly Tourist
Jamaica Kincaid

The thing you have always suspected about yourself the
minute you become a tourist is true: a tourist is an ugly human
being. You are not an ugly person all the time; you are not an
ugly person ordinarily; you are not an ugly person day to day.
From day to day, you are a nice person. From day to day, all
the people who are supposed to love you on the whole do.
From day to day as you walk down a busy street in the large
and modern and prosperous city in which you work and live,
dismayed, puzzled (a cliché, but only a cliché can explain you)
at how alone you feel in this crowd, how awful it is to go unnoticed, how awful it is to go unloved, even as you are surrounded by more people than you could possibly get to know
in a lifetime that lasted for millennia, and then out of the corner of your eye you see someone looking at you and absolute
pleasure is written all over that person's face, and then you
realize that you are not as revolting a presence as you think
you are (for that look just told you so). And so, ordinarily, you
are a nice person, an attractive person, a person capable of
drawing to yourself the affection of other people (people just
like you), a person at home in your own skin (sort of; I mean,
in a way; I mean, your dismay and puzzlement are natural to
you, because people like you just seem to be like that, and so
many of the things people like you find admirable about your-
selves—the things you think about, the things you think really
define you—seem rooted in these feelings): a person at home
in your own house (and all its nice house things), with its nice
back yard (and its nice back-yard things), at home on your
street, your church, in community activities, your job, at
home with your family, your relatives, your friends—you are
a whole person. But one day, when you are sitting somewhere, alone in that crowd, and that awful feeling of dis-
placedness comes over you, and really, as an ordinary person
you are not well equipped to look too far inward and set yourself aright, because being ordinary is already so taxing, and
being ordinary takes all you have out of you, and though the
words "I must get away" do not actually pass across your

lips, you make a leap from being that nice blob just sitting like a boob in your amniotic sac of the modern experience to being a person visiting heaps of death and ruin and feeling alive and inspired at the sight of it; to being a person lying on some far-away beach, your stilled body stinking and glistening in the sand, looking like something first forgotten, then remembered, then not important enough to go back for; to being a person marvelling at the harmony (ordinarily, what you would say is the backwardness) and the union these other people (and they are other people) have with nature. And you look at the things they can do with a piece of ordinary cloth, the things they fashion out of cheap, vulgarly coloured (to you) twine, the way they squat down over a hole they have made in the ground, the hole itself is something to marvel at, and since you are being an ugly person this ugly but joyful thought will swell inside you: their ancestors were not clever in the way yours were and not ruthless in the way yours were, for then would it not be you who would be in harmony with nature and backwards in that charming way? An ugly thing, that is what you are when you become a tourist, an ugly, empty thing, a stupid thing, a piece of rubbish pausing here and there to gaze at this and taste that, and it will never occur to you that the people who inhabit the place in which you have just paused cannot stand you, that behind their closed doors they laugh at your strangeness (you do not look the way they look); the physical sight of you does not please them; you have bad manners (it is their custom to eat their food with their hands; you try eating their way, you look silly; you try eating the way you always eat, you look silly); but they do not like the way you speak (you have an accent); they collapse helpless from laughter, mimicking the way they imagine you must look as you carry out some everyday bodily function. They do not like you. *They do not like me!* That thought never actually occurs to you. Still, you feel a little uneasy. Still, you feel a little foolish. Still, you feel a little out of place. But the banality of your own life is very real to you; it drove you to this extreme, spending your days and your nights in the company of people who despise you, people you do not like really, people you would not want to have as your actual neighbour. And so you must devote yourself to puzzling out how much of what you are told is really, really true (Is ground-up bottle glass in peanut sauce really a delicacy around here, or will it do just what you think ground-up bottle glass will do? Is this rare, multicoloured, snout-mouthed fish really an aphrodisiac, or will it cause you to fall asleep permanently?). Oh, the hard work all of this is, and is it any wonder, then, that on your return home you feel the need of a long rest, so that you can recover from your life as a tourist?

That the native does not like the tourist is not hard to explain. For every native of every place is a potential tourist, and every tourist is a native of somewhere. Every native everywhere lives a life of overwhelming and crushing banality and boredom and desperation and depression, and every deed, good and bad, is an attempt to forget this. Every native would like to find a way out, every native would like a rest, every native would like a tour. But some natives—most natives in the world—cannot go anywhere. They are too poor. They are too poor to escape the reality of their lives; and they are too poor to live properly in the place where they live, which is the very place you, the tourist, want to go—so when the natives see you, the tourist, they envy you, they envy your ability to leave your own banality and boredom, they envy your ability to turn their own banality and boredom into a source of pleasure for yourself.

He Rocked, I Reeled

Tama Janowitz

In high school, I took a remedial English class—maybe it wasn't remedial, exactly, but without my knowing it, I had signed up for some kind of English class for juvenile delinquents.

Well, it wasn't supposed to be a class for juvenile delinquents, but somehow everybody but me knew that that was who it was for; maybe it was listed in the course catalog as being for those students in the commercial program, the general program, whatever it was called to distinguish it from the academic precollege preparation program.

But anyway, on the first day I figured out who this course was directed at: The students were surly and wore leather jackets, and the girls all had shag hair-dos as opposed to straight and ironed, which was how the "nice" girls wore their hair.

Knowing me, I must have signed up for that class because it indicated that no work would be involved. And I was prepared for the worst, because somehow, having moved and switched schools so many times, I had been stuck in juvenile delinquent classes before.

The juvenile delinquent classes generally meant angry teachers and angry students who never read the books assigned and never spoke in class, which was no wonder because the teacher was generally contemptuous and sneering.

But this class ended up being different; the main thing was that the teacher, Mr. Paul Steele, didn't seem to know he was teaching students who weren't supposed to be able to learn. He assigned the books—by Sherwood Anderson, by Hemingway, by Melville—and somehow by the due date everyone had read them and was willing to talk about them.

Mr. Steele was a little distracted, a little dreamy, and most excellent. It was one of the few times up until that age I had a teacher who spoke to me—and the rest of the class—with the honesty of one adult talking to others, without pretense or condescension; there was no wrong or right, just discussion.

In college, I had another great course—in geology, a subject for which I had no interest. Once again, I had signed up for something that looked easy, a "gut" course to fulfill the science requirement.

But this guy—I believe his name was Professor Sand, an apt name for a geology teacher—was so excited and in love with rocks, with everything pertaining to the formation of the earth, that to this day rocks and everything pertaining to the formation of the earth still get me excited.

Oolitic limestone, feldspar, gypsum, iron pyrite, Manhattan schist—the names were like descriptions of food, almost edible, and as around that time I was starting to become interested in writing, the enthusiasm that the teacher had for the subject was transferred to me into an enthusiasm for language.

And the names of the different periods—the Jurassic, the Pre-Cambrian—even though I can't remember much about them, the words still hold mystery and richness.

At the end of the semester, there was a field trip up to the Catskills, to put into practice some of the techniques discussed in class. We were taken to a fossil bed of trilobites where, due to the particular condition of the sedimentary bed, only the trilobite bodies had been preserved over the millennia.

After a few minutes of listening to the professor's explanation, I bent over and picked up a piece of rock with a small lump sticking out of it and took it over to him.

To me, all I had found was a rock with a lump; but Professor Sand was totally amazed—I was the only one ever to find a fossilized trilobite complete with head.

Really, at that point there was little to stop me from becoming a geologist except for the fact that I knew I could never do anything involving numbers, weights or measurements, which I suspected would at some point have some bearing on the subject.

I remember another teacher, in graduate school, Francine du Plessix Gray, who taught a course called Religion and Literature—another subject in which I had no interest. But the way she spoke was so beautiful, in an accent slightly Frenchtinged. And because she was so interested in her topic, the students became interested, and her seminars were alive and full of argument.

Of course, I had many other fine teachers along the way, but the ones who stand out in my mind were those who were most enthusiastic about what they were teaching.

Many subjects in which I initially thought I was interested were totally destroyed for me by the teacher's dry, aloof, pompous, disengaged way of speaking.

But when the teacher was as excited about the topic—as if he or she was still a little kid, rushing in from the yard to tell a story—that was when the subject became alive for me.

"Ever Et Raw Meat?" and Other Weird Questions

Stephen King

It seems to me that, in the minds of readers, writers actually exist to serve two purposes, and the more important may not be the writing of books and stories. The primary function of writers, it seems, is to answer readers' questions. These fall into three categories. The third is the one that fascinates me most, but I'll identify the other two first.

The One-of-a-Kind Questions: Each day's mail brings a few of these. Often they reflect the writer's field of interest—history, horror, romance, the American West, outer space, big business. The only thing they have in common is their uniqueness. Novelists are frequently asked where they get their ideas (see category No. 2), but writers must wonder where this relentless curiosity, these really strange questions, come from.

There was, for instance, the young woman who wrote to me from a penal institution in Minnesota. She informed me she was a kleptomaniac. She further informed me that I was her favorite writer, and she had stolen every one of my books she could get her hands on. "But after I stole 'Different Seasons' from the library and read it, I felt moved to send it back," she wrote. "Do you think this means you wrote this one the best?" After due consideration, I decided that reform on the part of the reader has nothing to do with artistic merit. I came close to writing back to find out if she had stolen "Misery" yet but decided I ought to just keep my mouth shut.

From Bill V. in North Carolina: "I see you have a beard. Are you morbid of razors?"

From Carol K. in Hawaii: "Will you soon write of pimples or some other facial blemish?"

From Don G., no address (and a blurry postmark): "Why do you keep up this disgusting mother worship when anyone with any sense knows a MAN has no use to his mother once he is weened?"

From Raymond R. in Mississippi: "Ever et raw meat?" (It's the laconic ones like this that really get me.)

I have been asked if I beat my children and/or my wife. I

462

have been asked to parties in places I have never been and hope never to go. I was once asked to give away the bride at a wedding, and one young woman sent me an ounce of pot, with the attached question: "This is where I get my inspiration—where do you get yours?" Actually, mine usually comes in envelopes—the kind through which you can view your name and address printed by a computer—that arrive at the end of every month.

My favorite question of this type, from Anchorage, asked simply: "How could you write such a why?" Unsigned. If E. E. Cummings were still alive, I'd try to find out if he'd moved to the Big North.

The Old Standards: These are the questions writers dream of answering when they are collecting rejection *slips, and the ones they tire of quickest once they start* to publish. In other words, they are the questions that come up without fail in every dull interview the writer has ever given or will ever give. I'll enumerate a few of them:

Where do you get your ideas? (I get mine in Utica.)

How do you get an agent? (Sell your soul to the Devil.)

Do you have to know somebody to get published? (Yes; in fact, it helps to grovel, toady and be willing to perform twisted acts of sexual depravity at a moment's notice, and in public if necessary.)

How do you start a novel? (I usually start by writing the number 1 in the upper right-hand corner of a clean sheet of paper.)

How do you write best sellers? (Same way you get an agent.)

How do you sell your book to the movies? (Tell them they don't want it.)

What time of day do you write? (It doesn't matter; if I don't keep busy enough, the time inevitably comes.)

Do you ever run out of ideas? (Does a bear defecate in the woods?)

Who is your favorite writer? (Anyone who writes stories I would have written had I thought of them first.)

There are others, but they're pretty boring, so let us march on.

The Real Weirdies: Here I am, bopping down the street, on my morning walk, when some guy pulls over in his pickup truck or just happens to walk by and says, "Hi, Steve! Writing any good books lately?" I have an answer for this; I've developed it over the years out of pure necessity. I say, "I'm taking some time off." I say that even if I'm working like mad, thundering down homestretch on a book. The reason *why* I say this is because no other answer seems to fit. Believe me, I know. In the course of the trial and error that has finally resulted in "I'm taking some time off," I have discarded about 500 other answers.

Having an answer for "You writing any good books lately?" is a good thing, but I'd be lying if I said it solves the problem of *what the question means.* It is this inability on my part to make sense of this odd query, which reminds me of that Zen riddle—"Why is a mouse when it runs?"—that leaves me feeling mentally shaken and impotent. You see, it isn't just *one* question; it is a *bundle* of questions, cunningly wrapped up in one package. It's like that old favorite, "Are you still beating your wife?"

If I answer in the affirmative, it means I may have written—how many books? two? four?—(all of them good) in the last—how long? Well, how long is "lately"? It could mean I wrote maybe three good books just last week, or maybe two *on this very walk up to Bangor International Airport and back!* On the other hand, if I say no, what does *that* mean? I wrote three or four *bad* books in the last "lately" (surely "lately" can be no longer than a month, six weeks at the outside)?

Or here I am, signing books at the Betts' Bookstore or B. Dalton's in the local consumer factory (nicknamed "the mall"). This is something I do twice a year, and it serves much the same purpose as those little bundles of twigs religious people in the Middle Ages used to braid into whips and flagellate themselves with. During the course of this exercise in madness and self-abnegation, at least a dozen people will approach the little coffee table where I sit behind a barrier of books and ask brightly, "Don't you wish you had a rubber stamp?"

I have an answer to this one, too, an answer that has been developed over the years in a trial-and-error method similar to "I'm taking some time off." The answer to the rubber-stamp question is: "No, I don't mind."

Never mind if I really do or don't (this time it's my own motivations I want to skip over, you'll notice); the question is, Why does such an illogical query occur to so many people? My signature is actually stamped on the covers of several of my books, but people seem just as eager to get these signed as those that aren't so stamped. Would these questioners stand in line for the privilege of watching me slam a rubber stamp down on the title page of "The Shining" or "Pet Sematary"? I don't think they would.

If you still don't sense something peculiar in these questions, this one might help convince you. I'm sitting in the cafe around the corner from my house, grabbing a little lunch by myself and reading a book (reading at the table is one of the few bad habits acquired in my youth that I have nobly resisted giving up) until a customer or maybe even a waitress sidles up and asks, "How come you're not reading one of your own books?"

This hasn't happened just once, or even occasionally; it happens *a lot*. The computer-generated answer to this question usually gains a chuckle, although it is nothing but the pure, logical and apparent truth. "I know how they all come out," I say. End of exchange. Back to lunch, with only a pause to wonder why people assume you want to read what you wrote, rewrote, read again following the obligatory editorial conference and yet again during the process of correcting the mistakes that a good copy editor always prods, screaming, from their hiding places (I once heard a crime writer suggest that God could have used a copy editor, and while I find the notion slightly blasphemous, I tend to agree).

And then people sometimes ask in that chatty, let's-strike-up-a-conversation way people have, "How long does it take you to write a book?" Perfectly reasonable question—at least until you try to answer it and discover there *is* no answer. This time the computer-generated answer is a total falsehood, but it at least serves the purpose of advancing the conversation to some more discussable topic. "Usually about nine months," I say, "the same length of time it takes to make a baby." This satisfies everyone but me. I know that nine months is just an average, and probably a completely fictional one at that. It ignores "The Running Man" (published under the name Richard Bachman), which was written in four days during a snowy February vacation when I was teaching high school. It also ignores "It" and my latest, "The Tommy-knockers." "It" is over 1,000 pages long and took four years to write. "The Tommyknockers" is 400 pages shorter but took five years to write.

Do I mind these questions? Yes...and no. Anyone minds questions that have no real answers and thus expose the fellow being questioned to be not a real doctor but a sort of witch doctor. But no one—at least no one with a modicum of simple human kindness—resents questions from people who honestly want answers. And now and then someone will ask a really interesting question, like, Do you write in the nude? The answer—not generated by computer—is: I don't think I ever have, but if it works, I'm willing to try it.

Living with My VCR

Nora Ephron

When all this started, two Christmases ago, I did not have a video-cassette recorder. What I had was a position on video-cassette recorders. I was against them. It seemed to me that the fundamental idea of the VCR—which is that if you go out and miss what's on television, you can always watch it later—flew in the face of almost the only thing I truly believed—which is that the whole point of going out is to miss what's on television. Let's face it: Part of being a grown-up is that every day you have to choose between going out at night or staying home, and it is one of life's unhappy truths that there is not enough time to do both.

Finally, though, I broke down, but not entirely. I did not buy a video-cassette recorder. I rented one. And I didn't rent one for myself—I myself intended to stand firm and hold to my only principle. I rented one for my children. For $29 a month, I would tape "The Wizard of Oz" and "Mary Poppins" and "Born Free," and my children would be able to watch them from time to time. In six months, when my rental contract expired, I would re-evaluate.

For quite a while, I taped for my children. Of course I had to subscribe to Home Box Office and Cinemax in addition to my normal cable service, for $19 more a month—but for the children. I taped "Oliver" and "Annie" and "My Fair Lady" for the children. And then I stopped taping for the children—who don't watch much television, in any case—and started to tape for myself.

I now tape for myself all the time. I tape when I am out, I tape when I am at home and doing other things, and I tape when I am asleep. At this very moment, as I am typing, I am taping. The entire length of my bedroom bookshelf has been turned over to video cassettes, mostly of movies; they are numbered and indexed and stacked in order in a household where absolutely nothing else is. Occasionally I find myself browsing through publications like Video Review and worrying whether I shouldn't switch to chrome-based videotape or

have my heads cleaned or upgrade to a machine that does six
or seven things at once and can be set to tape six or seven
months in advance. No doubt I will soon find myself shopping
at some Video Village for racks and storage systems especially made for what is known as "the serious collector."

How this happened, how I became a compulsive videotaper, is a mystery to me, because my position on video-
cassette recorders is very much the same as the one I started
with. I am still against them. Now, though, I am against them
for different reasons: Now I hate them out of knowledge
rather than ignorance. The other technological breakthroughs
that have made their way into my life after my initial pig-
headed opposition to them—like the electric typewriter and
the Cuisinart—have all settled peacefully into my home. I
never think about them except when I'm using them, and
when I'm using them I take them for granted. They do exactly
what I want them to do. I put the slicing disk into the Cuisinart, and damned if the thing doesn't slice things up just the
way it's supposed to. But there's no taking a VCR for granted.
It squats there, next to the television, ready to rebuke any fool
who expects something of it.

A child can operate a VCR, of course. Only a few maneuvers are required to tape something, and only a few more
are required to tape something while you are out. You must
set the time to the correct time you wish the recording to begin and end. You must punch the channel selector. You must
insert a videotape. And, on my set, you must switch the "on"
button to "time record." Theoretically, you can then go out
and have a high old time, knowing that even if you waste the
evening, your video-cassette recorder will not.

Sometimes things work out. Sometimes I return home,
rewind the tape, and discover that the machine has recorded
exactly what I'd hoped it would. But more often than not,
what is on the tape is not at all what I'd intended; in fact, the
moments leading up to the revelation of what is actually on my
video cassettes are without doubt the most suspenseful of my
humdrum existence. As I rewind the tape, I have no idea of
what, if anything, will be on it; as I press the "play" button, I

have not a clue as to what in particular has gone wrong. All I ever know for certain is that something has.

Usually it's my fault. I admit it. I have mis-set the timer or channel selector or misread the newspaper listing. I have knelt at the foot of my machine and methodically, carefully, painstakingly set it—and set it wrong. This is extremely upsetting to me—I am normally quite competent when it comes to machines—but I can live with it. What is far more disturbing are the times when what has gone wrong is not my fault at all but the fault of outside forces over which I have no control whatsoever. The program listing in the newspaper lists the channel incorrectly. The cable guide inaccurately lists the length of the movie, lopping off the last 10 minutes. The evening's schedule of television programming is thrown off by an athletic event. The educational station is having a fund-raiser.

You would be amazed at how often outside forces affect a video-cassette recorder, and I think I am safe in saying that video-cassette recorders are the only household appliances that outside forces are even relevant to. As a result, my video-cassette library is a raggedy collection of near misses: "The Thin Man" without the opening; "King Kong" without the ending; a football game instead of "Murder, She Wrote"; dozens of PBS auctions and fundraisers instead of dozens of episodes of "Masterpiece Theater." All told, my success rate at videotaping is even lower than my success rate at buying clothes I turn out to like as much as I did in the store; the machine provides more opportunities per week to make mistakes than anything else in my life.

Every summer and at Christmastime, I re-evaluate my six-month rental contract. I have three options: I can buy the video-cassette recorder, which I would never do because I hate it so much; I can cancel the contract and turn in the machine, which I would never do because I am so addicted to videotaping; or I can go on renting. I go on renting. In two years I have spent enough money renting to buy two video-cassette recorders at the discount electronics place in the neighborhood, but I don't care. Renting is my way of deluding myself that I have some power over my VCR; it's my way of believing that I can still some day reject the machine in an ultimate way (by sending it back)—or else forgive it (by buying it)—for all the times it has rejected me.

In the meantime, I have my pathetic but ever-expanding collection of cassettes. "Why don't you just rent the movies?" a friend said to me recently, after I finished complaining about the fact that my tape of "The Maltese Falcon" now has a segment of "Little House on the Prairie" in the middle of it. Rent them? What a bizarre suggestion. Then I would have to watch them. And I don't watch my videotapes. I don't have time. I would virtually have to watch my videotapes for the next two years just to catch up with what my VCR has recorded so far; and in any event, even if I did have time, the VCR would be taping and would therefore be unavailable for use in viewing.

So I merely accumulate video cassettes. I haven't accumulated anything this mindlessly since my days in college, when I was obsessed with filling my bookshelf, it didn't matter with what; what mattered was that I believed that if I had a lot of books, it would say something about my intelligence and taste. On some level, I suppose I believe that if I have a lot of video cassettes, it will say something—not about my intelligence or taste, but about my intentions. I intend to live long enough to have time to watch my videotapes. Any way you look at it, that means forever.

My Grandmother's Illness
Mordecai Richler

The seventh summer of my grandmother's illness she was supposed to die and we did not know from day to day when it
would happen. I was often sent out to eat at an aunt's or at my
other grandmother's house. I was hardly ever at home. In
those days they let boys into the left-field bleachers of Delormier Downs free during the week and Duddy, Gas sometimes, Hershey, Stan, Arty and me spent many an afternoon
at the ball park. The Montreal Royals, kingpin of the Dodger
farm system, had a marvellous club at the time. There was
Jackie Robinson, Roy Campanella, Lou Ortiz, Red Durrett,
Honest John Gabbard, and Kermit Kitman. Kitman was our
hero. It used to give us a charge to watch that crafty little Jew,
one of ours, running around out there with all those tall dumb
southern crackers. "Hey, Kitman," we would yell, "Hey,
shmo-head, if your father knew you played ball on *shabus*—"
Kitman, alas, was all field and no hit. He never made the majors. "There goes Kermit Kitman," we would holler, after he
had gone down swinging again, "the first Jewish strike-out
king of the International League." This we promptly followed
up by bellowing choice imprecations in Yiddish.

It was after one of these games, on a Friday afternoon,
that I came home to find a crowd gathered in front of our
house.

"That's the grandson," somebody said.

A knot of old people stood staring at our front door from
across the street. A taxi pulled up and my aunt hurried out,
hiding her face in her hands.

"After so many years," a woman said.

"And probably next year they'll discover a cure. Isn't
that always the case?"

The flat was clotted. Uncles and aunts from my father's
side of the family, strangers, Dr. Katzman, neighbours, were
all milling around and talking in hushed voices. My father was
in the kitchen, getting out the apricot brandy. "Your grandmother's dead," he said.

"Where's Maw?"

471

"In the bedroom with...You'd better not go in."

"I want to see her."

My mother wore a black shawl and glared down at a knot of handkerchief clutched in a fist that had been cracked by washing soda. "Don't come in here," she said.

Several bearded round-shouldered men in shiny black coats surrounded the bed. I couldn't see my grandmother.

"Your grandmother's dead."

"Daddy told me."

"Go wash your face and comb your hair."

"Yes."

"You'll have to get your own supper."

"Sure."

"One minute. The *baba* left some jewellery. The necklace is for Rifka and the ring is for your wife."

"Who's getting married?"

"Better go and wash your face. Remember behind the ears, please."

Telegrams were sent, the obligatory long distance calls were made, and all through the evening relatives and neighbours and old followers of the Zaddik poured into the house. Finally, the man from the funeral parlour arrived.

"There goes the only Jewish businessman in town," Segal said, "who wishes all his customers were German."

"This is no time for jokes."

"Listen, life goes on."

My Cousin Jerry had begun to affect a cigarette holder. "Soon the religious mumbo-jumbo starts," he said to me.

"Wha'?"

"Everybody is going to be sickeningly sentimental."

The next day was the sabbath and so, according to law, my grandmother couldn't be buried until Sunday. She would have to lie on the floor all night. Two grizzly women in white came to move and wash the body and a professional mourner arrived to sit up and pray for her. "I don't trust his face," my mother said. "He'll fall asleep."

"He won't fall asleep."

"You watch him, Sam."

"A fat lot of good prayers will do her now. Alright! Okay! I'll watch him."

My father was in a fury with Segal.

"The way he goes after the apricot brandy you'd think he never saw a bottle in his life before."

Rifka and I were sent to bed, but we couldn't sleep. My aunt was sobbing over the body in the living room; there was the old man praying, coughing and spitting into his handkerchief whenever he woke; and the hushed voices and whimpering from the kitchen, where my father and mother sat. Rifka allowed me a few drags off her cigarette.

"Well, *pisherke*, this is our last night together. Tomorrow you can take over the back room."

"Are you crazy?"

"You always wanted it for yourself, didn't you?"

"She died in there, but."

"So?"

"I couldn't sleep in there now."

"Good night and happy dreams."

"Hey, let's talk some more."

"Did you know," Rifka said, "that when they hang a man the last thing that happens is that he has an orgasm?"

"A wha'?"

"Skip it. I forgot you were still in kindergarten."

"Kiss my Royal Canadian—"

"At the funeral, they're going to open the coffin and throw dirt in her face. It's supposed to be earth from Eretz. They open it and you're going to have to look."

"Says you."

A little while after the lights had been turned out Rifka approached my bed, her head covered with a sheet and her arms raised high. "Bouyo-bouyo. Who's that sleeping in my bed? Woo-woo."

My uncle who was in the theatre and my aunt from Toronto came to the funeral. My uncle, the rabbi, was there too.

"As long as she was alive," my mother said, "he couldn't even send her five dollars a month. I don't want him in the house, Sam. I can't bear the sight of him."

"You're upset," Dr. Katzman said, "and you don't know what you're saying."

"Maybe you'd better give her a sedative," the rabbi said.

"Sam will you speak up for once, please."

Flushed, eyes heated, my father stepped up to the rabbi. "I'll tell you this straight to your face, Israel," he said. "You've gone down in my estimation."

The rabbi smiled a little.

"Year by year," my father continued, his face burning a brighter red, "your stock has gone down with me."

My mother began to weep and she was led unwillingly to a bed. While my father tried his utmost to comfort her, as he muttered consoling things, Dr. Katzman plunged a needle into her arm. "There we are," he said.

I want to sit on the stoop outside with Duddy. My uncle, the rabbi, and Dr. Katzman stepped into the sun to light cigarettes.

"I know exactly how you feel," Dr. Katzman said. "There's been a death in the family and the world seems indifferent to your loss. Your heart is broken and yet it's a splendid summer day...a day made for love and laughter... and that must seem very cruel to you."

The rabbi nodded; he sighed.

"Actually," Dr. Katzman said, "it's remarkable that she held out for so long."

"Remarkable?" the rabbi said. "It's written that if a man has been married twice he will spend as much time with his first wife in heaven as he did on earth. My father, may he rest in peace, was married to his first wife for seven years and my mother, may she rest in peace, has managed to keep alive for seven years. Today in heaven she will be able to join my father, may he rest in peace."

Dr. Katzman shook his head. "It's amazing," he said. He told my uncle that he was writing a book based on his experiences as a healer. "The mysteries of the human heart."

"Yes."

"Astonishing."

My father hurried outside. "Dr. Katzman, please. It's my wife. Maybe the injection wasn't strong enough. She just doesn't stop crying. It's like a tap. Can you come in, please?"

"Excuse me," Dr. Katzman said to my uncle.

"Of course." My uncle turned to Duddy and me. "Well, boys," he said, "what would you like to be when you grow up?"

Complexion
Richard Rodriguez

Complexion. My first conscious experience of sexual excitement concerns my complexion. One summer weekend, when I was around seven years old, I was at a public swimming pool with the whole family. I remember sitting on the damp pavement next to the pool and seeing my mother, in the spectators' bleachers, holding my younger sister on her lap. My mother, I noticed, was watching my father as he stood on a diving board, waving to her. I watched her wave back. Then saw her radiant, bashful, astonishing smile. In that second I sensed that my mother and father had a relationship I knew nothing about. A nervous excitement encircled my stomach as I saw my mother's eyes follow my father's figure curving into the water. A second or two later, he emerged. I heard him call out. Smiling, his voice sounded, buoyant, calling me to swim to him. But turning to see him, I caught my mother's eye. I heard her shout over to me. In Spanish she called through the crowd: 'Put a towel on over your shoulders.' In public, she didn't want to say why. I knew.

That incident anticipates the shame and sexual inferiority I was to feel in later years because of my dark complexion. I was to grow up an ugly child. Or one who thought himself ugly. *(Feo.)* One night when I was eleven or twelve years old, I locked myself in the bathroom and carefully regarded my reflection in the mirror over the sink. Without any pleasure I studied my skin. I turned on the faucet. (In my mind I heard the swirling voices of aunts, and even my mother's voice, whispering, whispering incessantly about lemon juice solutions and dark, *feo* children.) With a bar of soap, I fashioned a thick ball of lather. I began soaping my arms. I took my father's straight razor out of the medicine cabinet. Slowly, with steady deliberateness, I put the blade against my flesh, pressed it as close as I could without cutting, and moved it up and down across my skin to see if I could get out, somehow lessen, the dark. All I succeeded in doing, however, was in shaving my arms bare of their hair. For as I noted with disappointment, the dark would not come out. It remained. Trapped. Deep in the cells of my skin.

Throughout adolescence, I felt myself mysteriously marked. Nothing else about my appearance would concern me so much as the fact that my complexion was dark. My mother would say how sorry she was that there was not money enough to get braces to straighten my teeth. But I never bothered about my teeth. In three-way mirrors at department stores, I'd see my profile dramatically defined by a long nose, but it was really only the color of my skin that caught my attention.

I wasn't afraid that I would become a menial laborer because of my skin. Nor did my complexion make me feel especially vulnerable to racial abuse. (I didn't really consider my dark skin to be a racial characteristic. I would have been only too happy to look as Mexican as my light-skinned older brother.) Simply, I judged myself ugly. And, since the women in my family had been the ones who discussed it in such worried tones, I felt my dark skin made me unattractive to women.

Thirteen years old. Fourteen. In a grammar school art class, when the assignment was to draw a self-portrait, I tried and I tried but could not bring myself to shade in the face on the paper to anything like my actual tone. With disgust then I would come face to face with myself in mirrors. With disappointment I located myself in class photographs—my dark face undefined by the camera which had clearly described the white faces of classmates. Or I'd see my dark wrist against my long-sleeved white shirt.

I grew divorced from my body. Insecure, overweight, listless. On hot summer days when my rubber-soled shoes soaked up the heat from the sidewalk, I kept my head down. Or walked in the shade. My mother didn't need anymore to tell me to watch out for the sun. I denied myself a sensational life. The normal, extraordinary, animal excitement of feeling my body alive—riding shirtless on a bicycle in the warm wind created by furious self-propelled motion—the sensations that first had excited in me a sense of my maleness, I denied. I was too ashamed of my body. I wanted to forget that I had a body because I had a brown body. I was grateful that none of my classmates ever mentioned the fact.

I continued to see the *braceros,* those men I resembled in one way and, in another way, didn't resemble at all. On the watery horizon of a Valley afternoon, I'd see them. And though I feared looking like them, it was with silent envy that I regarded them still. I envied them their physical lives, their freedom to violate the taboo of the sun. Closer to home I would notice the shirtless construction workers, the roofers, the sweating men tarring the street in front of the house. And I'd see the Mexican gardeners. I was unwilling to admit the attraction of their lives. I tried to deny it by looking away. But what was denied became strongly desired.

In high school physical education classes, I withdrew, in the regular company of five or six classmates, to a distant corner of a football field where we smoked and talked. Our company was composed of bodies too short or too tall, all graceless and all—except mine—pale. Our conversation was usually witty. (In fact we were intelligent.) If we referred to the athletic contests around us, it was with sarcasm. With savage scorn I'd refer to the 'animals' playing football or baseball. It would have been important for me to have joined them. Or for me to have taken off my shirt, to have let the sun burn dark on my skin, and to have run barefoot on the warm wet grass. It would have been very important. Too important. It would have been too telling a gesture—to admit the desire for sensation, the body, my body.

Fifteen, sixteen. I was a teenager shy in the presence of girls. Never dated. Barely could talk to a girl without stammering. In high school I went to several dances, but I never managed to ask a girl to dance. So I stopped going. I cannot remember high school years now with the parade of typical images: bright drive-ins or gliding blue shadows of a Junior Prom. At home most weekend nights, I would pass evenings reading. Like those hidden, precocious adolescents who have no real-life sexual experiences, I read a great deal of romantic fiction. 'You won't find it in your books,' my brother would playfully taunt me as he prepared to go to a party by freezing the crest of the wave in his hair with sticky pomade. Through my reading, however, I developed a fabulous and sophisticated sexual imagination. At seventeen, I may not have known how to engage a girl in small talk, but I had read *Lady Chatterley's Lover*.

It annoyed me to hear my father's teasing: that I would never know what 'real work' is; that my hands were so soft. I think I knew it was his way of admitting pleasure and pride in my academic success. But I didn't smile. My mother said she was glad her children were getting their educations and would not be pushed around like *los pobres*. I heard the remark ironically as a reminder of my separation from *los braceros*. At such times I suspected that education was making me effeminate. The odd thing, however, was that I did not judge my classmates so harshly. Nor did I consider my male teachers in high school effeminate. It was only myself I judged against some shadowy, mythical Mexican laborer—dark like me, yet very different.

GLOSSARY

Abstract and concrete are ways of describing important qualities of language. Abstract words are not associated with real, material objects that are related directly to the five senses. Such words as "love," "wisdom," "patriotism," and "power" are abstract because they refer to ideas rather than to things. Concrete language, on the other hand, names things that can be perceived by the five senses. Words like "table," "smoke," "lemon," and "halfback" are concrete. Generally you should not be too abstract in writing. It is best to employ concrete words naming things that can be seen, touched, smelled, heard, or tasted in order to support your more abstract ideas.

Allusion is a reference to some literary, biographical, or historical event. It is a "figure of speech" (a fresh, useful comparison) used to illuminate an idea. For instance, if you want to state that a certain national ruler is insane, you might refer to him as a "Nero"— an allusion to the Emperor who burned Rome.

Alternating method in comparison and contrast involves a point-by-point treatment of the two subjects that you have selected to discuss. Assume that you have chosen five points to examine in a comparison of the Volkswagen "Jetta" (subject A) and the Honda "Accord" (subject B): cost, comfort, gas mileage, road handling, and frequency of repair. In applying the alternating method, you would begin by discussing cost in relation to A + B; then comfort in relation to A + B, and so on. The alternating method permits you to isolate points for a balanced discussion.

Ambiguity means uncertainty. A writer is ambiguous when using a word, phrase, or sentence that is not clear. Ambiguity usually results in misunderstanding, and should be avoided in essay writing. Always strive for clarity in your compositions.

Analogy is a form of figurative comparison that uses a clear illustration to explain a difficult idea or function. It is unlike a formal comparison in that its subjects of comparison are from different categories or areas. For example, an analogy likening "division of labor" to the activity of bees in a hive makes the first concept

481

more concrete by showing it to the reader through the figurative comparison with the bees.

Antonym is a word that is opposite in meaning to that of another word: "hot" is an antonym of "cold"; "fat" is an antonym of "thin"; "large" is an antonym of "small."

Argumentation is a form of writing in which you offer reasons in favor of or against something. (See Chapter 11, pp. 404–406.)

Audience refers to the writer's intended readership. Many essays (including most in this book) are designed for a general audience, but a writer may also try to reach a special group. For example, William Zinsser in his essay "Simplicity" (p. 22) might expect to appeal more to potential writers than to the general reading public. Similarly, Linda Bird Francke's "The Ambivalence of Abortion" (p. 382) might have special relevance for young married women, and Elizabeth Wong's "The Struggle to Be an All-American Girl" (p. 131) could mean something particularly special to young Chinese-Americans. The intended audience affects many of the writer's choices, including level of *diction,* range of *allusions,* types of *figurative language,* and so on.

Block method in comparison and contrast involves the presentation of all information about your first subject (A), followed by all information about the second subject (B). Thus, using the objects of comparison explained in the discussion of the "alternating method" (see entry, p. 481), you would for the block method first present all five points about the Volkswagen. Then you would present all five points about the Honda. When using the block method, remember to present the same points for each subject, and to provide an effective transition in moving from subject A to subject B.

Causal analysis is a form of writing that examines causes and effects of events or conditions as they relate to a specific subject (see Chapter 10, pp. 358–360).

Characterization is the description of people. As a particular type of description in an essay, characterization attempts to capture as vividly as possible the features, qualities, traits, speech, and actions of individuals.

Chronological order is the arrangement of events in the order that they happened. You might use chronological order to trace the history of the Vietnam War, to explain a scientific process, or to present the biography of a close relative or friend. When you order an essay by chronology, you are moving from one step to the next in time.

Classification is a pattern of writing where the author divides a subject into categories and then groups elements in each of those categories according to their relationships to each other (see Chapter 8, pp. 281–282).

Clichés are expressions that were once fresh and vivid, but have become tired and worn from overuse. "I'm so hungry that I could eat a horse" is a typical cliché. People use clichés in conversation, but writers should generally avoid them.

Closings or "conclusions" are endings for your essay. Without a closing, your essay is incomplete, leaving the reader with the feeling that something important has been left out. There are numerous closing possibilities available to writers: summarizing main points in the essay; restating the main idea; using an effective quotation to bring the essay to an end; offering the reader the climax to a series of events; returning to the conclusion and echoing it; offering a solution to a problem; emphasizing the topic's significance; or setting a new frame of reference by generalizing from the main thesis. Whatever type of closing you use, make certain that it ends the essay in a firm and emphatic way.

Coherence is a quality in effective writing that results from the careful ordering of each sentence in a paragraph, and each paragraph in the essay. If an essay is coherent, each part will grow naturally and logically from those parts that come before it. Coherence depends on the writer's ability to organize materials in a logical way, and to order segments so that the reader is carried along easily from start to finish. The main devices used in achieving coherence are *transitions,* which help to connect one thought with another.

Colloquial language is language used in conversation and in certain types of informal writing, but rarely in essays, business writing, or research papers. There is nothing wrong with colloquialisms like "gross," "scam," or "rap" when used in conversational settings. However, they are often unacceptable in essay writing—except when used sparingly for special effects.

Comparison/contrast is a pattern of essay writing treating similarities and differences between two subjects. (See Chapter 6, pp. 211–212.)

Composition is a term used for an essay or for any piece of writing that reveals a careful plan.

Concrete (See *Abstract and concrete*)

Connotation/denotation are terms specifying the way a word has meaning. Connotation refers to the "shades of meaning" that a word might have because of various emotional associations it calls up for writers and readers alike. Words like "American," "physician," "mother," "pig," and "San Francisco" have strong connotative overtones to them. With denotation, however, we are concerned not with the suggestive meaning of a word but with its exact, literal meaning. Denotation refers to the "dictionary definition" of a word—its exact meaning. Writers must understand the connotative and denotative value of words, and must control the shades of meaning that many words possess.

Context clues are hints provided about the meaning of a word by another word or words, or by the sentence or sentences coming before or after it. Thus in the sentence, "Mr. Rome, a true *raconteur,* told a story that thrilled the guests," we should be able to guess at the meaning of the italicized word by the context clues coming both before and after it. (A "raconteur" is a person who tells good stories.)

Definition is a method of explaining a word so that the reader knows what you mean by it. (See Chapter 7, pp. 244–245.)

Derivation is how a word originated and where it came from. Knowing the origin of a word can make you more aware of its meaning, and more able to use it effectively in writing. Your dictionary normally lists abbreviations (for example, O.E. for Old English, G. for Greek) for word origins and sometimes explains fully how they came about.

Description is a type of writing that uses details of sight, color, sound, smell, and touch to create a word picture and to explain or illustrate an idea. (See Chapter 3, pp. 94–95.)

Dialogue is the exact duplication in writing of something people say to each other. Dialogue is the reproduction of speech or conversation; it can add concreteness and vividness to an essay, and can also help to reveal character. When using dialogue, writers must be careful to use correct punctuation. Moreover, to use dialogue effectively in essay writing, you must develop an ear for the way other people talk, and an ability to create it accurately.

Diction refers to the writer's choice or use of words. Good diction reflects the topic of the writing. Krutch's diction, for example, is rather formal, despite his purpose of expressing deeply felt emotions. Malcolm X's diction is more varied, including subtle descriptions in standard diction and conversational sarcasms. Levels of diction refer both to the purpose of the essay and to the writer's audience. Skillful choice of the level of diction keeps the reader intimately involved with the topic.

Division is that aspect of classification (see Chapter 8, pp. 281–282) where the writer divides some large subject into categories. For example, you might divide "fish" into salt water and fresh water fish; or "sports" into team and individual sports. Division helps writers to split large and potentially complicated subjects into parts for orderly presentation and discussion.

Effect is a term used in causal analysis (see Chapter 10, pp. 358–360) to describe the outcome or expected result of a chain of happenings. When dealing with the analysis of effects, writers should determine whether they want to work with immediate or final effects, or both. Thus, a writer analyzing the effects of an accidental nuclear explosion that happened in 1956 might choose to analyze effects immediately after the blast, as well as effects that still linger.

Emphasis suggests the placement of the most important ideas in key positions in the essay. Writers can emphasize ideas simply by placing important ones at the beginning or at the end of the paragraph or essay. But several other techniques help writers to emphasize important ideas: (1) key words and ideas can be stressed by repetition; (2) ideas can be presented in climactic order, by building from lesser ideas at the beginning to the main idea at the end; (3) figurative language (for instance, a vivid simile) can call attention to a main idea; (4) the relative proportion of detail offered to support an idea can emphasize its importance; (5) comparison and contrast of an idea with other ideas can emphasize its importance; and (6) mechanical devices like underlining, capitalizing, or using exclamation points (all of which should be used sparingly) can stress significance.

Essay is the name given to a short prose work on a limited topic. Essays take many forms, ranging from a familiar narrative account of an event in your life, to explanatory, argumentative, or critical investigations of a subject. Normally, in one way or the other, an essay will convey the writer's personal ideas about the subject.

Euphemism is the use of a word or phrase simply because it seems less distasteful or less offensive than another word. For instance, "mortician" is a euphemism for "undertaker"; "sanitation worker" for "garbage collector."

Fable is a narrative with a moral (see Chapter 4, pp. 131–132). The story from which the writer draws the moral can be either true or imaginary. When writing a fable, it is important that a writer clearly presents the moral to be derived from the narrative, as Rachel Carson does in "A Fable for Tomorrow."

Figurative language, as opposed to *literal,* is a special approach to writing that departs from what is typically a concrete, straightforward style. It involves a vivid, imaginative comparison that goes beyond plain or ordinary statements. For instance, instead of saying that "Joan is wonderful," you could write that "Joan is like a summer's rose" (a *simile*); "Joan's hair is wheat, pale and soft and yellow" (a *metaphor*); "Joan is my Helen of Troy" (an *allusion*); or a number of other comparative approaches. Note that Joan is not a rose, her hair is not wheat, nor is she some other person named Helen. Figurative language is not logical; instead, it requires an ability on the part of the writer to create an imaginative comparison in order to make an idea more striking.

Flashback is a narrative technique in which the writer begins at some point in the action and then moves into the past in order to provide necessary background information. Flashback adds variety to the narrative method, enabling writers to approach a story not only in terms of straight chronology, but in terms of a back-and-forth movement. However, it is at best a very difficult technique and should be used with great care.

General/specific words are necessary in writing, although it is wise to keep your vocabulary as specific as possible. General words refer to broad categories and groups, while specific words capture with more force and clarity the nature of a term. The distinction between general and specific language is always a matter of degree. "A woman walked down the street" is more general than "Mrs. Walker walked down Fifth Avenue," while "Mrs. Webster, elegantly dressed in a muslin suit, strolled down Fifth Avenue" is more specific than the first two examples. Our ability to use specific language depends on the extent of our vocabulary. The more words we know, the more specific we can be in choosing words.

Hyperbole is obvious and intentional exaggeration.

Illustration is the use of several examples to support our idea (see Chapter 5, pp. 169–170).

Imagery is clear, vivid description that appeals to our sense of sight, smell, touch, sound, or taste. Much imagery exists for its own sake, adding descriptive flavor to an essay, as when Richard Selzer in "The Discus Thrower" writes, "I unwrap the bandages from the stumps, and begin to cut away the black scabs and the dead, glazed fat with scissors and forceps. A shard of white bone comes loose." However, imagery can also add meaning to an essay. For example, in Francke's essay, the pattern of imagery connected with the setting and procedure of her abortion alerts the reader to the importance of that event in the author's life. Again, when Orwell writes at the start of "A Hanging," "It was in Burma, a sodden morning of the rains. A sickly light, like yellow tinfoil, was slanting over the high walls into the jail yard," we see that the author uses imagery to prepare us for the sombre and terrifying event to follow. Writers can use imagery to contribute to any type of wording, or they can rely on it to structure an entire essay. It is always difficult to invent fresh, vivid description, but it is an effort that writers should make if they wish to improve the quality of their prose.

Introductions are the beginning or openings of essays. Introductions should perform a number of functions. They should alert the reader to the subject, set the limits of the essay, and indicate what the thesis (or main idea) will be. Moreover, they should arouse the reader's interest in the subject, so that the reader will want to continue reading into the essay. There are several devices available to writers that will aid in the development of sound introductions.

1. Simply state the subject and establish the thesis. See the Rita Mae Brown essay (p. 271), and "The Three New Yorks" (p. 292), by E. B. White.

2. Open with a clear, vivid description of a setting that will become important as your essay advances. Save your thesis for a later stage, but indicate what your subject is. See the essay by Ehrlich (p. 121).

3. Ask a question or a series of questions, which you might answer in the introduction or in another part of the essay. See the Jordan essay (p. 255) and the Didion essay (p. 34).

4. Tell an anecdote (a short, self-contained story of an entertaining nature) that serves to illuminate your subject. See the Staples essay (p. 191).

5. Use comparison or contrast to frame your subject and to present the thesis. See the Goodman essay (p. 227).

6. Establish a definitional context for your subject. See the Scott essay (p. 246).

7. Begin by stating your personal attitude toward a controversial issue. See the Hall essay (p. 83).

These are only some of the devices that appear in the introductions to essays in this text. Writers can also ask questions, give definitions, or provide personal accounts—there are many techniques that can be used to develop introductions. The important thing to remember is that you *need* an introduction to an essay. It can be a single sentence or a much longer paragraph, but it must accomplish its purpose—to introduce readers to the subject, and to engage them so that they want to explore the essay further.

Irony is the use of language to suggest the opposite of what is stated. Writers use irony to reveal unpleasant or troublesome realities that exist in life, or to poke fun at human weaknesses and foolish attitudes. For instance, in "A Hanging," the men who are in charge of the execution engage in laughter and lighthearted conversation after the event. There is irony in the situation and in their speech because we sense that they are actually very tense—almost unnerved—by the hanging; their laughter is the opposite of what their true emotional state actually is. Many situations and conditions lend themselves to ironic treatment.

Jargon is the use of special words associated with a specific area of knowledge or a specific profession. It is similar to "shop talk" that members of a certain trade might know, but not necessarily people outside it. For example, in Bettelheim's essay there are several terms or applications of jargon relating to psychology, while the medical jargon in Kozol's essay helps him defend his opinion on a nonmedical subject. Use jargon sparingly in your writing, and be certain to define all specialized terms that you think your readers might not know.

Journalese is a level of writing associated with prose types normally found in newspapers and popular magazines. A typical newspaper article tends to present information factually or objectively; to use simple language and simple sentence structure; and to rely on relatively short paragraphs. It also stays close to the level of conversational English without becoming chatty or colloquial.

Metaphor is a type of figurative language in which an item from one category is compared briefly and imaginatively with an item from another area. Writers create metaphors to assign meaning to a word in an original way.

Narration is telling a story in order to illustrate an important idea (see Chapter 4, pp. 131–132).

Objective/subjective writing refers to the attitude that writers take toward their subject. When writers are objective, they try not to report their own personal feelings about their subject. They attempt to control, if not eliminate, their own attitude toward the topic. Thus in the essay by Roiphe (see pp. 361–362), we learn about the underlying causes of divorce, but the writer doesn't try to convince us of the rightness or wrongness of it. Many essays, on the other hand, reveal the authors' personal attitudes and emotions. In Donald Hall's essay (see pp. 83–87), the author's personal approach to the process of reading seems clear. He takes a highly subjective approach to the topic. Other essays, such as Kozol's (see pp. 414–419), blend the two approaches to help balance the author's expression of a strong opinion. For some kinds of college writing, such as business or laboratory reports, research papers, or literary analyses, it is best to be as objective as possible. But for many of the essays in composition courses, the subjective touch is fine.

Order   is the manner in which you arrange information or materials in an essay. The most common ordering techniques are *chronological order* (involving time sequence); *spatial order* (involving the arrangement of descriptive details); *process order* (involving a step-by-step approach to an activity); *deductive order* (in which you offer a thesis and then the evidence to support it); and *inductive order* (in which you present evidence first and build toward the thesis). Some rhetorical patterns such as comparison and contrast, classification, and argumentation require other ordering techniques. Writers should select those ordering principles that permit them to present materials clearly.

Paradox   is a statement that *seems* to be contradictory but actually contains an element of truth. Writers use it in order to call attention to their subject.

Parallelism   is a variety of sentence structure in which there is "balance" or coordination in the presentation of elements. "I came, I saw, I conquered" is a good example of parallelism, presenting both pronouns and verbs in a coordinated manner. Parallelism can also be applied to several sentences and to entire paragraphs (see the Syfers's essay, pages 407–409). It can be an effective way to emphasize ideas.

Personification   is giving an object, thing, or idea lifelike or human qualities. For instance, Ray Bradbury personifies Halloween when he writes that it "didn't just stroll into our yards" (see p. 182). Like all forms of figurative writing, personification adds freshness to description, and makes ideas vivid by setting up striking comparisons.

Point of view   is the angle from which a writer tells a story. Many personal or informal essays take the *first-person* (or "I") point of

view, as the essays by Malcolm X, Saroyan, Moon, Hughes, Orwell, Didion, Miller, and others reveal. The first-person "I" point
of view is natural and fitting for essays when the writer wants to
speak in a familiar and intimate way to the reader. On the other
hand, the *third-person* point of view ("he," "she," "it," "they")
distances the reader somewhat from the writer. The third-person
point of view is useful in essays where writers are not talking exclusively about themselves, but about other people, things, and
events, as in the essays by Kozol, Carson, and White. Occasionally, the second-person ("you") point of view will appear in essays, notably in essays involving process analysis where the
writer directs the reader to do something; part of Ernest Hemingway's essay (which also utilizes third-person point of view) uses
this strategy. Other point-of-view combinations are possible when
a writer wants to achieve a special effect. For example, Friedman's and Keillor's essays combine *first-* and *second-person*
points of view. The position that you take as a writer depends
largely on the type of essay you write.

Prefix   is one or more syllables attached to the front of another word
in order to influence its meaning or to create a new word. A
knowledge of prefixes and their meanings aids in establishing the
meanings of words and in increasing the vocabulary that we use in
writing. Common prefixes and their meanings include *bi-*(two), *ex-*
(out, out of), *per-*(through), *pre-*(before), *re-*(back), *tele-*(distant),
and *trans-*(across, beyond).

Process analysis   is a pattern of writing that explains in a step-by-step
way the methods for doing something or reaching a desired end
(see Chapter 9, pp. 322–323).

Proposition   is the main point in an argumentative essay. It is like a
thesis except that it usually presents an idea that is debatable or
can be disputed.

Purpose   refers to what a writer hopes to accomplish in a piece of
writing. For example, the purpose may be *to convince* the reader
to adopt a certain viewpoint (as in Joseph Wood Krutch's "The
Vandal and the Sportsman," p. 427), *to explain* a process (as in
Garrison Keillor's "How to Write a Personal Letter," p. 324), or
to allow the reader *to feel a dominant impression* (as in Gretel
Ehrlich's "A River's Route," p. 121). Purpose helps a writer to
determine which expository technique will dominate the essay's
form, as well as what kinds of supporting examples will be used.
Purpose and *audience* are often closely related.

Refutation   is a technique in argumentative writing where you recognize and deal effectively with the arguments of your opponents. Your own argument will be stronger if you can refute—prove false or wrong—all opposing arguments.

Root is the basic part of a word. It sometimes aids us in knowing what the larger word means. Thus if we know that the root *doc-* means "teach" we might be able to figure out a word like "doctrine." *Prefixes* and *suffixes* are attached to roots to create words.

Sarcasm is a sneering or taunting attitude in writing. It is designed to hurt by ridiculing or criticizing. Basically, sarcasm is a heavy-handed form of irony, as when an individual says, "Well, you're exactly on time, aren't you" to someone who is an hour late, and says it with a sharpness in the voice, a sharpness designed to hurt. Writers should try to avoid sarcastic writing and to use more acceptable varieties of irony and satire to criticize their subject.

Satire is the humorous or critical treatment of a subject in order to expose the subject's vices, follies, stupidities, and so forth. Syfers, for instance, satirizes stereotyped notions of wives, hoping to change these attitudes by revealing them as foolish. Satire is a better weapon than sarcasm in the hands of the writer because satire is used to correct, whereas sarcasm merely hurts.

Sentimentality is the excessive display of emotion in writing, whether it is intended or unintended. Because sentimentality can distort the true nature of a situation, writers should use it cautiously, or not at all. They should be especially careful when dealing with certain subjects, for example the death of a loved one, remembrance of a mother or father, a ruined romance, the loss of something valued, that lend themselves to sentimental treatment. Only the best writers—Thomas, Francke, Hughes, and others in this text—can avoid the sentimental traps rooted in their subjects.

Simile is an imaginative comparison using "like" or "as." When Orwell writes, "A sickly light, like yellow tinfoil, was slanting over the high walls into the jail yard," he uses a vivid simile in order to reinforce the dull description of the scene.

Slang is a level of language that uses racy and colorful expressions associated more often with speech than with writing. Slang expressions like "Mike's such a dude" or "She's a real fox" should not be used in essay writing, except when the writer is reproducing dialogue or striving for a special effect. Hughes is one writer in this collection who uses slang effectively to convey his message to the reader.

Suffix is a syllable or syllables appearing at the end of a word and influencing its meaning. As with prefixes and roots, you can build vocabulary and establish meanings by knowing about suffixes. Some typical suffixes are *-able* (capable of), *-al* (relating to), *-ic* (characteristic of), *-ion* (state of), *-er* (one who), which appear often in standard writing.

Symbol   is something that exists in itself but also stands for something else. Thus the "stumps" in paragraph 20 of Selzer's essay "The Discus Thrower" are not just the patient's amputated legs, but they serve as symbols of the man's helplessness and immobility. As a type of figurative language, the symbol can be a strong feature in an essay, operating to add depth of meaning, and even to unify entire essays.

Synonym   is a word that means roughly the same as another word. In practice, few words are exactly alike in meaning. Careful writers use synonyms to vary word choice, without ever moving too far from the shade of meaning intended.

Theme   is the central idea in an essay; it is also often termed the *thesis*. Everything in an essay should support the theme in one way or another.

Thesis   is the main idea in an essay. The *thesis sentence,* appearing early in the essay, and normally somewhere in the first paragraph, serves to convey the main idea to the reader in a clear way. It is always useful to state your central idea as soon as possible, and before you introduce other supporting ideas.

Title   for an essay should be a short, simple indication of the contents of your essay. Titles like "On Keeping a Notebook," "What to Listen for in Music," "The Ambivalence of Abortion," and "How to Write a Personal Letter" are the sorts of titles that convey the central subjects of these essays in brief, effective ways. Others, such as "Survival," "Night Walker," and "I Became Her Target" also convey the central idea, but more abstractly. Always provide titles for your essays.

Tone   is the writer's attitude toward his or her subject or material. An essay writer's tone may be objective ("Arizona 87"), ironic ("I Want a Wife"), comic ("Eating Alone in Restaurants"), nostalgic ("Moon on a Silver Spoon"), or a reflection of numerous other attitudes. Tone is the "voice" that you give to an essay; every writer should strive to create a "personal voice" or tone that will be distinctive throughout any type of essay under development.

Transition   is the linking of one idea to the next in order to achieve essay coherence (see *Coherence*). Transitions are words that connect these ideas. Among the most common techniques to achieve smooth transition are: (1) repeating a key word or phrase; (2) using a pronoun to refer back to a key word or phrase; (3) relying on traditional connectives like "thus," "for example," "moreover," "therefore," "however," "finally," "likewise," "afterwards," and "in conclusion"; (4) using parallel structure (see *Parallelism*); and (5) creating a sentence or an entire paragraph that serves as a bridge from one part of your essay to the next. Transition is best achieved when the writer presents ideas and details carefully and in logical order. Try not to lose the reader by failing to provide for adequate transition from idea to idea.

Unity   is that feature in an essay where all material relates to a central concept and contributes to the meaning of the whole. To achieve a unified effect in an essay, the writer must design an introduction and conclusion, maintain a consistent tone and point of view, develop middle paragraphs in a coherent manner, and always stick to the subject, never permitting unimportant elements to enter. Thus, unity involves a successful blending of all elements that go into the creation of a sound essay.

Vulgarisms   are words that exist below conventional vocabulary, and which are not accepted in polite conversation. Always avoid vulgarisms in your own writing, unless they serve an illustrative purpose.

Acknowledgments

Maya Angelou, excerpt from *I Know Why the Caged Bird Sings* by Maya Angelou. Copyright © 1969 by Maya Angelou. Reprinted by permission of Random House, Inc.

Margaret Atwood, "Survival," excerpt from *Survival: A Thematic Guide to Canadian Literature* by Margaret Atwood. Reprinted with the permission of Stoddart Publishing Co. Limited, Toronto.

James T. Baker, "How Do We Find the Students in a World of Academic Gymnasts and Worker Ants?" in *The Chronicle of Higher Education,* 1982. Reprinted by permission of the author.

Russell Baker, "The Two Ismo's," in *The New York Times,* June 5, 1982. Copyright © 1982 by The New York Times Company. Reprinted by permission.

James Baldwin, "If Black English Isn't a Language, Then Tell Me, What Is?" in *The New York Times,* July 29, 1979. Copyright © 1979 by The New York Times Company. Reprinted by permission.

Bruno Bettelheim, "Fairy Tales and Modern Stories," from *The Uses of Enchantment: The Meaning and Importance of Fairy Tales* by Bruno Bettelheim. Copyright © 1975, 1976 by Bruno Bettelheim. Reprinted by permission of Alfred A. Knopf Inc.

Ray Bradbury, "Tricks! Treats! Gangway!" in *Reader's Digest,* October 1975. Copyright © 1975 by Ray Bradbury. Reprinted by permission of Don Congdon Associates, Inc.

Rita Mae Brown, "To the Victor Belongs the Language," excerpt from *Starting from Scratch: A Different Kind of Writer's Manual* by Rita Mae Brown, copyright © 1988 by Speakeasy Productions, Inc. Used by permission of Bantam Books, a division of Bantam, Doubleday, Dell Publishing Group, Inc.

Rachel Carson, "A Fable for Tomorrow," from *Silent Spring* by Rachel Carson. Copyright © 1962 by Rachel L. Carson. Reprinted by permission of Houghton Mifflin Company.

Aaron Copland, "What to Listen For in Music," from *What to Listen For in Music*. Copyright © 1957 by McGraw-Hill, Inc. Reprinted by permission.

Joan Didion, "On Keeping a Notebook," from *Slouching towards Bethlehem* by Joan Didion. Copyright © 1966, 1968 by Joan Didion. Reprinted by permission of Farrar, Straus and Giroux, Inc.

Annie Dillard, "An American Childhood," excerpt from *An American Childhood* by Annie Dillard. Copyright © 1987 by Annie Dillard. Reprinted by permission of Harper & Row, Publishers, Inc.

Greg Easterbrook, "Escape Valve" in *The New York Times*, December 26, 1981. Copyright © 1981 by The New York Times Company. Reprinted by permission.

Nora Ephron, "Living with My VCR." Copyright © 1985 by Nora Ephron. Reprinted by permission of International Creative Management, Inc. First published in *The New York Times*, December 23, 1984.

Gretel Ehrlich, "A River's Route." Copyright © 1989 by Gretel Ehrlich. Reprinted by permission of the author.

Linda Bird Francke, "The Ambivalence of Abortion" in *The New York Times*, May 14, 1976. Copyright © 1976 by The New York Times Company. Reprinted by permission.

Leonid Fridman, "America Needs Its Nerds" in *The New York Times*, January 11, 1990. Copyright © 1990 by The New York Times Company. Reprinted by permission.

Bruce Jay Friedman, "Eating Alone in Restaurants," from *The Lonely Guy*. Copyright © 1979 by McGraw-Hill, Inc. Reprinted by permission.

Ellen Goodman, "The Tapestry of Friendships," from *Close to Home* by Ellen Goodman. Copyright © 1979 by The Washington Post Company. Reprinted by permission of Simon & Schuster, Inc.

Donald Hall, "Four Ways of Reading" in *The New York Times*, January 26, 1969. Copyright © 1969 by The New York Times Company. Reprinted by permission.

Ernest Hemingway, "Camping Out." Reprinted with permission of Charles Scribner's Sons, an imprint of Macmillan Publishing Company, from *Ernest Hemingway Dateline: Toronto* by Ernest Hemingway, edited by William White. Copyright © 1985 by Mary Hemingway, John Hemingway, Patrick Hemingway, and Gregory Hemingway. This article first appeared in *The Toronto Star Weekly*, June 26, 1920.

ical Society. Originally published in the *New England Journal of Medicine*. Reprinted by permission of Penguin Books USA, Inc.

Judith Viorst, "Friends, Good Friends—and Such Good Friends." Copyright © 1977 by Judith Viorst. Originally appeared in *Redbook*. Reprinted by permission of Lescher & Lescher, Ltd.

Eudora Welty, "Moon on a Silver Spoon." Reprinted and abridged by permission of the author and the publisher from *One Writer's Beginnings* by Eudora Welty, Cambridge, Mass.: Harvard University Press, copyright © 1983, 1984 by Eudora Welty.

E. B. White, "The Three New Yorks," from *Here Is New York* by E. B. White. Copyright 1949 by E. B. White. Reprinted by permission of Harper & Row, Publishers, Inc.

Roger Wilkins, "I Became Her Target," in *Newsday*, September 6, 1987. Reprinted by permission of the author.

Randall Williams, "Daddy Tucked the Blanket," in *The New York Times*, June 10, 1975. Copyright © 1975 by The New York Times Company. Reprinted by permission.

Elizabeth Wong, "The Struggle to Be an All-American Girl." Originally appeared in the *Los Angeles Times*. Reprinted by permission of Elizabeth Wong.

Malcolm X, "Prison Studies," from *The Autobiography of Malcolm X* by Malcolm X, with the assistance of Alex Haley. Copyright © 1964 by Alex Haley and Malcolm X. Copyright © 1965 by Alex Haley and Betty Shabazz. Reprinted by permission of Random House, Inc.

William Zinsser, "Simplicity," from *On Writing Well* by William Zinsser. Copyright © 1976 by William K. Zinsser. Reprinted by permission of the author.